HITCHCOCK

This new collection of writings on Alfred Hitchcock celebrates the remarkable depth and scope of his artistic achievement in film. It explores his works in relationship both to their social context and to the traditions of critical theory they continue to inspire. The collection draws on the best of current Hitchcock scholarship. It features the work of both new and established scholars such as Laura Mulvey, Slavoj Žižek, Peter Wollen and James Naremore, and displays the full diversity of critical methods that have characterized the study of this director's films in recent years. The articles are grouped into four thematic sections: "Authorship and aesthetics" examines Hitchcock as auteur and explores particular aspects of his artistry such as his use of the close-up, the motif of the double, and the neglected topic of humor. "French Hitchcock" considers the influential reception of the filmmaker's work by the critics at *Cahiers du cinéma* in the 1950s, as well as the more recent engagement with Hitchcock by French philosopher Gilles Deleuze. "Poetics and politics of identity" investigates how personal and social identity is both articulated and subverted through style and form in Hitchcock's works. The concluding section, "Death and transfiguration," addresses the manner in which the spectacle and figuration of death haunts the narrative universe of Hitchcock's films, in particular his subversive masterpiece, *Psycho*.

Richard Allen is author of Projecting Illusion (1995). He has edited numerous books on the philosophy and aesthetics of film including Hitchcock: Centenary Essays (1999) with Sam Ishii-Gonzáles. He is also author of a forthcoming book on Hitchcock entitled Hitchcock and Cinema: Storytelling, Sexuality and Style.

Sam Ishii-Gonzáles teaches aesthetics and film theory at New York University and the Film/Media Department at Hunter College. He is co-editor of *Hitchcock: Centenary Essays* (with Richard Allen, 1999) and has published essays on Luis Buñuel, David Lynch, and the painter Francis Bacon.

HITCHCOCK

Past and future

Edited by Richard Allen and
Sam Ishii-Gonzáles

Routledge
Taylor & Francis Group

LONDON AND NEW YORK

First published 2004
by Routledge
11 New Fetter Lane, London EC4P 4EE

Simultaneously published in the USA and Canada
by Routledge
29 West 35th Street, New York, NY 10001

Routledge is an imprint of the Taylor & Francis Group

© 2004 Richard Allen and Sam Ishii-Gonzáles editorial material
© 2004 individual chapters the contributors

Typeset in Perpetua by Taylor & Francis Books Ltd
Printed and bound in Great Britain by TJ International Ltd,
Padstow, Cornwall

British Library Cataloguing in Publication Data
A catalogue record for this book is available from the British Library

Library of Congress Cataloging in Publication Data
A catalog record for this book has been requested

ISBN 0–415–27525–3 (hbk)
ISBN 0–415–27526–1 (pbk)

CONTENTS

ILLUSTRATIONS

NOTES ON CONTRIBUTORS

Richard Allen is Associate Professor of Cinema Studies at New York University. He is the author of *Projecting Illusion* (1995) and co-editor of four books on the aesthetics and philosophy of film: *Film Theory and Philosophy* (1997), *Hitchcock Centenary Essays* (1999), *Wittgenstein, Theory and the Arts* (2001) and *Camera Obscura/Camera Lucida: Essays in Honor of Annette Michelson* (2003). He is the author of numerous articles on Hitchcock and is co-editor with Sidney Gottlieb of *Hitchcock Annual*.

Miran Bozovic is Associate Professor of Philosophy at the University of Ljubljana, Slovenia. He is the author of *Der grosse Andere: Gotteskonzepte in der Philosophie der Neuzeit* (1993), *An Utterly Dark Spot: Gaze and Body in Early Modern Philosophy*(2000), and editor of *The Panopticon Writings by Jeremy Bentham* (1995).

Sidney Gottlieb is Professor of English at Sacred Heart University, Fairfield, CT. He has edited *Hitchcock on Hitchcock: Selected Writings and Interviews* (1995), *Alfred Hitchcock: Interviews* (2003), and *Framing Hitchcock: Selected Essays from the* Hitchcock Annual (2002) with Christopher Brookhouse. He is co-editor with Richard Allen of *Hitchcock Annual*.

Sam Ishii-Gonzáles is a doctoral candidate in the Department of Cinema Studies at New York University and teaches aesthetics and film history at NYU, Hunter College. He is co-editor with Richard Allen of *Hitchcock Centenary Essays* (1999) and has published essays on the work of

Luis Buñuel, David Lynch, and the English painter Francis Bacon. His dissertation considers Deleuze's film semiotics in relation to the artistic practice of Fassbinder, Pasolini, and Warhol. It is entitled "Towards a Minor Cinema."

Adam Lowenstein is Assistant Professor of English/Film Studies and Associate Director of the Film Studies Program at the University of Pittsburgh. His essays have appeared in *Cinema Journal, Post Script,* and the anthology *British Cinema, Past and Present* (2000). He is author of "Shocking Representation; Historical Trauma, National Cinema, and the Modern Horror Film," forthcoming from Columbia Universtity Press.

Joe McElhaney is Assistant Professor of Film Studies at Hunter College/City University of New York. His book on Hitchcock, Fritz Lang and Vincente Minnelli is forthcoming from Temple University Press.

James Morrison teaches film and literature at Claremont McKenna College. He is the author of a critical study, *Passport to Hollywood: Hollywood Films, European Directors* (1998), and *Broken Fever* (2002), a memoir. He has completed a manuscript on Terrence Malick, and is working on a study of Hollywood, mass culture, and the sublime.

Laura Mulvey is Professor of Film and Media Studies at Birkbeck, University of London and Director of the AHRB Centre of British Film and Television Studies. Her essays have been published in *Visual and Other Pleasures* (1989) and *Fetishism and Curiosity* (1996). She is also the author of the BFI Film Classic book of *Citizen Kane.* She has co-directed six films with Peter Wollen as well as *Disgraced Monuments* with Mark Lewis (Channel Four, 1994).

James Naremore is Chancellor's Professor of Communication and Culture at Indiana University and the author of several books on modern literature and film, including *Filmguide to* Psycho (1973), *Acting in the Cinema* (1988), *The Films of Vincent Minnelli* (1993), and *More than Night: Film Noir in its Contexts* (1998).

Walter Raubicheck is Assistant Professor of English at Pace University and co-editor of *Hitchcock's Rereleased Films: From* Rope *to* Vertigo (1991).

Angelo Restivo is the author of *The Cinema of Economic Miracles: Visuality and Modernization in the Italian Art Film* (2002). His current work examines cinema, space, and visual culture in relation to the transition from Fordism to post-Fordism. He is Assistant Professor in the Department of English, East Carolina University.

Bettina Rosenbladt teaches German language and culture, including film, at Santa Clara University.

Daniel Antonio Srebnick is a musician and composer who lives in New York City. He has scored theatrical productions, films, and numerous television programs, he has also produced several records.

James M. Vest teaches French and Film Studies at Rhodes College in Memphis, TN, where he also participates in the interdisciplinary humanities program. He has authored two books on French literature and culture, *The French Face of Ophelia from Belleforest to Baudelaire* (1989)and *The Poetic Works of Maurice de Guérin* (1992), and has published articles on French literary topics and on approaches to teaching world literature. His essays on Hitchcock's French connections have appeared in *Hitchcock Annual,* the *Journal of the Midwest Modern Language Association,* and *The French Review.* He is currently completing a book on Hitchcock and France.

Patricia White is Chair of Film and Media Studies at Swarthmore College. She is the author of *Uninvited: Classical Hollywood Cinema and Lesbian Representability* (1999) and a member of the *Camera Obscura* editorial collective.

Peter Wollen is Chair of the Department of Film/TV at UCLA. He was the co-curator of *Addressing the Century: 100 Years of Art and Fashion* (1999) at the Hayward Gallery in London. His recent books include *Raiding the Icebox: Reflections on Twentieth Century Culture* (1992), a revised and expanded edition of *Signs and Meanings in the Cinema* (1998), and *Paris Hollywood: Writings on Film* (2002). His work in film includes co-writing the screenplay for Michelangelo Antonioni's *The Passenger* (1975), *Riddles of the Sphinx* (1977), co-directed with Laura Mulvey, and *Friendship's Death* (1988), which he both wrote and directed.

Slavoj Žižek, a philosopher and Lacanian psychoanalyst, is Senior Researcher in the Institute of Social Sciences at the University of Ljubljana, Slovenia. Recent books include *The Ticklish Subject: The*

Absent Centre of Political Ontology (1999), *The Art of the Ridiculous Sublime: On David Lynch's* Lost Highway (2000), *The Fright of Real Tears: Krzysztof Kieslowski Between Theory and Post-Theory* (2001), and *Welcome to the Desert of the Real* (2002).

ACKNOWLEDGMENTS

Richard Allen would like to thank the main people who made the Hitchcock Centenniel Conference at New York University possible. They are: Mary Schmidt Campbell, Dean of the Tisch School of the Arts, New York University; the conference and academic panel organizing committees comprising Walter Raubicheck and Walter Srebnick of Pace University, and Bill Simon and Anna McCarthy of New York University, who gave both of their organizational skills and scholarly insight; and finally, the staff of the Department of Cinema Studies at New York University: Ken Sweeney, Ann Harris, Ventura Castro, Cathy Holter, Angela Samson, and Julia Perlowski.

The editors wish to thank Sid Gottlieb for his encouragement and support in the production of this volume, Rebecca Barden, Helen Faulkner and Chantelle Johnson at Routledge for their patience and hard work, and, on a more personal note, David Owens and Bridget Sisk.

Permissions

Three of the essays in this volume have been previously published. Peter Wollen's "Hitch: A Tale of Two Cities" appeared in *Paris and Hollywood: Writings on Film* (London: Verso, 2002) and is reprinted with permission of the author. James Naremore's "Hitchcock and Humor" appeared in *Strategies,* vol. 14, no. 1 (May 2001), pp. 13–27 and is reprinted with permission of the editor and publisher, Taylor & Francis. Laura Mulvey's "Death drives" appeared in *Film Studies* (Spring 2000), pp. 5–14, and is reprinted with permission of the editor. In Daniel Srebnick's essay "Music and Identity: The Struggle for Harmony in *Vertigo,*" Bernard Herrmann's score for *Vertigo* is quoted with the permission of Famous Music Publishing.

HITCHCOCK CHRONOLOGY

List of Hitchcock films and key biographical dates

1899   Alfred Joseph Hitchcock born August 13 in lower-middle-class district of London's East End. He is the third child of William and Ellen Hitchcock. His father is a prosperous greengrocer, his mother a devout Irish Catholic.

1913   Completes his formal education after four years at a Jesuit school, Saint Ignatius College.

1914   Father dies age 52. Hitchcock lives alone with his mother until his marriage, twelve years later.

1915   Hitchcock begins working at Henley Telegraph and Cable Company. After working as a technician he is transferred to the advertising department. During this period he continues his education by taking evening classes for non-matriculated students at the University of London. He attends lectures on economics and political history as well as art history, drawing, and painting. Hitchcock is given a medical deferment from military conscription due to his weight and because of the involvement of his employers in the war effort.

1920   Hitchcock gets a part-time job as title-card designer for the Famous Players-Lasky, the London branch of an American production company. Within a few months he is offered full-time employment. He leaves Henley Telegraph and Cable for a career in motion pictures.

1922   Hitchcock assists the producer Seymour Hicks in completing *Always Tell Your Wife* after the director falls ill. He is then giving his own feature to direct, *Number Thirteen*, but it is not completed due to the poor financial situation of the studio (it shuts down shortly thereafter). The studio is taken over by producer Michael Balcon who forms Gainsborough Pictures. Over the next three years Hitchcock will serve as assistant director and co-scenarist on five films directed by Graham Cutts: *Woman to Woman, The White Shadow, The Passionate Adventure, The Prude's Fall* and *The Blackguard*. He takes on additional chores as editor (*The White Shadow*) and art director (*The White Shadow, The Passionate Adventure*). *The Blackguard* is lensed at the UFA studios in Berlin following a deal between Balcon and German producer Erich Pommer. It is during the making of this film that Hitchcock observes the shooting of F.W. Murnau's *The Last Laugh* (1924), a work that will have an enormous influence on his own filmmaking.

1925   After four years of apprentice work Hitchcock completes the direction of his first feature, *The Pleasure Garden*. He begins a nine-film collaboration with scenarist Eliot Stannard.

1926   *The Mountain Eagle*, like his first feature, is shot at Emelka Studios in Munich. There are no known prints of this film in existence. His third feature, *The Lodger*, would later be referred to (by the director himself) as the first "'true' Hitchcock film." Initially shelved, it is re-edited under the supervision of Ivor Montagu. *The Lodger* is a major critical and commercial hit. Hitchcock marries Alma Reville, who he met at Famous Players-Lasky in 1921 and who worked as editor on *Woman to Woman* (1923). Reville serves as assistant director on Hitchcock's first three features.

1927   After shooting *Downhill* and *Easy Virtue* Hitchcock moves from Gainsborough to British International Pictures where he makes his next ten features, beginning with *The Ring*.

1928   *The Manxman, The Farmer's Wife, Champagne*. Birth of his only child Patricia Hitchcock on July 7.

1929   *Blackmail*, shot both as a silent and, first British sound film (two years after the first American sound film, *The Jazz Singer*). Also directs *Juno and the Paycock,* for which Alma Reville writes the scenario. She is credited as scenarist on Hitchcock's next six films.

1930   Certain sections of *Elstree Calling,* and *Murder!*

1931   *Mary*, a German version of *Murder!*, and *The Skin Game*.

1932   *Number Seventeen* and *Rich and Strange*.

1933   Hitchcock produces *Lord Camber's Ladies*, his last venture with British International. Working as a freelance director, he makes

Waltzes from Vienna, at Gaumont-British studios for independent producer Tom Arnold. (He later would consider this one of the lowest ebbs of his career.) While shooting the film he is reunited with Balcon, now executive in charge of production for Gaumont-British. Hitchcock signs a five-picture deal with producer and studio.

1934 *The Man Who Knew Too Much*. First of several collaborations with Balcon and Montagu (producers) and Charles Bennett (screenwriter). It is this series of films which establish Hitchcock's reputation as "Master of Suspense."

1935 *The Thirty-Nine Steps*.

1936 *Secret Agent* and *Sabotage*.

1937 *Young and Innocent*.

1938 *The Lady Vanishes*. Hitchcock wins Best Director prize from New York Film Critics.

1939 *Jamaica Inn*, last film of his "British period": twenty-three films in fourteen years (nine of which are silent). Signs Hollywood contract with David O. Selznick, producer of *Gone with the Wind* (Best Picture Oscar, 1939).

1940 *Rebecca*. Hitchcock's first Hollywood film wins Best Picture Oscar for Selznick. Hitchcock is nominated for Best Director but loses to John Ford for *The Grapes of Wrath*. During his "Selznick period," Hitchcock makes ten films but only three are actually produced by Selznick Pictures (the others: *Spellbound* and *The Paradine Case*). Mostly, Hitchcock is loaned out by Selznick to other producers and studios for increasingly larger fees beneficial to Selznick alone. Hitchcock's second Hollywood film, *Foreign Correspondent* is, also nominated for Best Picture. It is made by the independent producer Walter Wanger.

1941 *Mr. and Mrs. Smith* and *Suspicion*. The latter wins Best Actress Oscar for Joan Fontaine, and begins Hitchcock's four-film collaboration with Cary Grant (the other three are *Notorious*, *To Catch a Thief*, and *North By Northwest*).

1942 *Saboteur*.

1943 *Shadow of a Doubt*. Hitchcock's mother, whose health had been in decline for several months, dies on September 26 while the film is in production. His brother would die a few months later under somewhat "mysterious" circumstances (according to biographer Donald Spoto).

1944 *Lifeboat*. Hitchcock receives his second nomination for Best

Director despite the controversy generated by the film's almost sympathetic portrayal of a Nazi sailor. As part of the war effort, Hitchcock directs two short films for the British Ministry of Information, *Aventure Malgache* and *Bon Voyage.*

1945   *Spellbound.* The first of three films made with Ingrid Bergman (along with *Notorious* and *Under Capricorn*). Hitchcock returns to England to supervise the making of a compilation documentary *The Memory of the Camps* detailing the horrors of the Nazi death camps. Hitchcock writes a detailed treatment and oversees the editing of footage shot by Allied cameraman. The documentary is not completed.

1946   *Notorious.* Hitchcock's first film with costume designer Edith Head. She collaborates with him again on *Rear Window* and all but four of the director's final thirteen works.

1947   *The Paradine Case.* Hitchcock's last film with Selznick.

1948   *Rope.* Hitchcock's first color work and arguably his most experimental. The feature was meant to consist entirely of ten-minute long takes. It begins a four-film collaboration with James Stewart (the others are *Rear Window, The Man Who Knew Too Much,* and *Vertigo*). *Rope* is made for Hitchcock's own production company Transatlantic Pictures, formed in collaboration with Sidney Bernstein. The company produces only two films, *Rope* and *Under Capricorn,* neither particularly successful.

1949   *Under Capricorn.*

1950   Hitchcock decides it is too risky to produce and finance one's own films. In the fifties he becomes an independent filmmaker signing multi-picture contracts with several different studios: Warner Bros. Paramount, Universal. *Stage Fright* is the first of five films made for Warner Bros.

1951   *Strangers on a Train.* Hitchcock's first genuine commercial success since *Notorious.* It is his first collaboration with cinematographer Robert Burks. Burks will shoot twelve of the next thirteen films. The exception is *Psycho,* which is shot with Hitchcock's television cameraman, John Russell.

1953   *I Confess.*

1954   *Dial M for Murder,* Hitchcock's experiment with 3-D, and *Rear Window.* Hitchcock receives his fourth nomination for Best Director for *Rear Window.* It is the first of six films made for Paramount and the first of four consecutive collaborations with the scriptwriter John Michael Hayes. It is edited by George Tomasini who will serve as editor on nine of the next ten Hitchcock films (the exception being: *The Trouble with Harry*).

1955 *To Catch a Thief, The Trouble with Harry.* The latter features music by the composer Bernard Herrmann. He will work on the next eight films, including *The Birds,* which has no musical score but which lists Herrmann as "sound consultant." *Alfred Hitchcock Presents*, a half-hour television series debuts on CBS. Hitchcock directs three episodes: "Revenge," "Breakdown," and "The Case of Mr. Pelham."

1956 *The Man Who Knew Too Much* and three episodes of *Alfred Hitchcock Presents*: "Back for Christmas," "Wet Saturday," and "Mr. Blanchard's Secret."

1957 *The Wrong Man* and three episodes of *Alfred Hitchcock Presents*: "One More Mile to Go," "Four O'Clock," and "The Perfect Crime." In Paris, Eric Rohmer and Claude Chabrol publish the first book-length study of the auteur.

1958 *Vertigo* and three episodes of *Alfred Hitchcock Presents*: "Lamb to the Slaughter," "A Dip in the Pool," and "Poison."

1959 *North by Northwest* and three episodes of *Alfred Hitchcock Presents*: "Banquo's Chair," "Arthur," and "The Crystal Trench."

1960 *Psycho.* Released by Paramount but shot at Universal. Due to reluctance on the part of his studio, Hitchcock offers to shoot it on a small budget and a short production schedule using members of his television crew. He also agrees to waive his usual salary ($200,000 plus bonuses) for 60 percent ownership of the negative. Paramount agrees, convinced that *Psycho* is minor Hitchcock. Instead, the film becomes the most commercially successful black-and-white motion picture since Griffith's *Birth of a Nation* (1915). Hitchcock receives his fifth, and last, nomination for Best Director. Directs two episodes of *Alfred Hitchcock Presents*: "Incident at a Corner," and "Mr.Bixby and the Colonel's Coat."

1961 Two episodes of *Alfred Hitchcock Presents*: "Horse Player" and "Bang! You're Dead."

1962 *Alfred Hitchcock Presents* is transformed into *Alfred Hitchcock Hour.* (Title change coincides with the show's return to CBS after a two-year run on NBC.) Hitchcock directs only one episode: "I Saw the Whole Thing." This version will run for two more years on CBS, then return to NBC for one final season. Show ends its run, after ten seasons, in 1965.

1963 *The Birds.* The first film of a multi-picture deal with Universal. Hitchcock makes his last six films for this studio. He also becomes a major stockholder in the company during this period, trading his rights to *Psycho* and the television series for 150,000 shares.

1964   *Marnie*. Hitchcock's last collaboration with Burks, Tomasini, and Herrmann. (Burks and Tomasini both die shortly after their work on this film is completed. Herrmann is hired to compose the music for *Torn Curtain* but is eventually fired. They never speak after this.)

1966   *Torn Curtain*.

1968   Hitchcock receives lifetime achievement award (Irving G. Thalberg Memorial) at the Oscars.

1969   Hitchcock develops *Kaleidoscope*, an Antonioni-esque experiment to be shot on location in New York City, but Universal does not back the project. The studio convince Hitchcock to make an international spy thriller: *Topaz*. It is a critical and commercial failure.

1972   *Frenzy*. Shot in London on a relatively small budget (and away from the prying eyes of the studio). Hitchcock originally asks Vladimir Nabokov to write the script. Nabokov declines. The screenplay is written instead by the playwright Anthony Shaffer (*Sleuth*). The film is a commercial success, finishing among the top moneymakers of the year.

1976   *Family Plot*. Hitchcock's final film, made when he is 75 years old. The director has a pacemaker installed shortly before the beginning of production.

1978   Hitchcock begins work on his fifty-fourth feature to be called *The Short Night*. There is extensive preparation on the script but due to the filmmaker's declining health the film is never made.

1980   Hitchcock dies April 29, a few months after receiving a knighthood.

INTRODUCTION

Richard Allen

On October 13–17, 1999, the Department of Cinema Studies at New York University, of which I was then the chair, organized a large-scale conference, "Hitchcock: A Centennial Celebration," to mark the centenary of Alfred Hitchcock's birth on August 13, 1899. The conference comprised both a large number of academic panels devoted to various aspects of Hitchcock's work and plenary sessions featuring a number of Hitchcock's film collaborators: the screenwriters Jay Presson Allen, Evan Hunter, Arthur Laurents, and Joe Stefano; and the actors Patricia Hitchcock, Janet Leigh, Eva Marie Saint, and Teresa Wright.[1] *Hitchcock: Past and Future* presents a selection of the academic papers presented at the conference. Some have been extensively revised and expanded, while others are printed here more or less as they were given at the time. The Hitchcock centenary seemed an opportune moment to reassert the significance and value of cinema as a form of artistic expression through a consideration of one of the medium's most widely celebrated and influential practitioners. Hitchcock is an exemplary figure in this context because he embodies what has always been at stake in defending film as an art form once it is conceded that film, given its thorough dependence on technical equipment, can actually be an art form. This is the relationship that the medium bears to a mass audience on account of its dependence upon technology and technical development to which stylistic innovation is, as Hitchcock recognized, partially wedded. Filmmaking at the highest technical standard requires on-going capital investment in order to be sustained on a consistent basis, and hence it presupposes a large and regular stream of revenue that only a mass audience can provide. Hitchcock's films demonstrate, perhaps better than the works of any other director, the achievements that are possible in film as a medium for reflecting upon the conditions of human existence in a context where the production of art is explicitly concerned with maintaining commercial appeal. The auteurist critics of *Cahiers du cinéma* were the first to recognize Hitchcock's exemplary status in this regard. Furthermore, while successive generations of ideological critics have sought to point out the ways in which Hitchcock's films inhabit narrative conventions that reproduce certain cultural stereotypes, they have nonetheless singled Hitchcock out for the self-conscious way in which he inhabits these conventions and calls into question the patterns of human behavior and interaction they reproduce.

It is worth reminding ourselves at this time what can be achieved in cinema, in particular in popular cinema, and what can be achieved by its study, even at the risk of further canonization of an already canonized figure.[2] For the idea of the study of films as works of art – that is, as objects valued in their uniqueness or specificity for what they are and for what they say – is under threat by certain contemporary scholars who seem intent on reducing the study of film to an analysis of how they are received by audiences, circulate in culture, and reflect or resonate with other kinds of cultural forms and social processes. Even when the valorization and explication of film as an art form is not explicitly dismissed as an elitist enterprise, it is nonetheless eschewed in favor of defining the medium in terms of social "effects" and the kind of "pleasures" it solicits, pleasures that are in principle equally available from numerous kinds of cultural objects. Either way, what is abandoned is the role of aesthetic judgment in discriminating exactly what is valuable about films and how they contribute to human culture, whether their value lies in formal qualities alone, or whether it lies in the cognitive function of films, their capacity to reflect upon, and to move their audience to reflect upon, the culture of which they are a part.

This is not the place to diagnose the pervasive skepticism about textual meaning, about the objectivity of value judgments, indeed about the possibility of human agreement itself that underlies the denigration of the study of cinema as an art form in the university just as it threatens humanistic understanding in general, suffice it to say that "Hitchcock: A Centennial Celebration" was conceived as an antidote to such a skepticism and the devaluation of the art of film it engenders.[3] I cannot claim, of course, that all the participants at the conference – the contributors to this volume in particular – share my diagnosis of the state of film studies or my conception of the role of Hitchcock and Hitchcock Studies as a possible antidote to it. There was, nevertheless, a spirit of celebration at the conference regarding Hitchcock's achievements in film, or what was achieved under Hitchcock's name, and it is reflected in the tone of many of the scholarly essays in this collection. For while they are undoubtedly methodologically diverse in a manner that reflects the range of papers that were presented at the conference, they are characterized by a concern to explicate, and, yes, to celebrate, the expressive and representational possibilities and parameters of Hitchcock's work, even as some of them seek to qualify an authorially-based understanding of it.

We have divided the material into four parts, although certainly some of the papers could be placed in more than one of these subdivisions. Part I consists of papers that investigate central topics in Hitchcock's aesthetics and reflect, as a result, upon Hitchcock's overall profile as auteur and some of the characteristics that distinguish the various phases of his career. Peter Wollen, in an essay of broad compass entitled "Hitch: A Tale of Two Cities (London and Los Angeles)," situates Hitchcock's identity as a filmmaker between the cultural polarities embodied in the contrast between London and Los Angeles. Although Hitchcock began his filmmaking career in Britain and made nearly half of his fifty-three films there, he worked for an American studio with American stars and always aspired to the ideal of technical perfectionism achieved in Hollywood filmmaking, as well as the power it wielded over a mass audience. Yet, as Wollen points out, Hitchcock's characteristic artistic preoccupations – his music-hall sense of humor, his view of murder as one of the fine arts, his preoccupation with sexuality as forbidden fruit, and his abiding interest both in the thriller genre and in aesthetic experimentation – were all bequeathed by the culture in which he was raised. While Hollywood amply provided him with the technical resources to realize his artistic concerns in a way that his home country could ill afford, Hitchcock remained thoroughly of the English middle-class in his habits and manners. Firmly ensconced in Bel-Air, Hitchcock consistently returned to British material and to British collaborators for inspiration.

James Naremore's groundbreaking paper "Hitchcock and Humor" addresses a central aspect of the filmmaker's work that has been thoroughly neglected in the critical literature.[4] Naremore demonstrates that Hitchcockian humor combines the orchestration of extreme anxiety with deflationary moments of comedy, often represented in the diegesis itself through iconoclastic laughter in a manner that is characteristic of the gallows humor or black humor theorized by Freud and celebrated by André Breton. Naremore notes some of the key practitioners of black humor who influenced Hitchcock – such as De Quince, Poe, Wilde, and O'Henry – and finds the fullest realization of this aesthetic in the short-story format of Hitchcock's television series. Hitchcock's television work, Naremore argues, is central to understanding his œuvre, for in this new medium Hitchcock was free to abandon the format of the wrong man narrative, which typically liberated the hero from the taint of villainy and restored the conventional moral order, in favor of "morbidly satiric" tales that were devoid of innocent characters and that frequently invited viewers to identify with the point of view of the criminal mind. In this way, Hitchcock prepared the ground for *Psycho*, a film that Naremore describes as "Hitchcock's most brilliant and frightening exercise in black humor."

Bettina Rosenbladt's contribution to the volume, "Doubles and Doubts in Hitchcock: The German Connection" undertakes a detailed examination of the murderous double in Hitchcock's works by probing the origins of this figure in German expressionist film and its literary forbears. Through a close reading of *The Cabinet of Dr. Caligari* (1919) and *Nosferatu* (1922), she shows how a doubling motif is sustained in both films through the interweaving of uncanny themes and elliptical narrative form. She suggests that they embody different iconographic traditions, both of which profoundly influenced Hitchcock. In the first, the figure of the double is given a psychological connotation through the pervasive mood of uncertainty and foreboding created by the use of light and shadow; in the second, the figuration of the double is given a more objective metaphysical weight by being connected with forces of nature. Through detailed interpretations of *The Lodger* and *Shadow of a Doubt*, Rosenbladt argues that "while the double increasingly loses much of its obvious otherness," it also "gains in uncanniness by its very likeness to other characters in the film and to ourselves." She also traces a distinct shift between the early works, where the films' complex doubling seems mainly to entertain the audience with Hitchcock's directorial brilliance and legerdemain, and the later work, in which complex doubling motifs prompt us to reflect upon the role of the family and the situation of women in modern America.

Joe McElhaney's essay "The Object and the Face: *Notorious*, Bergman, and the Close-Up" takes as its point of departure two seemingly opposed statements on Hitchcock made by Jean-Luc Godard over a forty-year period. While Godard, in 1957, celebrates Hitchcock's capacity, amidst a transparently fictive narrative, to document the human face and the emotion it registers in a manner akin to the neorealist filmmakers, he later (in *Histoires du cinéma*) claims that Hitchcock creates a world of structures and surfaces devoid of human content, and thus what we remember in his films are close-ups not of people but of objects. Through a detailed examination of Hitchcock's use of the close-up in *Notorious*, McElhaney argues that the key to the filmmaker's aesthetic lies in the expressive tension created between the subjectifying and objectifying aspects of the cinematic close-up that is dramatized in the way in which Hitchcock's camera engages Bergman's star persona. Bergman is an actress whose star persona, like that of the great silent film actresses, is embodied in her face. Yet it is a face that is antithetical, in its expressivity and mobility, to the glamorous, yet forbidding, mask-like persona of a Garbo. The pathos of *Notorious* lies in the manner in which Bergman's face, as it becomes related in a series of close-ups to a network of deadly gestures and objects, is increasingly drained of expression, as if de-natured or object-ified. In this way, the expressive dimension of Bergman's face is registered by Hitchcock's camera through its very occlusion. In conclusion, McElhaney compares Bergman's work with Hitchcock to her later films with Rossellini in order to challenge the conventional opposition (repeated by Godard) between neorealism and Hitchcock.

This part concludes with Sid Gottlieb's carefully researched essay on "Unknown Hitchcock: The Unrealized Projects," which draws attention to the remarkable range of ideas and plans for films that, for one reason or another, never came to fruition. Gottlieb surveys several projects that Hitchcock extensively developed, yet which remained unfilmed. He argues that they are of particular interest for the light they shed upon the director's enduring concerns: his improvisation and creativity; his attempts to refashion himself at various times during his career; his approach to collaboration, especially in pre-production; and finally, his attempts to negotiate the external constraints placed upon his productivity. Can these unrealized works give us insight into the films that Hitchcock did succeed in making? While Gottlieb resists categorizing Hitchcock as an "artist of the incomplete," the nature and range of his unrealized projects and ideas do suggest the extent to which the projects that were actually realized on film do themselves manifest degrees of incompletion, as Slavoj Žižek's discussion of alternative endings to Hitchcock's films in the final essay in the volume attests.

The French reception of Hitchcock has been of signal importance in critical assessments of the filmmaker's work, and the essays in Part II analyze different facets of this reception. In "To Catch a Liar: Bazin, Chabrol and Truffaut Encounter Hitchcock," James Vest focuses upon the extraordinary encounters between the cineastes of *Cahiers du cinéma* and the laconic director on location in the French Riviera to shoot footage for *To Catch a Thief* in the summer of 1954. As Vest points out, for the young critics of *Cahiers*, Hitchcock was a pivotal figure in their polemic on behalf of the director as auteur. Their mentor, André Bazin, was more skeptical both about auteurism and about the status of Hitchcock himself; nonetheless, he allowed eleven articles on the director to be published in a three-year period, and was the first to interview him for the magazine. Bazin was shocked both by the director's attitude on set and by Hitchcock's evasion of his questions, and the younger cineastes faired no better in subsequent interviews. It was Truffaut who most ingeniously handled the unresponsive filmmaker by concluding that the director himself was a Hitchcockian creature, a dissembler, who must be compelled to confess like his characters. Yet while Hitchcock initially made light of the claims of his French admirers, he nonetheless increasingly assumed the mantle of auteur that seemed expressly created for him. In this way, the ground was prepared for the series of interviews (or confessions) that resulted in Truffaut's book *Hitchcock* as well as the subsequent critical valorization of Hitchcock as master auteur.

Complementing Vest's historical study, Walter Raubicheck in "*Hitchcock, the First Forty-Four Films:* Chabrol's and Rohmer 'Politique des Auteurs' " undertakes a detailed re-evaluation of Claude Chabrol's and Eric Rohmer seminal 1957 monograph on the director. He argues that the central thesis of their work – "form does not embellish content, it creates it" – arises from a critical dialogue with André Bazin, who cannot account for Hitchcock's distinctive genius from the standpoint of his realist aesthetic. For Bazin, Hitchcock's style betrays an excessive allegiance to a constructivist school of montage and visual expressionism that imposes an interpretation upon "reality" rather than allowing this reality to (ambiguously) unfold, as it does in the mise-en-scène aesthetic of Welles. While Chabrol and Rohmer do not reject Bazin's aesthetic in the sense that their focus is nearly always on the content of the shot and how it is photographed rather than the relationships between shots, they conceive of realism in the cinema as something that arises from the organization of the material elements of film rather than as something that is "conditioned by the location of objects in space and time." Hitchcock's visual style, then, is not characterized by "shallow virtuosity" but a masterful blending of form with content in a manner that will provide a model for their own filmmaking practice.

While Vest and Raubicheck usefully remind us of the original and productive encounters between Hitchcock and his Parisian admirers, Sam Ishii-Gonzáles, in "Hitchcock with Deleuze," focuses on a more recent French reading of the director: the commentary on Hitchcock found in the philosopher Gilles Deleuze's two-volume study of cinema published in France in 1983 and 1985, respectively. Deleuze positions Hitchcock between the two representational systems that characterize the history of the medium: the movement-image (of classical cinema) and the time-image (of modern cinema). According to Deleuze, Hitchcock invents a new kind of image that he calls the "mental-image" or "relation-image" which makes the process of thought itself the object of signification. Hitchcock renders palpable percepts and affects, and in so doing he paves the way for the modern cinema of Antonioni, Godard, Resnais, *et al*. What is not clear in Deleuze, however, is the development or evolution of the mental-image in the filmmaker's work. Ishii-Gonzáles argues that this image develops over a period of years and reaches its perfection in the fifties, particularly in *Rear Window*, *The Wrong Man,* and *Vertigo*. It is in this trio of films most of all that we can understand Deleuze's claims for Hitchcock as avatar of both the classical cinema of perceptive, affective, and active montage and the modern cinema of time.

Part III explores the representation of personal and political identity in Hitchcock's works. This topic has been of central importance for critics who write from the standpoint of contemporary critical theory and for whom Hitchcock's films become an occasion to investigate the relationship between the social and aesthetic construction of identity, whether it is understood in the broadest terms (the idea of personal identity as a whole) or whether it is conceived more narrowly, say, in terms of a gendered subject or a subject defined by sexual orientation. Daniel Srebnick's essay, "Music and Identity: The Struggle for Harmony in *Vertigo*," approaches the topic of the formation of identity in more narrowly aesthetic terms, arguing that Bernard Herrmann's music for *Vertigo* provides a sonic evocation of the struggle for identity dramatized in the film. Herrmann contrasts music that has a stable tonal center, embodied in the main "love theme," with densely chromatic sequences that lack tonal stability and create a sense of musical dissonance. The listener struggles to find a stable or predictable harmonic structure (whether tonal or atonal) where the ear can rest. In this way, the score at once cues and expresses the psychological struggle of James Stewart's character Scottie Ferguson as he strives to reconcile the dictates of reason with those of desire. While this musical tension characterizes the overall architecture of Herrmann's score, it is exemplified, for Srebnick, in the ascending and descending E flat minor/major 7th arpeggios that open the film and later accompany Judy's transformation into Madeleine. These arpeggios, which pull the listener in opposing directions simultaneously, provide an aural evocation of Scottie's acrophobia and thereby express his deeper fear of ascending to the place where the narrative secret might be revealed and his own identity resolved.

In "The Silence of *The Birds*: Sound Aesthetics and Public Space in Later Hitchcock," Angelo Restivo takes as his point of departure Slavoj Žižek's psychoanalytic diagnosis of a shift in Hitchcock's work towards films whose formal construction undermines the fictions of subjective and social cohesion that are sustained in his earlier films. He asks: can we characterize the filmmaker's stylistic innovations in a manner that links them to wider developments in the social field and thereby provide a more precise historical grounding for Žižek's psychoanalytic claims? Restivo suggests that in his postwar films Hitchcock undertakes a reconfiguration of cinematic space by deploying "acousmatic" or disembodied sound (a concept first described by Michel Chion). Since the source of "acousmatic" sound is invisible, it has the potential to undermine the distinction between what is inside the legible, visible, public space of action and what is outside it. By reconfiguring, in this way, the relationship between social and psychic space, Hitchcock's films not only respond to the emergence of television but to the wider postwar shift in capitalist economy from modes of production to modes of consumption. As Restivo demonstrates through an analysis of the extraordinary sound design for *The Birds,* the reconfiguration of cinematic space in Hitchcock's works of this period do not merely reflect the changes taking place in culture at large but are themselves actively engaged (both formally and thematically) with these issues.

Adam Lowenstein's essay, "The Master, The Maniac, and *Frenzy*: Hitchcock's Legacy of Horror," challenges the assumption, enshrined in negative critical reactions to the film, that the explicitness of *Frenzy* is an aberration in Hitchcock's work, a departure from a restrained aesthetics of suspense that is assumed by many critics to distinguish his œuvre from the maniacal world of post-Hitchcockian horror that the film seems to herald. Instead, Lowenstein argues, *Frenzy* combines restraint and suspense with moments of terror in a manner that is characteristic of other Hitchcock works such as *Sabotage* and *Psycho*. But whereas *Sabotage* unwittingly violates audience sympathies in its moment of terror, *Frenzy* is designed to "foreground outrage," and while *Psycho* relies on artful suggestion at the moment audience sympathies are betrayed by the sudden murder of its heroine, *Frenzy*'s depiction of sexual violence is graphic and unadorned. *Frenzy* thus makes explicit the manner in which surface decorum in Hitchcock is always subtended by incipient violence. Lowenstein argues persuasively that while British critics, especially, felt that the film was dated in its portrayal of London, its apparent anachronisms serve to represent archetypes of British class identity that serve a deeper artistic purpose. For what *Frenzy* suggests in its systematic exposure of the brutality that lurks beneath the veneer of social propriety is nothing less than a critique of British national identity itself in which the proverbial stiff upper lip is revealed as a veneer of cynicism and hypocrisy, and the working-class milieu of Covent Garden, so often nostalgically or idealistically portrayed, is a place where murder is the real work that is done.

In "Hitchcock's Ireland: The Performance of Irish Identity in *Juno and the Paycock* and *Under Capricorn*," James Morrison argues explicitly against the commonplace assumption that Hitchcock is an a-political, if formally experimental director, by offering an extended meditation on the topics of national identity and colonialist domination in Hitchcock's two explicitly Irish-themed films: his 1930 adaptation of Sean O'Casey's *Juno and the Paycock* and his 1949 version of Helen Simpson's novel *Under Capricorn*. Both films, Morrison suggests, present national identity or allegiance as a species of performance or theatricality that challenge any essentialist conception of national affiliation. In *Juno and the Paycock*, Hitchcock consciously foregrounds O'Casey's own preoccupation with the delusory narcissism of Irish nationalism and presents it as the mirror image of English imperial domination. In *Under Capricorn*, the Irish protagonists are at once portrayed as complicit with, yet also subject to, colonial authority. Furthermore, through the use of long takes, Hitchcock at once suggests what the all-encompassing gaze of colonial authority excludes, (what remains off-screen), and conveys a sense of the impermanence or fictiveness of the colonial mansion that forms the central location of the film. In these ways, Hitchcock enacts a critique of Irish national identity through the experimental form in which his work is cast.

To conclude this part of the volume, Patricia White, in "Hitchcock and Hom(m)osexuality," interrogates from a lesbian perspective the growing body of queer theoretical writing on Hitchcock exemplified in D.A. Miller's seminal analysis of *Rope* and Lee Edelman's recent work on several Hitchcock films including *Rear Window*. The discourse of queer theory parallels the feminist critique of the authority of heterosexual masculinity and the male author. Yet by pre-empting the critique of gender oppression with the diagnosis of homophobia and the displaced, aestheticized expressions of homosexual desire that are complementary to it, queer theory reproduces the very indifference to female desire that was the original object of feminist critique, and re-establishes, albeit on different terms, the authority of the male author. White borrows Luce Irigaray's neologism "hom(m)osexuality" to diagnose the way in which male subjectivity, embodied in male-centered discourse, defines the field of sexuality, and the manner in which these queer readings of Hitchcock uphold the authority of masculinity, even as that masculinity is reconceived as an anal–homosexual form rather than a phallic–heterosexist one. In the final part of her chapter, White develops a counter-discourse to this masculinist definition of the field of sexuality by locating the presence of lesbian desire in Hitchcock's *Stage Fright*. As in *Rebecca*, the ostensible narrative is that of one woman trying to prove the guilt of another in a manner that restores patriarchy. But like that earlier film (based on a novel by Daphne du Maurier), *Stage Fright* simultaneously produces a counter-narrative about the obsession of one woman for another. This lesbian desire is invoked by the extraordinary presence of Marlene Dietrich, whose authorship of her own self-display for a female gaze far exceeds the control of Hitchcock, the male author.

The three chapters comprising the final part contemplate the manner in which the spectacle and figuration of death haunts the narrative universe of Hitchcock's films, in particular in his subversive masterpiece *Psycho*. Commencing with Godard's epigram "The cinema is death 24 times a second," Laura Mulvey, in "Death Drives," undertakes a subtle meditation on the death of cinema and the role of death in narrative film through a close analysis of Hitchcock's 1960 work prompted by a viewing of Douglas Gordon's video installation, *24-Hour Psycho*. For Mulvey, *Psycho* represents a turning point in the history of cinema, as well as Hitchcock's œuvre. While conventional narrative film is characterized by a fairy-tale plot whose forward-looking trajectory results in the formation of the couple that returns us to the place where it began (the family home), Hitchcock characteristically combines this plot with the story of a crime and the unmasking of a criminal in a spectacular death that coincides with the romantic union. In this way, even Hitchcock's more "conventional" films link the spectacle of death with the formation of the couple in a manner that undermines the facile optimism of romance. However, in the first part of *Psycho*,

Hitchcock strips away the armature of romance entirely by figuring the forward momentum of the romance plot as a "death drive," an ineluctable movement towards death and hence towards stasis that is given a literal rendition in the frozen shot of Marion's eye that closes the sequence. The second part involves a backward movement towards the realm of the uncanny embodied in the enclosed space of the maternal home where we arrive finally at the conflation of the inanimate with the animate in the form of living deadness that is, for Mulvey, the origin and condition of cinema itself.

In a learned and ingenious contribution to Hitchcock scholarship, "Of 'Farther Uses of the Dead to the Living': Hitchcock and Jeremy Bentham," Miran Bozovic identifies a progenitor of *Psycho*'s Norman Bates, and by extension Alfred Hitchcock, in the utilitarian philosopher Jeremy Bentham, who lived from 1748 to 1832. Bentham requested that his dead body be dissected so that it might have the greatest value for the living. Dissection, as Bozovic points out, had been legally restricted to the corpses of villains. This created an acute shortage of corpses that encouraged body theft, and, in the notorious case of Burke and Hare, murder itself. However, Bentham also made a still more radical suggestion. He proposed that after dissection his body be preserved and displayed as an "auto-icon," that is, as the best representation of Bentham himself. Indeed, Bentham went so far as to imagine a theater of preserved corpses in which dialogues between great figures of the past (including Bentham himself) would be staged "in person." Bozovic discovers in Norman Bates a figure that combines Bentham's novel idea of a theater of corpses with the older, delinquent "wild utilitarianism" of Burke and Hare who killed people in order to use their dead bodies. Norman's fate, he concludes, is rather like that of Burke whose body was preserved as a reminder of his crimes, although Norman is, in effect, stuffed while still alive, condemned to sit and stare vacantly like the preserved corpse of his mother with which he has become irrevocably assimilated.

The failure of Gus Van Sant's recent so-called shot-by-shot remake of *Psycho* prompts Slavoj Žižek to reflect upon what is unique or irreducible about Hitchcock's work. In his essay "Is There a Proper Way to Remake a Hitchcock Film?" he makes three proposals. First, Hitchcock's films are distinguished not by their narrative content but by patterns of visual, formal, material gestures or motifs (which Thomas Leitch has referred to as Hitchcock moments)[5] that cut across different narrative contexts, such as the motif of falling, or of the women who know too much, or the spiral. In Lacanian terms these motifs are not symptoms that mean something but *sinthoms*, gestures or patterns that are at once laden with emotional significance but semantically opaque. Secondly, as Žižek has argued elsewhere, a defining feature of the director's work is the inscription of an uncanny fantasmatic gaze, "the blind spot in the field of the visible from which the picture itself photo-graphs the spectator," and, in this context, he notes that

Lacan conducted Seminar I in the same year that *Rear Window* was released. Finally Hitchcock's films are characterized by their endings that resonate with alternative possibilities in a manner that anticipates digital media where the narrative world that is realized is explicitly acknowledged as only one from a set of possible options. Remakes, Žižek concludes, should either uncannily double Hitchcock's works, revealing their difference by their very sameness (in this respect Van Sant's *Psycho* is a failed masterpiece), or else they should stage one of the alternative scenarios that subtend the ones realized by Hitchcock, a paradigm for which is the eruption of the pre-ontological chaos of the Real exemplified in Coppola's *The Conversation*.

I am grateful to Sam Ishii-Gonzáles and Steven Schneider for their comments.

Notes

1   The most valuable material from the collaborators' panels has been published in successive volumes of The *Hitchcock Annual*. See "An Interview with Jay Presson Allen," *Hitchcock Annual* 2000–1, pp. 3–22, reprinted in Sid Gottlieb and Christopher Brookhouse (eds.) *Framing Hitchcock: Selected Essays from the Hitchcock Annual*, Detroit: Wayne State University Press, 2002, pp. 206–20; "Working with Hitch: A Screenwriter's Forum with Evan Hunter, Arthur Laurents, and Joe Stefano," *Hitchcock Annual* 2001–2, pp. 1–37; and "Working with Hitchcock: A Collaborators' Forum with Patricia Hitchcock, Janet Leigh, Eva Marie Saint, and Teresa Wright," *Hitchcock Annual 2002-3*, pp32-66
2   Some of the dangers as well as the benefits of the development of "Hitchcock Studies" are discussed by Sid Gottlieb in the Introduction to *Framing Hitchcock*, pp. 13–18.
3   I diagnose some of the problems raised by skepticism in the study of the arts together with Malcolm Turvey in "Wittgenstein's Later Philosophy: A Prophylaxis Against Theory" in Allen and Turvey (eds.) *Wittgenstein, Theory and the Arts*, London: Routledge, 2001, pp. 1–35.
4   The recent publication of Susan Smith's book *Hitchcock: Suspense, Humor and Tone*, London: BFI, 2000, has further compensated for the lack of critical attention to humor in Hitchcock's work.
5   See Thomas Leitch, "The Hitchcock Moment," in Gottlieb and Brookhouse, *Framing Hitchcock*, pp. 180–96.

Part I

AUTHORSHIP AND AESTHETICS

Chapter 1

Hitch
A tale of two cities London
and Los Angeles

Peter Wollen

This is an essay written against compartmentalization – specifically, the national compartmentalization of Hitchcock into "English" and "American." Hitchcock began his film career in 1920 when, after showing some samples of his work as a title card designer, he was hired by the new Famous Players-Lasky studio in Islington, a district in the north of London. This was an American-owned and managed studio and in his first three years of employment Hitchcock designed the titles and worked in other capacities for no less than eleven films. Just as it seemed that he might be able to make the transfer to direction, however, the American owners pulled out. The empty studio was rented to independent producers, this time actually English, one of whom, Michael Balcon, eventually launched Hitch on his long career as a director. Hitchcock subsequently made five pictures at Islington for Balcon and Gainsborough, still working, however, with then-famous American stars such as Virginia Valli, Carmelita Geraghty, and Nita Naldi. Thus, from the very start, Hitchcock, although based in his native London, with excursions to Germany, was closely connected to Los Angeles, first through his American employers and then through the presence of Hollywood stars on the set of his "English" films.

His time with Balcon was followed by nine years working for John Maxwell and British International at Elstree, another London suburb. It was during this period that Hitchcock triumphantly negotiated the transition to sound with his 1929 film, *Blackmail*. He continued working for Maxwell through 1932 before he returned to Balcon to make the first version of *The Man Who Knew Too Much*, which he re-made over twenty years later for Paramount as an American film. The second Balcon period secured Hitchcock's place as Britain's leading director, as he successfully completed a string of hits for Gaumont-British, culminating in *The Thirty-Nine Steps* and *Sabotage*, the first classic Hitchcock thrillers, which established Hitch as the "master of suspense." His very last picture for Balcon, *The Lady Vanishes*, further developed the mix of spy film and screwball comedy on which Hitch had built his reputation. Soon afterwards he was invited to Los Angeles where, basically, he recycled the same genre mix for his new Hollywood producers, eventually working with Cary Grant (rather than Robert Donat) as the star of *North by Northwest*. Grant – also, of course, from England – quickly became his preferred Hollywood actor.

We tend to think of Hitchcock's Englishness in terms of his childhood in Leytonstone, his rise upward through the class structure to Shamley Green in Surrey, his bullying "little man" sense of the world, his old-fashioned music hall sense of humor, his smirking taste for double entendre, his keen attention to social embarrassment, his Orwellian view of murder as one of the fine arts, and his fascination with sexuality as forbidden fruit. No doubt these are qualities rooted in his childhood as the son of a Catholic shopkeeper, as he nurtured aspirations towards becoming a sophisticated man of the world in a merciless English social scene to which he felt fundamentally unfitted by his class and his cultural background, his private fears, and his all too public rotundity and weight. But it was in England too that Hitchcock, so staunchly middle-brow in so many of his tastes, also acquired his cultivated interest in modern art, his perfectionism, his willingness to experiment, and his fascination with new techniques, to which he always turned with immediate enthusiasm. It was another side of England, the artistic sophistication that Hitchcock acquired through his social superiors at the London Film Society, which stimulated his abiding interest in experiment, which led him towards the dream sequences in *Spellbound* and *Vertigo*, the rolling camera in *Rope*, the virtuoso montage in *Psycho*, the use of the Kuleshov Effect in *Rear Window*, the electronic soundtrack in *The Birds,* and the unachieved collaboration with Len Lye on *The Secret Agent*.

Hitchcock became an American citizen in 1955, sixteen years after he had embarked for New York on the *Queen Mary*, together with his wife Alma (whom he met at Famous Players-Lasky), their daughter Pat, their cook, their maid, and Hitchcock's indispensable personal assistant Joan Harrison, who had been intimately involved in all Hitchcock's projects since 1935, the year he had first hired her as a secretary. Harrison stayed with Hitch when he left for the United States, working on his films right through to *Shadow of a Doubt*. Although she did leave in the late 1940s, in order to pursue her own independent career, she returned again to the fold in the 1950s, to take charge of the nostalgically named Shamley Productions, where she was responsible for organizing Hitch's extremely successful television series, *Alfred Hitchcock Presents*. Shamley Green, it is worth noting, was Hitchcock's last address in England, a lovingly restored Tudor cottage set in the countryside on the outskirts of London, which he reluctantly had to give up following his mother's and brother's death, since it was impractical to leave it empty.

For a long period of time after his arrival in America, however, Hitchcock was continually moving back and forth across the Atlantic – to make short films for the war effort, stung by taunts that he had fled the country in its hour of need, then back to Hollywood. He returned again to shoot *Under Capricorn* for the independent production company Transatlantic Pictures, which he had set up with Sidney Bernstein, an old friend from Film Society days, in order to escape the clutches of the monomaniacal Hollywood producer, David Selznick. In 1955, Hitchcock was back in London again, where he was introduced to Charlie Chaplin by Bernstein. Chaplin explained that he considered himself to be a citizen of the world and that consequently he saw no particular point in changing the nationality that he had arbitrarily acquired at his birth. Hitchcock argued that, as an American taxpayer, he felt that he was under a moral responsibility to become a citizen of his adopted country. However, as John Russell Taylor points out,[1] the very next film he made was *The Trouble With Harry*, a quintessentially English project, albeit transposed into an American setting – New England, of course.

If we look back at Hitchcock's very first English picture, *The Pleasure Garden* – actually Anglo-German – we find a film in which the two leading parts were both played by American female stars. When his English producer, Michael Balcon, saw the finished film, he commented that the picture seemed completely American in its lighting and style. Hitch responded that this was only to be expected, since the bulk of his cinematic experience, both in the industry and as a filmgoer, had actually been of American films. He wanted, in fact, to combine a view of the world that was quintessentially English with a professionalism and an overall look that were basically American. The stories that appealed most to Hitchcock, even when he was in America, were very English, both in style and atmosphere – du Maurier, for instance, or the spy thriller – and when they had American sources he Anglicized them through his own detailed work on the script and through his choice of collaborators who understood and tolerated his predilections. On the other hand, he also wanted the gloss and sophistication and technical polish of Hollywood. He wanted both London and Los Angeles.

When we recall the earlier "English" Hitchcock we think of black-and-white films that were typically based on West End stage hits, although the later Pinewood films were already veering towards the melodramatic thriller (Buchan, Maugham, Conrad, du Maurier). When we think of "American" Hitchcock we think of films in color, largely based on short stories or slim and fast-paced novels (Highsmith, Woolrich, Boileau and Narcejac, Bloch). In comparison, English Hitchcock can look awkwardly dated and confined – disjointed, like a

Nevinson painting, all jagged, angular, to use a phrase of Hitchcock's – while the later American Hitchcock seems more streamlined, more expansive, more hypnotic.[2] But, in the last analysis, English Hitchcock was always already striving to be American and Hollywood Hitchcock was always already drawing on a whirlpool of paranoia, sadism, voyeurism, and schizophrenia triggered by the very English obsessions and fears that Hitch brought with him from Leytonstone and Shamley Green to Bel-Air and Scotts Valley.

In retrospect, it is striking how many of Hitchcock's American studio projects were set in Britain or based on British source material. *Rebecca* was adapted from a du Maurier novel, *Foreign Correspondent* was set in London, *Suspicion* was based on a book by Francis Iles, the story idea for *Saboteur* was credited to Hitchcock himself, *Rope* came from a Patrick Hamilton play, *The Man Who Knew Too Much* was a re-make of the earlier English version, *North by Northwest* recycled *The Thirty-Nine Steps*, and so on, via J. Trevor Story's *The Trouble With Harry*, right through to *The Birds*, which came from Daphne du Maurier short story; *Marnie*, a Winston Graham novel originally set in Devon; and *Frenzy*, a thriller set in London, adapted from a novel by La Bern, a favorite author for directors of English spy films and crime thrillers. Similarly, his most successful source for television was the work of Roald Dahl. Working closely on these and other projects were Hitchcock himself, Alma (of course), Joan Harrison, Angus MacPhail, Charles Bennett, Raymond Chandler, Keith Waterhouse and Willis Hall.

One further footnote – perhaps most significant of all – Hitchcock, shortly after his arrival in Los Angeles, repaid the debt he owed from Islington days to both Jane Novak (star of *The Blackguard*, written by Hitch, directed by Graham Cutts) and Betty Compson (star of *Woman to Woman,* directed by Cutts, with Hitchcock as assistant director) by giving them each small parts in, respectively, *Foreign Correspondent* and *Mr. and Mrs. Smith*. Thus Hitchcock began his career as an English director in Hollywood by making an explicit connection to the American beginnings of his London career. The truth is that Hitchcock made every effort to Americanize himself professionally while he was still in England and then defiantly stuck to his English habits once he was ensconced in America.

There is a telltale story which Hitchcock recounted to John Russell Taylor. Towards the end of his career, he embarked on *Torn Curtain*, a project inspired by a very English spy story, but was prevailed upon by the studio, Universal, to cast Paul Newman opposite Julie Andrews – who was, at least, English. Newman, however, posed a serious problem. First, he was a Method-influenced actor and Hitchcock loathed not so much actors as such, but Method actors, as a particularly troublesome category. Hitch never forgot the horrors of his earlier experience with Montgomery Clift. Second, and much more unforgivably, Newman flaunted his shamelessly laddish American-ness. John Russell Taylor tells the story as follows: "The first real social encounter between Hitch and Newman got them off on the wrong foot. Hitch invited Newman home to a small dinner party. The first thing Newman did was to take off his jacket at table and drape it over the back of his chair. Then he refused Hitchcock's carefully chosen vintage wine and asked for beer instead. And, to make matters worse, he insisted on going and getting it himself out of the refrigerator and drinking it from the can." As Taylor notes, "the whole of the shooting was overshadowed by the judgments reached that evening."[3]

Lurking beneath this story, of course, was the question of social class. Hitchcock had acquired fame and wealth and, with them, he had cultivated an idealized upper-class lifestyle. Although he by no means came from a poor background – his father was a shopkeeper whose successful business was eventually incorporated into the nationwide chain store Mac Fisheries – he was still fascinated, from his earliest years, by the social style and mores of the traditional British upper classes. His enthusiastic attendance at London Film Society screenings had given him an entrée into the more sophisticated world whose values he envied, the world of Ivor Montagu and Adrian Brunel. In a way, his interest in Murnau or Eisenstein or vintage René Clair was related to his taste for champagne and Parisian cuisine. At the same time, he developed an ambivalent fascination with upper-class women. The problem with English actresses, he told an interviewer in 1935, was that "it is always their desire to appear a lady and, in doing so, they become cold and lifeless. Nothing pleases me more than to knock the ladylikeness out of chorus girls." In comparison, he thought, "many of the American stars have come from the poorest of homes. They have had the common touch, and they have never lost it."[4]

In fact, Hitchcock took these attitudes with him on the ship to America. His favored male alter egos – Farley Granger, James Stewart or Cary Grant – always appeared as sophisticates, whatever their real origins may have been, whereas when the women were dressed up as ladies they were then tormented for it, just as Madeleine Carroll was in *The Thirty-Nine Steps*. In fact, long before he got to America, Hitch had fantasies of humiliating female American stars – "If I were directing Claudette Colbert (whom I consider one of the loveliest women in American films), I should first show her as a mannequin. She would slink through the showroom in her elegant, French way, wearing gorgeous gowns as only such a woman can. She would be perfectly coiffured, perfectly made-up. Then I would show her backstage. As she disappeared through the curtains, I'd make her suck down a piece of toffee or chewing gum which she had kept in her mouth all the time she was looking so beautiful."[5] Of course, this particular fantasy, which Hitch justified as "a touch of realism," was nothing to what he was able to do when he actually got to Hollywood. Nor did he ever get the chance to direct Claudette Colbert, although she was his first choice for the female lead in *Foreign Correspondent*.

Shortly after Hitch's marriage to Alma (at the fashionable Brompton Oratory) and his honeymoon in fashionable St. Moritz, Michael Balcon suggested to Hitchcock that he might move to Mayfair, traditionally the "society" core of central London. Hitchcock rejected the idea, explaining "'I never felt any desire to move out of my own class."[6] Instead he moved into a maisonette, at the top of ninety-two stairs – no elevator – in a nondescript stretch of Cromwell Road. After he arrived in Los Angeles, however, Hitchcock acquired a house in fashionable Bel-Air, albeit a "snug little house" (in his words)[7] rather than a grandiose residence – John Russell Taylor describes it as "an English-style cottage (or what passed locally for one)." There he read the English papers, "sometimes weeks out of date" and "wearing invariably English, invariably formal clothes, in defiance of the climate and that noonday sun to which only mad dogs and Englishmen are impervious."[8] Despite his success, Hitchcock always stayed fundamentally middle class in his tastes and aspirations, except (perhaps) in the area of food and wine (where he cherished the opportunity of becoming a *bon viveur* in the old Edwardian style) and art (where he added Braque and Dubuffet to the Klee and Sickert already in his collection).

I think Hitchcock was happier in Los Angeles than he was in London, largely because he was able to play the waggish and eccentric Englishman without the self-consciousness that would have overcome him in England, as if the Southland gave him license to turn himself into something of a caricature without the shame he might have felt in London. In fact he made his image into a trademark, much as Chaplin had done before him – a comparison, I think, that was always in Hitchcock's mind. In his 1965 article on "Film Production" for the *Encyclopaedia Britannica,* he singled out a select group of directors as having a personal style – Lubitsch, Chaplin, DeMille, Griffith, Ince, Lang, and Murnau – all of them, like Hitch, directors from the silent era: three Americans and four Europeans who ended up in LA.[9] When Hitchcock reminisced about the silent days in 1936, he proudly quoted an English newspaper as saying, back in 1924, that *Woman to Woman* was "the best American picture made in England" – a film on which Hitchcock had worked, on his own account, as script-writer, set designer, *and* production manager.[10] "'In the beginning', he explained, 'I was American-trained' and, as he put it, 'therein lies my debt to America'."[11] Hitchcock repaid that debt richly when he finally arrived in the United States, but in English cultural coinage, by bringing to Los Angeles a vision of the world, a psycho-pathology and an obsession with filmmaking as an art that were profoundly English in their roots.

While Hitch was making *North by Northwest* he fantasized, apparently in a tipsy moment, that one day movies could be dispensed with altogether and the audience would be wired with electrodes to produce the requisite responses as the director, in John Russell Taylor's words, would "play on them as on a giant organ console."[12] This, I believe, was his ultimate dream of Hollywood. He was interested, of course, in all three of the main requisites for filmmaking – money, professionalism, and technology – and he found all three readily available in Los Angeles, whereas in London there was always somehow a bit of a problem. America permitted him to make the very English films he could only dream about making in England, yet that dream was itself rooted in his early experiences of Hollywood and his fascination with it. Where else could he make the great leap forward that he felt the cinema required if his dreams were to be fully realized? Hitchcock needed Los Angeles but, in the depths of his dreams and nightmares, he never left London. In America Hitch insulated himself in a private world of his own – a world that emerged into the public sphere in the form of his Hollywood masterpieces – yet his Los Angeles self could never escape from its London other. The two were inextricably interlocked from the beginning to the end of his career. To steal his own phrase, it was always a case of "Handcuffed, key lost!"

Notes

1 John Russell Taylor, *Hitch*, New York: Da Capo Press, 1996.
2 For Hitchcock's interest in modernist painting see Dominique Paini and Guy Cogeval (eds.) *Hitchcock et l'Art*, Paris: Mazzotta, for the Centre Pompidou, 2001.
3 Taylor, *Hitch*, p. 276.
4 Alfred Hitchcock, "Women are a Nuisance: An Interview with Barbara J. Buchanan," in Sidney Gottlieb (ed.) *Hitchcock on Hitchcock: Selected Writings and Interviews*, Berkeley and Los Angeles: University of California Press, 1995, p. 80. Originally published as "Alfred Hitchcock Tells a Woman that Women are a Nuisance," in *Film Weekly*, London, September 20, 1935.
5 Hitchcock, "Women are a Nuisance," in Gottlieb, *Hitchcock on Hitchcock*, p. 80.
6 Taylor, *Hitch*, p. 81.
7 Donald Spoto, *The Dark Side of Genius: The Life of Alfred Hitchcock*, New York: Ballantine Books, 1983, p. 266.
8 Taylor, *Hitch*, p. 174.
9 Alfred Hitchcock, "Film Production," in Gottlieb, *Hitchcock on Hitchcock*, pp. 216, 217. Originally published in *Encyclopaedia Britannica*, vol. 15, 1965, pp. 907–11.
10 The film critic of the *Daily Express*, London, 1924, cited in Alfred Hitchcock, "Close Your Eyes and Visualize," in Gottlieb, *Hitchcock on Hitchcock*, p. 246. Originally published in *The Stage*, London, July 1936.
11 Ibid.
12 Taylor, *Hitch*, p. 234.

Chapter 2

HITCHCOCK AND HUMOR

James Naremore

One of my earliest boyhood memories from an Alfred Hitchcock movie is of a scene in the American version of *The Man Who Knew Too Much* (1956), in which James Stewart, searching for a gang of assassins who have kidnapped his son, visits a Camden Town taxidermist named "Ambrose Chappell." The scene begins in typical Hitchcock fashion, with a slow tracking shot from Stewart's point of view as he approaches the taxidermist's shop at the end of a sinister alleyway. Inside, he encounters a shabby and benign-looking group of tradesmen, but the atmosphere is uneasy because we already know that people in this movie are not always what they seem, and because the stuffed animals arrayed about the room lend a menacing, rather eerie quality to the mise-en-scène. Stewart threatens the shop owner, accusing him of being a kidnapper, and when the taxidermists call the police, a scuffle breaks out. But then, in the midst of the fight, everything turns into a vaguely uncanny form of slapstick. Stewart realizes too late that the taxidermists are innocent, and the taxidermists alternately try to protect their stuffed animals and use them as weapons against Stewart, whom they regard as a madman. As Stewart struggles to escape, he catches his hand in the open mouth of a stuffed tiger, and at one point a fat little man threatens him with a dead sawfish. The sequence ends with a clever flourish of Bernard Herrmann's music and a huge close-up of a snarling lion that gazes ferociously at the audience.

What impressed me as a boy about this scene was that it was frightening, perverse, and funny *at the same time*. On some inarticulate level I was aware that I had experienced a quick shift in dramatic tone, but the scene also involved an intertwining of my laughing and screaming impulses; it began with a menacing tension that led to fearful laughter, then achieved a sublation of fear, and then capped everything with a scary surprise in the form of a lion who seemed to be saying "Boo." It did all of this, moreover, while making me pleasurably aware that the emotional machinery was being manipulated by a clever, behind-the-scenes entertainer.

Looked at today, the struggle in the taxidermist's shop no longer strikes me as quite so clever, and I doubt that anyone could argue that it marks an especially important moment in Hitchcock's career. Although it remains an entertaining diversion, it probably doesn't have a strong emotional efficacy for contemporary audiences, who are likely to find the stuffed creatures in Ambrose Chappell's shop much less spooky and witty than the ones in Norman Bates's parlor. I suspect, however, that everyone would agree that the scene is characteristic of Hitchcock; indeed, the emotional effects I've been trying to describe are among the chief things that enable us to distinguish him from, say, a director such as Fritz Lang, who was an equally great exponent of stories about crime and suspense.[1]

In retrospect, it seems odd to me that Hitchcock's critics have never paid close attention to his habit of mingling suspense and humor. As Gilberto Perez has recently noted, the analytic literature on Hitchcock is now so large that it threatens to outstrip his true importance: "for he would have to be incomparably the greatest of all filmmakers to merit the amount of critical and academic attention bestowed on him, well in excess of any other director's share and giving no sign of diminution."[2] (Then again, one could argue that he *is* the greatest filmmaker, for that very reason.) And yet, while the literature says a great deal about how Hitchcock creates suspense, shock, and psychological unease, it says relatively little about how he also produces jokes and laughter. Thus, in the useful introduction to *Hitchcock on Hitchcock*, editor Sidney Gottlieb briefly surveys the many critical approaches that have been taken with regard to the director and then remarks, "It surprises me that we still have not had a full treatment of the comic Hitchcock."[3] We do of course have important commentaries by Lesley Brill and Stanley Cavell on Hitchcock's uses of pastoral or romantic comedy; and, as Gottlieb observes, we have Thomas Leitch's fine book on Hitchcock as trickster and game-player.[4] But there is an especially important aspect of Hitchcock's work, described by British director Bruce Robinson as an "ability to make anxiety amusing," that everyone recognizes and almost nobody analyzes.[5] In what follows, I want to offer some thoughts about this kind of amusement, which is significant enough to justify adding a few more pages to the library of critical commentary.

Let me emphasize that my chief interest here is in the affective quality of "amusing anxiety," or in what I shall call "humor," as opposed to the broader and more generic notion of comic cinema. At the outset, however, a few words about comedy seem appropriate. A useful place to begin is with the fact that some of Hitchcock's favorite themes and narrative structures are equally well suited to tragic, melodramatic, or comic treatments. The mistaken identity plot, for example, can be found in both Sophocles and Plautus, and in both *The Wrong Man* and *North by Northwest*. By the same token, the characteristic emotional effects of a Hitchcock movie – suspense and surprise – are typical of both the cliff-hanging thriller and the practical joke. American director Andrew Bergman, a contemporary exponent of classic Hollywood's screwball tradition, makes a similar point when he observes that "what [Hitchcock] did in these thrillers is very close to what one attempts in comedy – placing ordinary characters in extraordinary situations."[6]

Actually, the ordinary/extraordinary formula can account for most films of the classic studio era, regardless of their ostensible genres. The standard Hollywood movie in the period is a modern variation on what classical scholars call "Greek New Comedy," a formula that Northrop Frye describes as follows: "What normally happens is that a young man wants a young woman, that his desire is resisted by some opposition … and that near the end of the play some twist in the plot enables the hero to have his will." [7] In Hollywood's case, this formula produces a boy-meets-girl story about beautiful but "ordinary" people in unusual circumstances, which usually ends with a kiss and a fadeout – a resolution that can sometimes appear both chaste and coyly suggestive, balancing the conflicting demands of traditional marriage and sexually liberated capitalism. As Dana Polan has argued, the formula is so pervasive that "each and every genre (and each and every scene within the films) is easily rewritable, the tone of each work easily transformable into its opposite."[8] Hence a picture about a sheriff who defends a town from outlaws can be treated seriously, as in *High Noon* (1952), or amusingly, as in *Rio Bravo* (1959), and the difference is largely a matter of tone rather than plot.

Hitchcock was the sort of director who enjoyed playing variations of tone within a given film, and classic Hollywood's all-purpose plot conventions tended to facilitate his style, enabling him to shift easily from light comic banter to melodramatic danger, sometimes within a single scene. Even so, he directed only one Hollywood film that was not about murder or death: the screwball comedy *Mr. and Mrs. Smith*, scripted by Norman Krasna and starring Carole Lombard and Robert Montgomery. This picture appeared late in the screwball cycle and was overshadowed by two other examples that have become legendary: Howard Hawks's *His Girl Friday* (1940) and Preston Sturges's *The Lady Eve* (1941). Perhaps for that reason, critics have usually regarded it as an oddity or as a project unsuited to Hitchcock's particular talents. But in fact, he had already made two straightforward comedies in England: *Champagne*, which Raymond Durgnat describes as "a kind of playgirl's *Sullivan's Travels*,"[9] and *Rich and Strange*, which is a fairly lighthearted treatment of suburban marriage.

In a recent essay, Lesley Brill has demonstrated that Hitchcock's American pictures, for all their atmosphere of anxiety and death, have a surprising number of important things in common with those of Preston Sturges; even a somber film such as *Vertigo* (1958), he notes, deals with many of the same themes as *The Lady Eve*.[10] Dana Polan takes this argument further, showing how most of Hitchcock's pictures could be rewritten as generic screwball comedies, just as screwball comedy itself could be rewritten in a more troubling mood. For example, the funniest scene in *Mr. and Mrs. Smith* takes place in a nightclub where Robert Montgomery undergoes a series of public humiliations during a failed attempt to show his estranged wife that he has a date that is more impressive than hers. As Polan observes, the scene is replete with what we usually regard as anxious Hitchcockian themes: "sexuality as a battle of gazes; public space as an agonic site overrun by a crowd turned mob, mocking one's every project; the self as finally nothing but vulnerable materiality."[11] These same themes are not far beneath the surface in the most hilarious moments of Sturges's *The Lady Eve*, but they can also be found in the most agonizing non-comic scene in Hitchcock's *Rebecca* when Joan Fontaine discovers she has worn the wrong dress to a ball. Consider as well *The Thirty-Nine Steps*, which places Robert Donat in all kinds of public situations where he has to put on an act, and which keeps veering from screwball romance to melodramatic danger to perverse anxiety. An equally obvious case in point is *Rear Window*, which derives much of its fascination from the way it interjects harrowing violence into a New-Comic plot. Probably the most extreme example (though it doesn't quite succeed in its comic/romantic moments) is *The Birds* (1963), which was designed by Hitchcock and screenwriter Evan Hunter to start out as a screwball comedy (spoiled heiress Tippi Hedren meets small-town bachelor Rod Taylor) and then become an apocalyptic horror movie; notice, moreover, that the two different modes of the film are linked by sly jokes, such as the bird-in-a-cage imagery of the opening scene, which is echoed later when the heroine is trapped in a phone booth and attacked by seagulls.

If we accept Northrop Frye's theory of fictional modes in *Anatomy of Criticism*, the tale of murder itself has an inherently comic tendency. It begins in the era of Sherlock Holmes as what Frye calls a "low mimetic" sharpening of attention to detail, so that "the dullest and most neglected trivia of daily living leap into mysterious and fateful significance," and quickly merges with the thriller "as one of the forms of melodrama."[12] In its melodramatic form, it deals with the "triumph of moral virtue over villainy," and is always in danger of becoming "advance propaganda for the police state" (p. 47). Nevertheless, Frye notes, the genre tends to be surrounded by "a protective wall of play," and the more serious and melodramatic it becomes, the more likely it is to be looked at ironically, with "its pity and fear seen as sentimental drivel and owlish solemnity." From this point, it easily develops toward the opposite pole of melodrama, which Frye describes as "comic irony or satire," or as the tendency to define "the enemy of society as a spirit within that society" (p. 47).

The scene I've described from *The Man Who Knew Too Much* can be viewed as a condensed and rather apolitical illustration of the process Frye has charted. It begins in melodrama, with the search for an innocent child who is kidnapped by terrorists from Morocco or from somewhere in the Balkans, and it quickly modulates into comedy, irony, and satire, with an American tourist wrestling a bunch of English shopkeepers. In Hitchcock's more darkly romantic or serious work, this same propensity toward dramatic irony creates a remarkable blend of melodrama and satire, so that it is often difficult to say where one feeling ends and the other begins. Isn't it vaguely amusing, in a rather detached and absurdist fashion, that the doctor in charge of an insane asylum should turn out to be psychotic? Or that a sailor from a sunken Nazi submarine should be rescued by a lifeboat filled with Americans and then turn out to be the most capable person aboard? Or that a beautiful woman should start out a film as an alcoholic and then almost die from drinking poisoned coffee? The list of these situations could be greatly lengthened; the ones I've mentioned are from, respectively, *Spellbound*, *Lifeboat*, and *Notorious* and they comprise what most people think of as Hitchcock "touch" – a feeling of iconoclastic laughter lurking behind classically wrought stories about romance, murder, and suspense.

The iconoclasm can be latent or overt. In nearly three decades of showing Hitchcock films to American college students, I've found that two scenes from his work are guaranteed to produce big laughs: the moment in *Strangers on a Train* when the villain Bruno Anthony uses his cigarette to explode a child's balloon, and the moment in *North by Northwest* when the hero Roger Thornhill finds himself standing over the dead body of a UN diplomat holding a bloody knife and being photographed by newspaper reporters. In each case, a suspenseful melodrama quickly spins on its heels and becomes a comic satire, and in each case the audience's laughter derives in part from the feeling that melodramatic convention is being reversed, mocked, or amusingly exaggerated. One might say that the audience takes pleasure in a deliberately "inappropriate" laughter that exposes the solemnity and sentiment of the ordinary murder story.

This effect is all the more interesting when we consider that most of the laughter depicted inside Hitchcock's films, at the level of the diegesis, is also inappropriate, but in a more discordant and disconcerting way. Consider the laughter (or perhaps the grimace) on the face of the painted clown in *Blackmail* (1929); or the laughter of Bruno Anthony in *Strangers on a Train* when he looks at his mother's abstract painting and thinks it resembles his father; or the laughter of Roger Thornhill's mother and nearly everybody aboard a crowded elevator in *North by Northwest* ("You gentlemen aren't *really* trying to kill my son, are you?"); or – most troubling of all – the laughter of Rose Balestrero in *The Wrong Man* as she stands in a tenement hallway and descends from depression and anxiety into madness.

One of the most subtle uses of this sort of ironic laughter can be heard in a sound transition in *Sabotage* at the climax of the scene in which little Stevie Verloc is killed by a bomb. Viewers of *Sabotage* may remember that the story as a whole begins with a saboteur's failed attempt to blow up a power station. On the next day, newspaper headlines sneer at the bomber's ineptitude and proclaim "London Laughs." The agents who control the saboteur warn him that "London must not laugh again tonight," and indeed, at least on the surface, there is nothing amusing about the second attack. Hitchcock pulls out all the melodramatic stops, showing us a tow-headed boy, a puppy, and a little old lady riding along in a bus while a time-bomb ticks away in a package the boy is holding. Suspense is generated by cross-cutting between the bus and the moving hands of the city's clocks, and the pace of the cutting steadily accelerates until the moment when, somewhat to our surprise, the bus and the boy are blown to smithereens. The sequence ends with a visual and sound dissolve that takes us from the exploded bus to Winnie Verloc's parlor, where the sound of the explosion melts into polite, rather strained laughter among her guests – a laughter that, in this context, resembles nothing so much as the sound of broken glass or shattered debris. (Whenever I've isolated the sequence in the classroom my students have broken into laughter themselves as if they were sharing in the director's joke.)

With examples such as these, we have moved some distance from pure comedy and have entered the domain of a macabre form of amusement that has special names. In *Jokes and Their Relation to the Unconscious* (1905), Sigmund Freud calls it simply "humor," a term I am adopting for this essay, even though in the English language it usually needs a modifier such as "gallows humor." Freud himself illustrates it with a joke about a condemned man being led off to the gallows on a Monday who is overheard to say, "What a way to start the week!" He also cites instances of humor from *Simplicissimus*, a famous comic weekly published in Munich, and from the frontier writings of Mark Twain. All such joking, he explains, functions as "*an economy in the expenditure of affect.*"[13] Unlike the witty or "crazy" forms of comedy, humor arises only when "there is a situation in which, according to our usual habits, we should be tempted to release a distressing affect and if motives then operate upon us which suppress that affect *in statu nascendi*" (p. 228). This ability to suppress the unpleasant feeling, Freud writes, is "one of the highest psychical achievements," enjoying "the particular favor of thinkers" (p. 228). It involves "something like magnanimity" by virtue of the humorist's "tenacious hold upon his customary self and his disregard of what might overthrow that self and drive it to despair" (p. 229).

In 1928, Freud returned to the same theme in a short paper entitled simply "Humor," in which he observes that "the essence of humor is that one spares oneself the affects to which the situation would naturally give rise and overrides with a jest the possibility of such an emotional display."[14] As with wit and the comic, Freud finds something "*liberating*" about humor; but the humorous attitude also contains what he calls a "fine and elevating" quality, resulting chiefly from a "triumph of narcissism" and "the ego's victorious assertion of its own invulnerability" (p. 217). In every case of humor, he writes, the ego "refuses to be hurt by the arrows of reality or to be compelled to suffer." Instead, the narcissistic aspect of the psyche insists "it is impervious to wounds dealt by the outside world, in fact, that these are merely occasions for affording it pleasure" (p. 217). This attitude, Freud emphasizes, is quite different from emotional resignation; it is "rebellious," signifying "the triumph not only of the ego, but also of the pleasure principle," which is strong enough to assert itself in the face of "adverse real circumstances" (p. 217).

At another juncture in the same essay Freud elaborates on the psychic process that creates humor, showing how it involves "the subject's removing the accent [of emotion] from his ego and transferring it onto his [protective or parental] super-ego" (pp. 218–19). Humor can therefore be described as the dialectical opposite of wit, which "originates in the momentary abandoning of a conscious thought to unconscious elaboration." If wit is "the contribution of the unconscious to the comic," humor is "a contribution to the comic made through the agency of the super-ego" (p. 220). Perhaps for that reason, Freud notes, humor does not always require an audience; it can be experienced purely subjectively, usually by social outsiders who "narcissistically" defend themselves against pain. It is also what Freud terms a "rare and precious gift," for "there are many people who have not even the capacity for deriving pleasure from humor when it is presented to them by others" (p. 221).

Another, equally familiar, name for gallows humor is "black humor," which is the English translation of what the surrealist André Breton, a disciple of Freud and the major theorist of subversively dark literary comedy, called "*humour noir*." The immediate ancestor of this term, Breton tells us, is "*umour*," borrowed from the English "humor" and coined by Jaques Vache, a veteran of trench warfare in World War I and an important contributor to the surrealist movement, whose *Lettres de guerre* (Letters from the Front, 1920) were published shortly after Vache and one of his friends had taken part in a double suicide, or perhaps a murder-suicide. ("I object to being killed in wartime," Vache had written. "I will die when I want to die … But then I'll die with someone else. Dying alone is too boring.") Breton's *Anthologie d'humor noir* (Anthology of Black Humor*)*, which was compiled in the mid-1930s but was not published until 1940 at a time when Breton claimed that the historical situation was appropriate, contains excerpts from Vache's book, along with samples from the work of over forty other black humorists. In the introduction to the volume, Breton quotes Freud's account of gallows humor and also calls attention to Hegel's earlier notion of "objective humor," an extreme form of the Romantic or aesthetic sensibility, involving both a repudiation of external circumstance and a love of detachment or "external contemplation."[15] According to Breton, objective humor is closely related to *humour noir*, which constitutes "*a superior revolt of the mind*" against bourgeois convention (p. xvi).

For Breton, black humor is the "mortal enemy of sentimentality" (p. xix) and the essential element or keynote of every worthwhile modern art and philosophy. The purpose of his anthology is to define such humor and give a sense of its genealogy by using short examples drawn from a wide range of literary sources: Jonathan Swift ("the first black humorist"), the Marquis de Sade, Edgar Allan Poe, Charles Baudelaire, Friedrich Nietzsche, Arthur Rimbaud, André Gide, Alfred Jarry, Franz Kafka, and many others.[16] Breton also notes in passing that black humor can be seen at the cinema – for example, in the early comedies of Mack Sennett, in certain of Chaplin's less sentimental pictures, and, of course, in Buñuel's *Un Chien Andalou* (1928) and *L'Age d'or* (1930).

I myself would argue that black humor is one of the hallmarks of modernist art and that Alfred Hitchcock, who is not mentioned by Breton, was not only one of its great practitioners but also the artist most responsible for bringing a spirit of surrealist laughter into the vernacular modernism of Hollywood movies. Hitchcock was certainly not alone in producing such laughter, as one can see from almost any film directed by Billy Wilder, but more than any of his contemporaries Hitchcock came to be identified with black humor which he repeatedly packaged as mass entertainment. His propensity toward the effect is perhaps least evident during his first years in America, when he collaborated with David O. Selznick and was restrained from turning the opening scenes of *Rebecca* into a series of jokes; but the humorous feeling isn't entirely absent during that period, partly because Selznick's swooning romanticism and taste for *amour fou* have a natural affinity with the surrealist sensibility. In *Rebecca*, for example, the title character is a woman who, even in death, seems to laugh mockingly at the earnestness and sentiment of Maxim de Winter and his new wife. Even in Hitchcock's overtly propagandistic wartime work, which includes *Lifeboat* and the two short films he made for the British Ministry of Information in 1944 (*Bon Voyage* and *Adventure Malgache*), the sense of detached irony and objective humor almost undercuts the patriotic messages. Ultimately, his career as a whole can be described in terms of different degrees or shadings of black humor, a quality that unifies such different pictures as *The Trouble With Harry* and *Psycho*, which Thomas Leitch has claimed are "the two most disparate films in Hitchcock's entire *œuvre.*"[17] In some of his most glamorous comedies, such as *To Catch a Thief*, the dark jokes are slickly eroticized, most notably in the famous seduction scene when heiress Grace Kelly offers her jewelry to cat-burglar Cary Grant. (When he was making this film, Hitchcock complained to André Bazin about "the necessity of renouncing adult, masculine humor in order to satisfy American producers.").[18] In his non-comic pictures about romantic obsession, such as *Under Capricorn* and *Vertigo*, which were among his least commercially successful productions, the fetishism is less conducive of laughter and the feeling of humor derives chiefly from the twists of the plots. In his spy thrillers, such as *The 39 Steps*, dark humor mingles with sexual innuendo and utopian romance, and the movement between these modes is often treated like a dialectical montage.

One characteristic of black humor, as both Freud and Breton observed, is a somewhat elevated or "objective" tone. Hitchcock managed to convey this feeling both through his fastidious control of cinematic enunciation (as in the lofty, bird's-eye shots that are an obvious feature of his style) and through his carefully constructed persona, which audiences found especially amusing. Then, too, his films sometimes steered close to the sardonic effects of high literary modernism. A passage from Eliot's *The Waste Land* (1922) could serve as an ironic epigraph to a light entertainment such as like *Rear Window*: "Oh keep the dog far hence, that's friend to men,/Or with his nails he'll dig it up again." In other films, Hitchcock seems rather like a slick, slyly commercial practitioner of the kind of nightmarish wit we find in Kafka. (Whether or not he ever read Kafka, his celebrated thrillers of the 1930s were filmed at the very moment when *The Trial* and *The Castle* were first translated into English, and when the influence of Kafka was pervasive in British art.) And when he depicts the lowest fringes of the middle class, as in parts of *Sabotage* and in *The Wrong Man*, he has something in common with the spooky, quotidian humor of W.H. Auden, the leading poet of Britain's "Age of Anxiety." Consider Auden's "As I Walked Out One Evening" (1937) which uses a nursery-rhyme meter to create a sense of dread: "The glacier knocks in the cupboard,/The desert sighs in the bed,/And the crack in the teacup opens/A lane to the land of the dead."

Today, black humor is ubiquitous, appearing in everything from museum exhibits to television commercials. No doubt it has always played some role in American popular and commercial art; in the 1930s, for example, at about the same time that Hitchcock became an international celebrity, Charles Addams began drawing cartoons for the *New Yorker*. But if I had to name the period when black humor fully entered the consciousness of the American mass public and reached a kind of saturation point on the marketplace, I would say the 1950s – a supposedly complacent decade that produced such phenomena as Vladimir Nabokov's best-selling *Lolita* (1955); E.C. comic books, whose entire line was based on the grisliest forms of black humor; and the *Alfred Hitchcock Presents* television series, which might as well have been subtitled *Anthologie d' humour noir.*

(There are connections between these apparently different examples: Nabokov once discussed the possibility of writing a screenplay for Hitchcock, and E.C.'s horror comics used a ghoulishly comic narrator who made jokes somewhat in the manner of Hitchcock himself.) This was also the period when Hitchcock gave his name to *Alfred Hitchcock's Mystery Magazine*, a widely circulated "pulp" journal formed on the model of *Ellery Queen's Mystery Magazine*, which specialized in darkly comic or ironic stories about murder by such gifted writers as Henry Slesar, Roald Dahl, and Stanley Elkin. The television series drew material from many of the same writers, and in one instance Robert Stevenson directed an episode based on Evelyn Waugh's "The Man Who Liked Dickens," a horror story from the 1930s that Waugh himself had rewritten for the last chapter of one of the most savage dark comedies in modern literature, *A Handful of Dust* (1934).

When the television show debuted in 1955, Hitchcock told the press that it would be "bringing murder into the American home, where it has always belonged."[19] Over the next ten years he made good on his promise, at the same time becoming a paradoxical kind of star – a popular, even beloved figure who took a dandified, darkly satiric approach to many of the things the nation was supposed to hold dear. The series was supervised by Joan Harrison and Norman Lloyd, and James Allardice wrote the commentaries that Hitchcock delivered so wittily; but to conclude that Hitchcock himself had little to do with its success, as some commentators have done, would be a bit like arguing that Bob Hope or Jack Benny were mere figureheads on their own broadcasts. Hitchcock directed some of his most perfect and characteristic films for the program, and he contributed a comic persona and a set of generic expectations that he had developed throughout the previous decade, not only in films but also on the radio, where he made frequent guest-star appearances.

On July 22, 1940, shortly after coming to America, Hitchcock "directed" and played host for a radio adaptation of his British silent film, *The Lodger*, which became the pilot episode for "Suspense," a long-running CBS exercise in *noir* that was in many ways a precursor of his series *Alfred Hitchcock Presents*. (The subsequent host of "Suspense" was an anonymous and unfunny character called "The Man in Black.") Throughout the 1940s he made witty appearances on "Information Please," a popular quiz show that featured celebrities and public intellectuals; and in 1951 he hosted a weekly, half-hour broadcast entitled "Murder by Experts," featuring "tales by the leading writers of mystery fiction." In these venues and others, he perfected the upper-crust manner and the propensity toward gallows humor that would ultimately find their greatest popular expression on television. By the end of the 1950s, he had become a brand name that signified a refined, black-comic sense of bloody murder, and a character who, in Thomas Leitch's words, was "ironic, aloof, anecdotal, manipulative and fond of witty reversals, even if they make nonsense of the stories that have led up to them."[20]

If *Alfred Hitchcock Presents* was closely attuned to Hitchcock's previously established star image, it was also, inevitably but no doubt unintentionally, very much in keeping with some of the writings that had been collected in André Breton's surrealist anthology of 1940. For example, Breton had published an excerpt from Thomas De Quincey's nineteenth-century memoir, *On Murder Considered as One of the Fine Arts* (1827 and 1839), which treats the theme of murder from an aesthetic rather than a moral point of view. A prototypical dandy, De Quincey insists that there is a properly artistic way to go about committing mayhem: "As to old women, and the mob of newspaper readers," he writes, his tone anticipating Nietzsche and a host of modernist intellectuals, "they are pleased with anything, provided it is bloody enough. But the mind of sensibility requires something more."[21] This humorous, iconoclastic argument became the foundation of a literary tradition, and it was an acknowledged influence on Oscar Wilde's "Pen, Pencil and Poison" (1889), which tells the true story of Thomas Wainewright – an aesthete, "a forger of no mean or ordinary capabilities, and ... a subtle and secret poisoner almost without rival in this or any age." (When a friend criticizes Wainewright for doing away with a young woman, he responds in distinctly Wildean fashion: "Yes, it was a dreadful thing to do, but she had very thick ankles.")[22] Hitchcock probably knew the Wilde essay, and he certainly knew De Quincey, whom he once quoted in an address to the Film Society of Lincoln Center.[23] Indeed Peter Wollen has suggested that *Murder Considered as One of the Fine Arts* was as important to Hitchcock's work as the short fiction of Edgar Allan Poe, laying the foundations for criminal connoisseurship and providing a direct inspiration for films such as *Rope* (1948).[24] Equally important, De Quincey also provided the inspiration for Hitchcock's public persona and the famous speeches he delivered on television.

Another influential name in the Breton anthology was the popular turn-of-the-century American author O. Henry, who wrote short tales with ironic or surprise endings. The structure (if not the tone) of the typical O. Henry story is in many ways similar to the half-hour broadcasts on *Alfred Hitchcock Presents* and it reminds us as well of Hitchcock's earliest, perhaps most revealing, artistic creations: the short fictional pieces he wrote for the "house" magazine of W.T. Henley's Telegraph and Cable Company, in the days before he entered the movies. As Patrick McGilligan has recently shown, there were at least seven of these stories, and most of them were constructed like jokes with a sudden revelation in the last lines that throws humorous light on everything that has gone before. The jokes tend to be playfully grim or frightening, involving fantasies of death or sexual humiliation that are banished by the surprise endings. As one instance of what McGilligan calls a narrative "turnaround," consider "The

Woman's Part," a 1919 entry told from the point of view of a husband who seems to be passively, secretly watching his wife and her lover discuss a murder and then embrace one another. In the last line of the story, we discover that the husband is viewing the scene from the cheap seats in a theater and that his wife is acting in a melodrama.[25]

In his commentaries for the *Anthologie d' humour noir*, Breton pointed out that both De Quincey and O. Henry deserved to be called black humorists because they shared an instinctive "benevolence and compassion" for the criminal classes.[26] *Alfred Hitchcock Presents* had the same attribute; in fact, as Christopher Anderson has pointed out, it might be the only network television show in American history that consistently invited its audience to identify with the point of view of criminals.[27] A more darkly funny and unorthodox project than Hitchcock's feature films, which depicted criminal psychology through the "wrong man" device and always ended by restoring the world to conventional order, the television show was virtually devoid of innocent characters. Its most memorable programs were based on the kind of morbidly satiric material that was quite rare in movie theaters and sometimes its criminals went completely unpunished. Remarkably, only one episode was deemed too dark for the network. "The Sorcerer's Apprentice" featured Brandon DeWilde as a mentally handicapped youth who, after watching a magician, accidentally saws someone in half. (This program was never broadcast by CBS but it can now be seen on TV nostalgia channels where the Hitchcock series is in syndication.)

Critics have often suggested that other episodes of the television show were "saved" only because Hitchcock's closing remarks lightened the atmosphere and provided a conservative resolution. Hitchcock himself told *TV Guide* that his commentary offered "a necessary gesture to morality." But did audiences really believe it when he told them that the Barbara Bel Geddes character in "Lamb to the Slaughter" had been captured by police when she tried to kill her second husband with a prematurely defrosted leg of lamb? Surely not, because the show's fun derived from the fact that people sometimes got away with murder. By the same token, Hitchcock got away with jokes about the sponsors. ("Crime does not pay – even on television," he remarked on the first episode. "You must have a sponsor.") This was an old device from network radio, practiced by Fred Allen, Phil Harris, and even Orson Welles. But Hitchcock was different because his tone was more contemptuous and because he never spoke the name of an advertiser or endorsed a product. Throughout the series he maintained the comic attitude of a British eccentric who was a victim of vulgar commerce, and his audience seems to have loved him for it.

Alfred Hitchcock Presents led directly to *Psycho*, Hitchcock's most brilliant and frightening exercise in black humor, which shaped his public identity in later years. This film invites audiences to identify first with a thief and then with a murderer, and its entire mechanism of suspense, surprise, and bloody horror is

33

structured like a practical joke – although at times, especially in the performance of Anthony Perkins as Norman Bates, it also achieves an impressive blending of menace and pathos. In interviews, Hitchcock always emphasized the film's amusing qualities. At one point he told François Truffaut that an English newspaperwoman who lacked a sense of humor had described *Psycho* as the work of a "barbaric sophisticate." He seemed intrigued or even pleased by the description. "If *Psycho* had been intended as a serious picture," he remarked, "it would have been shown as a clinical case with no mystery or suspense ... The only question then is whether one should always have a sense of humor in dealing with a serious subject. It seems to me that some of my British films were too light and some of my American movies have been too heavy-handed, but it's the most difficult thing in the world to control that so as to get just the right dosage."[28]

The "right dosage" would soon become impossible for Hitchcock to calculate. He never fully entered the pure unalloyed world of black comedy that we find in Jim Thompson's novels or Stanley Kubrick's movies, but he had moved so close to that world that he could no longer easily return to the polished entertainments of his earlier career. *Psycho* was a watershed film, marking a shift away from Hollywood's restrained, New-Comic formulas and foreshadowing the 1970s trend toward gross-out – a form that not only embraces bad taste but also "transforms revulsion into a sought after goal."[29] There is no space in this essay to review the many determinants of the cultural change so I shall merely refer interested readers to William Paul's excellent *Laughing / Screaming*, which explains the "striking inversion" whereby "low-class genres became high-class product."[30] As a result of the inversion, black humor lost some of its aura of sophistication; moreover, the supposedly "higher" forms of satire and irony were challenged by what Paul describes as a repressed "Old-Comic" tradition of farce, ribaldry, and forthright vulgarity. In this environment, Hitchcock's work began to seem slightly antiquated.

Looked at today, against the background of the gross-out slasher films it influenced, *Psycho* clearly belongs to a more repressed and hierarchical period. Until this point Hitchcock's art had usually depended upon a formally controlled, "classy" atmosphere that was inflected with rebellious black humor. In *Psycho* he experimented with what was regarded at the time as an exploitation genre and he was more frank than ever about lower-body anxieties; but he also created an austere, black-and-white example of "pure cinema" in which violence was indirect and "barbarity" was offset by irony and wit. Thus, even though *Psycho* was a carnivalistic experience for its original audiences, Hitchcock's most admiring critics were able to give it cultural capital and art-movie status by comparing it with the writings of Swift and Conrad.[31]

In subsequent years, as his reputation flourished and as the movie industry changed, Hitchcock's films grew manifestly darker and perhaps more serious;

but the disjunction between his grim jokes and his apparently light genres became more stark and difficult to manage. The bird attacks in *The Birds*, the rape scene in *Marnie*, the protracted killing of an enemy agent in *Torn Curtain*, and the rape-murder in *Frenzy* tend to overpower the respective conventions of the screwball comedy, the romantic melodrama, the spy story, and the "wrong-man" thriller. Hitchcock's aloof irony remains, but violence ruptures the glamorous surface to such a degree that the humor dies or grows sour. Paradoxically, just at the moment when black comedy dominated the culture at large (and just at the moment when Brian De Palma was refashioning many of Hitchcock's motifs for a younger audience), Hitchcock seemed no longer willing or able to sustain the complex atmosphere of his most admired films. The important point to emphasize, however, is that in a lifetime that spanned two world wars and the major social upheavals of the twentieth century his artistry had always derived from his special ability to treat horror with humor. Few directors have been so entertaining or have enjoyed such serene and orderly careers, even though the serenity was achieved by virtue of a detached, aesthetic, willfully amused response to primal anxieties. At some level Hitchcock must have agreed with a remark by Thomas De Quincy, who seems almost to define the Freudian version of black comedy: "The reader will think I am laughing … Nevertheless I have a very reprehensible way of jesting at times in the midst of my own misery."[32]

Notes

1   Lang's work is not entirely devoid of comedy (he directed a Brechtian musical, *You and Me* [1938] which is basically comic), and certainly his films have satiric and ironic qualities. And yet the tone is different from Hitchcock. In his splendid book, *The Films of Fritz Lang: Allegories of Vision and Modernity*, London: BFI, 2000, Tom Gunning makes several interesting comparisons between Hitchcock and Lang. Lang, he argues, "is less concerned with the psychological complexity of characters … than with their interface with social systems, with technology and politics" (pp. xi–xii). This may help to explain the more abstract and somber feeling he evokes.

2   Gilberto Perez, *The Material Ghost: Films and Their Medium*, Baltimore: Johns Hopkins University Press, 1988, p. 9.

3   Sidney Gottlieb (ed.) *Hitchcock on Hitchcock: Selected Writings and Interviews*, Berkeley and Los Angeles: University of California Press, 1995, p. xxiii.

4   Stanley Cavell, "*North by Northwest*," in Marshall Deutelbaum and Leland Poague (eds.) *A Hitchcock Reader*, Ames: Iowa State University Press, 1986, pp. 249–61; Lesley Brill, *The Hitchcock Romance: Love and Irony in Hitchcock's Films*, Princeton: Princeton University Press, 1988; Thomas M. Leitch, *Find the Director and Other Hitchcock Games*, Athens: University of Georgia Press, 1991.

5   Bruce Robinson quoted in *Hitchcock*, a supplement to *Sight and Sound*, London: BFI, 1999, p. 35.

6   Andréw Bergman quoted in *Hitchcock*, a supplement to *Sight and Sound*, p. 30.

7   Northrop Frye, *Anatomy of Criticism: Four Essays*, Princeton: Princeton University Press, 1957, p. 163.

8   Dana Polan, "The Light Side of Genius: Hitchcock's *Mr. and Mrs. Smith* in the Screwball Tradition," in Andréw S. Horton (ed.) *Comedy / Cinema / Theory*, Berkeley: University of California Press, 1991, p. 137.

9   Raymond Durgnat, *The Strange Case of Alfred Hitchcock*, Cambridge: MIT, 1974, p. 83.

10 Lesley Brill, "Redemptive Comedy in the Films of Alfred Hitchcock and Preston Sturges: 'Are Snakes Necessary?'," in Richard Allen and S. Ishii-Gonzáles (eds.) *Hitchcock Centenary Essays*, London: BFI, 1999, pp. 205–20.

11 Polan, "The Light Side of Genius," p. 134.

12 Frye, *Anatomy of Criticism*, pp. 46–7. Subsequent citations appear in parentheses in the text.

13 Sigmund Freud, *Jokes and Their Relation to the Unconscious*, trans. James Strachey, New York: Norton, 1960, pp. 228–9. Subsequent citations appear in parentheses in the text.

14 Sigmund Freud, "Humor," in *Standard Edition of the Complete Works of Sigmund Freud*, vol. XX, trans. James Strachey, London: Hogarth Press, 1953, p. 216. Subsequent citations appear in parentheses in the text.

15 André Breton (ed.) *Anthology of Black Humor*, trans. Mark Polizzotti, San Francisco: City Lights Books, 1997, p. xvi. As in his earlier book, *The Political Position of Surrealism* (1935), Breton predicts here "that the black sphinx of *objective humor* [cannot] avoid meeting, on the dust-covered road of the future, the white sphinx of *objective chance*, and that all human creation [will] be the fruit of their embrace" (p. xvi). This statement could almost serve as a recipe for a film like *Strangers on a Train*. Subsequent citations appear in parentheses in the text.

16 Given this list of names, black humor might appear to be solely the product of white males. In fact, we can find examples of it within all races and genders; most contemporary African-American comics employ it, and it has a long tradition in Jewish comedy (as Freud probably knew).

17 Thomas M. Leitch, 'The Outer Circle: Hitchcock on Television," in Allen and Ishii-Gonzáles, *Hitchcock Centenary Essays*, p. 60.

18 Quoted in André Bazin, "Hitchcock vs. Hitchcock," in Albert J. LaValley (ed.) *Focus on Hitchcock*, Englewood Cliffs, NJ: Prentice Hall, 1972, p. 65.

19 Hitchcock quoted by Alex McNeil, 'Alfred Hitchcock Presents," in *Total Television*, fourth edition, New York: Penguin, 1996, pp. 23–4. Information on the Hitchcock show in this and the following paragraphs comes from the same source. I am grateful to Michelle Hilmes for data on Hitchcock's radio appearances.

20 Leitch, "The Outer Circle," p. 65.

21 De Quincy, *On Murder Considered as One of the Fine Arts*, quoted by Breton, *Anthology of Black Humor*, p. 56.

22 Oscar Wilde, "Pen, Pencil and Poison, A Study in Green," in *The Complete Works of Oscar Wilde*, New York: Harper & Row, 1989, p. 1004.

23 See Brigitte Peucker, "The Cut of Representation: Painting and Sculpture in Hitchcock," in Allen and Ishii-Gonzáles, *Hitchcock Centenary Essays*, pp. 141–56.

24 Peter Wollen, "*Rope*: Three Hypotheses," in *Hitchcock Centenary Essays*, pp. 75–85.

25 Patrick McGilligan, "Alfred Hitchcock Before the Flickers," *Film Comment*, July/August 1999, 22–31.

26 Breton, *Anthology of Black Humor*, p. 189.

27 I am grateful to Christopher Anderson for pointing this out to me. His extended commentary on the Hitchcock show will figure in his forthcoming book on crime and American television. For a commentary on the series that is similar to my own, see Leitch, "The Outer Circle."

28 Francois Truffaut, with the collaboration of Helen G. Scott, *Hitchcock*, revised edition, New York: Simon & Schuster, 1984, pp. 201–2.

29 William Paul, *Laughing/Screaming: Modern Hollywood Horror and Comedy*, New York: Columbia University Press, 1994, p. 10. Subsequent citations appear in parentheses in the text.

30 Paul, *Laughing/Screaming*, p. 33.

31 See the commentaries on *Psycho* by Durgnat, *The Strange Case of Alfred Hitchcock*, and Robin Wood, *Hitchcock's Films Revisited,* New York: Columbia University Press, 1989.

32 Thomas De Quincey, *Confessions of an English Opium Eater*, quoted by Breton, *Anthology of Black Humor*, p. 54.

Chapter 3

DOUBLES AND DOUBTS IN HITCHCOCK
The German connection

Bettina Rosenbladt

I imagine my ego as being viewed through a lens: all the forms which move around me are egos; and whatever they do, or leave undone, vexes me.[1]

E.T.A. Hoffmann

Figure 3.1: Production still of *The Cabinet of Dr. Caligari* (1919)

In the last cameo of all his films, Hitchcock appears as the shadowy mirror image of Caligari's shadow, the duplicitous figure in the German expressionist film *The Cabinet of Dr. Caligari* (Robert Wiene, 1919). It demonstrates Hitchcock's lifelong interest in central themes of German films of the Weimar period as well as their particular stylistics. Caligari, it will be remembered, is the itinerant hypnotist who exhibits his medium Cesare at fairgrounds during the day and at night wills him to murder people. Simultaneously, he may also be an upstanding citizen, director of an insane asylum.

It is tempting to take this image as a metaphor of how Hitchcock saw his role vis-à-vis the public: on the surface he appears as the respectable bourgeois, the meticulous professional and committed family man, but at the same time he leads a shadow existence as the fearsome manipulator who sends out multiple Cesares – figments of his imagination – willing them to perform on screen the acts he secretly desires to see happen but fears to commit himself. Publicity photos emphasize this approach to his public persona: he is shown pouring poison into Ingrid Bergman's cup in *Notorious* or threatening Janet Leigh in the shower in *Psycho*.

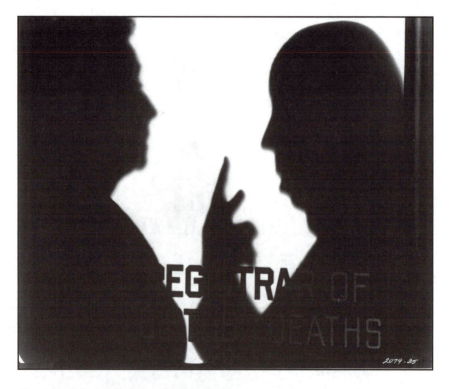

Figure 3.2: Hitchcock in *Family Plot* (1976)

Hitchcock's gesture of posing as his own double – and, by extension, as double of his fictional creatures – has analogies in his films. His screen world is peopled with characters that lead double lives, have split personalities or are followed by shadow twins. Figures such as the two Mrs. de Winters from *Rebecca,* the Guy/Bruno pair from *Strangers on a Train,* Judy/Madeleine from *Vertigo*, or Norman Bates/Mrs. Bates from *Psycho* come immediately to mind, and there are many others.

My interest in looking at Hitchcock with German eyes, so to speak, was first sparked by the resemblance of the central double figure of Uncle Charles/Niece Charlie in *Shadow of a Doubt* with certain double constructions of German Romanticism. In stories dating back to that time, fragments of the shattered self, as in the Hoffmann epigraph above, are projected out into the world where they turn into separate characters acting on their own, mostly to the annoyance of the original self. In this chapter, I would like to explore this connection further. By comparing *The Lodger* and *Shadow of a Doubt* with a number of German films of the 1920s that most likely served as channels for Romantic motifs in Hitchcock, I will trace the theme of the doubled/split character from Hitchcock to the German films and from there further back in time to the German Romantic past.[2]

Hitchcock's Catholic upbringing, his Jesuit schooling, and in general his growing up in a culture steeped in Victorian values, with their sharp separation of good and evil, must have instilled in him a heightened awareness of their interrelationship and the dual nature of man. We also know that he was familiar with and fond of the important texts of the literature of the double, such as the works of Poe, Stevenson's *Dr. Jekyll and Mr. Hyde* or Wilde's picture of *Dorian Gray.* Other ways of treating the theme were shown in the German films of the Weimar period. Their shadow worlds of madness, murder, and mayhem are teeming with double figures. Foreign films were screened regularly in London, and Hitchcock enjoyed watching them. In his conversations with Truffaut he singles out one picture that had impressed him most of all: Fritz Lang's *Der müde Tod* (1921; *Tired Death*, known as *Destiny*).[3] We don't know what, in particular, Hitchcock liked about it. It is very lyrical, beautifully lit, using superimpositions to suggest the interpenetration of life with death. It is also a doubles story of sorts: Death initially misrepresents himself as a wandering stranger who, after arriving in town, convinces the town dignitaries to sell him a piece of land so he can establish "a garden" – much like Nosferatu in Murnau's film negotiates the purchase of a town house in Wisborg. In view of various Hitchcock films where horror, fate or death irrupt with suddenness in ordinary people's lives, he must have liked the idea of Death sitting down among the people in a tavern to drink a glass of beer and then going ahead with establishing his inexorable reign right there, among them, in close proximity to their everyday world.

Destiny, coming so shortly after the war when hundreds of thousands of young women had lost their husbands or lovers, shares with other German films of the period the themes of death, love, fate, and sacrifice, often presented, as in Lang's film, in fairy-tale images from German Romanticism. In the early twenties, Hitchcock had the opportunity to experience first hand the culture that gave rise to these kinds of cinematic visions and to study how the films were made. This visit was to be pivotal for Hitchcock's career.

The occasion was the filming of *The Blackguard*, a British-German venture, at the UFA studios in Berlin in 1924. According to Spoto, Hitchcock supervised "virtually everything" in that production, and while there, absorbed lessons in filmmaking that lasted a lifetime.[4] Spoto quotes Hitchcock as saying:

> Those were the great days of the German pictures. [...] Germany was beginning to fall into chaos. Yet the movies thrived. The Germans placed great emphasis on telling the story visually – if possible with no titles, or at least very few. [...] My models were forever after the German filmmakers of 1924 and 1925.[5]

I think it is obvious that we should not assume that these "lessons" came to fruition instantly. We can observe, rather, that Hitchcock would integrate various elements – German and others – gradually and ever more purposefully into his own style of filmmaking.[6] In fact, the two films Hitchcock himself directed in Germany in 1925 in another German-British venture, *The Pleasure Garden* and *The Mountain Eagle,* were rejected as "too English" by the German public, if mainly for reasons of content.[7] Reviewers in the trade press praised Hitchcock's sets and his lighting style, but criticized, surprisingly, his use of intertitles. "The many titles take away part of the suspense. This overabundance of explanatory words almost makes the film into an illustrated novel" wrote one reviewer, and he was not alone in his assessment.[8]

Hand in hand with the appropriation of elements of film style, we can imagine, went the absorption of aspects of Germany's literary and folkloric past. Spoto tells us that Hitchcock familiarized himself with stories of German Romantic writers such as Ludwig Tieck, E.T.A. Hoffmann, and the fairy tales of the Grimm Brothers.[9] It is also possible that Hitchcock, in later films, drew upon his real-life exposure to the chaotic world of post-World War I Germany. The country was torn apart by contradictions. Amid great anxiety after the lost war, economic difficulties, and political strife, Berlin had become "the amusement capital of the world,"[10] where all kinds of entertainment where to be had, licentious sex flourished, and crime was rampant.[11] Of particular interest to Hitchcock may have been the German obsession with sexual murder at that time. A number of bestial serial murderers terrorized the public, with the press helping to whip up a panic. At the same time, artists such as George Grosz and Otto Dix produced innumerable explicit and violent paintings and drawings with *Lustmord* (sexual murder) as their subject.[12] The causes for this outburst are difficult to fathom. Among possible reasons mentioned are the brutalizing effects of the recent war, of course. Fear of and hatred for women may also have been motivated by the fact that they had survived the war in far greater numbers and with their bodies intact; for many women the war had in fact been an empowering experience. Pressed into employment for the war effort, women had gained in independence and assertiveness. Calculated provocation and commercial success, however, are also cited as factors for producing *Lustmord* art.[13]

Hitchcock's third film, *The Lodger*, was made right after his return to England. It centers on a man who may or may not be a pathological sex murderer. The film is based on a Jack the Ripper novel by Marie Belloc Lowndes, but it is not unlikely that additional sources of inspiration were combined.[14] Jack the Ripper, the icon for sexual murder, does not show up in German film before Pabst's *Pandora's Box* (1928), except for a short episode in Paul Leni's *Waxworks*. The German title *Das Wachsfigurenkabinett* and its brilliant expressionistic style – constructed abstract sets, the characters in form and costume matching the decor, long winding staircases, chiaroscuro lighting, superimpositions, bracketed by the mad chaos of the fairground setting in the frame tale – invoke *Das Kabinett des Dr. Caligari,* but in structure and content *Waxworks* is an imitation and parody of Lang's *Destiny*. From it, Hitchcock may have taken the parodic impulse. (The mad fairground atmosphere crops up later in *Strangers on a Train*.) Jack the Ripper is not named but is obliquely present in two of the period's most famous films that are much more powerful in impact: *Caligari* and *Nosferatu*.

In the title character of *The Lodger*, we meet the first in a long line of self-divided males who are directly or indirectly guilty of murdering women. In this film, Hitchcock focuses less on the deeds of his protagonist than on the question whether the murderer who signs himself as "The Avenger" and the lodger are the same person. He may be a two-faced person who is a charmer during the day and a killer at night (he may even have killed his sister in incestuous jealousy), or he may be a basically decent man who, traumatized by the loss of his sister, hunts down a murderous alter ego he is planning to kill. That double commits the murders and, toward the end of the film, is ostensibly caught in the act. We never learn for certain, however, if he actually is The Avenger, leaving open the option, even beyond the happy ending, that Daisy has married a serial murderer.

Serial murder and undecidable guilt are themes in *Caligari*. A direct link to Hitchcock's film suggests itself through the figure of the lodger. When he first presents himself at the door, with his face half-covered, making his wide-eyed gaze all the more startling, he reminds one instantly of Cesare in *Caligari*, particularly at the moment when Caligari first wakes him from his hypnotic sleep.[15]

The lodger's slow, deliberate, trance-like movements contrast throughout the film with the other more realistically acting characters. His good looks, his gentleness, and sorrowful eyes are reminiscent of the androgynously beautiful and sad Cesare who, when he is not in his catatonic state, moves his pliable body in harmony with the painted plant-like shapes of the decor. A closer look at *Caligari* will show further parallels.

The Cabinet of Dr. Caligari opens as a young man, Francis, narrates to an older man what happened to him many years ago. In a flashback, we see how his friend Allen gets murdered by a shadowy figure. Previously Cesare, a somnambulist exhibited in the fairground by the sinister-looking showman Caligari, had predicted Allen's death. The following night, Jane, the girlfriend of Francis (and Allen), is attacked at knifepoint by Cesare, who tries to abduct her but who expires from the effort. Francis follows up on his suspicion that Caligari is involved. He finds him in the local insane asylum – as the director. A number of further scenes reveal, however, that Francis himself is a patient in the asylum. The story told, then, is the story of a madman. The film ends as the asylum director, with a long gaze into the camera – as if wanting to hypnotize the viewer into believing his words – benignly declares that he now knows what is wrong with Francis and he will be able to cure him.

The film is a visual riot. Everything is stylized, from the painted sets suggesting houses and interiors in distortion, to the costumes and acting of the characters. The precariously leaning walls decorated with jagged shapes create a nervous and aggressive atmosphere that is only occasionally tempered by softer round shapes in and around Jane's house, the feminine sphere. Light and shadow are painted onto the sets, but in ways that defy natural laws. The actors wear clothes and make-up mostly in whites and blacks, sometimes in designs that match the decor. Some characters wear more black, others more white, but all share in both colors, indicating the co-presence of the inherent polarities in each character.

Like *Destiny*, *Caligari* must be considered against the background of the recent war. The set designers, like the expressionist painters before the war, can be seen as giving "expression of inner meaning through outer form,"[16] as translating shell shock and postwar trauma into the strange distorted images.[17]

But the sets are also meant to reflect the splintered identity of the mad protagonist. There are innumerable doubles in the film. If we single out the most obvious ones, a kind of hierarchy results. At the top is Francis as the teller of the tale; he may have invented the whole story as a cover for his own guilt over the jealous murder of his friend and rival for the affection of his girlfriend Jane. Under this premise, Francis is split into a daytime gentleman self and a night-time killer, who projects his killer fantasies onto the evil agency of Caligari. Caligari is split into the respected asylum director and the sinister fairground showman. In addition, he is doubled by Cesare, his instrument who, while he (Cesare) is out committing murders, is doubled by a life-size doll occupying the box in which he usually rests. The killer is doubled by a murderer caught in the act but who turns out to be innocent of the murders Cesare has committed.

The result is a narrative that allows for multiple interpretations, much like a kaleidoscope that reveals a different pattern with each turn.[18] Guilt can be transferred and denied ad infinitum, from one double to the next, up and down, hierarchical structure: is Cesare the guilty one because he does the deed, or is it Caligari who directs him with the power of his mind? Or is Caligari a victim of Francis who pursues him for a crime he actually committed himself? Depending upon from which perspective one looks at them, all involved are victims and perpetrators, making it impossible to apply moral judgments: the frames of reference have been obliterated. But the source of desire, too, cannot be clearly located. When Cesare drops his knife, overcome by the beauty of the sleeping woman in front of him, we do not know if he defies Caligari's orders, acts vicariously for him or if he acts on Francis's behalf. Richard McCormick sees here "an anarchic moment in the film at which three elements – woman, desire, and the 'monster' – come together to threaten [...] even the evil authority exerted by Caligari,"[19] reaffirming "the close affinity between monster and woman in early horror films" in Linda Williams's analysis of these films.[20] Thus, the moment Cesare drops his knife could be linked to an earlier scene in the film. The preceding afternoon, Caligari had given Jane a private "exhibition" of his very phallic Cesare, and she had been quite excited by the view.

The flashback adds to the general slippage of boundaries: can we dismiss it as the ravings of a lunatic, or does it represent, on the contrary, an enhanced version of reality on the premise, based on a lingering notion going back to Romanticism, that madmen, like sleepers and hypnotics, have a more immediate access to "the Truth"?[21] There is no outside "objective" agency to help us decide. Overall, the unusual visual experience, the suspense and the intricate two-frame narrative make the film both irritatingly undecidable and highly entertaining: a formula on which many of Hitchcock's films are based.[22]

Caligari is significant for Hitchcock for three reasons, not all of them immediately important for *The Lodger:* the visual aspect, the presentation of the double, and the way in which the story is told. Visually, *Caligari* and *The Lodger* have not much in common. The mise-en-scène in Hitchcock's film is realistic. Distortions are used sparingly, usually in a subjective context but not necessarily as point-of-view shots. One example concerns the lodger's nightly outings. As the landlady wakes up at night, we see her window reflected against the wall of her bedroom in a *Caligari*-style black/white sharply angled shape. It is through this very window that she peers and, catching sight of the lodger walking away into the night, feels her suspicions about his identity intensifying. These shots are embedded in a sequence with other "abstract" chiaroscuro shots of the hallway and the staircase.[23] In the way it is presented, the landlady's observation is characterized as subjective, as not reliable as a basis for judgment. Similarly, we see Joe's growing conviction of the lodger's guilt developing out of string of subjective associations superimposed on a footprint in the dirt in front of him: he feels he is on the "right track" now. Thus, while *Caligari* is a construct of intersecting subjective spaces, *The Lodger* plays in a realistic realm that from time to time is punctured by subjective moments, throwing into doubt our own ability to read correctly what we see on screen. In films throughout his career, however, Hitchcock would make ample use of *Caligari*'s "abstract" graphic shapes, which he produces with the camera using light, shadow, and camera angles, to express moods of foreboding, feelings of anguish, and confinement, or to "paint" guilt on someone's face by dividing it – he does it here, in *The Lodger* – or by shading it with bars as in the scene in *Strangers on a Train*, when Bruno announces to Guy that he has murdered his wife and Guy is shown to be complicit in that deed.

The double figure in *The Lodger* is embodied in just one character, not in three as in *Caligari* (Francis–Caligari–Cesare). The lodger's character oscillates between various identities as the suspect of vicious crimes and an example of virtue as brother, son, and lover, culminating in images of him in Christ-like suffering poses as an innocent wrongly persecuted. He is a somewhat "embryonic" double figure. He not only barely registers as an outside manifestation: a fleeting shadow, a person seen from behind, an unseen character caught by the police; he also exhibits not that much inner conflict between his various parts. In later films, Hitchcock will present the different modes of the double figure much more explicitly. For example, in *Strangers on a Train*, Guy's murderous second self assumes an independent identity in Bruno; in *Psycho*, the inner self is palpably present in the powerful "mother." So in order to make visible the lodger's dividedness, Hitchcock employs other means, such as cutting the lodger's face in two by lighting at repeated instances, particularly when he relates the death of his sister,[24] or by allowing the viewer to attribute opposite motivations – one benign, one possibly murderous – to ambiguous gestures, such as the one when he picks up the poker to stoke the fire and we think momentarily that he might smash Daisy's skull with it.[25]

The flashback, too, is handled differently. In *Caligari*, it is retroactively discredited as untrustworthy by the fact that a madman narrates it. In *The Lodger*, however, we have no basis on which to discount its truth – and no basis to assert it, either. We remain suspicious because of the way Hitchcock makes the lodger appear as less than forthcoming. He leaves important blind spots: whose hands turned off the lights? What actually happened to the sister who, at the moment of death, was in the lodger's very arms?[26]

Both films present their story in such a way that there is more than one way to understand it. That is why, in his interview with Truffaut, Hitchcock doesn't really seem to care if the viewer thinks the lodger is guilty or not.[27] The idea, rather, is to show the fluidity between the criminal and the average person, between deviancy and normalcy.

This melting of boundaries and character oscillation is a prominent theme in German Romantic literature. To relate just one extreme example: in 1808, Heinrich von Kleist wrote the story of a young widow who, in a time of war, is saved by a dashing nobleman from rape by soldiers. A little later she finds herself miraculously pregnant and is devastated when she eventually learns, from the perpetrator himself, that the man who saved her, whom she adores and loves as her guardian angel, took advantage of her after she had fainted during the enemy attack. The story caused a scandal when it first appeared.[28]

Caligari bears a particularly strong resemblance to the stories E.T.A. Hoffmann wrote in the first decades of the nineteenth century. His protagonists are young men who are always on the brink of going mad – like Francis – from their inability to adjust to the dreary unimaginative everyday life in the repressive climate, politically and otherwise, of the *Biedermeier* times in Germany. Hoffmann's central characters, often artists, strive for a self-realization that would allow them both to transcend their dull materialistically oriented existence and to acknowledge the dark forces that philistine society considers demonic and destructive. From the fantasy worlds they create for themselves out of frustration, double figures arise who promise a more fulfilled life, or who threaten – and often lead to – madness and death. The double, as we encounter it in Romantic literature, is a physical projection of the hidden self, of the "otherness," which cannot be accommodated in the prevailing value system.

The title figure of *Caligari* looks like an embodiment of a character out of Hoffmann's tales, such as *The Golden Pot* (1813) or *The Sandman* (1816). Caligari's old-fashioned attire and top hat designate him as a figure of displacement in time and space with slightly supernatural attributes. His huge glasses are metaphors, not as we might assume for wisdom or clear-sightedness, but for the disturbed or refracted view of reality by the alienated individual. Among Hoffmann's contemporaries who thought optical instruments – including glasses – were unnatural and therefore somehow "magic" was Goethe. He believed the artificially enhanced view of the world to be out of harmony with one's inner world, leading to skewed perceptions. Caligari's other prop, his phallic stick, also has an equivalent in Hoffmann. It appears in the hand of one of the sinister double figures of *The Sandman*, in an illustration drawn quite suggestively by Hoffmann himself. It demonstrates that cognitive and carnal knowledge are always important stakes for the divided self. (Hitchcock will make such a stick an important part of Uncle Charles's attire in *Shadow of a Doubt*.)

Hoffmann's significance for *Caligari* and similar films lies not least in the construction of the stories to allow several conflicting readings. In *The Golden Pot*, bourgeois reality and a fantasy world intersect continually without being harmonized. They are engaged in a conflict that is never resolved. In *The Sandman*, the hero's tribulations can be understood psychologically (the persecuting doubles are nothing but projections of an insane mind) or metaphysically (man is subject to a dark force outside of himself against which he is powerless). For both readings, although they are obviously incompatible, the text offers ample proof.

Hitchcock no doubt drew inspiration from *Caligari* for the *Lodger* and for many subsequent films. And yet, whenever the question of the "German influence" came up in interviews, the name Hitchcock invariably mentioned was that of Murnau. During his stay in Berlin he had had the opportunity to watch him on the set and he admired his work greatly.[29] Among Murnau's many qualities as a filmmaker was his talent to conjure, via technology applied with clinical precision, a menacing atmosphere to provoke archaic fears – a talent Hitchcock himself would develop to perfection later in his career. *Nosferatu,* Murnau's 1922 version of the Dracula story, is a film in this vein. It shares with *The Lodger,* similar to *Caligari,* a double figure of the ghostly mass murderer type.

The "hero" in *Nosferatu* is the young recently married burgher Thomas Hutter, who goes on a business trip abroad for adventure and financial gain in a real-estate deal. His customer Count Orlok is a *nosferatu* (or "undead one"). In a nocturnal blood-sucking episode with him, the vampire becomes Hutter's double. They return simultaneously to Hutter's old and Nosferatu's new home in Wisborg, where Hutter's distraught wife Ellen seems to await "both husbands." Nosferatu brings the plague with him and spreads death everywhere. To save the town and her husband from destruction, Ellen gives herself to the vampire in one long night, and both perish.

The fairy-tale simplicity of the story is deceiving. Images and intertitles are often at odds and allow multiple readings. Printed narration in the film comes from various sources. There are pages from a chronicle, letters, diaries, the ship's log, and snippets of dialogue. Comparing the novel *Dracula*, the basis for the screenplay, with *Nosferatu*, Judith Mayne has shown how the film inverts Bram Stoker's narrative strategies of piecing together a complete picture from multiple points of view in journals and letters.[30] In the film, the narration doesn't come together. The documents themselves may be mystifying, like Nosferatu's missive which contains strange letters and symbols. Often, tangential information is given, whereas more important events are left unexplained. In other instances, the words clearly contradict the images. In the key scene of Nosferatu's first night-time attack on Hutter that is intercut with Ellen sitting up in alarm in bed in Wisborg and calling out to her husband, the narrator comments: "Hutter, far away, had heard her cry of warning." What we see, instead, is Nosferatu reacting to her cry by turning away from Hutter, who doesn't even stir in his sleep. It is as if the words are meant to distract from the subliminal message – which is just too awful to be fully realized – encoded in the images.

In contrast to *Caligari*, *Nosferatu* was filmed on location. Murnau's high-angled shots of narrow town streets nevertheless create a similarly claustrophobic atmosphere, expressing the constricted living conditions of the town's inhabitants. An unceasing wind that stirs in the trees and sweeps through the flowers speaks of transience and imparts a nervous, unsettled mood. Somehow we understand the haste with which Hutter leaves this uneasy flowery paradise and embarks on his trip. In this and other respects, Hutter resembles figures in the stories by Ludwig Tieck, particularly *Blonde Eckbert* (1797) and *The Runic Mountain* (1802). Feeling trapped by the narrowness of their little towns or villages, tired of repetitive ordinariness, these fairy-tale heroes escape from their communities' well-kept gardens into the rough mountains in search of the unknown and the secret of life. Their voyage away from human habitation into the wilderness parallels and partly symbolizes the gradual progression into the depths of their souls. The transition from actually experienced outside nature to the landscapes of the mind is deliberately blurred. In the frightening, and at the same time fascinating, natural environments they encounter otherness in the form of slightly supernatural beings, strange men, powerfully alluring women or frightful old hags who metamorphose androgynously into one another. So like in a dream, regardless of how far they travel, at their destinations the protagonists are always greeted by a different alter ego they are unable to recognize as such. In their blindness they will attempt to murder their doubles; instead, they fall into madness and themselves perish. In Murnau's film, nature equally serves as psychic space. The gradual opening of natural vistas during Hutter's voyage show the liberating effect it has on his mind. As he enters Count Orlok's realm, nature, however, becomes wild and threatening. In Count Orlok's castle, the high towers, steep winding stairs, heavy arches and dark passageways suggest that we are following Hutter deeper and deeper into the hidden spaces of his psyche, until he comes upon, down in the crypt, the staring image of his double.[31] Unable to deal with this encounter, he chooses flight, again.

Ellen, too, leaves her cramped interiors to be outside, near the edge of the water. There she is waiting, as the intertitle tells us, "for her beloved," who must be the Nosferatu part of her husband since she knows that Hutter is returning by land. To her, then, Nosferatu appears in an aspect of limitlessness and freedom, as expressed in the wide expanse of the sea and the fiercely blowing wind. The crosses near her in the sand indicate transcendence, glimpses of the infinite, rather than death, as they do in the paintings of Caspar David Friedrich

(1774–1840), a German Romantic painter whom Murnau invokes here and whose landscapes are more like visionary statements than "copies" of the natural world. Friedrich's insistence on painting what "the inner eye"[32] sees and the priority he accords mood over subject link him with Expressionist art.[33]

Murnau's images have opened a secret channel of communication between Nosferatu and Ellen. Ellen, a liminal figure – we always see her near doors, windows, the beach, ever ready to step beyond, to reach out for what is on the other side – meets Nosferatu somewhere in an infinite space in anticipation of their more "physical" encounter.

Nosferatu appears to be more than just Hutter's double. In structure, he somewhat resembles Caligari who is split into a human and a demonic half, and functions also as a projected double of another character. Nosferatu, the physical projection of Hutter's hidden self, also has two constituents. He starts out as Count Orlok, Hutter's respectable business partner who negotiates contracts. With that persona goes a hat that disappears once the contract is signed and Nosferatu metamorphoses into his other half, the vampire.

The vampire's nature is indeterminate and encompasses everything that is alive. He reigns in untamed nature; he is madness (through the real-estate agent Knock, his representative in Wisborg), sickness, unrestrained sexuality, and death. When Hutter finds him in his casket in the crypt, his face looks as inertly wooden as the splintered box top. He is variously associated with animals: rats, coyotes, flies, and spiders, but also with in-between creatures such as carnivorous plants. Moreover, in his yearning for Ellen he is human-like and finally even acquires a soul: moments before he vanishes into thin air, we see his reflection in the mirror. Nosferatu is all pervasive and ultimately uncontrollable. He unleashes all those elements that tend to remain hidden in darkness because they disrupt the unimpeded flow of civil life. Murnau's depiction of the helplessness of the town's establishment – the harbor officials, the professor, the doctor – in the face of Nosferatu's irrational threat runs counter to the positivistic belief of the time that science and rational management could attain complete control over the environment. So instead of being one man's shadow – Hutter functioning as a typical representative of provincial narrowness – Nosferatu is the shadowy underside of repressed bourgeois society.

Does the film's ending indicate a resolution of the tensions it presents? The images leading to the film's formal closure with the death of both Ellen and Nosferatu are deeply ambiguous. Ellen's inner struggle before she throws open the windows as a signal to Nosferatu of her readiness for him, and the impossible mixture of revulsion and abandon with which she offers her throat, invite more than one interpretation. The view of the woman in the claws of the monster could inspire horror less for the woman so violated, but rather for the uneasily realized implication that the woman may actually enjoy the experience. As in

Caligari, where hints of complicity between female desire and the "monster" are perceivable, we could see Ellen as in league with the vampire and condemn her body – not a new idea in the portrayal of femininity in Western culture – as a site of pollution that needs to be eradicated together with her demon lover, thus turning Nosferatu into a kind of Avenger. Does Ellen's presentation in the film encourage such a reading? In her openness to Nosferatu we see, I think, her ability to absorb the contradictions between her day-to-day existence and the incommensurable. Her attunement to Nosferatu's anarchic irrational nature is like an attunement to the natural vicissitudes of life. In telling symbolism she is dressed in black during the day and in white at night, a motif that links her with the characters in *Caligari*. In the image of Ellen's and Nosferatu's embrace the spiritual and the sensual, including its beastliness, are merging.

Yet the transformative power of her act, first for her husband and then for society, is doubtful. Hutter's despair at his wife's death and the professor's resigned withdrawal from this site of mourning contradict again the cheery message of the chronicler claiming that "At that very hour the Great Death ceased."[34] The ending remains inconclusive.

Hitchcock transports the vampire from the spiritual realm to the mundane. Hitchcock's "vampire," the lodger, is not ugly and he doesn't come to buy a deserted house but to rent a room. What links the two films is the lodger's relationship with Daisy. The mesmeric intensity with which he fixates her from the moment he sees her recalls Nosferatu's yearning gaze in Ellen's direction. It has the same ambiguity: does Nosferatu desire Ellen in order to consume her, or does he hope to be consumed by her in a redemptive gesture that will end his cursed existence? Similarly we may ask if the lodger's obvious fascination with Daisy's "golden curls" threatens to trigger a murderous assault on her, or if rather he senses that she is the person to deliver him from the cause of his anxieties.

The allusions to the lodger's vampiric nature are at times quite funny, as in the scene where he sits in the audience of Daisy's fashion house, absolutely fascinated by her appearance, but gentleman that he is, he does not fail to light the cigarette of a young woman seated nearby. Much to the lady's dismay, who clearly wants his attention, he goes through the motions totally mechanically, without even for a second diverting his eyes from Daisy. Another vampire joke may occur in the last scene when Daisy's parents visit the lodger's mansion and Daisy's mother hands the lodger the toothbrush he forgot back at the house. Is the clueless mother encouraging her vampire-son-in-law to take good care of his fangs for the crucial night ahead?

On a more serious plane, in *The Lodger,* just like in *Nosferatu,* the arrival of the "stranger" brings to a head the tensions already inherent in the environment. People are brought face to face with their hidden selves. Daisy finds that she doesn't really love her law-and-order boyfriend Joe. She discovers her sensuality but also her capacity for compassion that leads to the lodger's "redemption." She learns that she is a separate being from her parents. I have seen the usually unflappable Daisy hesitate just once in the entire film. It occurs right after the handcuffed lodger has escaped into the darkness and told her to meet him "by the lamp post." The mother has fainted. Daisy is torn momentarily between helping and comforting her and helping the lodger. Her lover wins, as he must. But with her job involving dressing/undressing and displaying her body, she is portrayed as a "new woman" and marked early on as incipient transgressor against the traditional values of her parents' household, dominated by her nurturing cookie-baking mother.[35] That she should line up with the dark outsider against the other three traditionalists in the house and stay with him until he sheds his dark clothes for angelical white ones in the hospital room seems only natural. I don't think she ever once considers the lodger to be a criminal.

Joe is confronted with his deficiencies as a lover, resembling Hutter in this respect. He also has to face his professional fallibility: he allowed self-interest, his love for Daisy, to cloud objective judgment and guide his actions, thus contributing to a near fatal miscarriage of justice, demonstrating once again how desire for and of woman is envisioned as disrupting the lawful order established by man.

Everyday Londoners are shown as indirectly complicit in the sexual murders. They appear as avid witnesses when another victim has been felled by the Avenger, as eager consumers of news about murder via radio, paper, and gossip, and as potential murderers themselves when they hunt down the lodger and seem prepared to lynch him. Similarly, the Wisborgers unleashed their pent-up aggressiveness against the real-estate agent Knock, Nosferatu's stand-in and designated scapegoat. When they could not get their hands on him, they ended up tearing a scarecrow to pieces. Newspaper people are guilty of sensationalizing and profiting from the crimes, inciting the public to irrational behavior. Hitchcock himself appears both among the newspaper people and the potential lynchers, creating here his lifelong "double" role as Hitchcock the filmmaker and Hitchcock the man, as portrayer and "virtual" perpetrator of villainy.

The emblems for what may be the root cause of the Avenger's twistedness and crimes, however, hang on the walls in the home of Daisy's parents, a couple of exemplary respectability. We may ridicule as kitsch the pictures that cause so much anguish in the lodger, but the camera shows how they push and pull him with what they frame: the half-naked women in provocative poses seem to beckon, but their etherealized Madonna faces prohibit approach.[36] In connection with some of Murnau's asexual heroines, Jo Leslie Collier points out how Romanticism's tendency to idealize created a paradoxical image of woman that was passed on to subsequent generations: "[T]he woman [man] most desired was the one he could never, must never have sexually;" he writes; having sex with her "was tantamount to a perversion: pleasure gained from the degradation of a saint."[37] The pictures may serve as a summary of the hypocrisy and perverse logic of Victorian culture toward sex.

There remains one disturbing aspect of the film. Much is made of the suffering of the lodger, but the Avenger's victims' suffering is totally ignored. Their beautiful detached golden curled heads, back lit lovingly, could be screaming in sexual ecstasy just as well as in fear of death. The effect is intended, I am sure, for just another ambiguity, a first instance of the motif of marriage as murder or death as love, in a Hitchcock film, with many more to come. Does the film constitute an interesting filmic exercise with no bearing on the experiences of real women?

Shadow of a Doubt shares many story elements with *The Lodger,* but made nearly twenty years later, it is the confident statement of a filmmaker who is sure of his art. The figure of the serial murderer is less abstract, his victims are brought into focus and we are given a semblance of an answer as to what the Avenger avenges. It is a surprisingly sympathetic look at women's lot in modern America.

The two Charlies have long been understood as the two poles of a double figure. The first serious analysis of the film, by François Truffaut in 1954, revealed its basic dualistic structure.[38] The very opening invests the two main characters – Uncle Charles and his niece Charlie who has been named after him – with, so to speak, equal protagonist rights. Following shots of their respective cities, houses, windows of their rooms, they are introduced in mirror-like fashion as resting on their beds, both in a depressed mood. Other dualities involve major and minor characters, doubled sequences, plus a variety of specific doubled shots and camera movements.[39]

Subsequent interpretations, building on this dual basic structure, invariably encountered difficulties in evaluating Young Charlie's twinship with her evil Uncle. Does Charlie, as McLaughlin suggests, become "in the obscure equation proposed by the insinuating camera movement, a criminal, too,"[40] who becomes guilty not only by association but through the fact that she actually "triggers [the] process"[41] of luring her Uncle into her family? Or is she, as Sterritt believes, linked "with the common noir motif of a 'spider woman' who tempts and ensnares a male victim"?[42] Rothman, in contrast, argues that Charles and Charlie could possibly "both be viewed as acting out of love and a shared condition of innocence."[43]

The problem with these interpretations is the assumption that doubles are necessarily based on mutually exclusive dual opposites. To be viable as a whole – that is to say, as the composite identity of the two (or multiple) parts – the condemnation of one side of the equation seems to be required, or, in Rothman's interpretation, the "good" somehow needs to absorb the "bad," mysteriously erasing the difference between the two. To grasp the dynamics of the relationship of the two Charlies it helps to interpret it along the lines of the split figures in the texts of the Romantics. There the various component parts are inseparably intertwined, involved in a complicated dialectic that receives its dramatic impact precisely from the inescapably simultaneous existence of complementary opposites.

Uncle Charlie resembles all of the double figures we have considered so far. He is a person's "projection" – Charlie's – and he is split into daytime and nighttime halves. There is also the "man in the East" who corresponds to the murderer getting caught in *Caligari* and *The Lodger*. Uncle Charlie's dark side has some supernatural attributes. On his bed in Philadelphia he looks "undead" and when he stiffly rises the movement recalls Nosferatu's spectral emergence from his wooden box aboard the ship. He transcends spatial limitations in his "magic" escape from the detectives in Philadelphia and his telepathic communication with young Charlie. Later he causes a (garage) door to close by itself – a "trick" Nosferatu was especially good at. Other indications of his nature as a shadow character include the pollution he spreads visually when his train first arrives, and the other vapors he produces, such as his cigar smoke or the car exhaust fumes. His demonic nature is further hinted at through the fact that he refuses to be photographed. And just like Caligari, Nosferatu, and the lodger, he arrives as a "stranger" in town, intrudes into a middle-class family, and threatens to disrupt the bonds of its members.

Similarities extend to the portraiture of the physical environment of the middle-class world as oppressive. In *Nosferatu*, architectural images weigh down on the inhabitants of the town. The city of London, in *The Lodger*, is plunged into fog and darkness for most of the time. In *Shadow of a Doubt* the parallel opening seems to invite a contrastive comparison between Uncle Charles's big city world of Philadelphia and the wholesome environment of Santa Rosa. The opening shot of Philadelphia with the wide span of the bridge and the river beneath suggests an openness to the world that is lacking in the small town of Santa Rosa, giving Uncle Charles an exotic air that will prove so attractive to young Charlie. A junkyard, however, hints at metropolitan filth, and Uncle Charles's place at the tenement house reminds us of the lonely disconnected lives whose sad city existence he shares. Uncle Charles's room itself, in keeping with his somewhat "unreal" nature, seems shifting and unstable. Solid walls are made diaphanous by reflections of sunlit windows and doors appear to lead through windows. Throughout this film Hitchcock uses lighting to produce *Caligari*-like effects, not, however, as in *The Lodger*, to express unreliability of perception, but to translate the characters' feelings of being unsettled or confined, transforming, as Murnau had done, the physical world into psychic space. The effects are much more pervasive and pronounced here than in *The Lodger*, and they are smoothly and functionally integrated in the overall mise-en-scène.

The town of Santa Rosa itself looks initially like a sunny paradise. But it grows progressively darker and more ominous after Uncle Charles's arrival. Big bulky trees throw huge shadows, dwarfing people around them. At night in particular, leafy shadows, trembling from a restless wind (which seems to blow in from *Nosferatu*'s world), form mobile patterns on the walls which are eerily reminiscent of the painted vegetative shapes on the houses in *Caligari*.

In young Charlie's home we notice unsettling features. Thin vertical blocks of light and shadow, reflections of the banister and of window bars, visually transform the house into a place of confinement, echoing the shapes we saw on the walls in Uncle Charles's room in Philadelphia. The materiality of the house is weighing down its inhabitants. "We don't own the house, the house owns us," Emma says at one point. Moreover, just as the family is "imprisoned" at home, Joe, the father, is at his workplace. When the two Charlies visit him there, he peers at them through the solid bars of his window.

As the narrative unfolds in this constricted space, young Charlie feels – as she later explains to Graham – "in the dumps." Existential dissatisfaction is often the trigger that produces the double figure, like in *Nosferatu* or in the Romantic stories. Hitchcock's choosing Charlie as the subject of the double represents a significant shift from *The Lodger*. Daisy, we remember, has a job and thus apparently doesn't suffer from Charlie's kind of emptiness and lack. Women almost never figure as the subject of a double. In the triangles of desire that often develop in doubles stories, a man and his double will be rivals over a female, as in *Caligari*, *Nosferatu* or *The Lodger*. A split male may also experience a divided desire for two different females, one a Madonna, the other a whore. This type of female double, however, as Hitchcock's *Vertigo* makes abundantly clear, is a construct of the male subject. Indeed, Uncle Charles himself constructs a dichotomy between good town women and bad city women, or good mothers and bad widows.

Hitchcock then bestows on Charlie a degree of humanity – that is the "privilege" to experience a crisis of subjectivity, resulting from longing for self-realization – which men like to reserve for themselves. Charlie is searching for a way to transcend the purely material existence of "dinner, then dishes, then bed" that characterizes her mother's world. So to "save" her from a bottomless pit of meaninglessness young Charlie conjures up her dashing uncle who, when he is not traveling, lives in a big city, has interesting stories to tell, and aims at "lightening up the stuffy atmosphere" in the town. Her awakening sensuality also welcomes the special attentions he accords her. He becomes her ideal of desirable virility, and at the same time, since there are no female models of autonomous selfhood around for her to emulate, an example for the kind of self she might want to grow into.

Unlike the sinister Caligari, the vampire in *Nosferatu*, and even the lodger who is persecuted, Uncle Charles does not remain a stranger in town for long. For his good looks and smooth behavior he is almost instantly adopted as one of their own by the townspeople. Some welcome him because of his money; for others, such as Mrs. Potter, he seems to promise future love. People somehow feel "completed" by his presence, driving home the point again that the double is always already at home in the environment it invades.

Emma in particular welcomes Charles as a missing part of herself. He represents her lost past, her identity as Emma Spencer Oakley, reawakening maternal and sisterly feelings for her former little brother. But he also rekindles her libido, her animal nature, which has succumbed to years of neglect in a dull marriage. (It is embodied in that ghastly dead animal fur shawl Charles presents her with.) In one telling scene Charles and Emma lock eyes as he is fiddling with the "phallic" champagne bottle, pointing it at her while she starts to giggle uncontrollably. Her husband Joe shifts his eyes from one to the other, deeply embarrassed. It looks like an incestuous act.

Besides reflecting people's desires, Charles also illuminates the community's dark side. Joe is shocked when Charles suggests that embezzling goes on in banks and that he, Joe, might aspire someday to replace his boss. Charles takes Charlie into a bar where the pervasiveness of social injustice is exposed in the character of Louise, who figures as Charlie's underprivileged alter ego, and where the boisterous soldiers remind us that it is a time of war. It may even occur to us that there is a relation between serial killing and waging war. Uncle Charles's function here is the same as that performed by Nosferatu and the lodger: exposing the hidden face of the average, the ordinary.

All this serves as background for the main story. The film traces the trajectory of young Charlie's maturation. What happens to the ring Uncle Charles gives to his niece marks the stages of this process. It is a powerful symbol on a number of levels. The sexual meaning is strongly suggested by the way Uncle Charles slips the ring on Charlie's finger. Just like the implied incestuous encounter Charles had with Emma, this solemn moment propels us back in history to a time of pagan fertility rites: the sacred marriage between mother and son, or brother and sister. Incest is intimately tied to the doubles theme. We find it both in the biographies and the writings of the Romantic poets all over Europe. It translates the Romantic individual's longing for union with a brother- or sister-"spirit" which finds its fulfillment in incestuous coupling with the twin or sibling of the opposite gender. It also served to demonstrate the Romantics' defiance of bourgeois conventions and taboos. In Hitchcock's film, all of these elements are present. We sense the primordially anarchic wanting to bubble up from underneath a thin layer of carefully constructed civilized life; but for Charlie the ring-giving also clearly means a longed-for spiritual union. The handsome Uncle

Charles, on the other hand, may also point to the reality of incest committed by uncles on their pretty nieces all over America, then as well as now. The real and the symbolic are so tightly interwoven here as to make it impossible to separate out the various levels.

The ring also can be taken as the symbol for the gradual integration of Charlie's fractured identity. Interestingly, it doesn't mean much to her initially when she believes it to be a gift from her "savior," representing happiness. After she has learned that death is inscribed on it she disavows it and Uncle Charles takes it back, breaking the union of their souls. What follows is an initiation-like descent into the hell of her own darkness where Charlie has to face death and her own murderous potential (as when she admits to her uncle that she is prepared to "kill you myself"). She is discovering and embracing "the vampire" in herself – indeed she momentarily turns into one after the library scene: she sleeps all the next day "like a log" and comes back to life only after sundown. So not until she is ready to fully accept her hidden self does she lay claim on the ring deliberately. At that point, it becomes a source of power. Wearing it, she can use it to exorcise Uncle Charles's evil presence.[44]

This moment of her triumph, however, is also the moment of her defeat. Parallel to her disengagement from her male double, Charlie discovers her fated kinship with other women. The object that so powerfully ties and unties the relationship of the dual protagonists involves a third person. The ring had been the property of a human being with a real life and a horrible end. It gives away its secret the instant Charlie has discovered the inscription (for once Uncle Charles hasn't paid attention to those little details!) by starting to "sing": the "Merry Widow" tune arises in Charlie's mind, a secret message not from Uncle Charles who desperately wants the tune and its title to remain hidden but from the victim. We are given a full account of the victim's life in the library scene. Elsie B. Michie argues that the real horror of that moment lies less in the discovery that Uncle Charles really is the Merry Widow Murderer – we had suspected that all along – but in the story of his victims. Implied in the inscription of the ring, furthermore, is the (symbolic) first death of "the beautiful Thelma Schenley," who, when she received the ring ceased to be "TS" but became "BM": Mrs. Bruce Masterson. This prefigures Charlie's own fate: "The scene in the library is thus finally horrifying because inscribed on the ring and in the newspaper article is the story not just of Uncle Charlie's crimes or even of the suffering of his victims but of the path Charlie must follow if she is to become a wife and mother."[45]

In the penultimate scene, Charlie wears the ring as a signal for Uncle Charles to leave town. At the same time she acknowledges her defeat, that she is resigned to giving up her desire to lead a self-determined life. In that scene, her fate is shown as merged with that of her mother, just as it was shown as merged with that of the widows in the earlier scene. Mother and daughter have a similar stake in Uncle Charles, implied in the incestuous link he has with both of them. Thus, his leaving town affects them in parallel ways: Charlie will lose her own identity when she becomes Graham's wife, Emma will lose hers again, after she had retrieved it for a while through Uncle Charles presence, who took her back in time to the days when she was "Emma Spencer Oakley." Hitchcock affectionately shows her "little death which seems to be taking her out of the film"[46] when he fades to black while she is in mid-sentence giving her tearful speech about the pleasures of pre-marital life: "You see – we were so close growing up. And then Charles went away and I got married, and … Then you know how it is. You sort of forget you're you. You're your husband's wife …" Having gained her self, Charlie loses it in the same instance.

Young Charlie's confrontation with her double has brought her self-knowledge but it has also afforded her a glimpse into the dark heart of patriarchy. Hitchcock shows the different deaths women die in this kind of society: there are the symbolic ones when women get married but there is also the real one Uncle Charles inflicts on the widows and that he wants to inflict on Charlie. Why must Uncle Charles kill women? The nature of his crime, his sexual pathology, is his deep-seated fear of the "Dionysian" side of man, represented here in a rather faint echo in the recurring image of the dancing couples. Music and dance, originally expressions of a positive life force, of sensuality, of the opposite of what the domesticated repressed burgher embodies, appear in the film in the somewhat muted form of a festive crowd moving to the giddy rhythms of the waltz. As the soundtrack suggests, in Uncle Charles's mind the music quickly turns dissonant. His "virility," his supposedly independent and adventurous lifestyle, is based on murdering what he perceives to be a threat to the established patriarchal order. That threat emanates not just from fun-loving, carefree humans, but is embodied, more specifically, in the "Merry Widow": the laughing, independent woman, the "phallic" female. (Uncle Charles's most recent victim was a "musical comedy star.")

The phallic female is but one aspect of the Great Mother that continues to strike fear into the hearts of men in patriarchy. The widows, the "useless women," may conjure for Uncle Charles an even more dreadful aspect of her: the pre-Christian archetypal image of the Crone, "the negative aspect of the all-powerful Mother, who embodied the fearful potential for rejection, abandonment, death."[47] Throughout Christian times men tried to deny that negative archetype, witch persecutions being one manifestation of that effort, but "modern male prejudices against aging women represent another manifestation of the same effort."[48] It seems then that part of the "attempt to deny death is the possibility of inflicting death on others in order to purge it from oneself."[49] Uncle Charles the Avenger tries to defeat Death by death.

Hitchcock gives his film a fairy-tale ending: the "bad guy" dies and gets buried, while for the "good guys" there is the promise of a wedding. But Hitchcock makes sure we don't take the ending at face value. In the last images of the film we see Uncle Charles's funeral cortège, accompanied on the sound-track by excessive laudatory comments on the beauty of his character. It makes us realize that Charles's violent death is not really his end: as the people in the town bury his body but eulogize his spirit, they are ensuring that the monster will rise again from his grave and continue to haunt them. At the same time Charlie is shown standing in front of the church, physically and mentally sepa-rated from the rest of the congregation by a secret that will be hard to bear in the long run. She is holding hands with Graham, her prospective bridegroom, who meekly looks up to her, echoing what she says but hardly comprehending. The happiness of this marriage is compromised from the beginning. While Charlie is intact physically, her spirit, her dreams, and desires have been buried together with her double. Her self is sadly diminished. She is stuck in the rut she talks about at the beginning of the film. To drive this point home, Hitchcock makes Graham mouth the same words of "comfort" her father had used then: "It's not as bad as that."

This type of ironic closure, which makes it obvious that nothing has been resolved and points beyond itself at unresolved issues outside the cinematic or literary text, is among the features remaining constant it seems from one work to the next involving the otherwise notoriously protean doubles motif. For the Romantics, narrative non-closure was the consequence both of a philosophical stance and an aesthetic program developed amid the dramatic changes in almost all areas of their existence in the aftermath of the French Revolution and the Napoleonic Wars. As the old order had collapsed and the new was slow in consol-idating, people felt adrift and disoriented. To compensate for the dissolution of stable social and other frameworks the Romantics experimented with new holistic models of being, thinking and creating. For Friedrich Schlegel (1767–1829), the main theoretician of the Romantic movement, the universe was "an infinite and infinitely bewildering chaos," constantly in flux and in the process of becoming.[50] For him the challenge for the Romantic artist consisted in finding a way to express the universe in all its "infinite plenitude"[51] in the work of art – an impossibility really since how can the artist, a finite being, ever hope to grasp the infinite and give it shape in finite form? He could do so only by way of approximation, in an infinite process of creating a system of paradoxes held in continual tension: "[Art] was, to [Schlegel], the dialectic fusion not of one pair of opposites, but of many pairs, all of which, shading off into each other in subtle nuances, were the periphery, as it were, of the same mysterious center that was the heart of the paradox,"[52] making manifest the "the essential 'duplicity' of art, which reflected the 'duplicity' of man and the 'duplicity' – the infinite plenitude and infinite unity – of the world itself."[53] There could be no end to this process, much less a successful, "happy" one since "a Romantic ending is always only a temporary one. [...] The individual text, as a moment in the infinite approximation, becomes at the same time a monument of a necessary failure."[54] Romantic heroes and their doubles fail spectacularly in the stories of Tieck and Hoffmann, as we have seen, because they are incapable of grasping this duplicity, of first recognizing and then balancing it. If narrative closure does occur in these texts it is achieved on a utopian plane (*The Golden Pot*) or is tinged with irony (*The Sandman*).

Beyond its metaphysical dimension the German Romantic version of the double figure derives much of its power from a solid grounding in empirical psychology and what could be termed "proto-psychoanalysis." Theoretical and practical research, speculation and "an intensive regimen of experiments in self-contemplation or introspection"[55] led the Romantics to results that in many ways anticipate the findings of both Freud and Jung.[56] The double figure in literature is closely linked to the preferred field of research of the Romantics, the repressed "night side" of the self which they insist on accepting as an integral part of a person instead of condemning it as a site of "sickness."

Given this set of particular circumstances for the rise of the motif of the double in German Romanticism, how can we tie together the various manifestations of the figure in the different works we have considered? Its resurgence in the German films of the 1920s can be attributed to a host of different reasons. First to consider are the surprisingly similar socio-political conflicts in Germany in the 1820s and the 1920s, albeit modified somewhat by different historical realities.[57] The recent war had again disrupted to the core everything that had anchored people's existence, from the political and social order to moral codes and models of gendered behavior in intimate relationships. Men in particular were affected by loss of autonomy and social status, undermining their identities. In films such as *Caligari* and *Nosferatu,* we see men's shattered selves threatened by fantastic authority figures with whom women obscurely seem to conspire, displacing men's anxieties from a broader social context where they often originated, more explicitly onto the sexual realm.[58] More importantly perhaps the new medium of film offered possibilities for the depiction of twilight worlds and monstrous double figures the Romantics quite literally could only have dreamt of. Again in anticipation of Freud, the Romantics had engaged intensely in dream analysis, regarding dream images and dream "narratives" as "language of abbreviations and hieroglyphs" for subconscious motivations which they understood as distorted or even inverted versions of the dreamer's conscious thoughts.[59] In film the impalpable world of moving images could be projected and be taken in directly through the eyes by the viewer, and he could experience the inverted dream world as if it were emanating from his own subconscious. In a film like *Caligari,* then, the spectator could be drawn into the world of the movie, turning himself into one more double of the ones he saw on screen. These types of effects could be achieved with very little investment. In *Nosferatu*, however, Murnau shows what could be done by using film technology proper: most of the cinematic special effects – negative footage, fast-motion and other trick photography – are associated with the monster itself. In addition, Murnau uses the double channel structure of film (at that time) to set up a contrast between language and vision, having the written word take on the role of the conscious mind trying to obfuscate transmission of the "unspeakable" encoded in the "subconscious" medium of the images.

We get an idea of how much the German theme and the German methods must have resonated with Hitchcock's own artistic aims and personal temperament in the way he combines these elements with homegrown British material for *The Lodger*. By fashioning a narrative where the "happy" ending can be said to be as valid as its opposite, and where the hero along the way effortlessly metamorphoses from criminal to saint (and perhaps back), the budding director brings out brilliantly the paradoxical nature the motif was endowed with in its prior German Romantic embodiments. With Hitchcock, though, the double increasingly loses much of its obvious otherness while it also gains in uncanniness by its very likeness to other characters in the film and to ourselves, the spectators. Moreover, in his cameos and publicity photos, Hitchcock places himself into the world of the film, often, as we have mentioned, as a double of the villain. (In *Shadow of a Doubt*, on the train Uncle Charles is riding to Santa Rosa, a character creates a link between the film's bad guy and the Hitchcock character by remarking that he looks as "sick" as Uncle Charles.) In Hitchcock's fictional universe both the director himself and the audience become potentially complicit in the crimes depicted. Even in *The Lodger*, where the paradoxical structure of the double motif succeeds above all to prove to the world Hitchcock's virtuosity, social criticism is presented by addressing the issues of hypocritical attitudes to sex and to sensationalism involving sex and violence in the media and the public at large.

In *Shadow of a Doubt* these types of criticisms become much more acute and urgent, pointing to the underlying unresolved, unresolvable, problems that stand in the way of closure to the romance narrative. First among these is misogyny, of course, which is presented as ubiquitous and inescapably inherent in patriarchical society. Furthermore, class distinctions are touched upon, as noted above, in the character of Louise. Charlie's encounter with her occurs in the bar-room sequence that, according to Mladen Dolar, is marked structurally as the center of the film.[60] The bar is "a place like hell" (as Dolar puts it) where Uncle Charles fittingly gives his "the world is a sty" speech to Charlie, reminding us that he considers it his mission to eliminate "useless women" and in that way clean up the world a bit. The presence of soldiers in this sequence, who have been conscripted to vanquish Hitler and his helpers, who likewise thought it necessary to purge the world of useless "degenerate" undesirables such as Jews and gypsies and homosexuals, to my mind subtly but insistently links Uncle Charles's thinking to that of the fascists. At the same time Hitchcock may hint at the futility of a military campaign abroad if someone with a mindset like Uncle Charles could be embraced so fully at home, thus narrowing the moral distance between the average Santa Rosians and the Nazis and blurring comforting borders.

Hitchcock is clearly concerned with concrete issues in society. Can we still claim, then, as we did at the beginning of this chapter, that Hitchcock is an unscrupulous showman who sadistically exploits his audience? Or is he rather the doctor who shows us the symptoms so we can find a remedy? He is, I think, in true doubles fashion, a bit of both. There is no doubt in my mind that Hitchcock has a sadistic streak and that he revels in his artistry to devise ever-new ways of scaring and shocking the viewer. However, in doing so he appeals to the "little Hitchcock" in all of us who succumb delightedly to *Angstlust*, the pleasure in fear. At the same time there is always a more serious subtext, carefully camouflaged, which betrays a social critic and perhaps even a metaphysician who invites us to reflect on the world's and our own "duplicity," which must be accepted as fundamental to existence.

Notes

1 Quoted in Otto Rank, *The Double, A Psychoanalytic Study* (1914), ed. Harry Tucker, Chapel Hill: University of North Carolina Press, 1971.

2 I would like to thank Richard Allen without whose miraculously untiring trust and encouragement this paper would never have materialized. My thanks also go to Sam Ishii-Gonzáles for his enlightening comments on an early draft.

3 François Truffaut, *Hitchcock*, revised edition, New York: Touchstone, 1985, p. 26.

4 Donald Spoto, *The Dark Side of Genius: The Life of Alfred Hitchcock*, New York: Ballantine Books, 1983, p. 74.

5 Spoto, *The Dark Side of Genius*, p. 74ff.

6 Sidney Gottlieb gives an excellent overview of the German influence on the style, techniques ,and themes in Hitchcock's early work. In addition he delineates his relationship with Murnau, Dupont, and Lang and points out how Hitchcock's "idea of cinema" was influenced by the German model. See Sidney Gottlieb, "Early Hitchcock: The German Influence," *Hitchcock Annual* 1999–2000: 100–30.

7 See Joseph Garncarz, "Stofflich englisch und stilistisch deutsch," in *Obsessionen, Die Alptraumfabrik des Alfred Hitchcock,* Filmmuseum der Landeshauptstadt Düsseldorf, Marburg: Schüren Verlag, 2000, pp. 83–97; and Anhang, "Wir Deutschen sind nicht so auf das gute Ende erpicht wie die Angelsachsen," in *Hitchcock in Deutschland – Quellentexte 1924/26*, pp. 127–47.

8 Original: "[…] dass in den vielen indirekten Titeln ein Teil der Spannung vorweggenommen wird. Diese Überfülle der erläuternden Worte läßt den Film fast zu einem illustrierten Roman werden," in Garncarz, "Stofflich englisch und stilistisch deutsch."

9 Spoto, *The Dark Side of Genius*, p. 77ff.

10 See Anton Kaes, Martin Jay and Edward Dimendberg (eds.) *The Weimar Republic Sourcebook*, Berkeley: University of California Press, 1995, p. 553.

11 Theodore Price has interesting things to say about this aspect of Hitchcock's stay in Germany. His book also contains useful lists of German silent films together with plot summaries and lists of their major themes that he then matches with Hitchcock films. See Theodore Price, *Hitchcock and Homosexuality, His 50-Year Obsession with Jack The Ripper and the Superbitch Prostitute – A Psychoanalytic View*, Metuchen, NJ: The Scarecrow Press, 1992, pp. 288–354.

12 Maria Tatar analyses the phenomenon in *Lustmord: Sexual Murder in Weimar Germany*, Princeton: Princeton University Press, 1995.

13 See Beth Irwin Lewis, "Lustmord: Inside the Windows of the Metropolis," in Katharina von Ankum (ed.) *Women in the Metropolis. Gender and Modernity in Weimar Culture*, Berkeley: University of California Press, 1997, p. 203.

14 I am indebted for essential insights into *The Lodger* to Richard Allen, "*The Lodger* and the Origins of Hitchcock's Aesthetic," *Hitchcock Annual* 2001–2, 38–78. For a detailed account of the various sources and how they were transformed by Hitchcock, see pp. 45–52.

15 This moment has been described repeatedly in detail. See William Rothman, *Hitchcock, The Murderous Gaze*, Cambridge, MA and London: Harvard University Press, 1982, p. 15ff; Richard Allen, "Hitchcock or the Pleasures of Metaskepticism," in Richard Allen and S. Ishii-Gonzáles (eds.) *Hitchcock Centenary Essays*, London: BFI, 1999, p. 223. In "*The Lodger* and the Origins of Hitchcock's Aesthetic," Allen details Hitchcock's complex staging of the lodger's entrance (see pp. 56–9).

16 "Modern Expressionism in Germany, Austria, and the Scandinavian countries was an offshoot of Romanticism and [...] had its roots in late nineteenth-century Symbolism and Post-Impressionism. Its essence was the expression of inner meaning through outer form." See H.H. Arnason, *The History of Modern Art*, third edition, New York: Prentice Hall, Abrams, 1986, p. 131.

17 We must keep in mind, though, that at the time of the film's making Expressionism as a movement in the arts was waning and entered the cinema largely for fashionable and, it must be admitted, commercial reasons. See Richard McCormick, *Gender and Sexuality in Weimar Modernity. Film, Literature, and "New Objectivity,"* New York: Palgrave, 2001, p. 7: "[Expressionism] was an artistic movement that began in German painting around 1905, became important in literature around 1910, flourished just before and during the war (especially in the theater), but by 1920 was nearly exhausted. Only then, when this once revolutionary aesthetic had begun to degenerate into fashionable, decorative visual style, did it enter the cinema, and by 1924 it was pretty much over there, too." See also part one, chapter three of Thomas Elsaesser, *Weimar Cinema and After*, London and New York: Routledge, 2000, p. 61ff. and passim. In his monograph on *The Cabinet of Dr. Caligari*, David Robinson insists that the film "was made, knowingly and strategically, [...] with the 'art' element calculated as an extra [...] box-office attraction." See David Robinson, *Das Cabinett des Dr. Caligari* , London: BFI, 1997, p. 43. We encounter here a very Hitchcockian tension between box-office calculation and claim to high art. It would be naïve to insist however that commercial considerations in filmmaking necessarily have to compromise artistic integrity.

18 Elsaesser describes this mode of narration very appropriately as an "anachronistically displayed *Rashomon* effect" (*Weimar Cinema and After*, p. 103).

19 McCormick, *Gender and Sexuality in Weimar Modernity*, p. 25ff.

20 Referred to in Patrice Petro, *Joyless Streets: Women and Melodramatic Representation in Weimar Germany*, Princeton, NJ: Princeton University Press, 1989, p. 148.

21 The later claim that the framing device was imposed on the film by the director against the wishes of the scriptwriters, most emphatically propagated by Siegfried Kracauer in his *From Caligari to Hitler*, has long been discounted. See John Barlow, *German Expressionist Film*, Boston: Twayne Publishers, 1982.

22 According to one reviewer at the time the film provoked a mixture of "mirth and incomprehension" among the spectators. See Frederick W. Ott, *The Great German Films*, Secaucus, NJ: Citadel Press, 1986, p. 52.

23 For a detailed analysis of this sequence see Charles Barr, *English Hitchcock*, Moffat, Scotland: Cameron & Hollis, 1999, pp. 36–8.

24 See Rothman, *Hitchcock: The Murderous Gaze*, p. 42ff.

25 See Rothman, *Hitchcock: The Murderous Gaze*, pp. 23–5, and Allen, "*The Lodger*," p. 61ff.

26 Rothman analyzes this sequence in *Hitchcock: The Murderous Gaze*, p. 46; Allen, in "*The Lodger*," pp. 65–8. Žižek points out the basic incompatibility of the flashback with Hitchcock's use of the subjective camera. Conventionally the flashback, as used in *film noir* for example, functions to relate a subject's recollection to social reality. In Hitchcock this doesn't happen: "Hitchcock, the director of the subjective camera *par excellence* who, for that very reason, experiences such difficulties handling the flashback: in those rare cases when he resorts to it (*Stage Fright, I Confess*), the result is deeply ambiguous and strange, and the flashback as a rule proves false." "'In His Bold Gaze My Ruin Is Writ Large'" in Slavoj Žižek (ed.) *Everything You Always Wanted to Know About Lacan (But Were Afraid to Ask Hitchcock)*, trans. Martin Thom, London and New York: Verso, 1992, p. 260 ff.

27 See Trufffaut, *Hitchcock*, p. 43.

28 Eric Rohmer made the story – *Die Marquise von O* – into a film in 1976 (same title).

29 Spoto, *The Dark Side of Genius*, p. 75ff.

30 Judith Mayne, "Dracula in the Twilight: Murnau's *Nosferatu* (1922)," in Eric Rentschler (ed.) *German Film and Literature, Adaptations and Transformations*, London: Methuen, 1986, pp. 25–39.

31 Charles Jameux beautifully describes this "voyage comme connaissance de soi" in his *F.W. Murnau*, Paris: Éditions Universitaires, 1965.

32 Friedrich's advice to a young painter: "Close your physical eye that you may first see your picture with the inner eye. Then bring to light what you have seen in darkness so that it may affect others from the outside in." See Peter Krieger, "Caspar David Friedrich," in *Galerie der Romantik*, third edition, Berlin: Nationalgalerie Staatliche Museen zu Berlin Preußischer Kulturbesitz, 1997, p. 41. See also note 16 above.

33 See Angela Dalle Vacche, "F.W. Murnau's Nosferatu. Romantic Painting as Horror and Desire in Expressionist Cinema," in *Cinema and Painting: How Art is used in Film*, Austin: University of Texas Press, 1996. Dalle Vacche has researched Murnau's indebtedness to various painters in great depth.

34 *Nosferatu* has received a host of interpretations. In his careful reading Gilberto Perez sees Nosferatu as an allegory of the death we all have to learn to accept. See "The Deadly Space Between," in *The Material Ghost*, Baltimore and London: Johns Hopkins University Press, 1998, pp. 123–48. *Nosferatu* has also repeatedly been attacked as being anti-Semitic. See Elisabeth Bronfen, "The Vampire: Sexualizing or Pathologizing Death," in Rudolf Käser and Vera Pohland (eds.) *Disease and Medicine in Modern German Cultures*, Ithaca: Cornell Studies in International Affairs, 1990, p. 85.

35 For the characterization of Daisy as "new woman" see Allen, "*The Lodger*," p. 71.

36 See Rothman, *Hitchcock: The Murderous Gaze*, pp. 19–20.

37 Jo Leslie Collier, *From Wagner to Murnau: The Transposition of Romanticism from the Stage to the Screen*, Ann Arbor: University of Michigan Press, 1988, p. 110.

38 *Cahiers du cinéma* 39, October 1954, pp. 48–9; referred to in Mladen Dolar, "Hitchcock's Objects," in Žižek, *Everything You Always Wanted to Know About Lacan*.

39 For complete lists of all the doublings see Eric Rohmer and Claude Chabrol, *Hitchcock: The First Forty-Four Films*, trans. Stanley Hochman, New York: Ungar Publishing Co., 1979, pp. 72–3; Spoto, *The Dark Side of Genius* pp. 276–7; Dolar, "Hitchcock's Objects," pp. 31–2.

40 James McLaughlin, "All in the Family," in Marshall Deutelbaum and Leland Poague (eds.) *A Hitchcock Reader*, Ames: Iowa State University Press, 1986, p. 142.

41 McLaughlin, "All in the Family," p. 150.

42 David Sterritt, *The Films of Alfred Hitchcock*, Cambridge: Cambridge University Press, 1993, p. 59.

43 Rothman, *Hitchcock: The Murderous Gaze*, p. 242.

44 For a different but interesting summary of the journey of the ring see Dolar, "Hitchcock's Objects," note 39.

45 Elsie B. Michie, "Hitchcock and American Domesticity," in Jonathan Freedman and Richard Milington (eds.) *Hitchcock's America,* New York and Oxford: Oxford University Press, 1999, p. 47.

46 Bill Krohn, *Hitchcock at Work*, London: Phaidon, 2000, p. 69.

47 Barbara Walker, *The Crone: Woman of Age, Wisdom and Power*, San Francisco: Harper & Row, 1985, p. 12.

48 Walker, *The Crone*, p. 13.

49 Walker, *The Crone*, p. 13.

50 Hans Eichner, *Friedrich Schlegel*, New York: Twayne Publishers, 1970, p. 68.

51 Eichner, *Friedrich Schlegel*, p. 68.

52 Eichner, *Friedrich Schlegel*, p. 70.

53 Eichner, *Friedrich Schlegel*, p. 70.

54 Original: "… ein romatisches Ende immer nur ein vorläufiges sein kann. [J]eder einzelne Text [wird] als Moment der unendllichen Annäherung gleichzeitg auch Monument eines notwendigen Scheiterns" in Detlef Kremer, *Romantik*, Stuttgart and Weimar: Verlag J.B. Metzler, 2001, p. 97.

55 Dennis McCourt, *Going Beyond the Pairs: The Coincidence of Opposites in German Romanticism, Zen, and Deconstruction*, Albany: State University of New York Press, 2001, p. 25. In this fascinating book McCourt identifies German Romanticism as the site where Eastern and Western philosophy and religion meet. He includes such literary figures as Rilke and Kafka in his analysis. Perhaps a place for Hitchcock could be found in the mix as well.

56 "[T]here is hardly a single concept of Freud or Jung that had not been anticipated by the philosophy of nature and Romantic medicine." Henri Ellenberger, *The Discovery of the Unconscious. The History and Evolution of Dynamic Psychiatry*, New York: Basic Books, 1970, p. 205. Ellenberger gives an excellent overview of the Romantics' exploits in the field. For a summary of these issues see Kremer, *Romantik*, p. 80ff.

57 See Elsaesser, *Weimar Cinema*, p. 66ff.

58 McCormick analyzes this type of displacement in Weimar films in his *Gender and Sexuality in Weimar Modernity*, p. 96 and passim.

59 Gotthilf Heinrich Schubert is the main capacity in this field. Freud considered Schubert's *Symbolik des Traums* (1814) as precursory for his *Dream Analysis*. See Kremer, *Romantik*, p. 81ff.

60 "The double scenes are roughly centered around this pivotal one which has no double and serves as their hinge" (Dolar, "Hitchcock's Objects," p. 38).

Chapter 4

THE OBJECT AND THE FACE
Notorious, Bergman and the close-up

Joe McElhaney

JEAN-LUC GODARD: And something which is very astonishing with Hitchcock is that you don't remember what the story of *Notorious* is, or why Janet Leigh is going to the Bates Motel. You remember one pair of spectacles or a windmill – that's what millions and millions of people remember. If you remember *Notorious,* what do you remember? Wine bottles. You don't remember Ingrid Bergman. When you remember Griffith or Welles or Eisenstein or me, you don't remember ordinary objects. He is the only one.

JONATHAN ROSENABUM: Just as with neorealism, as you show, you remember only people.

GODARD: Yes, it's exactly the contrary. You remember feelings, or the death of Anna Magnani. It's very clear.[1]

But is it so very clear? In Hitchcock, does the human disappear or become secondary to a cinema of the object in the way that Godard describes? And does this world necessarily stand opposed to that of neorealism, if we are to understand neorealism as a cinema of "feelings" which leaves us primarily with images of the people who inhabit it?

Much of what follows in this essay was provoked by these 1998 interview statements of Godard's, given in relation to the Hitchcock segment of Godard's video and book series *Histoire(s) du cinéma*. Godard's attempt here is to locate Hitchcock's status as "a poet on a universal level" in a way that no other director was able to match and which pivots around the powerful role of the object.

Through these objects, which seem to override conventions of narration, psychology, and logic, Hitchcock became "the greatest creator of forms of the twentieth century and ... it is forms which tell us, finally, what there is at the bottom of things." The preceding quote is taken from the soundtrack to the video. When accompanied by a brilliant montage of objects from Hitchcock films, the argument has its undeniable pull, as hypnotic and compelling as the dead Mabuse's whispered instructions to Dr. Baum to commit acts of terrorism in Fritz Lang's *The Testament of Dr. Mabuse* (1932).

Nevertheless, upon awakening from the trance induced by this poetic flow of images and words, certain questions begin to arise. For if Hitchcock's cinema is one in which the object has assumed such a magisterial role that it has allowed its auteur to "take control of the universe," this still does not adequately account for the seemingly never-ending fascination with these films. If we turn to a much earlier reading of Hitchcock by Godard we find a different approach, equally germane to my purposes here. In his 1957 review of *The Wrong Man*, Godard's emphasis is not on Hitchcock's opposition to neorealism but with that film's "neorealist notations," the manner in which the film negotiates its way between a narrative situation that is wildly coincidental and fantastic and a manner of presentation strongly documentary in impulse. Throughout this review, the close-up receives special attention for the way in which it brings forth the film's project, particularly in relation to Henry Fonda's face.[2] This shift in Godard's take on Hitchcock, separated by a period of roughly forty years, is indicative of a voluminous body of literature on Hitchcock and the manner in which it has likewise attempted (over roughly the same period) to locate the fascination of Hitchcock's cinema within essentially two positions: Hitchcock either as a moralist, philosopher, and humanist, or as a filmmaker of structure and surface. While extremely important work has emerged out of these two traditions, it must be clear by now that neither of them alone is adequate.

In Truffaut's interview book with Hitchcock, there is a quote in relation to *Strangers on a Train* (1951) which is often cited as an example of Hitchcock's fascination with matters of pure form: "Isn't it a fascinating design? One could study it forever." However, there is a quote in relation to the same film that is not cited as often. Commenting on problems in the writing and casting of the romantic leads and its weakening effect on the final film, Hitchcock says: "The great problem with this type of picture, you see, is that your main characters sometimes tend to become mere figures."[3] In other words, a brilliant surface and formal structure are, however alluring, still not enough. The ideas of the film must also be embodied in the actors, the structure must contain within it human forms as well. Throughout Hitchcock's cinema the face of the actor has assumed a particular importance in this regard. In 1965, working out of a statement of Ingmar Bergman's, Hitchcock wrote that everything in cinema "begins with the actor's face. It is to the features of this face that the eye of the spectator will be guided, and it is the organization of these oval shapes within the rectangle of the screen, for a purpose, that exercises the director."[4]

Hitchcock often explained that to be an actor in his films, normal displays of personality and dramatic skill were not always required. The essential skill was to be able to "do nothing extremely well," while adding that this was "by no means as easy as it sounds."[5] What is important is not to repeatedly signify thoughts and emotions through explicit facial expressions and gestures as though these alone were the final repository of meaning. (His difficulties with more Method-oriented actors such as Montgomery Clift and Paul Newman were precisely along these lines.) At the same time (and in spite of his own frequently stated admiration for this so-called Kuleshov effect), a simple neutrality or blankness of expression in the midst of brilliant montage will often not suffice either. First, the face itself must also be iconographically appropriate. Hence his unhappiness with faces he felt were temperamentally unsuited to the material at hand, as with Robert Cummings in *Saboteur* (1942) who "has an amusing face, so that even when he's in desperate straits, his features don't convey any anguish."[6] Second, the face must possess an intrinsic level of expressiveness and be sufficiently malleable in order to be absorbed back into the montage structure, a quality Hitchcock felt was lacking in Sylvia Sidney during the montage set piece of Verloc's murder in *Sabotage* (1936). Sidney's absence of telegraphed surface emotion resulted in Hitchcock finding it "rather difficult to get any shading" into her face.[7] In short, the actor must become at once a plastic element – an object or surface – *and* one of flesh and blood. In either case, the close-up functions as the most privileged of techniques for displaying the possibilities of this cinematic face.

Almost no Hitchcock film uses the close-up as frequently and systematically as *Notorious*: 119 close-ups and 72 extreme close-ups, a combined total of 191 shots in a 101-minute film.[8] Why this need for the camera to be up close so often? My argument will be that the persistence of the close-up in *Notorious* is symptomatic of a much larger reawakened interest in the close-up during this period. In discussing with Truffaut the increased fashion for "psychological pictures" that were being turned out by other filmmakers during the 1940s, Hitchcock estimates that "eighty per cent of the footage was shot in close-ups or semiclose shots." While feeling that the directors of these other films did this out of "an instinctive need to come closer to the action" rather than part of a conscious formal strategy, Hitchcock explained that with *Lifeboat* (1944) he wanted to make use of this trend in a much more deliberate manner. (Unfortunately Hitchcock does not elaborate except to note that this approach eventually became "the television technique.")[9]

While there are several possible explanations for this historical shift in attention paid to the close-up, my concern will be with two. In one of these, the silent cinema becomes a touchstone in rethinking the possibilities of the close-up for the sound era, both in terms of the face and of the face's relationship to the object. In the other, the face is situated in relation to realism as that term was understood during the immediate postwar period, pre-eminently through Italian neorealism. Here the face is not a glamorous or abstract surface (as it often was during the silent era) but an index of thought and revelation in the widest social sense, offered up for microscopic examination and revealed through the lens of the camera. The careers of Ingrid Bergman and Hitchcock (both together and apart) are of major significance in relation to this history. Bergman's presence in *Notorious* is central, so much so that to see the film (even in polemical terms) as being about wine bottles raises some major interpretive and historical problems.

At the time of the release of *Notorious*, Bergman was at the height of her fame. In 1946, film exhibitors voted her the most popular female star in Hollywood. The enormous financial success of *Notorious* served as yet another confirmation of her appeal. If nothing else, the repeated close-ups she receives are a testament to her stardom. As spectacle they are often ravishing, prime examples of the Hollywood close-up of the female star in which the primary objective is to beautify the face. Even a cinematographer of the period as unconventional as John Alton would write in 1949 that "*feminine close-ups or portraits should always be beautiful,*" while adding that such close-ups serve as "the jewels of the picture."[10] Hitchcock's cinema is full of these "jewels," forming a gallery of beautiful faces stretching across his body of work. Still, there is a sustained intensity to the camera's fixation with Bergman in *Notorious* that deserves special attention. In order to address this, we must first examine some of the historical circumstances surrounding the film.

The year 1946 stands out as the most profitable in Hollywood's history and a period in which its dominance as a spectacle-producing industry was second to none. But this dominance was increasingly being called into question. Among its other perceived problems, Hollywood's methods were regarded as those in which individual authorship became lost within the production of technically polished but anonymous entertainments and a cineam in which most often an individual producer or a studio exerted the stongest control.[11] Hitchcock's difficult relationship with producer David O. Selznick was marked by perpetual struggles between the two men over the outcome of the final product, struggles which Selznick usually won: none of the Selznick-produced Hitchcock films were ones in which the director later claimed to have any great personal investment. *Notorious* began as a Selznick project before he sold the entire package over to RKO Radio, where Hitchcock was able to work with the kind of freedom he had previously enjoyed on only one other American film, *Shadow of a Doubt* (1943). If, as Béla Balázs has argued, "close-ups are the pictures expressing the poetic sensibility of the director,"[12] then for Hitchcock the close-ups in *Notorious* partly serve as a form of authorial intervention, away from Selznick's interfering hand. The close-up now becomes not only a way of bringing something closer to the camera but of much more vividly creating a sense of an imprint, both of what is being filmed and of who is doing the filming. That *Notorious* was exceeding certain classical norms in this regard was something noted at the time. In her 1947 review of the film, Dilys Powell wrote that *Notorious* "might be described as an exercise in the close-up," and while praising the ability of the actors to convey so much through facial expression, she also found that "the movement of the camera is overruling."[13] As with many major directors who began during the silent era, Hitchcock never abandoned the basic impulses of his cinematic origins in which there was a need not simply to make films and express oneself but also to search for the fundamental nature of cinema. Central here was the close-up's role in filming objects and the camera's power to "mystically" bestow life upon them. The question of the object and the fragment was particularly crucial to alternative European cinemas during the 1920s. But it was also during the 1920s when Balázs's writings on the close-up first appeared, and his work on the face, in particular, is one of the cornerstones of classical film theory. Balázs posits a utopian cinematic world which allows for "the universal comprehensibility of facial expression and gesture" transcending the limitations of words.[14] The real power of silent cinema resides in the camera's intimacy with its subjects in which "the very atoms of life and their innermost secrets revealed at close quarters" take precedence over spectacle.[15] As is well known, Hitchcock was aware of these issues surrounding the close-up and of the films that sometimes put them into practice. It is obvious from the beginning of his career that the close-up is being asked not simply to serve as a classical narrative tool and fluidly insinuate itself into a causal chain but to signify in an extreme manner. The close-ups of faces and objects standing out so strongly in his early films are consistent with the ways in which the silent cinema of the 1920s privileged close-ups of this nature. At the same time, Hitchcock very quickly established his own particular articulation of the relationship between face and object.

In a film such as *Champagne* (1929), for example, an extreme close-up of the cork of a champagne bottle pops into the camera, the fluid covering the lens. A cut to another extreme close-up, taken from the side of the champagne bottle, shows the liquid being poured into a glass. This gradually becomes an optical point-of-view shot, as the camera pans behind the glass and we see through the glass as the champagne is being swallowed by a still-unseen character. The view that is shown here is of a dance floor on a ship, with the thick circular pattern at

The object and the face

the bottom of the glass giving us a parody of an optical view through a lens, before the glass is finally lowered. This is followed by a close-up of the face of the man to whom this point-of-view shot belongs as he looks directly into the camera. The object here finds itself the subject of the three strong looks central to Hitchcock's cinema: the look of the camera, which often brings these objects close to the lens (so insistent in this particular shot); the look of the character expressed through the optical point-of-view shot (again, quite extreme here); and the look of the spectator to whom this shot is obviously addressed – the pop of the cork threatening to symbolically pop out the eye of the spectator who instead gets a bit indirectly soaked as the fluid covers the camera's lens. *Champagne* was Hitchcock's penultimate silent film. In later years, he repeatedly expressed his devotion to a "pure cinema" which had its basis in the silent era, employing strictly visual means to convey information in opposition to the sound era's over-reliance on "photographs of people talking."[16] This sentiment is a persistent influence of the essentialist discourses on film from the 1920s and which the example of Hitchcock's own filmmaking practice considerably complicates. He adapted quickly and easily to the introduction of sound, transposing the formal concerns of his silent films with a minimal amount of struggle. In this regard, there is a fair amount of continuity in the ways in which close-ups are used in his silent films and in his sound. At the same time, *Notorious* clearly follows a certain pattern of development in Hitchcock from the mid-to-late 1940s, in which the close-up was appearing with increased frequency and self-consciousness. Furthermore, the film emerges when certain discourses about the close-up begin to draw attention to what is felt to be the current inadequacies of the device, particularly as it is being practiced by contemporary Hollywood.

It is during this period when Eisenstein makes his well-known distinction between the American and Soviet conceptions of the close-up. For the Americans, the close-up is a quantitative question of presentation, spectacle, and viewpoint within a traditional system of decoupage, while for the Soviets it is a qualitative question of signification, meaning, and designation (shots are not close up to the Soviets but large scale) and bound up with montage.[17] For Eisenstein, the limitation of D. W. Griffith's (and, by extension, much of American cinema's) conception of the close-up is that it always confines itself to the level of "*representation and objectivity*, and nowhere does Griffith try through the *juxtaposition* of shots to shape *import and image*."[18] In a 1945 essay on the strengths and limitations of contemporary film criticism, Eisenstein complains of the dominance of a certain medium-shot sensibility in which only "a generalized concept of the event" is created in the spectator's mind. Within the world of the medium shot, the spectator is completely uninterested in matters of authorship, of film construction. Instead, the spectator is only "moved by the living play of emotions." By contrast, the long-shot view, as a formal device, "conveys the general scope of the phenomenon." But in the close-up "the spectator plunges into the most intimate matters on the screen: a flinching eye-lash, a trembling hand, fingertips touching the lace at a wrist ... All these at the required moment point to the person through those details in which he ultimately conceals or reveals himself." Eisenstein argues for the importance of a critical approach to cinema that is likewise "close up," capable of breaking down a film and breaking into it in an attempt to understand its components. While conceding the importance of both the long- and medium-shot views, Eisenstein argues that it is the close-up view of all of a film's "component links" which must assume priority.[19] The same year, Eisenstein argues for the importance of objects (and for Eisenstein objects here include the actor) being filmed in such a way that they take "root in the very tissue of the work" and that all matters of framing and lighting "must aim toward not merely *figuring* the object but also *revealing* its signifying and emotional aspect."[20] Hitchcock's understanding of the close-up does bear some relationship to Eisenstein's, however removed Hitchcock might be from Eisenstein's concerns in other ways. Even Hitchcock's language when describing close-ups – his preferred term of "BIG HEAD" for extremely close shots of faces, for example – suggests an Eisensteinian concern with scale rather than simple proximity.[21]

Hitchcock criticism has often drawn attention to the role of the object as either something exchanged and transferred among characters (such as the key to the wine cellar in *Notorious* which passes from Alex's key chain to Alicia to Devlin and then back again) or as an object turned "against nature" in such a way that its apparent innocuousness becomes infused with violent and lethal connotations (again, the key to the wine cellar or the bottles themselves, some of which contain not wine but uranium ore). However, *Notorious* marks a crucial moment in Hitchcock's body of work in which objects are not simply exchanged, and not simply turned against nature, but are situated in such a way that they assume wide-ranging implications within the film as a whole, revealing their "signifying and emotional aspect." One of the film's great set pieces illustrates this.

This is the sequence in which Alicia finally realizes that she is being poisoned by Alex Sebastian (Claude Rains) and his mother (Leopoldine Konstantine), and which contains one of the film's most famous shots: that of the poisoned coffee cup as it almost completely fills up the foreground space. The use of such over-scaled props is not without precedent in Hitchcock. There are the glasses of brandy containing poison in *The Lady Vanishes* (1938) and the gun being fired into the camera at the end of *Spellbound* (the latter evoking the shot of the exploding cork from *Champagne* described earlier). But there is a certain compressed intensity to this particular object in *Notorious* that its predecessors do not fully possess. In the earlier films, the over-scaled props never quite get beyond a certain anecdotal level in which the danger to the protagonists is an external element suddenly introduced into the film for the purpose of suspense. In *Spellbound* the object is not even turned against nature but is, by its very nature, a lethal one. The moment in which it simultaneously fires into the face of the character holding it and out into the audience evokes the "attractions" quality of early cinema, like the final shot of *The Great Train Robbery* (Edwin S. Porter, 1903) but done in close-up and as a form of optical point-of-view. In *Notorious*, the coffee cup is not simply placed within the film's environment in order to assume a menacing role (as happens with the brandy glasses in *The Lady Vanishes*). Instead, the sense of menace is one that has been slowly permeating the film from the beginning. The shot is not only the most extreme use of an object in the film but also a culminating moment in one of the film's crucial motifs: in a film so strongly centered around the consumption of liquids and poisons, a world in which the heroine's own well-being is threatened by her relationship to these liquids (her alcoholism, her knowledge about the wine bottles which leads to her being slowly murdered through poisoned coffee), this shot, arriving just before her moment of revelation about being poisoned, has the effect of surpassing – to make use of Eisenstein's language for a moment – "the limits of situation." Arguably what we have here is a large-scale shot of the cup that has "taken root in the very tissue of the work" and not a mere close-up.

How the shot achieves its particular impact, however, is equally based on other factors, in particular the way that the face functions in relation to the object. The shot itself is not quite a close-up in the conventional sense. The faces of both Alicia (sitting on the left of the frame) and Dr. Anderson (Reinhold Schünzel, in profile on the far right) are also visible in what may be more accurately defined as a medium shot. Nevertheless, the effect is of extraordinary proximity, achieving all the impact of an extreme close-up while simultaneously functioning as a medium shot showing Alicia, sinking into the chair on the far left, being overwhelmed by the poisons contained within the cup. Bergman's face, both in this shot and throughout the first half of the sequence, is marked by its almost completely withdrawn, mask-like quality. The poisons have so permeated Alicia's system by this point that her face, eyes hooded and barely registering what is going on around her, has lost its expressive connotations. The cup assumes an increasingly expressive function as Alicia's mental alertness is threatened with literal extermination. Throughout Hitchcock's work, the expressive possibilities of the face are often contrasted with the utterly passive and inexpressive object, a world of pure matter or surface; or a contrast will be established between an expressive face and an inexpressive or impassive one: the transparent face of the heroine of *Rebecca*, for example, with that of the stone-faced Mrs. Danvers. Sometimes the stone face may be literally realized, as in the faces of the Statue of Liberty in *Saboteur* or Mount Rushmore in *North by Northwest* (1959); or the face may have turned to bone and dust, as in the skull of Mrs. Bates in *Psycho*.

The fact that in *Notorious* the face being effectively drained of life is Ingrid Bergman's is of a particular significance.

Bergman (like Hitchcock) arrived in Hollywood in 1939, at a time when a certain melancholia increasingly begins to manifests itself in film theory and criticism.[22] What recurs throughout these writings is that there is not simply a decline in expressive visual power brought on by sound. We are also witnessing a cinema in which the face no longer carries the same iconographic boldness that it did during the silent era. Whether this historical opposition between the face in silent and sound film is completely accurate *as* history is not of primary concern here. What *is* of some significance is that this attitude did exist, and that the sound film is regarded as one that is creating obstacles for the possibilities of a uniquely cinematic conception of the face. For Balázs writing in the 1940s, the silent film possessed a "microphysiognomy" in the way that it filmed the face that the so-called talking film seriously threatens.[23] What Balázs sees as particularly debilitating for the face in sound cinema is its relationship to the spoken word. A fundamental incompatibility is seen between a face in close-up and a face that then opens its mouth to speak. Once it does this it merely becomes a "sound-producing instrument" in which the mouth, because of being "in active movement, often appears grotesque."[24] However, neither explicitly in his writings and interviews nor implicitly in his films does Hitchcock directly express this kind of melancholia. Even his statements about the ideals of "pure cinema" are not melancholic but (like Eisenstein's) actively critical, still strongly connected to the possibilities of film practice. And in *Notorious* he has a female star who raises major issues in terms of the history of the cinematic face caught in a crucial historical moment.

No other film star so acutely represented the difficult state of transition from the face in silent cinema to that of sound as Bergman's great Swedish predecessor, Greta Garbo. Regardless of her success in sound films, Garbo remains the silent film star *par excellence* in terms of the connotations of her face. Early in her career Bergman was often compared to Garbo, and, like Garbo, Bergman is a star around whom a fetish for the face has become a central aspect to her cult. As John Kobal would later write, "Bergman's appeal was drawn from her face."[25] By the 1940s, Bergman not only succeeds but *replaces* Garbo as a great European/Hollywood female star, correcting the problem areas of Garbo's persona (aloofness, exoticism, sexual ambiguity) for an American wartime public. While the "perfection" of Bergman's face does suggest some of the ideal, mask-like qualities of Garbo, the specific uses to which Bergman puts her face are of a different order. Bergman represents a significant moment during the sound period when the mask-like grandeur of the silent star gives way to what Edgar Morin has called "the quiet face," which attempts to "reconcile the permanent expression of the mask with the thousand tiny lifelike expressions which constitute 'naturalness.'"[26] As a *femme fatale* in *Notorious* Bergman represents a trend that gradually emerges after 1930 in which the silent icon of the vamp is increasingly humanized, becoming the "*good–bad girl*."[27] While Garbo played the title role of the *femme fatale* quite seriously in *Mata Hari* (George Fitzmaurice, 1932), more than a decade later Bergman assumes a similar kind of role in *Notorious* much more ironically: "Mata Hari," Alicia describes herself at one point, "She makes love for the papers."

Bergman was explicitly marketed by Selznick as "the first natural movie star" after Bergman refused to undergo Selznick's initial attempts to conventionally glamorize her. In a newsreel from the late 1940s she and Hitchcock are shown arriving at Heathrow Airport to begin production on what would be their final film together, *Under Capricorn* (1949). Even the newsreel cameraman for this short cannot resist a very tight close-up of her face while the narrator describes her as "the Swedish-born actress, wearing no make-up yet looking lovelier than Hollywood pictured her." Many of her Hollywood films share in a general fascination with Bergman's face, irresistibly returning to it in close-up. The close-ups that Bergman receives during this period serve to confirm her heavily promoted "naturalness," turning it into an enormously attractive spectacle.[28] Bergman's close-ups are both acts of seduction for the viewer and pieces of evidence definitively establishing this "new" kind of beauty.[29] Many of the early sequences of *Notorious* show Bergman in a disheveled state: drunk or hung over, strands of hair getting stuck in her mouth or flying in front of her eyes. When she wakes up with a hangover, she finds her hairpiece lying next to her on the bed, as though such surface tools of glamour are somehow incompatible with the persona. (Of course in all cases she looks quite beautifully and carefully disheveled.) By its very nature, then, Bergman's face is incapable of assuming the nature of a Garbo-like mask but must continually connote its naturalness and be in motion through this combination of radiance and eroticism.

But the recurrence of Bergman close-ups and the emphasis on facial expression as the very center of her performances is also traceable to a completely mundane matter in terms of her body. Bergman, at 5'9", was unusually tall for an actress, often as tall or more so than her leading men. As a way of getting around the problem, there tends to be an avoidance of long and medium-long shots of her in Hollywood films, thereby avoiding the potential risk of placing her side-by-side with a leading man over whom she might tower.[30] The bulk of Bergman's expressive power as an actress, then, is forced to occur from the waist up. In this regard, we may think of her as the purest of Hitchcock's actors in that the movements of her body, by the very limitations imposed upon it, must often be repressed or controlled, resulting in the face becoming the primary expressive tool. Pascal Bonitzer has isolated the repression of the gestural as being a central component of the "revolution" in cinema of which Hitchcock's work stands as exemplary. Within this revolution, the comparative bodily freedom and carniva-lesque anarchy of early cinema gives way to a cinema engaged in a "progressive domestication of the actor's body."[31] The discovery of the close-up of the face (in which a maximum amount of emotional power is often achieved through a minimal amount of facial gesture), and of the expressive possibilities of editing in general, results in the actor's body assuming an increasingly controlled function. While the face had been a central component of Hitchcock's work from the beginning of his career, with Bergman Hitchcock worked for the first time with a star whose identity was closely linked with her face, one strongly marked by its naturalistic qualities. In linking *Under Capricorn* with *Notorious*, Eric Rohmer and Claude Chabrol see both films as being "the story of a face, that of Ingrid Bergman. It is to this face that the homage of the most beautiful effects is made."[32] Bergman's face is not simply functional for Hitchcock, shaped by the dynamics of montage, but is also innately expressive so that his films with her seem to be (whatever their other concerns) *about* the face. Consequently in *Notorious* a crucial part of the process of Alicia's investigation in her role as a new kind of Mata Hari takes place around the face as well.

Perhaps the most notable moment in this regard occurs when Alicia first visits the home of Sebastian. In this sequence we are introduced to a number of crucial supporting characters, all of whom are not only introduced through, but also initially defined by, their faces in an overt manner, with the close-up often serving as a pivotal moment. Shortly after her arrival, in Alicia's point-of-view shot, Madame Sebastian makes her entrance down a long flight of stairs, moving in a single camera set-up (with brief cutaways to Alicia looking) from long shot into extreme close-up. A brief series of shot/reverse shots follows, as Alicia and Madame Sebastian converse in very tight close-ups about the trial of Alicia's father. We are offered a bold visual contrast here between the youthful beauty of Alicia and the considerably older and more imposing visage of the mother. The close framing works to heighten our sense of Alicia being intimidated by Madame Sebastian, a face-to-face encounter in which the tight smile on the older woman's face barely conceals her intense hostility and suspicion. She remarks on Alicia's beauty while also comparing Alicia's face to that of her father's. At the same time, the close framing works to create an atmosphere of implied interrogation, in which Madame Sebastian is scrutinizing Alicia's face for signs of duplicity. She questions Alicia as to her failure to testify at her father's trial. Alicia's excuse – that her father did not want her on the stand – only intensifies Madame Sebastian's suspicion. Konstantine's performance as Madame Sebastian here, her manner of raising a single eyebrow and slightly closing one eye as she says, "I wonder why?" in relation to Alicia's excuse for her absence, also heightens the sense of interrogation. This moment is interrupted by the appearance of Alex and his introduction to Alicia of the Nazi members of his group. Avoiding the shot/reverse shot structure here until the very end of the introduction, Hitchcock only shows us the various men stepping forward into Alicia's close-up point-of-view shot as they kiss her hand and we see each of their faces.[33] It is a very theatrical form of introduction, almost a way for each of them to take a bow before the performance begins rather than after. More to the point, each of them is marked by their highly distinctive facial make-ups, a way of indelibly printing them on the mind of both Alicia (who is there for American intelligence in order to take note of and remember everyone who is present) and the spectator. Some of these men conform to stereotype (in particular, Ivan Triesault's Eric Mathis) and some do not (the standout here being Eberhard Krumschmidt's bungling Emil Kupka, who is finally murdered by Mathis). The last of these introductions is Dr. Anderson (whose entrance breaks Alicia's extended point-of-view shot, and there is a cut to a reverse angle as we see her glowing smile upon meeting him). Anderson's face is quite benign and friendly, and Alicia later describes Anderson to Devlin as having a "kind face" with "a crease in the forehead." However, Anderson is, in fact, a brilliant and powerful Nazi scientist named Otto Renzler.

Furthermore, with *Notorious* Bergman may be seen as the first major female star of Hitchcock's in Hollywood who assumes a role which is also strongly erotic, becoming the central figure in a film in which (as Truffaut tells Hitchcock) "you were regarded not only as the master of suspense, but also as an expert on physical love on the screen."[34] Unlike Grace Kelly or Tippi Hedren later, this erotic component never strongly manifests itself for Hitchcock in a fetishistic response to clothes, hair, and other body parts. With Bergman, eroticism begins and ends with the face. Ingmar Bergman, for example, has spoken of the experience of seeing her Hollywood films during the 1940s: "In her face – the skin, the eyes, the mouth – especially the mouth – there was this very strange radiance and an enormous erotic attraction."[35] This mouth becomes a centerpiece in the famous extended kissing sequence from *Notorious* that may be seen as an indirect response to Balázs's difficulties with the mouth in sound cinema. Neither Alicia nor Devlin ever directly face the camera here but either have their backs to it or are shown in profile. They continually talk (in low voices) and kiss in a tight, two-shot close-up that follows them across the terrace and into the apartment in a single take as Devlin makes a phone call.

What is also significant about the sequence is its placement in the film. Up to this point, much of the interplay between Alicia and Devlin has centered around the act of looking into and interpreting each other's faces: her extended look into his face at the party in Miami as well as the extreme intimacy of the shot/reverse shots in her cabin as they look at one another; her desire to "wipe that grin" off of his face as they are speeding along the highway; the quick scan that he gives to her face in profile as she looks out the window of the plane as they are about to land in Rio; the cafe sequence in Rio when she speaks of trying to interpret what is going on "behind that copper's brain." With the kissing sequence on the terrace, the act of looking into and interpreting a face gives way to a purely erotic moment of physical contact through faces and mouths constantly rubbing against one another. The sequence is at once frankly modern and sophisticated in its eroticism and about as simple and "primitive" in its appeal as the cinema gets.

In *Notorious*, it is not Bergman who is asked "to do nothing extremely well" but her co-star, Cary Grant. Grant's general strengths as an actor stand in marked contrast to those of Bergman. Like Bergman, Grant is an actor strongly associated with Hitchcock. But if Bergman is primarily an actor of the face in which a gestural body is typically downplayed, Grant's central expressive tool is his body. Grant is essentially a comic actor, and like all great performers who work within this mode, his body's relationship to the decor and to the objects that surround him is fundamental to his appeal. In all of his other films for Hitchcock there is a frequent emphasis on Grant's body in motion, with close-ups used much more sparingly than in *Notorious*. Camera distance is primarily in the medium to long shot range in order to capture this relationship between Grant's body and his environment, with the favored method of shooting his face being the medium close-up which still allows for a certain kind of gestural freedom. But in *Notorious*, not only is his face frequently impassive but also his bodily movements are unusually restricted. Throughout the film as a whole, Grant consistently underplays. In close-ups, his face is often rigid, a kind of surface in its own right and marked by its absence of telegraphed thought and feelings in contrast to Bergman. In the first cafe sequence in Rio, Hitchcock employs a standard shot/reverse shot for the conversation between them, generally alternating medium and full close-ups. In the shots showing Alicia talking to Devlin, Bergman is often quite animated, gesturing with her hands, folding and unfolding them, placing them over her face in embarrassment. By contrast, Grant's Devlin barely gestures or moves at all, with one hand folded on top of the other, as though attempting to restrain them, and his face shows little clear emotion.

While both gesture and the mobile body have definite functions in Hitchcock, they take place not only in a controlled manner but are most often situated within a structure of contrast and relations.[36] Again the poisoning sequence is crucial. Gesture here is highly controlled. Alicia sits in a mammoth wing chair that greatly restricts both her movements and her vision. Madame Sebastian's slow gesture of pouring the coffee as the camera follows her from her chair over to Alicia acquires the stateliness of a ritual. Every gesture in this sequence is tied to death. What is particularly disturbing here is not simply that Alicia is being poisoned but that Bergman's face is drained of the very qualities that give it its apparently singular nature. It no longer seems radiantly natural or erotic but almost dead. Alex even directly refers to Alicia's need to "put the roses back" into her cheeks. Beyond this, Alicia's face has lost almost all of its capacity to be a functioning Hitchcock face, which is to say that it has lost its ability to not only connote the act of looking but (always its corollary in Hitchcock) the act of thought and perception. The famous mouth barely moves, the eyes are hooded and hardly seem to notice anything around them. It is not until Alex interrupts Dr. Anderson as he is making suggestions to Alicia about improving her health that Alicia's face seems to come to life. The shot in which it does is as startling as the shot of the enormous coffee cup. In close-up, Bergman almost imperceptibly tilts her head and quickly shifts her eyes in Alex's direction, "doing nothing extremely well." Prior to this, the spectator has been given an excess of information about the circumstances of Alicia's poisoning in order to create suspense: when will Alicia realize what is happening to her? The giant coffee cup not only conveys the extreme amounts of poison in Alicia's system, threatening to overwhelm her, but the size of the cup may also be seen as a figuration of this excessive amount of knowledge given to the spectator, one which the spectator no longer desires to have but wants Alicia to possess instead. In a second, the close-up of Alicia breaks this tension, quickly followed by three optical point-of-view shots: of the cup and two subjective tracking shots into the face of her mother-in-law (who looks directly into the camera) and her husband (who pretends to be reading a paper and avoids her look). Throughout *Notorious*, the face both reveals and conceals, becomes a stabilizing and destabilizing presence, is both a mask and (particularly in the case of Bergman's Alicia) an index of thought and emotion.

But if *Notorious* captures Bergman at her peak, it was also the last popular success she would enjoy during the 1940s. Several major failures followed *Notorious*, culminating with *Under Capricorn*. Following that final film for Hitchcock, Bergman made *Stromboli, terra di dio* (1949), working with a film-maker whose methods would seem to be diametrically opposed to Hitchcock's and to Hollywood's: Roberto Rossellini. Several years earlier she had seen Rossellini's *Open City* (1945) and *Paisà* (1946). It is this kind of cinema towards which Bergman herself is now drawn as she tires of what she perceives to be Hollywood's overly slick and professional methods: "I've had ten years of doing the same kind of beautiful, romantic movies. Now I want to do something realistic. I want to do something like *Paisan*."[37]

It is tempting to see Hitchcock and Rossellini's approach as being utterly opposed to one another, and *Notorious* would initially seem to be unrelated to the late wartime and postwar drive towards realism which Rossellini's cinema exemplified. The film is obviously shot on studio sets with the actors standing or sitting in front of enormous rear projection screens for outdoor scenes and the beautifully textured indoor lighting is of an entirely different nature from the kind of work found in *Open City*.[38] In comparison with the meticulous montage and beautifully constructed scenario of *Notorious*, the Rossellini of a film such as *Europa '51* (1952) has elliptical cutting, poor dubbing, and a blunt and sometimes didactic scenario that would no doubt have made the formalist in Hitchcock cringe, not only in terms of its structural awkwardness but also in the explicitness of its ideology. To call a film *Europa '51* clearly signposts it as a work that directly wishes to testify on the state of postwar European culture, and on a major scale. Indeed, much of Rossellini's work has this kind of social and historical ambition, one which Hitchcock's work tends to avoid. The political implications of a film such as *Notorious* are significant and available to be read as such by anyone wishing to do so. At the same time, these issues are situated in such a way that they may also be seen as *insignificant*, as simply a pretext – for the story of a complicated romantic triangle, for the filmmaker's own attention to matters of form and style. (This was, in fact, the position that Hitchcock himself adopted when discussing the film.) But for all their differences, many of them fundamental, we may also see Rossellini and Hitchcock as being complementary opposites.

First, realism itself is not by any means antithetical to Hitchcock. If contrast is arguably the fundamental structuring element to Hitchcock's work, then every drive towards artifice, the "slice of cake" that Hitchcock sometimes called his cinema, will invariably be countered with a drive towards realism, the "slice of life." Throughout his career, Hitchcock drew upon various strategies associated with film realism, pre-eminently a sense of verisimilitude in the re-creation of middle- and working-class culture in films like *Blackmail* (1929), *Shadow of a Doubt,* and *The Wrong Man* (the latter with its "neorealist notations"). For all of its studio artifice, *Notorious* uses two methods often linked with the language of film realism: the long take and improvisation, particularly in the famous extended kissing scene on the terrace.[39] The degree to which this long take is "realistic" is an endlessly debatable point. But the extreme proximity of the camera to the actors and the sense of intimacy and tactility that it creates; the almost unbearable sense of duration that emerges through the extended take; and the partially improvised dialogue, at once awkward and naturalistic, all of this is far from being incidental to the developments of film realism during the 1940s, even if it is not precisely articulated in the same manner as Rossellini. Second, for all of the mystificatory prose that has been printed about Rossellini's respect for reality, for people, and for "things as they are," his films often feel strongly *constructed*. Some of his most notable sequences, such as the capture of the tuna in *Stromboli*, are highly accomplished examples of montage. The camerawork in *Europa '51* is almost as assured as that in *Notorious*, with expressive lighting effects and a fluid and intricate use of the crab dolly for interiors, while his final film with Bergman, *La Paura* (1956), is as visually expressionistic and melodramatic as anything by Hitchcock.[40]

Europa '51, then, may be seen as in some ways a continuation of *Notorious* and not simply its antithesis. In both films, Bergman's characters undergo a symbolic trial-by-fire following the loss of crucial male figures – the father in *Notorious*, the son in *Europa '51* – her relationship to both of them strongly tied to World War II and the process of adjustment after it. In response to these deaths, the two women are called upon to bear witness to postwar situations of the utmost social and political urgency. If, for Hitchcock in *Notorious*, objects play a crucial role in relation to the issue of circulation and exchange, at once urgent and the "empty" place of the MacGuffin, for Rossellini in *Europa '51* such objects as the toy train given to Irene's son, the political books given to her by her Communist cousin, and the cardboard boxes which rhythmically roll off the assembly line of the factory in which she temporarily works, are lifeless and usually discarded. Both Alicia and Irene ultimately suffer from what one might crudely term an excess of revelation. They have seen (and done) too much according to the logic of their social worlds and are punished for this: Alicia through poisoning and Irene through being sentenced to a mental institution when the profoundly Christian deeds she undertakes after her son's death are misinterpreted by her family as a form of insanity. And in both films, it is the face of Bergman in close-up that becomes the privileged vehicle through which the concerns of the films are largely articulated. For both Rossellini and Hitchcock, the act of looking, conveyed through the protagonist's gaze at her environment, face filmed in close-up as she does this, is central to the process of their awakening. They both must learn to *see*, even if in Rossellini this process is far more agonizing than it is in Hitchcock and initially produces a complete inability on the part of the protagonist to fully process what it is she is looking at. As André Bazin writes of Bergman in *Europa '51*, "Her drama lies far beyond any psychological nomenclature. Her face only outlines a certain property of suffering."[41]

The year after *Notorious*, Rossellini filmed a version of Jean Cocteau's play *The Human Voice* in which Anna Magnani's face was shot frequently in close-up. Rossellini described it as a "study of the human face, the penetration into the hidden wrinkles of a physiognomy."[42] For Rossellini, the camera eye here was microscopic and he defined this as "a moral approach which also becomes an aesthetic fact."[43] Indeed, it is important to take note of an increased tendency during the postwar period towards a de-glamorization of the face, not only in Italian neorealism but also in cinema worldwide. The face is not only "close up" but it is now often literally a face without make-up, a face which belongs to the dying, to the mentally unbalanced, a face which desperately sweats and offers itself up for exposure.[44] In her films with Rossellini, Bergman often finds her own face caught up in these new kinds of situations. She is no less beautiful here (particularly in *Stromboli*) than she is in her Hollywood films, but the context has shifted. Rather than casting Bergman in roles which valorize her naturalness, so common during her Hollywood period, Rossellini tends to give her roles that are marked by a certain unsympathetic and (particularly strong in their later films together) artificial quality, in which a Nordic or non-Mediterranean woman is suddenly forced to confront the mystery of a Southern culture so alien to her. Her face is now subjected to another intense form of implied interrogation, as thorough as that in *Notorious* but of a different order.

As we have already seen, near the end of *Notorious,* Alicia's great moment of revelation takes place when she looks from the poisoned coffee cup into the faces of her husband and mother-in-law. This revelation is so intense that she finally collapses, as much from this knowledge as from the poison itself. At the end of *Europa '51*, Irene has been sent to an asylum. But the asylum also becomes a space within which she achieves her greatest moment of lucidity and connection with the world around her. This plays itself out for Rossellini in Irene's simultaneous rejection of the object (the various blots of the Rorschach test handed to her by a psychiatrist which she refuses or is unable to interpret) and an acceptance and serious contemplation of the face. The faces that Alicia looks into (both here and in the earlier dinner party sequence) are masks, concealing violence and murder; the faces that Irene looks into are those of the other women in the asylum who, unlike Irene, truly suffer from mental diseases, their madness explicitly (and almost expressionistically) written on their faces. In both films, the act of looking into these faces is marked by bravura camera movements tied to optical point of view: the fast tracks into Alex and his mother and the nervously gliding dolly movement across the floor of the asylum as Irene not only looks at the women but the women all look back at her. In a pivotal moment, Irene comforts a suicidal woman, their two faces meeting in close-up, each of them initially shown in the other's point-of-view shot. Irene eventually takes the woman's face in her hands, touching her forehead and offering comfort, before finally laying her head next to the woman's on the bed. Alicia is rescued from the space that threatens to obliterate her and is literally taken into Devlin's arms as the formation of a romantic couple is tentatively put into place. Her face has exhausted itself and by the end of the film there is no need to closely examine it any longer. Significantly, it is not *Notorious* but *Europa '51* which ends with a close-up of Bergman, seen from behind the bars of the asylum after she has made a decision to stay behind its walls and to care for others. Until the very end, Irene's face continues to signify, and while she is not rescued into the safety of the couple (an option which she pointedly rejects when she sends her husband away), she now responds to what she calls "a great spiritual force," the kind of revelation which Alicia never achieves.

To use the camera in the manner of Rossellini, to insist upon its microscopic intensity is at once too literal for Hitchcock and too metaphysical, upsetting the relation between realism and abstraction that is at the heart of his cinema. While incorporating some strategies of film realism, Hitchcock's cinema largely operates within a controlled formalist framework. As Bonitzer has written, Hitchcock's art was "an art of structures, which demanded that 'cinema' take precedence over all else, any notion of realism, and certainly over any existentialist effusions on the part of the protagonists."[45] Rossellini, for all of his use of artificial and even expressionist devices, largely creates works that open onto a conception of not simply the real and the visible but also the invisible, the "great spiritual force" that so often galvanizes his protagonists.

This is not to suggest that Rossellini's approach to the face and the close-up is more profound than that of Hitchcock. Rather, what we have here are two canonical filmmakers working at a contemporaneous moment during which a questioning is taking place of some of the fundamental principals of filmmaking and in which the close-up assumes a major function. Furthermore, each of these directors is working with a film star whose image allows for these issues to be explored with an extraordinary richness. Rather than following Godard's lead here, creating binary oppositions between Rossellini and Hitchcock, it may be best to see their work during this period as a great implied dialogue on the possibilities for the close-up, a dialogue between artifice and realism, revelation and transcendence, the face and the object – a dialogue that is at once closely bound up with this immediate history and utterly fundamental to the larger history of cinema itself.

Notes

1 Jonathan Rosenbaum, "Godard in the Nineties: An Interview, Argument and Scrapbook," *Film Comment*, vol. 34, no. 5, September/October 1998, p. 58.

2 Jean-Luc Godard, *Godard on Godard*, ed. and trans. Tom Milne, Martin Secker & Warburg Limited, 1972, pp. 49–55.

3 Francois Truffaut, with the collaboration of Helen G. Scott, *Hitchcock*, revised edition, New York: Simon & Schuster, 1984, p. 198.

4 Alfred Hitchcock, "Film Production," in Sidney Gottlieb (ed.) *Hitchcock on Hitchcock: Selected Writings and Interviews*, Berkeley and Los Angeles: University of California Press, 1995, p. 218. Originally published in *Encyclopaedia Britannica*, vol. 15, 1965, pp. 907–11.

5 Hitchcock says: "[The actor] should be willing to be utilized and wholly integrated into the picture by the director and the camera. He must allow the camera to determine the proper emphasis and the most effective dramatic highlights" (Truffaut, *Hitchcock*, p. 111). This has its corollary in the writings of Béla Balázs when he states, "Even the best film actors are told by the director when a close-up is about to be made: 'Do what you like as long as you don't "act." Don't do anything at all, just feel and imagine the situation you are in and what then appears in the face of its own accord as it were and flexes the muscles in gesture is enough' " (*Theory of the Film*, trans. Edith Bone, London: Dennis Dobson Ltd, 1952, p. 77).

6 Truffaut, *Hitchcock*, p. 145.

7 Truffaut, *Hitchcock*, p. 111.

8 These figures are taken from Barry Salt, *Film Style and Technology: History and Analysis*, second edition, London: Starword, 1992, p. 222. Other Hitchcock films broken down in

such a way by Salt include *The Lodger* (29 extreme close-ups, 94 close-ups), the 1934 version of *The Man Who Knew Too Much* (35 extreme, 48 close), *The Lady Vanishes* (24 extreme, 72 close), *Foreign Correspondent* (22 extreme, 126 close), and *Vertigo* (15 extreme, 113 close).

9 Truffaut, *Hitchcock*, p. 155.

10 John Alton, *Painting with Light*, Berkeley: University of California Press, 1995, p. 97, originally published in 1949.

11 See Parker Tyler, *Magic and Myth of the Movies*, New York: Simon & Schuster, 1970; originally published in 1947. Tyler argues that Hollywood's primary realm is not the creation of art but the creation of myth, a kind of modern technological folklore in which individual traces of authorship are usually irrelevant, as they would be in any other kind of folk art.

12 Balázs, *Theory of the Film*, p. 56.

13 Dilys Powell, *The Golden Screen: Fifty Years of Films*, ed. George Perry, London: Headline, 1989, p. 65. Lindsay Anderson, writing five years after the release of *Notorious*, even complains of the "large and boring close-ups" which dominate a film that Anderson considers to be one of the director's worst, along with the two that immediately followed it, *The Paradine Case* (1947) and *Rope* (1948). Anderson finds that in these films Hitchcock has begun to explore technique "as an end in itself." See Anderson, "Alfred Hitchcock," in Albert J. LaValley (ed.) *Focus on Hitchcock*, Englewood Cliffs, NJ: Prentice Hall, 1972, p. 57. originally published in 1949.

14 Balázs, *Theory of the Film*, pp. 44–5.

15 Balázs, *Theory of the Film*, p. 31.

16 Truffaut, *Hitchcock*, p. 61.

17 Sergei Eisenstein, "Dickens, Griffith, and the Film Today," in *Film Form: Essays in Film Theory*, ed. and trans. Jay Leyda, New York: Harcourt Brace Jovanovich, 1949, pp. 237–8.

18 Eisenstein, "Dickens, Griffith, and the Film Today," p. 240.

19 Sergei Eisenstein, "A Close-Up View," in *Film Essays and a Lecture*, ed. and trans. Jay Leyda, Princeton, NJ: Princeton University Press, 1982, pp. 151–2.

20 Cited by Jacques Aumont in *Montage Eisenstein*, trans. Lee Hildreth, Constance Penley, and Andrew Ross, London: BFI and Bloomington and Indianapolis: Indiana University Press, 1987, p. 93.

21 See Leonard Leff, "Ingrid in the Lion's Den: Cutting *Notorious*," *Film Comment*, vol. 35, no. 4, July–August 1999, p. 28.

22 See, for example, Parker Tyler's writings on "the human mask" in *The Hollywood Hallucination*, New York: Simon & Schuster, 1970, pp. 222–9. originally published in 1944. Tyler's friend, Joseph Cornell, shares in much of this melancholia about the face, particularly that of the female star. See his 1941 essay on Hedy Lamarr, "Enchanted Wanderer: Excerpt from a Journey Album for Hedy Lamarr," in Paul Hammond (ed.) *The Shadow and Its Shadow: Surrealist Writings on the Cinema*, second edition, Edinburgh: Polygon, 1991, p. 222; originally published in 1942.

23 Balázs, *Theory of the Film*, p. 65: "In the sound film the part played by this 'microphysiognomy' has greatly diminished because it is now apparently possible to express in words much of what facial expression apparently showed. But it is never the same – many profound experiences can never be expressed in words at all."

24 Balázs, *Theory of the Film*, pp. 68–9. Within the context of Hollywood itself at this time, *Sunset Boulevard* (Billy Wilder, 1950) may be seen as a moment in which this discourse about sound cinema's impoverished relationship to silent cinema reaches its mythical apogee.

25 John Kobal, *People Will Talk*, New York: Alfred A. Knopf, 1986, p. 452.

26 Edgar Morin, *The Stars*, translated by Richard Howard, New York: Grove Press, 1961, p. 157.

27 Morin, *The Stars*, pp. 24–5.

28 Balázs writes, "The microscopic close-up is an inexorable censor of 'naturalness' of expression; it immediately shows up the difference between spontaneous reaction and deliberate, unnatural, forced gesture" (*Theory of the Film*, p. 77).

29 In her Swedish films prior to coming to Hollywood, there is not this fetish for naturalism in terms of face and make-up. In the Swedish version of *Intermezzo* (Gustav Molander, 1936) Bergman's face is covered with far more make-up than in the Hollywood version made three years later, and in the earlier version she even has plucked eyebrows. It is the *absence* of plucked eyebrows that became part of her "natural" Hollywood look and Selznick's publicity machine made much use of this absence during the early 1940s. In a 1939 memo, Selznick writes about a conversation he had with the actress Ann Rutherford who told Selznick "that all the girls she knows are letting their eyebrows grow in as a result of Bergman's unplucked eyebrows." See Rudy Behlmer (ed.) *Memo from David O. Selznick*, New York: The Viking Press, 1972, p. 137.

30 In a memo sent to Gregory Ratoff, the director of Bergman's Hollywood debut, *Intermezzo* (1939), Selznick instructed Ratoff on careful photography of Bergman, which included "avoiding long shots, so as not to make her look too big" (Behlmer, *Memo from David O. Selznick*, p. 134). In *Notorious*, Hitchcock takes full advantage of the disparity in height between Bergman and Claude Rains by *emphasizing* her height over his rather than attempting to hide it. "It's rather touching," Truffaut told Hitchcock, "the small man in love with a taller woman" (Truffaut, *Hitchcock*, p. 172).

31 Pascal Bonitzer, "Hitchcockian Suspense," in Slavoj Žižek (ed.) *Everything You Always Wanted to Know About Lacan (But Were Afraid to Ask Hitchcock)*, trans. Martin Thom, London and New York: Verso, 1992, p. 17.

32 Eric Rohmer and Claude Chabrol, *Hitchcock: The First Forty-Four Films*, trans. Stanley Hocman, New York: Ungar Publishing Co., 1979, p. 102.

33 According to Bill Krohn, Hitchcock originally intended for the sequence to be constructed in shot/reverse shot and it was filmed this way. During the editing, he removed all of Alicia's reaction shots except for the last one so that "the unbroken subjective shot of the Nazis approaching the camera adds yet another unsettling touch to the endangered heroine's first visit to the Sebastian house." See Krohn, *Hitchcock at Work*, London: Phaidon, 2000, p. 96.

34 Truffaut, *Hitchcock*, p. 261.

35 Quoted in Ingrid Bergman and Alan Burgess, *Ingrid Bergman: My Story*, New York: Delacorte Press, 1980, p. 467.

36 James Naremore notes that the close-up became the most important technical device in an increased drive towards naturalism in performance style within cinema in that it often allowed for Stanislavskian "gestureless movements." Citing Pudovkin, Naremore also notes that much of the concern with controlled gesture, the relative immobility of the actor's body and the strong importance given to the close-up of the face has its basis in Soviet cinema. See Naremore, *Acting in the Cinema*, Berkeley: University of California Press, 1988, pp. 39–40.

37 Laurence Leamer, *As Time Goes By: The Life of Ingrid Bergman*, New York: Harper & Row, 1986, p.151.

38 This second unit footage on *Notorious* was shot by the Hollywood cinematographer most associated with the trend towards realism in the film image during the 1940s, Gregg Toland. Toland was the original cinematographer on *Intermezzo* but was fired by Selznick for his unsatisfactory work in shooting Bergman's close-ups. The primary cinematographer on *Notorious*, Ted Tetzlaff, was noted primarily for his flattering work with female stars, particularly Carole Lombard.

39 According to Krohn, Hitchcock encouraged Bergman and Grant to deviate from the scripted dialogue for this sequence since he apparently wanted something more spontaneous and natural to be spoken here than what already existed in Ben Hecht's script (*Hitchcock at Work*, p. 97).

40 Jose Luis Guarner has compared *La Paura* to Hitchcock's work, specifically *Vertigo* (1958) and *Marnie* (1964). See *Roberto Rossellini*, trans. Elisabeth Cameron, New York: Praeger, 1970, pp. 72–3.

41 André Bazin, *Bazin at Work*, ed. Bert Cardullo, trans. Alain Piette and Cardullo, New York and London: Routledge, 1987, p. 139.

42 Cited by Tag Gallagher, *The Adventures of Roberto Rossellini*, New York: Da Capo Press, 1998, p. 232. Bergman later appeared in a television version of *The Human Voice* (Ted Kotcheff, 1966).

43 Gallagher, *The Adventures of Roberto Rossellini*, p. 232.

44 A few examples will suffice here as objects of further study: *T-Men* (Anthony Mann, 1947), *Stray Dog* (Akira Kurosawa, 1949), *Beyond the Forest* (King Vidor, 1949), *Panic in the Streets* (Elia Kazan, 1950), *Pickup on South Street* (Sam Fuller, 1953).

45 Pascal Bonitzer, "*Notorious*," in Žižek, *Everything You Always Wanted to Know About Lacan*, p. 152. Bonitzer also argues that Ingmar Bergman "is the filmmaker furthest removed from Hitchcock." More than thirty years after making *Notorious*, Hitchcock saw Ingrid Bergman in *Autumn Sonata* (Ingmar Bergman, 1978) and was distressed over the treatment her face received in the film. Ingmar Bergman had not protected his female star ("She looks old. They've shot her badly"). Instead, with microscopic intensity but minus Rossellini's concern with the transcendent, the film exposed her aging face to the camera. The film would turn out to be her last theatrical feature and was made at a time when Bergman was dying. Hitchcock left before the film was over, announcing: "I'm going to the movies." See David Freeman, *The Last Days of Alfred Hitchcock*, Woodstock, New York: The Overlook Press, 1984, pp. 55–6.

Chapter 5

UNKNOWN HITCHCOCK
The unrealized projects

Sidney Gottlieb

I've always admired the bravado of T.S. Eliot and his ability to disarm and reorient a hyper-intelligent and perhaps jaded audience with a deceptively simple proposition. Only ten paragraphs into his essay "Tradition and the Individual Talent," for example, he stuns his readers, in the manner of the Metaphysical poets he often modeled himself after, with a "suggestive analogy": "I, therefore, invite you to consider," he says, "the action which takes place when a bit of finely filiated platinum is introduced into a chamber containing oxygen and sulphur dioxide."[1] Similarly, I'd like to propose a catalytic reorientation via what I hope will be a suggestive analogy. I invite you to consider what happens when we juxtapose these two images: Michelangelo's *Captive* (see Figure 5.1), his bold gesture of enormous confidence and haunting nervousness, hovering on a tremulous threshold, not quite statue, but more than rock; and Hitchcock's early minimalist drawing (see Figure 5.2), a few pen strokes that sketch an unfinished – perhaps resolutely and perennially unfinished – man, himself, an emblem of his witty and Protean self-representation and art. While this juxtaposition by no means fully describes or explains Hitchcock as either man or artist, it may, like Eliot's chemical experiment described above, provoke a useful critical flare-up, and focus our attention specifically on those aspects of Hitchcock's career that define him – part Michelangelo, part captive – as an artist of the unfinished and interrupted, the diverted and emergent.

Figure 5.1: Michelangelo's *Captive*

In emphasizing those qualities in my essay I mean to complement and complicate rather than entirely subvert the still-current image of Hitchcock, often cultivated by Hitchcock himself, as the self-directed maker of masterpieces and master of the art of success. I do not mean to deflect attention from his completed body of work and remarkable achievements, often measured by analyses of the unity, coherence, structural integrity, and directorial control they display. But his true legacy is not only, as it were, the product but the process, and the often embedded "incompleteness" of his work; a comprehensive view of what is often called his "trajectory" should, I believe, take into account his "roads not taken," the opportunities he had as well as those he took, and the ways his artistic ambitions were often restricted, redirected, and frustrated by a variety of internal and external forces; and a full appreciation of his "completed" films should

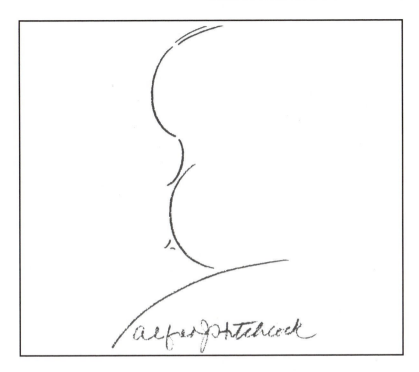

Figure 5.2: Hitchcock's early minimalist drawing

recognize the intimate relationship between these "slices of cake," as he called them, and the bits and pieces he never quite pulled together, which were nevertheless far from inconsequential, much more than, as the analogy almost requires, "crumbs."

The title of my essay requires a bit of explanation. First, the two halves of the proposition are not identical: "unknown Hitchcock" is a substantially broader category, which includes the "unrealized projects." While the title implicitly promises revelations, which I indeed hope to deliver, I should begin by acknowledging that while this subject has been beneath the critical radar for a long time, it is currently gaining much-deserved attention. When I began work on this project some years ago, there was an air of "discovery" around it, but it has since become a hotbed of activity, and the media have been alerted. For example, when James Cameron's *Titanic* was front page news, various syndicated columnists referred to Hitchcock's planned but unmade film of the same name for Selznick in the late 1930s – although they unfortunately didn't give any details of the inventive visual designs that Hitchcock envisioned for his film.[2] Not long ago, hot on the scent of reports of "new" Hitchcock discoveries, the British style magazine *The Face* featured a section of photographs from what seems to have been nominated as Hitchcock's most intriguing unrealized project, referred to as both *Frenzy* and *Kaleidoscope* – which also figures prominently in Dan Auiler's important examination and presentation of *Hitchcock's Notebooks* and the section on "unproduced projects" at Steven DeRosa's fascinating and regularly updated website on Hitchcock and his writers.[3] And increasing scholarly and critical interest in Hitchcock's unrealized projects – the best current example of which is Joseph McBride's nicely detailed essay on Hitchcock's long-standing plan to film J.M. Barrie's *Mary Rose*[4] – is complemented by reports of serious studio interest in filming such Hitchcock projects as *Frenzy/Kaleidoscope* and *No Bail for the Judge*, as well as a version of *Suspicion* more faithful to the original Francis Iles novel, as well as to what Hitchcock often reported was his original intention for the film.[5]

"Unknown Hitchcock" is rapidly becoming more "known," and the phrase deserves careful use and definition. It remains a handy one, but should not unnecessarily call to mind yet another mysteriously and ominously "dark" side of Hitchcock's genius. Exploring this territory may indeed heighten our sense of Hitchcock's various blockages, untamable themes, and "failures," but also our sense of his enormous creative energy, and his ceaseless, probing, and productive collaborative work, much like the "Unknown Chaplin" revealed by Kevin Brownlow and David Gill. Perhaps instead of "unknown," I might have used the term "Invisible Hitchcock" to stress from the very beginning my debt to Jonathan Rosenbaum's important work on the "Invisible Welles," which surveys Welles's many unreleased, unfinished, and planned but not fully executed films.[6] Hitchcock is far less in need of "defending" in certain ways than Welles – especially from any claim that he had a "fear of completion" or was irrepressibly self-sabotaging – but I often have Welles in mind as I consider Hitchcock and the legacy of his "unrealized projects," and the broader topic of how unrealized projects figure in the career, reputation, and self-definition of other directors as well.

Finally, the term "unrealized projects" remains somewhat loose and problematic: unrealized in what ways and for what reasons? "Unrealized projects" is the designation used in cataloging more than 250 folders of items in the Hitchcock Collection at the Margaret Herrick Library, Academy of Motion Picture Arts and Sciences, and part of what I hope to do here is, at least in some preliminary and provisional way, define this term, especially to account for the wide variety of material it is used to describe; briefly "theorize" it (that is, offer some broad comments on it as a conceptual and critical category); survey at least some of the relevant material; and offer a few suggestions about the role of such works in Hitchcock's career and what I propose may be new ways of assessing this career.[7]

It may be useful to start concretely by giving examples of the wide range of materials that should, I think, be considered as – or at least as we examine – Hitchcock's "unrealized projects," using the term very broadly to cover a continuum of projects that Hitchcock worked on in one way or another and at various levels of involvement, proposed or had proposed to him, but that were never undertaken, materially completed, or released. Each of these types of "unrealized project" has its own valence and its own particular kind of relevance to our understanding of Hitchcock's workaday world and his cinematic ambitions, intentions, and designs – as well as the designs people had for and on him.

I would include at least at the periphery of the unrealized projects (and certainly as part of an investigation of "unknown Hitchcock") scripts, story ideas, and proposals presented to Hitchcock, not the thousands of unsolicited proposals that flooded his office (and were duly recorded in documents preserved in the archives), but material by writers he admired and worked with, like Sean O'Casey (*The Park*, turned into his play *Within the Gates*, and similar to the "day in the life of a city" project, discussed below, that Hitchcock frequently mentioned in interviews), Angus MacPhail (folder 1057), Samuel Taylor (*In Another Country*, folder 1127), and Richard Condon (folder 1281). And perhaps it is not stretching the bounds of the unrealized project too far to consider the opportunities Hitchcock had to direct various films – films he perhaps could have made but for one reason or another did not. Some of these proposals are fascinating, although it is not always clear how seriously Hitchcock considered them: Selznick evidently wanted Hitchcock to direct Ingrid Bergman in *Intermezzo*, and proposed *The Lost Weekend*, *The Spiral Staircase*, and *The Turn of the Screw*, among many other titles. He also at one point in the early 1940s was eager to film *Mein Kampf*, with Ben Hecht as a scriptwriter and Hitchcock as the director. Hal Wallis planned a version of *The Constant Nymph* directed by Hitchcock and featuring Laurence Olivier and Vivien Leigh. There was talk of him directing Margaret Sullavan in *Back Street*, Joan Crawford in *A Woman's Face*, and Norma Shearer in *Escape*, and John Houseman wanted Hitchcock to direct *Letter from an Unknown Woman*. 20th-Century Fox evidently sought him for *How Green Was My Valley*, and Val Lewton, working for Selznick, proposed Hitchcock to direct *Les Miserables* and *Treasure Island*. He was offered *Wages of Fear*, but, as he explained somewhat cryptically, "the publishing house in Paris screwed up the deal."[8] And John Russell Taylor reports, incredible as it may seem, that Hitchcock was asked to step in and finish directing *Cleopatra*.[9] In the very least such material usefully outlines some of Hitchcock's roads not taken, and tells us something intriguing about how he was "conceptualized" by various studio executives and producers: that he was not pigeonholed as only a director of thrillers, for example, and that his name came up frequently in plans to make romantic and women-centered melodramas.

We should also consider properties he pursued and acquired, and the archival documentation of these activities illustrates Hitchcock's indefatigable search for new material and how his office was geared up to handle this process of screening and discovery. Stephen Rebello quotes interesting comments by several people who worked with Hitchcock on his search for material:

> H.N. Swanson ... put it this way: "Hitch never casually looked for 'something different.' He was *relentless*." Another longtime Hitchcock associate, agent Michael Ludmer, insisted, "We scoured everything – plays, novels, short stories, newspaper clippings. ... Since one couldn't second-guess what little spark might turn him on, it was terribly back-breaking tracking material for him."[10]

Rebello goes on to note, "Hitchcock depended on [Peggy] Robertson to wade through prospective material. In a year in which the Hitchcock office logged 2,400 submissions, Robertson passed on only thirty to the boss."[11] Even with an efficient filtering process in place, Hitchcock's involvement was substantial, and though it was sometimes draining and frustrating – as he relates in a humorous sketch titled "Journal of Mr. Hitchcock after his Explorations through the Jungle of Story Agents and Tellers of Tales" (folder 1285, dated 5/21/51) – we soon become aware of the extent to which such a persistent and far-ranging casting of his net was part of the routinized basis of Hitchcock's artistic inspiration, whether or not it resulted in a finished film.

It is thus pertinent to consider stories, novels, plays, and scripts Hitchcock expressed an interest in filming, even when his proposals didn't go very far: these include such titles as John Buchan's *Greenmantle* (another of his Richard Hannay novels), John Van Druten's play *London Wall*, Leslie Charteris's *The Saint in New York*, and Francis Iles's *Malice Aforethought* (which he did preside over as a radio show). The folders contain many traces of projects that piqued his interest: for example, in early 1954, the stories of *Beyond a Reasonable Doubt* and *The Blackboard Jungle* were submitted to him, along with *The Bad Seed* (folder 1286). Months later he expressed an interest in the latter and asked the studio to look at it but he notes, "I feel they will say 'too downbeat.'" We hear nothing further of it in the files, but it is an intriguing blip on the screen – as intriguing as his passing on the potentially extremely Hitchcockian *Beyond a Reasonable Doubt*, filmed shortly after by Fritz Lang (in 1956, the year of Hitchcock's own film *The Wrong Man*).

More substantial in defining the category of the unrealized projects is Hitchcock's regular mention of what he called "Films We Could Make" (the title of one of his early essays, published in 1927) or "Films I'd Like to Make" or, phrased more negatively, films "the censor wouldn't pass" – an early version of the recurrent kind of title of anthologies of stories that came out under his name much later, such as "Stories They Wouldn't Let Me Show on Television," and so on, comically asserting his continuing awareness of restrictive pressures on him, enforced by censors, studios, and audiences, the multiple components of the "they" who won't let him do what he wants to do. Some of the proposals in his essays and interviews might surprise even knowledgeable Hitchcockians: he envisions making abstract art films, visual tone poems of "rhythmic movement and light and shade," elements of which he did integrate into various films;[12] films on controversial topics and events rather than "local rather quiet history,"[13] such as the General Strike of 1926, which he wanted to shoot not as "a wishy-washy picture" but as "a magnificently dynamic motion picture," with "fistfights between strikers and undergraduates, pickets, and all the authentic drama of the situation";[14] anti-establishment films on corporate, legal, and judicial incompetence and injustice, as in his planned "anti-capital punishment film where the prison governor revolts and refuses to hang his man";[15] and films that intensify drama and "realism" by moving down the social scale to "that more colorful belt of beings, the middle class, and observing their unhampered attitude to life" – even the title of the essay from which this last statement is drawn, "More Cabbages, Fewer Kings," conveys the extent to which Hitchcock's "middle class" veered toward the lower end of the scale and encompassed a very broad spectrum of "the men who leap on buses" and "the girls who pack into the Tube."[16]

These and other such proposals are also to a certain extent fantasies, unmakeable as envisioned under present circumstances but worth dreaming about and describing: as part of a process of consolation (a film described is to some extent a film "seen," although not made), an expression of resentment at and resistance to the conventional and clichéd (in film form and in some of the ideology embedded in or reflected by it), and an effort to educate the public and define himself and his public persona as a particular kind of exceptional and unique cinematic artist. Hitchcock's comments on "Films I'd Like to Make" remind us of the "strategic" – that is, the expressive and performative as well as theoretical and aesthetic – function of Hitchcock's "unrealized projects," and we need to be alert to the intricacies and multiple functions of Hitchcock's discourse on and of these projects and proposals.[17]

Throughout his career Hitchcock made many brief statements and proposals about properties, incidents, topics, and stories that he had an interest in filming, ranging from simple descriptions, such as "Have you ever considered what an interesting film might be written round, say, the engineer of Tower Bridge who lets the bridge up and down!"[18] to graphic narrations of various criminal cases he wanted to adapt (both fictional, as in Lord Dunsany's story "Two Bottles of Relish," and real, as in the case of Adelaide Bartlett), to somewhat more involved outlines of scenarios that intrigued him: like the story he told Selznick about a young woman, to be played by Ingrid Bergman, kidnapped and chained to a close male friend for six months[19]; the story he showed great interest in about a ventriloquist who is a bigamist, murders his first wife, and then becomes haunted by guilt and delusions;[20] his plans to film Robert Thomas's play *Trap for a Solitary Man* about a woman who disappears, and then returns only to find that her husband insists that she is not his wife; his recurrent interest in the Crippen case, particularly as it was novelized by Ernest Raymond as *We the Accused*, a legal and police procedural about, in Hitchcock's words, a rather "kindly" murderer "who did nothing worse than rid himself of a bitch of a wife" – piece by piece, as it turns out;[21] and his ideas for a "first-rate comedy on the making of a movie" and the "really good Cold War suspense movie" he told Truffaut about.[22]

All these proposals are worth compiling and examining in detail, but perhaps even more fascinating and important are those that shade into what might be called Hitchcock "moments," self-standing but also germinative ideas and images, plots and stories that captivated his imagination, defined and exemplified the "cinematic" for him (a cinema of attractions, inventions, and, some might say, of obsessions), and at least tentatively implicated him in an aesthetic somewhat surprising for a greengrocer's son who dressed like a banker and worked in a factory producing merchandise.

One of the interesting things about these "moments" is that they are so well known. Perhaps everyone reading this essay could draw up a list of them: the film about twenty-four hours in the life of a city; the film shot in a telephone booth; various versions of the assembly-line sequence, ending with the discovery of a corpse or a couple making love; the drop of blood covering the petal of a flower; the extended high note by an opera singer turning into a scream.[23] Leaving aside for now the fact that some of these "moments" did make their way into his films in transformed or deflected ways, and the evidence that many of his films seem to have originated in and developed from the expansion of such "moments" – *North by Northwest* and *Family Plot* are particularly good examples of this process – let me suggest how these "unrealized" plans deepen our sense of what Thomas Leitch suggestively calls Hitchcock's "cinema of moments."[24]

Hitchcock mentioned these moments frequently in his interviews, and repeatedly brought them to the attention of critics and the public. He used them as witty set pieces and mini-dramas, continuing variations on his "films I'd like to make" routine. But perhaps it is not too far-fetched to think of his constant describing and retelling these moments as a mode of production as well as performance and expression: films without film, as the early Soviet filmmakers "made" when they had no film stock, and as later surrealist, avant-garde, and otherwise experimental artists, poets, and novelists envisioned, knowing that the category of the "cinematic" can stretch beyond the limits of celluloid. Some of Hitchcock's "moments" are so vivid, so strikingly visualized and shaped, and so accessible that critics and scholars often refer to them almost as though they are in actuality Hitchcock films: in the very least, they are treated as solid evidence of Hitchcock's cinematic imagination. These "moments," then, stand on a kind of threshold, not quite realized – that is, in the form of feature-length released films – but not completely unrealized, insofar as they are given structure, material form (via performance and print), and currency, an alternate kind of exhibition. Critics like to identify Hitchcock and the camera: far more than that, these "moments" perhaps allow us a glimpse of Hitchcock's imaginative embodiment of the entire cinematic apparatus – functioning as writer, director, producer, camera, projector, distributor, and exhibitor – an intimation of a "myth of total cinema" based on omnipotence of thought and real opportunities to enact one's cinematic tales to interested audiences and critics, a distinctively Hitchcockian blend of oneiric power and public relations which might rightly be called "public dreaming."

Furthermore, these "moments" move him from the craft and business of the completed and saleable commodity to an aesthetic of the unfinished, aligning him, however tentatively, with a long-standing tradition of, in Lucien Goldmann's words, "paradoxical masterpieces, achieved by [their] inachievement."[25] Such moments are the quintessential expression of Hitchcock's repeated credo, "I wish I didn't have to shoot the picture," and might usefully be considered in the context of the long-standing artistic attraction to the fragment, the sketch, the torso, the relic, the vision, the miniature: each testifying more to the epiphany of inspiration than the details of completion, each asserting that problems of construction, once solved, need not be elaborated, and that high ambitions are distorted, conventionalized, or trivialized by anything other than partial, suggestive, or synecdochal representation.[26] I don't want to lose sight of Hitchcock's fascination for mechanical details and his delight in execution, or suggest that he characteristically strains for the ineffable or the patently unrealizable. Nor do I want to overstate Hitchcock's attraction to the indeterminate – I haven't yet been able to ease my suspicions and fears of a postmodern Hitchcock, characterized by a yielding to the indeterminate, willful or otherwise, that would undoubtedly categorize *all* his projects as "unrealized." But I can well imagine Hitchcock nodding in agreement to Picasso's well-known words on material creation and the ironies of "executing" a work:

> Have you ever seen a finished picture? A picture or anything else? Woe unto you the day that you are finished! To finish a work? To finish a picture? What nonsense! To finish it means to be through with it, to kill, to rid it of its soul, to give it its final blow: the most unfortunate one for the painter as well as for the picture.[27]

Picasso's way of saying, in short: I wish I didn't have to paint the picture.

Hitchcock's professed attraction to an aesthetic of the unfinished, though, did not lead him to the next step of affirming as a rule that "I Wish I Didn't Have to

Shoot the Picture … So I Didn't." Many of his unrealized projects went into a high level of development, documented by extensive correspondence, anecdotal material, synopses, treatments, and even several generations of scripts (some credited to Hitchcock, and several with his comments, annotations, and questions written in or appended). I've been trying to suggest that there are multiple categories of Hitchcock's unrealized projects: to coin a phrase, some are born incomplete, some achieve and even aspire to incompletion, and some have incompletion thrust upon them. It is this last category that becomes particularly prominent as we look at a substantial list of projects that Hitchcock worked on energetically, and clearly designed and intended as finished, released films, not as fragments, rough drafts, exercises, or "moments," but which never made it that far. By examining these we get a remarkably expanded and in some respects new view and understanding of key aspects of Hitchcock, including the following:

- We gain access to Hitchcock's continuing elaborations of his enduring interests, themes, situations, and characters. Some of the projects, admittedly, fall into old grooves and repeat earlier efforts but others intensify, re-dramatize, and re-conceive his perennial concerns.
- We get a glimpse of the often-unappreciated wide range of his interests and ambitions. Hitchcock often talked about how he was trapped by his success in the genre he became associated with, well aware of the centripetal pull of being the Godfather of the suspense thriller: just when you think you are out, audiences and studio executives pull you back in. He did attempt to escape such a pull - and trap. In *Finding the Director*, Leitch traces Hitchcock's characteristic process of perennially breaking old molds and reinventing himself as he moved from one completed film to the next by going off in new directions with new material, new themes, and new cinematic styles and conceptualizations and visualizations of his role as a director.[28] Examining some of the unrealized projects in particular – *Perjury*, *R.R.R.R.*, and the unmade *Frenzy* come first to mind – deepens our understanding of Hitchcock's attempts at various points in his career to substantially refashion himself as a filmmaker, and dramatizes the extent to which his lifelong claim of trying to avoid the cliché frequently involves a not always successful struggle to avoid the Hitchcock cliché also.
- Examining the unrealized projects also gives us a valuable insight into Hitchcock's working method. Archival material in general often allows us to watch the director at work, but the archival material on the often problematic and difficult unrealized projects in particular expands our understanding of Hitchcock's routine, his characteristically intense rumination, collaboration (with screenwriters, researchers, and Alma in particular – the "unknown Alma" is a fascinating subject that awaits serious consideration),

extremely meticulous pre-production work, planning, and a perhaps somewhat unique "questioning process": his habit of raising question after
question about the details relevant to the story, setting, and characters,
anticipating the objections of those he called "the plausibles" but also establishing a basis for what might be called the "hyperreality" beneath and
counter-pointing the more obvious non-naturalistic "formalism" and stylistic
extravagance of his work.

• Similarly, we gain insight into unheralded aspects of his creative process: to
put it bluntly, unless we include improvisation and free play as components
of Hitchcock's working method and routine, we will end up with a distorted
notion of his way of making films. Hitchcock is not often praised or even
recognized as an improviser, but as he somewhat defensively clarified in
various interviews, he simply wasn't a great believer in improvisation in
front of the camera.[29] Archival records that document the stages before
shooting, though, frequently show a Hitchcock overflowing with ideas,
suggestions, proposals, and other mercurial elements of what too often is
thought of as his compulsive arranging and pre-planning.[30] Particularly with
the unrealized projects we get an intimate view of his far-ranging and often
spontaneous attempts to generate and shape material that was in one way or
another unusually resistant and challenging.

• Finally, we gain an invaluable look at internal and external pressures on
Hitchcock at work, some of which combined, as mentioned above, to thrust
incompletion upon him. An examination of the unrealized projects brings to
the fore intriguing evidence of why certain types of material continued to
prove intractable to his efforts, his inability to find writers to help give form
to his intentions (some of which were, to say the least, difficult to manage
and shape, and some of which simply did not lend themselves to satisfactory
treatment), and conflicts regarding what constituted a viable project: with
censors (including Hitchcock's own internalized view of what some
censoring body would and would not let him get away with) and with
studios (which possessed the annoying and dispiriting power, always threatened and occasionally wielded, to "just say no" to a project). Even studying
the completed films reminds us that Hitchcock's was always and inevitably
an "art of compromise," but especially because the "text" of an unrealized
film is an assortment of process-oriented documents, production records,
and memos as well as scripts, we are constantly alerted to the details of
Hitchcock's working environment, a system of simultaneous and uneven
levels of freedom and constraint, privacy and surveillance, personal and
artistic, but also corporate and public, responsibility.

Where specifically do we gain such insights into Hitchcock? I'll close with a quick survey of some of the existing information about key unrealized projects from different periods of his career, commenting briefly on some of their technical and stylistic as well as thematic components.

Perjury (folders 1301–4), based on the novel *The False Witness* by Marcel Auchard, with several scripts from 1938, including one co-authored by Hitchcock, is a fascinating dark tale full of twists and turns, as though he were remaking *Young and Innocent* (just released) as *Young and Guilty*, in the manner of a work of French poetic realism: an association keyed for me by the French character names, but especially by the milieu of corruption, unstable identity, grotesque play-acting (staged primarily by the police), the wrong man motif, the senseless death of a young boy, and the evocative, impressionistic description of the sad ending of the story, the death of an attractive young woman who took money to provide an alibi for a murderer, and then recanted her testimony, putting her in trouble with everyone, including the police, the criminal, and her neighbors. Early on, the script includes a provocative note: "Bishop enters, to some confusion. He looks exactly like Alfred Hitchcock" (folder 1302). One wishes he had turned to this project rather than *Jamaica Inn*, but he did come back to a complex story of a woman's entrapment shortly afterward in *Suspicion*.

The Lodger is often identified as the first "true" Hitchcock film, and in the early 1940s, he contemplated remaking it (folder 1131). Patrick McGilligan has suggested to me that this is one of the few "genuinely unrealized projects, that is, with the rights or script attached" before the 1950s, "for the very good reason that Hitchcock never bought the rights to anything himself or wrote a script without production go-ahead."[31] I would qualify some of these statements, but he rightly calls attention to the importance of this project. RKO was interested in making *The Lodger*, but "only with LAUGHTON directed by HITCHCOCK" (George Schaefer, memo of December 12, 1940, folder 1131), but gave up these plans upon learning that Selznick "expects to make this himself." Hitchcock and Myron Selznick, his agent, owned the rights to the story and there were evidently serious plans to make the film, which included hiring Alma to work on the script. (Unfortunately there is no indication of how the remake would compare with the earlier film. It is tempting to think that Hitchcock may have at least envisioned a version where he did not have to compromise his wish to portray a "guilty" lodger, as in the novel – an issue he was confronting on another front at this time during the making of *Suspicion*.) Word of this project must have got out: it even attracted the interest of Bela Lugosi who inquired about the possibility of appearing in the proposed film. But, according to McGilligan, "David O. Selznick wouldn't give his permission without a script ... and in the end Hitchcock gave up his share [of the rights] for money he desperately needed ... to the people who made the Laird Cregar version."

Hamlet seems an unlikely choice of subject for Hitchcock but correspondence on his proposed version of the play dates from as early as 1945, and several years later his plans were newsworthy items (folder 1125). Hitchcock envisioned his version as a "modern ... psychological thriller" in contemporary language, and, incredibly, as a vehicle for Cary Grant, as star and co-producer. The project was held up by a legal suit, not settled until 1954, instituted by a disgruntled professor who claimed proprietary rights to a modern version of the story. Although Hitchcock went no further with this project, in some ways a Hitchcock–Shakespeare connection is not so far fetched. There are allusions to *Hamlet* (obviously in *Murder!*, which includes soliloquies and a play within a play designed to catch a murderer, and also, if we are to be persuaded by Stanley Cavell, in *North by Northwest*[32]) and a variety of Shakespearean references and inflections throughout Hitchcock's films (and television work, including most obviously "Banquo's Chair"). Shakespeare is a central figure in the culture in which Hitchcock steeped himself, and perhaps represented an important model for him of the reachable ambition to be both commercially and critically successful, equally at home with high and low audiences.

The Knave of Newgate (folders 1128–30) is a project that Hitchcock considered from as early as 1946 on until the mid-1950s, when he evidently asked Ernest Lehman to work on it. On the surface it is a costume drama of an early eighteenth-century desperado, filled with action, abductions, jail-breaks, and "an innocent but high-spirited lady of good family." But the commentaries on the treatments push the proposed script from a rollicking rogue's tale to a revelation of the "authentic facts," a debunking of the mythic tales of Jack Sheppard and a "nightmarish" atmosphere akin to the illustrations of Cruikshank. Hitchcock's few costume dramas do indeed have their nightmarish moments that go beyond the often-facile conventions of gothic films. Auiler describes Hitchcock's striking opening for the film: "A crying baby, who is being christened, is unconsoled until his mother's breast is unveiled – a large smile, then he goes to suckle. Hitchcock would then shoot a closeup of the baby's head, which we then see is now a young man's head, as we pull away from the couple, who are amorously engaged."[33]

The Dark Duty (folders 1051–51), a best-selling novel by Margaret Wilson, was evidently of long-standing interest to Hitchcock: press releases announce it as his next film after *Under Capricorn* for Transatlantic Pictures in 1949 but as early as 1938 he mentioned in one of his essays his desire to make an anti-capital punishment film about the governor of a prison who refuses to execute a convicted man, and, according to Auiler, he reconsidered it again in 1963.[34] Hitchcock typically is not particularly kind in his films to representatives of legal or governmental authority, but he was perhaps attracted here, as in *I Confess*, to the central figure's crisis of conscience that flouts conventional wisdom – and the great price he pays for this manifestation of faith and morality.

The Bramble Bush (folders 1046–49), a novel by David Duncan, who also worked on the script, attracted Hitchcock as early as 1949. It was planned as a Transatlantic Pictures release but then put off until late 1952 when, now at Warner Bros, he worked on it extensively with George Tabori. Hitchcock described it succinctly, although without much enthusiasm, to Truffaut as "the story of a man who stole another man's passport without knowing that the passport owner was wanted for murder."[35] The plot is much more intricate than Hitchcock lets on here, and though he was never able to get a script that satisfied him, it showed much promise for, in Tabori's words, its "combination of sex and suspicion between the Hero and Heroine," which recalled *Notorious*, and for its ominous and existentially charged "wrong man" motif. The uncanny similarity to *The Passenger* (1975) – which Auiler says confidently, although without any supporting evidence, was based on this story[36] – illustrates that Hitchcock didn't actually need Antonioni to be Antonioni-esque.

The Queen and the Rebels is an even less likely candidate as a project for Hitchcock than *Hamlet*, but several folders document his interest in it in 1956 (folders 1161–2). There is no trace of script work done for or by Hitchcock on this play by Ugo Betti, which he owned the rights to and evidently thought of putting on stage in New York. But we find here evidence of Hitchcock's attraction to a modernist playwright and specifically to a political play that focuses on the fluidity of identity and the spectacle of masquerade: a "coarse and selfish adventuress" pretends to be a queen, allowing the real queen to escape. Her motivation is at first to spite her lover, a sentry on guard, but she is then swept up by a sudden awareness of the political power of theatricality. It might well have turned into a film that looked backward to *The Great Dictator* and *To Be or Not to Be*, and forward to *General Della Rovere*.

Flamingo Feather, a novel by Laurens Van Der Post, was taken very seriously by Hitchcock in 1956–7 as a potential project, illustrated by the extensive material preserved in the archives (folders 1053–64). With either Paramount or Hitchcock (or both) somewhat enthused by the remake of *The Man Who Knew Too Much*, some of which was shot in Africa, and visions of Hitchcock's return to the glory days of the action-adventure thrillers, Hitchcock and Angus MacPhail worked long and hard trying to make something of what MacPhail called "the insidious spell of John Buchan," the "essence" of which is "the theme of the romantic, poetic, mysterious Quest" (folder 1054). Hitchcock had some interesting visual ideas, particularly about filming "the Great Dream of the Takwena" tribe as a dramatic opening, and the novel has a curious similarity to Buchan's *Greenmantle*, a particular favorite of Hitchcock's, which similarly traipses across many exotic settings and envisions impending worldwide disorder in the form of religious revivalism manipulated by villainous politicians. But Hitchcock put it down as unworkable and turned to his other recently purchased property, which became *Vertigo*. When prompted by Truffaut he admitted that he dropped the project because of its "political aspects," but in a broad sense this was perhaps part of its initial attraction.[37]

No Bail for the Judge is rightly considered by DeRosa to be one of the most fascinating of Hitchcock's unrealized projects and it is no surprise that Hitchcock worked on it so carefully and extensively (*c.*1954–9), and also that it is still being mentioned as a project of interest to filmmakers. (The most recent reports indicate that a production team including Ron Rotholz and Julia Roberts will make a film based on a revised and Americanized version of the script originally prepared for Hitchcock by Samuel Taylor.) The original novel by Henry Cecil is about a judge, for once, in the position of a "wrong man," falsely accused on circumstantial evidence of killing a prostitute. But more prominent in the script is his daughter and her efforts to clear him, which involve her with a charming gentleman burglar whom she cons and flirts into helping her and an aristocratic pimp with whom she gets in over her head. In a key scene, she impersonates a prostitute to get closer to this pimp who may be helpful in the case, but she must confirm her false identity by having sex with him. This is not a scene of physical coercion or assault, as some critics (including DeRosa) have termed it, but a far more complex and ironic encapsulation of Hitchcock's recurrent interest in the clash of love and duty, sexual victimization that is not always a matter of assault, and the voyeuristic spectacle of "putting the woman through it." Various reasons are given why work on this film was halted: Audrey Hepburn, cast for the judge's daughter, became pregnant and Hitchcock was unwilling to go on without his new brunette rather than blonde heroine; or Hepburn was horrified by the scene in the park with the pimp, and she left the project, giving her pregnancy as her excuse; or unresolvable problems arose with the censor over the prominence of prostitution and perjury in the film. Whatever the reasons, after spending much time and money – one report indicates more than $200,000 – the project was abandoned.[38]

Blind Man was an original script by Ernest Lehman (written in the summer of 1960 through early 1961) that revolved around several ideas easily trivialized: a man gaining sight via a transplant operation, and the long-standing belief that the eyes of a murdered person somehow recorded the last moments of life, including presumably the image of the murderer.[39] This would have been enlivened, though, by special optical effects designed by Hitchcock, an important scene set in Disneyland, potentially yet another of Hitchcock's assessments of classically great and ominously foreboding American landscapes (a setting Disney refused to allow), and the overall conceptualization of the film as a vehicle for Jimmy Stewart that may have imaginatively reprised elements of earlier roles as he investigates whether or not a murder took place (as in *Rear Window*) and wanders in the midst of mysteries, visions, and split selves, with often painful and disorienting results (as in *Vertigo*).

R.R.R.R. is based on an idea which Hitchcock said in an interview that he had had "since 1935."[40] In the fall of 1964 through to the summer of 1965 Hitchcock planned, in his words, a "comedy melodrama ... a murder movie with overtones of comedy,"[41] set in a big hotel run by a newly arrived family of Italian crooks who plot, against the wishes of their reformed and respectable relative who brought them over, to steal a valuable collection of coins rated with the high numismatic value of R.R.R.R. Hitchcock worked with Agenore Incrocci and Furio Scarpelli, who had written *Big Deal on Madonna Street* and other artistically respected and profitable films of the new European cinema, but was never able to come up with a satisfactory script, blaming Incrocci and Scarpelli's slipshod construction and the "language barrier" that he felt hindered the intelligibility of the script. This unrealized project helps call our attention to an intriguing "Italian component" of Hitchcock's attempt to refashion himself after the failure of *Marnie*: this includes his work with Ignore and Scarpelli, current masters of the comic thriller; his startling discovery of Antonioni, which led him to re-evaluate his own methods – after screening *Blow-Up* he commented to Howard Fast that "These Italian directors are a century ahead of me in terms of technique! What have I been doing all this time?"[42] – and his continuing fascination for Italian neorealism, particularly De Sica's *Bicycle Thief*, a quintessential "chase film" for Hitchcock which he wanted to use as a model for a transformed notion of the adventure thriller to help differentiate himself from the recent crop of imitators making such films as *Charade*, *The Prize*, and *That Man From Rio*. With the specific example of De Sica in mind, he told Richard Condon (with whom he was working on another project) that "The picaresque story, in other words, should no longer be the fantasy, but to some extent using actuality at the same time selecting real, but bizarre, surroundings" (folder 1281). A final element of what DeRosa nicely calls Hitchcock's "Italian Connection" is his attempt to get Cesare Zavattini to work on a screenplay of "a dramatic idea something along the lines of ... *Notorious*."[43] Hitchcock was unable to finish any of these projects or move in any of these directions and turned instead to *Torn Curtain*, a disappointment on almost every level.

The final project in my survey, *Frenzy/Kaleidoscope* (*c.*1967–8), is particularly intriguing because of its startling subject matter, because there is so much material available on it – multiple scripts, including one by Hitchcock; comments by Truffaut on a late script;[44] and many records of story conferences – and also because the project went so far into development: it was evidently storyboarded, test-footage and both color and black and white stills were shot (and still exist), and it was heavily pitched to Universal Studio as the next Hitchcock feature and even publicized as such at Universal Studio tours (folders 1067–1123). Based on the true story of a compulsive killer of women, enlivened with the addition of the complex relationship between the killer and the policewoman – with dark motives of her own – who tracks, seduces, and traps him, it would also have been cinematically experimental as well as Hitchcockian: he envisioned it at least in part in a consciously updated visual style and setting – under the influence of neorealist, cinema verité, and Antonioni films, especially *Blow-Up*, which he had evidently just screened[45] – blended with "classic" Hitchcock touches, including a startling title sequence of kaleidoscopic colors almost emanating from the killer as a young boy (perhaps introducing a visual motif that would be used later as well), and a murder set in the bowels of a Mothball Fleet of dead (that is, retired) ships, in what might have been Hitchcock's last great image of the dark heart of the American landscape. Universal not only rejected this project but also indicated their shock and horror at it and Hitchcock was deeply hurt and disappointed, perhaps in ways that affected the remainder of his career. There is high drama and, I think, great critical interest in what I might title "The Making of the Unmade *Frenzy*," a story that begs to be told, and should be told, I think, without reducing it simply to a tale of an aging artist flailing about with uncontrollable impulses and intractable material or an heroic artist crushed one last time by a crass studio system. To fully understand this episode of Hitchcock's career, and his "unrealized projects" in general, we must confront the key question posed to him by one of his most insightful and challenging interviewers, Charles Thomas Samuels – "Why can't Alfred Hitchcock make anything he wants to?" – and Hitchcock's fascinating response: "That's a privilege I have, but one mustn't take advantage of it. My contract gives me complete artistic control. I can make any film I like, up to three million dollars. But such privileges are a responsibility to the studios, which I obviously cannot, and would not, take advantage of. I don't have the right kind of conceit."[46] An examination of the making and unmaking of *Frenzy* – Elaine Scarry's phrase fits Hitchcock's world of pain and creativity very nicely[47] – illustrates some ways that Hitchcock himself put "blots" on his clear horizons, and dramatizes that he, no less than Scottie Ferguson, knew something about the vertigo that comes from the competing claims of freedom, power, and responsibility.

I've had to leave much out of this preliminary survey, including his work with Lehman on *The Wreck of the Mary Deare*, interest in a courtroom drama and murder story *The Attorney* by Harold Masur, and extensive involvement with such projects as John Buchan's *The Three Hostages*, Elmore Leonard's *Unknown Man #89*, *Dead Run*, scripted by Richard Condon, part of a series of films sponsored by the World Health Organization of the United Nations, and *The Short Night,* announced as early as 1968 but lingering on and becoming dramatically enmeshed in what screenwriter David Freeman calls "The Last Days of Alfred Hitchcock." The list could go on and on, and I hope will be expanded in further studies of this important aspect of Hitchcock's life and career.

With this hope in mind, let me conclude here simply and provisionally: Hitchcock frequently disparaged these "unrealized projects" and perhaps influenced critics to consider them as curiosities at best, and at worst as illustrations of Hitchcock "running for cover." Taylor, for example, describes them as somewhat inconsequential: "There was always a certain amount of wastage, in the shape of properties worked on which never somehow reached the screen – though even here Hitch was persistent."[48] My high regard for these projects is far less grudging. I am by no means trying to argue for their centrality to our understanding of Hitchcock, simply their great value: in demonstrating his often uncredited conceptual and stylistic range, versatility, and ambition; emblematizing key moments of imaginative re-invention and triumph as well as practical failure and disappointment; highlighting the stresses of the studio system and commercial environment within which he worked, but also his internalization of and in some ways self-determined and needless capitulation to them; and otherwise helping to sketch out in fascinating detail the complexities of Hitchcock at work.

Acknowledgments

I would like to thank Faye Comstock, at the Margaret Herrick Library, and Ned Comstock, at the USC Library for the Performing Arts, for their invaluable help as I worked on the archival material of Hitchcock's unrealized projects. I have also benefited greatly from discussions with and other kinds of support from Richard Allen, Dan Auiler, Steven DeRosa, Rick DiLoreto, Mark Estrin, Leonard Leff, Patrick McGilligan, Ken Mogg, Eric Monder, and Jenni Sherwood. Howard

Fast talked at length with me on several occasions about working with Hitchcock on the unrealized *Frenzy* and Elmore Leonard sent me a copy of *Unknown Man #89* and told me what he recalled about Hitchcock's interest in his novel. Bill Luhr and David Sterritt commented extensively and insightfully on an earlier version of my essay and invited me to present this material to the Columbia University Seminar on Cinema and Interdisciplinary Interpretation. There simply aren't enough words to thank properly the seminar members and especially Tom Leitch, the respondent on that night, for their warm support and astute criticism.

Notes

1 T.S. Eliot, "Tradition and the Individual Talent," in *Selected Essays of T.S. Eliot*, New York: Harcourt, Brace & World, 1964, p. 7.

2 For Hitchcock's comments on the Titanic film, see Peter Bogdanovich, *Who the Devil Made It*, New York: Knopf, 1997, pp. 506–7, and Richard Schickel, *The Men Who Made the Movies*, New York: Atheneum, 1975, pp. 271–303. Charles Barr considers it as "one of the most tantalizingly attractive of all unmade films" in " 'A Marvelously Dramatic Subject': Hitchcock's *Titanic* Project," *Hitchcock Annual* 2000–1, pp.100–14.

3 Rupert Howe, "Love Thru a Lens," *The Face*, no. 31, August 1999, pp.130–4, with photographs by Arthur Schatz; Dan Auiler, *Hitchcock's Notebooks: An Authorized and Illustrated Look Inside the Creative Mind of Alfred Hitchcock*, New York: Avon, 1999, esp. pp. 544–54; Steven DeRosa, Hitchcock and His Writers, http://members.aol.com/vistavsion.

4 Joseph McBride, "Alfred Hitchcock's *Mary Rose*: An Old Master's Unheard *Cri de Coeur*," *Cineaste*, 24, no. 2, 2001, pp.24–8.

5 These items, along with others on Hitchcock-related projects, are reported on the MacGuffin website: http://www.labyrinth.net.au.

6 Jonathan Rosenbaum, "The Invisible Orson Welles: A First Inventory," *Sight and Sound*, summer 1986, 164–71.

7 Specific references are to folder numbers in the Hitchcock Collection in the section archived as Unrealized Projects. Most of these folders are headed by the title of the project, arranged in alphabetical order and numbered sequentially. I have gleaned additional information about Hitchcock's unrealized projects and films he proposed or were proposed to him from many sources, especially Donald Spoto, *The Dark Side of Genius: The Life of Alfred Hitchcock*, New York: Ballantine Books, 1983; John Russell Taylor, *Hitch*, New York: Berkley Books, 1985; and François Truffaut, with the collaboration of Helen G. Scott, *Hitchcock*, revised edition, New York: Simon & Schuster, 1984. I want to acknowledge my great debt to these books but to avoid piling up references I cite them specifically only when the information I refer to cannot be easily located via an index or chapter title in their respective books.

8 Arthur Knight, "Conversation with Alfred Hitchcock," *Oui*, February 1973, p. 68.

9 Taylor, *Hitch*, p. 329n.

10 Stephen Rebello, *Alfred Hitchcock and the Making of* Psycho, New York: Harper Perennial, 1991, p. 17.

11 Rebello, *Alfred Hitchcock and the Making of* Psycho, p. 19.

12 Alfred Hitchcock, "Films We Could Make," in Sidney Gottlieb (ed.) *Hitchcock on Hitchcock: Selected Writings and Interviews*, Berkeley and Los Angeles: University of California Press, 1995, p. 167. The title sequences in *North by Northwest* and *Psycho* are good examples of such elements integrated into Hitchcock's films. He also embeds abstract pictorial art in

various films, including *Suspicion*, *The Trouble with Harry*, and *The Birds*. Even late in his career, in his interview with Charles Thomas Samuels, Hitchcock continued to compare himself "to an abstract painter": "I'm not self-indulgent where content is concerned. I'm only self-indulgent about treatment. ... My favorite painter is Klee" (*Encountering Directors*, New York: G.P. Putnam's Sons, 1972, p. 239). Peter Wollen restores much-needed attention to Hitchcock as perennially an experimental filmmaker, deeply influenced by the London Film Society coterie of the 1920s and their avant-garde programming. See "*Rope*: Three Hypotheses," in Richard Allen and S. Ishii-Gonzáles (eds.) *Hitchcock Centenary Essays*, London: BFI, 1999, especially pp. 77–81.

13 Hitchcock, "Director's Problems," in Gottlieb, *Hitchcock on Hitchcock*, p. 190.

14 Hitchcock, "The Censor Wouldn't Pass It," in Gottleib, *Hitchcock on Hitchcock*, pp. 197, 198. Spoto reports that Hitchcock was also at one time interested in another politically controversial topic and considered the "possibility" of making "a film about General James Wolfe, a British hero of Quebec" (*Dark Side of Genius*, p. 246).

15 Hitchcock, "The Censor and Sydney Street," in Gottlieb, *Hitchcock on Hitchcock*, p. 194, evidently describing *The Dark Duty*, discussed later.

16 Hitchcock, "More Cabbages, Fewer Kings," in Gottlieb, *Hitchcock on Hitchcock*, p. 177.

17 Jonathan Rosenbaum's comment on Eric von Stroheim's manner of treating *Greed* is relevant to an understanding of Hitchcock's treatment of some of his unrealized projects: "Judging from many of Stroheim's own statements, it appears that he regarded the film [*Greed*] – at least in retrospect, and in public – as an act or gesture or idea (or a species of acts or gestures or ideas) more than as a material object, and subsequent accounts of the film by others have usually adopted this romantic bias" (*Greed*, London: BFI, 1993, p. 12).

18 Hitchcock, " 'Stodgy' British Pictures," in Gottlieb, *Hitchcock on Hitchcock*, p. 170.

19 Spoto, *Dark Side of Genius*, p. 258.

20 Described in detail in Spoto, *Dark Side of Genius*, p. 267.

21 Samuels, *Encountering Directors*, pp. 239–40.

22 Truffaut, *Hitchcock*, pp. 172–3, 249. The former, according to Annette Insdorf, was "realized" by Truffaut as *Day for Night* (*François Truffaut*, New York: Simon & Schuster, 1989, p. 188). The latter is another bit of evidence of Hitchcock's fascination with Cold War politics, an interest that emerges in several of his more fully developed "unrealized projects" such as *The Short Night*. For much information on this film and one version of the script, see David Freeman, *The Last Days of Alfred Hitchcock*, Woodstock: Overlook Press, 1984.

23 There are many fascinating but lesser-known "moments" as well, illustrating how habitually he manufactured and described such scenes. For example, he told a reporter about a film he wanted to make opening with Keystone Cops coming out of a tunnel, hit on the head one by one by a criminal; the comedy turns to disturbing pathos, though, with a close-up of the bloody head of a cop, then a quick cut to "his family in agony over his misfortune" ("The Hitchcock Formula," *New York Times*, February 13, 1938). In his well-known interview with Pete Martin, he outlined another brief darkly comical plot: "Someday I'll have a character dash into a hospital, pretend to be a patient, lie down on one of those litters on which they wheel you into the operating room, and before it's over, I'll have him operated on" ("Pete Martin Calls on Hitchcock," *The Saturday Evening Post*, July 27, 1957, pp.36–7, 71–3; reprinted in part in Harry M. Geduld (ed.) *Film Makers on Film Making*, Bloomington: Indiana University Press, 1967, pp. 123–34, quoted at p. 134. And his comments in an interview on his idea about a bomb in a baseball is worth quoting at length because it is not as well known as some of the others (and may have some bearing on a television drama he did direct entitled "Bang! You're Dead"):

> "I suggested a story about a fanatic old man who works in a baseball factory. He makes up one and puts dynamite in it. The ball with dynamite becomes the central character.

The ball goes out on the field, we follow it to the umpire, who throws it to the pitcher, who then strikes out three men in a row to win the game. ... Imagine the suspense! The ball is given to the club's director, and he puts it on a sideboard in his office with other trophies.

At the very end I wanted to have a cleaning woman come in and jiggle the ball by accident, and it rolls and rolls toward the edge. It's about to fall down and explode, and she catches it in the very last shot."

He sighs. "We never worked it out."

(Richard Gehman, "The Chairman of the Board," Film Study Center, Museum of Modern Art, Hitchcock clippings folder, #2, no source or page given).

Given the number and appeal of these "moments," it is no surprise that various people suggested that Hitchcock make a film of his most imaginative ones strung together. Richard Condon, for example, proposed this several times (letters of November 2 and 25, 1964, in folder 1281). Hitchcock respectfully – and wisely – declined.

24 Thomas M. Leitch, "The Hitchcock Moment," *Hitchcock Annual* 1997–98, pp. 19–39.

25 Lucien Goldmann, quoted in Marjorie Levinson, *The Romantic Fragment Poem: A Critique of Form*, Chapel Hill: University of North Carolina Press, 1986, p. 231, n. 1.

26 For interesting discussions of the tradition of the unfinished, see David Rosand, "Composition/Decomposition/Recomposition: Notes on the Fragmentary and the Artistic Process," in Lawrence D. Kritzman (ed.) *Fragments: Incompletion and Discontinuity*, a special issue of *New York Literary Forum*, 1981, pp. 17–38.

27 Quoted in Rosand, "Composition/Decomposition/Recomposition," p. 20.

28 Thomas M. Leitch, *Finding the Director and Other Hitchcock Games*, Athens: University of Georgia Press, 1991.

29 For example, he told Arthur Knight: "When people ask 'Don't you ever improvise on the set?' my answer always is, 'With all those electricians around and all the set dressers and so forth, you're going to start to compose a scene or rewrite a scene?' Now I say, if I'm going to improvise, I prefer to improvise in an office" ("Conversation with Alfred Hitchcock," p. 119).

30 Bill Krohn's *Hitchcock at Work*, London: Phaidon, 2000, is an excellent example of this revised view of Hitchcock, based on meticulous archival research rather than anecdotes about and preconceptions of Hitchcock's methods.

31 Patrick McGilligan, personal e-mail, October 22, 1999. He will discuss Hitchcock's work on proposed and unrealized projects in detail in his forthcoming critical biography.

32 Stanley Cavell, "*North by Northwest*," in Marshall Deutelbaum and Leland Poague (eds.) *A Hitchcock Reader*, Ames: Iowa State University Press, 1986, pp. 249–61.

33 Auiler, *Hitchcock's Notebooks*, pp. 551–2.

34 Auiler, *Hitchcock's Notebooks*, p. 551.

35 Truffaut, *Hitchcock*, p. 209.

36 Auiler, *Hitchcock's Notebooks*, p. 552.

37 Truffaut, *Hitchcock*, p. 249.

38 On various occasions late in his career Hitchcock indicated that he was resigned to this way of working. For example, in an interview with Bryan Forbes, he noted that "In the last two years, I've abandoned two projects, and the point is you get so far and you realize it's not going to work out, so it's better to lose $150,000 or $200,000 than two million. Just dump it, and let it go" (John Player Lecture, March 1967, untranscribed audiotape, National Film Theatre, London).

39 Material for *Blind Man* is in the Ernest Lehman Collection at the University of Southern California Library for the Performing Arts, box 32, containing not only several versions of the script but interesting notes by Lehman about the genesis of the story and his work on it with Hitchcock. Greg Garrett discusses *Blind Man* as well as *The Wreck of the Mary Deare* and

The Short Night in "The Men Who Knew Too Much: The Unmade Films of Hitchcock and Lehman," *North Dakota Quarterly*, 61, no. 2, spring 1993, 47–57.

40 Samuels, *Encountering Directors*, p. 249.

41 Quoted in Spoto, *Dark Side of Genius*, p. 513.

42 Quoted in Spoto, *Dark Side of Genius*, p. 526.

43 Steven DeRosa, "The Italian Connection," at http://members.aol.com/vistavsion.

44 Truffaut's comments are in a letter to Hitchcock included in *François Truffaut: Correspondence 1945–1984*, ed. Gilles Jacob and Claude de Givray, New York: Cooper Square Press, 2000, pp. 317–22, where he notes that the script "certainly contains the germ of a great film, a film of the stamp of *Shadow of a Doubt*, *Strangers on a Train* and *Psycho*" (p. 317).

45 David Hemmings, who had recently appeared in *Blow-Up*, was on a list of actors to consider for the main role, along with Michael Sarrazin and David Warner, perhaps most identified at this time with his offbeat role in *Morgan* (folder 1100).

46 Samuels, *Encountering Directors*, pp. 249–50.

47 Elaine Scarry, *The Body in Pain: The Making and Unmaking of the World*, New York: Oxford University Press, 1985.

48 Taylor, *Hitch*, p. 282.

Part II

FRENCH HITCHCOCK

Chapter 6

TO CATCH A LIAR
Bazin, Chabrol, and Truffaut encounter Hitchcock

James M. Vest

Ten years separate the Allied incursion into Normandy in June 1944 from the invasion of the Riviera in June 1954 by the crew of *To Catch a Thief*. During that decade France was attempting to recover from war and the ignominies of the Occupation, struggling to define its role in a new order while adjusting to a mixed legacy of tradition, collaboration, resistance, and liberation. In that decade Cartesianism, with its grounding in common sense, iterated observations, and inductive argumentation leading toward substantiable generalizations, was forced to confront Sartrean existentialism with its emphasis on the immediacy of an observer's gaze and of situation-based choices. In the shadow of the atomic bomb, French intellectuals also grappled with fallout from Artaud's theories of cruelty and Camus's representations of the absurd. Amid this social and intellectual turmoil French Catholicism reoriented itself, struggling for renewal by targeting teenagers and young adults via organized screenings and discussions of films. That decade also saw the demise of two stalwart film magazines, *La Revue du cinéma* and *L'Ecran Français*, and the birth in 1951 of their pace-setting successor, *Cahiers du cinéma*. It encompassed the rise of television as well as the advent of Cinerama, Cinemascope, and Vistavision. It also witnessed the flowering of dynamic Ciné-Clubs throughout France and the emergence of the Cinémathèque movement, anchored in Paris and Toulouse, dedicated to the preservation and renaissance of what Jean Cocteau and Eric Rohmer called the youngest muse.[1]

During that ten-year span some two dozen Hitchcock films were screened in France, including several from the British period and others that had been *verboten* during the Occupation, in addition to current releases. This allowed French moviegoers to view and assimilate many more Hitchcock movies than most of their counterparts elsewhere. As a result of concentrated viewings, some French *cinéphiles* began to discern pictorial and thematic tendencies in Hitchcock's films that encouraged them to develop theories centering on patterns of couplings, culpability, and confession. Chief among them was Rohmer, who voiced his observations on Hitchcock in the final issues of the venerable *Revue du cinéma* and subsequently in *La Gazette du cinéma* and in *Cahiers*.[2] Rohmer's increasingly positive views of Hitchcock were seconded by Claude Chabrol and François Truffaut, who, when they were both in their early twenties, began writing regularly for *Cahiers* under the critical eye of their mentor and intellectual sparring partner, André Bazin. To multiple viewings of numerous Hitchcock films, Rohmer and company brought youthful enthusiasm, informed by systematic Cartesian typologies, encouraged by evolving Catholic emphases, and imbued with the potentialities of existential self-expression. Soon they would encounter an arresting example of the absurd in an enigmatic personage called Alfred Hitchcock.

When Hitchcock came to France to do location shooting for *To Catch a Thief* in the summer of 1954, his month-long stay presented a unique opportunity for those aspiring film critics and would-be filmmakers to put to the test their theories about his recurrent themes and images, as well as about the degree of control he exerted over his films. Truffaut had recently launched his highly controversial "Politique des auteurs" and was intent on establishing Hitchcock as a certified auteur, that is the more or less autonomous creator of a cohesive cinematic œuvre.[3] At the same time, Chabrol was keen to test and refine an emerging theory about Hitchcockian *leitmotifs* including, most notably, a recurrent struggle between good and evil involving the transfer of guilt. Peripherally and somewhat reluctantly involved in these discussions was the co-founder of *Cahiers* and *doyen* of French film critics, the redoubtable Bazin. Although personally supportive of Chabrol, Truffaut, and other young Turks who persisted in elevating the director of *Rope*, *Stage Fright*, and *I Confess* to the rank of auteur, on the professional plane Bazin viewed them as extremists, dubbing them "Hitchcockiens fanatiques."[4]

The French *cinéphiles'* first personal contacts with the laconic filmmaker were extremely disturbing. When they mentioned the persistent themes of guilt transferal or the dualistic metaphysics that some discerned in his works, Hitchcock blithely claimed to have no idea what they were talking about. When they inquired about his exercise of authorial freedom he recounted stories about the front office and box office. This awkward *contretemps* forced substantial reconsideration of the *Cahiers* writers' theoretical positions and claims. When the human being did not correspond to their image of him, the absurdity of the situation was palpable, and a sense of disbelief alloyed with annoyance pervaded their writings from this period. Noting that one had to work very hard indeed to get Hitchcock to say something interesting, Chabrol would chafe at his inability to get past the director's defenses, while Truffaut would be brutally curt: Hitchcock was hiding something.

Bazin was the first to encounter Hitchcock, and their initial meetings were unsettling on several levels. The most respected of French film critics did not come unprepared to his meetings with the director. Himself the author of several essays on Hitchcock films in *L'Ecran Français, Arts, France Observateur,* and *Radio, Cinéma, Télévision,* Bazin was also thoroughly familiar with the numerous articles on Hitchcock published in *Cahiers* under his editorship, including substantive essays by Alexandre Astruc, Jean-Luc Godard, and Rohmer.[5] These articles, based on a comparative methodology involving examinations of clusters of images across films, articulated the grounds for a sweeping, radical thesis that Bazin was prepared to try out on Hitchcock.

The Hitchcockians' essentially Cartesian process, which Rohmer labeled analogical, worked in the following manner. Noting a room filmed through a drinking glass in *Champagne* and through a milk glass in *Spellbound* and recalling another glass of milk conspicuously positioned in *Suspicion* as well as poisoned drinks foregrounded in *Notorious* and *Under Capricorn, Cahiers* writers were led to speculate on the symbolic importance of such objects for Hitchcock. They were then compelled toward an increasingly encompassing vision of this director's predilection for using objects to concretize morally supercharged contexts. Similar procedures led to an increasingly coherent theory of physical settings with symbolic overtones (e.g., sites usually associated with amusement used as loci for mayhem) and of distinctive camera effects. A growing sense of the whole led to claims for pervasive unity among films that collectively could be viewed as an œuvre. Underlying this theoretical framework were expressions of hope that the Hollywood period would indeed transform Hitchcock into a true auteur, "un véritable auteur de films."[6]

Despite Bazin's personal reluctance to see in Hitchcock anything more than a gifted technician with poor taste who had sold out to the American studio system, during the first three years of his editorship *Cahiers* ran eleven articles dealing with nearly twenty Hitchcock films screened in first run, in re-issue, or in retrospectives. The fact that Hitchcock was allowed so much space reflected the magazine's commitment to principles of open intellectual debate as well as growing appreciation among the French moviegoing public for this eminently discussable, sometimes controversial, filmmaker. That Bazin would be willing to test the Hitchcockians' theses for them in the crucible of personal contact with the director attested to his tenacious good will and the courage to assay his own convictions.

While Hitchcock was shooting *To Catch a Thief* on the Riviera, Bazin traveled to Nice and interviewed him for *Cahiers* and for his protégés. The resulting article, "Hitchcock contre Hitchcock," appeared in the October 1954 issue of *Cahiers*. Its title succinctly recapitulated the shock of first encounter. Bazin was taken aback by the fact that during the hours of filming he witnessed in the flower market at Nice, Hitchcock intervened in the action only twice and otherwise seemed uninvolved in the shooting (p. 27). Serious critic that he was, Bazin also expressed discomfort with his perception that Hitchcock's jesting responses to his questions tended more to obscure than to clarify (p. 28). In a burst of classical rhetorical verve, Bazin resorted to vigorous metaphors of conflict to describe his exasperation at his interviewee's camouflage tactics and "pirouettes" (pp. 26, 27, 30). Bazin was so disconcerted by the answers he received from Hitchcock that he requested and was granted a second interview at Cannes to clarify certain points.

The centerpiece of Bazin's article was a report of the crucial moment when he accosted Hitchcock with an idea that was both unexpected and unpredictable in order to get the director to admit the existence and the weightiness of an ethical strand running through his work: "de lui faire admettre l'existence et le sérieux d'un thème moral dans son œuvre" (pp. 30–1). When the moment seemed right, Bazin laid out the claim advanced by Chabrol and Truffaut to have discerned a theme common to Hitchcock's works – that of the identification of a weaker character with a stronger one – which, because of its moral and intellectual implications, moved these films beyond the realm of simple suspense-thrillers to encompass something more intellectually compelling (p. 30). To reinforce his point Bazin cited examples from *Shadow of a Doubt*, *Strangers on a Train*, and *I Confess*. Bazin remarked that his interlocutor listened attentively and smiled broadly as the import seemed to sink in. But Hitchcock soon changed the subject. The sessions concluded with Bazin unable to turn the conversation back to essentials.[7]

Bazin returned to Paris and, while composing his now famous article, discussed with Chabrol and Truffaut his disconcerting interview experiences. Meanwhile, reports on the making of *To Catch a Thief*, its stars, and its director continued to appear in the French media, which emphasized Cary Grant's dressing and shopping preferences, Grace Kelly's hairstyles and clothes, the director's gastronomic indulgences, and the role of French participants in the making of the film rather than technical or theoretical matters.[8] The "Hitchcockiens fanatiques" were understandably nonplussed by much of what they heard and read, and thought of themselves as trapped in a Balzacian world of vanishing illusions.

A few weeks later when Hitchcock was in Paris, Chabrol received a phone call from Truffaut inviting him to come along to a press conference at the director's suite in the fashionable Hotel George V.[9] The two young writers were to represent *Cahiers du cinéma* at what turned out to be an exceedingly frustrating, yet productive, event. Upon being ushered into an elegant, spacious room, they felt disadvantaged by their youth and inexperience and were exasperated by a *Cahiers* tape recorder that, refusing to function, delayed proceedings for several minutes.[10] Most of all they were disappointed by the attitude of their interviewee, who talked about the Mediterranean sun rather than giving serious answers to their probing questions (p. 40). After a repetition of one of Hitchcock's oft-told anecdotes, Chabrol felt the time might be right to uncloak his assault weapons, "dévoiler quelques batteries." He blurted out, "Do you believe in the devil?" Hitchcock looked him in the eye fixedly with what Chabrol registered as a somewhat astonished air, replied that the devil is in each of us, then shifted the conversation back to *Rear Window*. As the interview hour was drawing to an end, Chabrol asked how closely the director worked on the preparation of his screenplays. Very closely indeed was the answer: from beginning to end including the layout of individual scenes (p. 41). Just as the two thought they had something of substance to support their auteurist views, the session concluded. As the group prepared to leave, Hitchcock shook hands with each person in attendance, ending with Chabrol and Truffaut.

On their way back to the *Cahiers* office Truffaut convinced Chabrol to call Hitchcock and ask whether he would entertain a few more questions. The very civil voice on the other end of the line indicated that he would be leaving soon but would try to answer the questions over the phone. Hearing the first one – "What is the figure in your carpet?" – Hitchcock became convinced that this Frenchman's questions could not be easily disposed of and invited him up for five minutes. Chabrol found Hitchcock attending to his papers while a small graying woman – "Alma Reville, je suppose" – was readying the luggage (p. 42).

Chabrol asked as succinctly as he could about the theme of the search for God that he and several of his colleagues had found in Hitchcock's works. Perhaps because of Chabrol's limitations in English, his self-styled "anglais un peu macaronique" (p. 42), or perhaps because Hitchcock heard what he wanted to hear, the director replied, all the while looking at Chabrol sympathetically, "Search of *good*? Oh yes, yes; there is a search of good." When Chabrol clarified his meaning, "Not good; God Himself," Hitchcock looked rather surprised and added, "God! ... Maybe, but it is unconscious." (These phrases are reported in English in the French text [pp. 42–3], as is "larger than life" [p. 44], below.) Unwilling to accept such an answer, Chabrol persisted, citing the cases of Hitchcock's characters caught in a net of evil who were able to escape only through confession (p. 43). His questions elicited agreement – sincere confession, yes, contrition – and an unsettling smile as Hitchcock added that he became aware of such things only after the fact, insisting that for him the screenplay was secondary to the form of the film, that he made the script conform to that overview in his head, and that the situations treated in his films were indeed universal. Hitchcock added that he saw things "larger than life" (p. 44). Chabrol translated this last phrase back to Hitchcock as "Métaphysique?" to which Hitchcock replied "Thank you" and went on to explain why he preferred melodrama. When the last suitcase was latched Chabrol took his leave.

A description of this encounter appeared in the October 1954 issue of *Cahiers*, along with an interpretative article, "Hitchcock devant le mal," in which Chabrol applied Catholic doctrine and existentialist tenets to Hitchcock's works, asserting that the director consistently showed characters who were, in both the Augustinian and Sartrean senses, free and who chose to do evil.[11] Their crime was not so important as, again borrowing Sartrean terminology, their struggle and their choices.[12] What mattered was their decision to accept responsibility. In these interviews and this article lay the seeds of the first book-length study of Hitchcock's films, co-authored by Chabrol and Rohmer.

Truffaut also wrote an article for the same issue of *Cahiers* entitled "Un Trousseau de fausse clés," in which he took Hitchcock to task for some of the troubling events mentioned by Chabrol and Bazin.[13] Whereas Chabrol spoke of disingenuousness, Truffaut asserted bluntly that Hitchcock was not telling the truth: "Hitchcock a menti" (p. 50). This article took the form of an open letter addressed to Bazin, in which Truffaut expressed his discomfort with Hitchcock's portrayal of himself in his recent interviews as a willing victim of his own lack of comprehension (p. 45). Truffaut thought Hitchcock was playing with Bazin, just as he played with Chabrol; thus when Bazin saw him as speechless, Hitchcock was silently thinking of a way to make Bazin believe that he had revealed something to him that he did not know (p. 46). But Bazin was not Hitchcock's only dupe. Truffaut was forced to acknowledge the great embarrassment of the Hitchcockians who wanted no part of an unreflecting genius, "un génie inconscient" (p. 47). Truffaut insisted that Hitchcock's American films developed the theme of the transfer of identity and that they did so with a psychological force that surpassed even his British films in which doubles figured prominently. Truffaut then offered an extended analysis of *Shadow of a Doubt,* showing how in every phase it exhibited this theme through plays on the idea of duality, thus giving expression to the extraordinarily balanced construction of a film whose creator surely must have been conscious of this pattern and of the thematics that underlay it (p. 49).[14] Conclusion: Hitchcock must be lying (p. 50).

But why should Hitchcock dissemble? Truffaut asserted that Hitchcock had built his career and indeed his life on misunderstandings, "le malentendu," choosing to be known as the master of suspense rather than as a Catholic filmmaker, and preferring a perverse form of modesty to self-acclaim. Thus Hitchcock would insist that his only good film was his most recent one, and yet when Chabrol asked him what was his worst American movie, he said they all were. Consequently, for Truffaut, the logical conclusion was that Hitchcock was indulging in rank "mensonges," that is, lies (p. 51).

Truffaut's argument took a peculiar twist that would have profound long-term impact. According to Truffaut, Hitchcock was in fact a Hitchcockian creature and thus extremely reluctant to explain himself. Nevertheless, Truffaut claimed, one day the director would be compelled to act like other Hitchcock characters who sealed their eternal destiny, "leur salut," through confession (p. 51). Truffaut himself would do everything in his power to make that happen. The concept of the famous marathon interview which Truffaut would conduct with Hitchcock eight years later may be traced to that proposition, couched in terms of a right-eous threat.

Hitchcock's initial reaction was to pooh-pooh the French critical enterprise. During an interview at the time of the London premier of *To Catch a Thief*, the director claimed not to recognize himself in what the young *Cahiers* Turks were writing about him – "I must admit that some of those articles made me wonder 'is this really me they're discussing?'" – and asserted that the inclusion of Catholic themes in his films must be purely "instinctive rather than deliberate."[15] Perhaps Hitchcock sensed in these determined young critics representatives of a system that was at once intriguing and foreign to him, one to which he was reluctant to subscribe. He later claimed during another interview that he preferred to leave certain things unexplained and that there was "nothing more stupid than logic," then added pointedly, "Descartes can go soak his head."[16]

Convinced of their insights, the *Cahiers* writers persisted. Hitchcock, who shared with them a strong interest in reputation building, welcomed the flurry of international notice and quickly warmed to the epithet auteur. When he was in Paris thereafter, representatives from *Cahiers* enjoyed exclusive interviews. Hitchcock's own claims to auteur status became more overt and categorical. In his next interview with Truffaut and Chabrol he stated emphatically that he had never filmed from someone else's script: "je n'ai jamais tourné le scénario d'un autre. Jamais."[17] In the same interview he acquiesced to the assertion that most if not all of his American films depicted paired relationships.[18] One might wonder whether Hitchcock was playing into these critics' hands, or handling them in his own image-enhancing way, or both.

Intense critical reaction to the Hitchcockians' claims ensued. Whose fault was it, asked Rohmer, if others insisted on seeing Hitchcock as merely a technician and if he himself refused to discuss the deep metaphysical sense of his own themes with Chabrol and Bazin? The pages of *Cahiers* bore the weight of an avalanche of responses, including dissenting comments by Jean Desternes, a highly skeptical editorial by Bazin entitled "Comment peut-on être Hitchcocko-Hawksien?," Chabrol's rebuttal, and Gérard Genette's impassioned defense of what he called Hitchcock's Jansenism.[19] Genette's prediction that exegesis of Hitchcock's cinema had just begun proved potently prophetic.[20]

Aftershocks were felt for decades. The concepts disputed in the pages of *Cahiers* spawned books on Hitchcock not only by Rohmer and Chabrol but also by *Cahiers* contributors from Jean Douchet to Bill Krohn.[21] Hitchcock acceded to Truffaut's invitation to extensive interviews in the 1960s and to others thereafter. In 1963 Penelope Houston took the *Cahiers* writers' approach and ideas to task in a point-by-point attack.[22] In 1970 *The American Scholar* published Charles Thomas Samuels's carefully articulated blast against the position articulated by Rohmer and associates, which prompted much debate.[23] Nearly two decades after the Hitchcockians had thrown down the gauntlet, Robin Wood, writing under the nom de plume George Kaplan, would revisit Truffaut's assessment of Hitchcock as consummate liar as a point of departure for his analysis of Hitchcock's later films.[24] The Truffauldian thesis would be advanced by Robert Kapsis and others who have studied Hitchcock from cultural, psychological, and sociological perspectives.[25]

Thus the debates that raged in the 1950s laid the foundations for numerous extended studies of Hitchcock – the man, the work, the image – not only by French critics including René Prédal, Noël Simsolo, and Bruno Villien,[26] but also by Anglophone critics as diverse as Maurice Yacowar, Donald Spoto, William Rothman, Lesley Brill, Tania Modleski, Robert Corber, Theodore Price, Thomas Leitch, Paula Marantz Cohen, Susan Smith, and others who have examined Hitchcock's creations in terms of preponderant themes and variations, of nuanced differences within a coherent vision.[27] Even revisionist studies emphasizing Hitchcock's evolving creative processes or the contributions of his collaborations, including those by Dan Auiler and Steven DeRosa, owe a major debt to those French writers who initially formulated a conception of Hitchcock's films as œuvre and of the creator himself as auteur.[28]

Acknowledgements

Research for this project was facilitated by a couple of Faculty Development Grants from Rhodes College, 1998 and 2002. For their assistance the author is indebted to Nancy Vest, Cecelia Vest, Stéphanie Carrez, Paul Williford, and Mark Winokur. A large debt is also owed to Kenan Padgett, Annette Cates, and William Short of Burrow Library at Rhodes College, to Joe Rees of Duke University Library, to the reference, newspaper and periodicals, and microforms staff at the Library of Congress, and to the staff of the British Film Institute, Bibliothèque du Film, Bibliothèque de l'Arsenal, and Bibliothèque de France.

Notes

1 A drawing by Cocteau, who was known both for his films and for his theories of poetic composition in the broadest sense, including cinema and graphic design, bore the phrase "Vive cette jeune muse, cinéma!" alongside a sketch of an ecstatic young woman encircled by stars. Rohmer referred to cinema as a youngster among the arts, "le dernier-né des arts." Cf. Eric Rohmer, 'Le Celluloïd et le marbre (III): De la métaphore," *Cahiers du cinéma*, no. 51, October 1955, 6. In this essay the shortened form *Cahiers* will be used to refer to *Cahiers du cinéma*, and translations from the French will be my own.

2 Eric Rohmer, "Festival Hitchcock: *Notorious*," *Revue du cinéma*, n.s. 3, no. 15, July 1948, pp. 70–2; 'Etude technique de *La Corde*," *Gazette du cinéma*, no. 1, May 1950, 1 and 3; "Le Soupçon," *Cahiers*, no. 12, May 1952, pp. 63–6; "De Trois Films et d'une certaine école," *Cahiers*, no. 26, August–September 1953, pp.18–25. For further details see James M. Vest, "The Emergence of an Auteur: Hitchcock and French Film Criticism, 1950–1954," *Hitchcock Annual* 2001–2, pp. 108–24.

3 Despite Bazin's better judgment and after several delays, *Cahiers* published Truffaut's inflammatory polemic, "Une Certaine Tendance du cinéma français" (no. 31, January 1954, pp.15–29), which attacked traditional, commercial French filmmaking and proposed instead a renewed cinema of *auteurs* modeled on Cocteau, Renoir, Vigo, Gance, and Méliès, all of whom exercised a significant degree of control over their films and produced a distinctively coherent body of work. Truffaut also believed that certain Hollywood directors, notably Hitchcock and Howard Hawks, could be classified as auteurs, a stance that made his views even more controversial in France.

4 André Bazin, "Hitchcock contre Hitchcock," *Cahiers*, no. 39, October 1954, 30; elsewhere in the same article Bazin referred to them as zealots, "des Hitchcockiens maximalistes," who counted among the director's wildest devotees, "ses plus farouches partisans" (p. 25). Subsequent citations appear in parentheses in the text.

5 Alexandre Astruc, "Au-dessous du volcan," *Cahiers*, no. 1, April 1951, pp. 29–32 and "Alibis et ellipses," *Cahiers*, no. 2, May 1951, pp. 50–1; Jean-Luc Godard, "Suprématie du sujet," *Cahiers*, no. 10, March 1952, pp. 59–61; Eric Rohmer, "Soupçon," pp. 63–6, and "De Trois Films," pp. 18–25.

6 Rohmer's descriptor "mode analogique" appeared in "De Trois Films," p. 22. The specific examples mentioned in this paragraph as well as the final quotation are taken from Raymond Borde and Etienne Chaumeton, "Flash-back sur Hitchcock," *Cahiers*, no. 17, November 1952, pp. 55–8.

7 Bazin recounted one of Hitchcock's joking parting shots in response to a query about the pre-planning of his films: how could he possibly have given a French journalist an hour of his time during shooting if he had needed to think about his movies at the same time? ("Hitchcock contre Hitchcock," p. 32).

8 For example: coverage in the Parisian daily, *L'Aurore*, July and July 1954. This aspect will be treated in more detail in my book *Hitchcock and France* (forthcoming, Praeger).

9 Bazin gave the time frame in general terms, "quelque temps plus tard à Paris" ("Hitchcock contre Hitchcock," p. 30) while Truffaut indicated it was in August 1954. Cf. François Truffaut and Claude Chabrol, "Entretien avec Alfred Hitchcock," *Cahiers*, no. 44, February 1955, pp. 31.

10 Claude Chabrol, "Histoire d'une interview," *Cahiers*, no. 39, October 1954, pp. 39. Subsequent citations appear in parentheses in the text.

11 Claude Chabrol, "Hitchcock devant le mal," *Cahiers*, no: 39, October 1954, pp. 18–24; the title could be rendered into English as "Hitchcock Confronts Evil."

12 Chabrol, "Hitchcock devant le mal," pp. 18–22.

13 François Truffaut, "Un Trousseau de fausses clés," *Cahiers*, no. 39, October 1954, pp. 45–53; translated into English as "Skeleton Keys," *Film Culture*, spring 1964, no. 32; reprinted in

Cahiers du Cinéma in English, 1966, no. 2. Subsequent citations (to the original) appear in parentheses in the text.

14 Truffaut attempted to situate *To Catch a Thief* in this same context based on what he knew of its plot. Truffaut mistakenly thought that Cary Grant's character would head a quasi-official band of thieves of international status, thereby avoiding police interference; he also pointed out that Hitchcock told reporters, anxious to discover who the copycat thief might be, that it was Charles Vanel, who played the restaurateur Bertani ("Un Trousseau de fausses clés," p. 50).

15 Catherine de la Roche, "Conversation with Hitchcock," *Sight and Sound*, vol. 25, no. 3, Winter 1956, p. 157.

16 Orana Fallaci, "Alfred Hitchcock," in *The Egotists*, Chicago: Regnery, 1963, p. 250.

17 Truffaut and Chabrol, "Entretien avec Alfred Hitchcock," p. 29.

18 Truffaut and Chabrol, "Entretien avec Alfred Hitchcock," p. 21.

19 Eric Rohmer, "A Qui la faute?", *Cahiers*, no. 39, October 1954, p. 6; Jean Desternes, "L'Amour en couleurs," *Cahiers*, no. 42, December 1954, pp. 27–31, 77; André Bazin, "Comment peut-on être Hitchcocko-Hawksien?", *Cahiers*, no. 44, February 1955, pp. 17–18; Claude Chabrol, "Les Choses sérieuses," *Cahiers*, no. 46, April 1955, pp. 41–3; Gérard Genette, "Courrier des lecteurs," *Cahiers*, no. 52, November 1955, pp. 59–60.

20 Genette, "'Courrier des lecteurs," p. 60.

21 Eric Rohmer and Claude Chabrol, *Hitchcock*, Paris: Editions Universitaires, 1957; Jean Douchet, *Alfred Hitchcock*, Editions de l'Herne, Collection "L'Herne-Cinéma" no. 1, 1967; Bill Krohn, *Hitchcock at Work*, London: Phaidon, 2000.

22 Penelope Houston, "The Figure in the Carpet," *Sight and Sound*, vol. 32, no. 4, Autumn 1963, pp. 158–64

23 Charles Taylor Samuels, "Hitchcock," *The American Scholar,* vol. 39, no. 2, Spring 1970, pp. 295–304.

24 George Kaplan, "Lost in the Wood," in Don Whittmore and Philip Alan Cecchettinni (eds.) *Passport to Hollywood*, New York: McGraw-Hill, 1976, pp. 48–9.

25 Robert E. Kapsis, *Hitchcock: The Making of a Reputation*, Chicago: University of Chicago Press, 1992.

26 René Prédal, "La Peur et les multiples visages du destin, ou de quelques aspects de la thématique hitchcockienne," in Michel Estève (ed.), *Alfred Hitchcock*, Etudes Cinématographiques 84/87, Paris: Minard-Lettres Modernes, 1971, pp. 85–140; Noël Simsolo, *Alfred Hitchcock*, Paris: Seghers, 1969; Bruno Villien, *Hitchcock*, Paris: Colona, 1982.

27 Maurice Yacowar, *Hitchcock's British Films,* Hamden, CT: Archon Books, 1977; Donald Spoto, *The Art of Alfred Hitchcock: Fifty Years of His Motion Pictures,* revised edition, New York: Anchor, 1992; William Rothman, *Hitchcock, The Murderous Gaze,* Cambridge, MA and London: Harvard University Press, 1982; Lesley Brill, *The Hitchcock Romance: Love and Irony in Hitchcock's Films,* Princeton: Princeton University Press, 1988; Tania Modleski, *The Women Who Knew Too Much: Hitchcock and Feminist Theory,* New York: Methuen, 1988; Robert J. Corber, *In the Name of National Security: Hitchcock, Homophobia, and the Political Construction of Gender in Postwar America*, Durham NC: Duke University Press, 1993; Theodore Price, *Hitchcock and Homosexuality: His 50-year Obsession with Jack the Ripper and the Superbitch Prostitute – A Psychoanalytic View,* Metuchen, NJ: The Scarecrow Press, 1992, pp. 288–354; Thomas M. Leitch, *Find the Director and Other Hitchcock Games,* Athens: University of Georgia Press, 1991; Paula Marantz Cohen, *Alfred Hitchcock: The Legacy of Victorianism,* Lexington: University Press of Kentucky, 1995; Susan Smith, *Hitchcock: Suspense, Humour and Tone*, London: BFI, 2000.

28 Stephen DeRosa, *Writing with Hitchcock: the Collaboration of Alfred Hitchcock and John Michael Hayes*, New York: Faber & Faber, 2001; Dan Auiler, *Vertigo: The Making of a Classic*, New York: St. Martin's Press, 1998; Jean-Pierre Esquenazi, *Hitchcock et l'aventure de Vertigo: l'invention à Hollywood*, Paris: CNRS, 2001.

Chapter 7

HITCHCOCK THE FIRST FORTY-FOUR FILMS
Chabrol and Rohmer's "Politique des Auteurs"

Walter Raubicheck

To go back to Chabrol and Rohmer's groundbreaking text is to reacquaint oneself with a seminal moment in film criticism and theory. What strikes today's reader, in addition to the famous "transfer of guilt" thesis for which it has been cited continuously in Hitchcock studies, is its insistence on Hitchcock as a true innovator of cinematic forms that embody this theme. Certainly the authors return again and again to the idea that the "wrong" men in Hitchcock's films are tainted by a universal guilt. However, the book insists on the director's ability to convey this psychological/metaphysical state through a visual style that makes use of both montage and expressionism. In doing so they hope to demonstrate that Hitchcock is an auteur who belongs in the same rank as their mentor André Bazin's favorite director, Orson Welles.

Although in many ways they belonged to Bazin's school of mise-en-scène criticism, these two *Cahiers du cinéma* critics clearly felt the need to question some of the implications of his aesthetics. Bazin's desire for a film practice that would capture "reality" in all its phenomenological certainty led him to devalue Hitchcock, whose virtuosity stuck him as shallow and whose work, for Bazin, was limited by what he considered to be the "detective story" genre, which did not contain the thematic consistency heralded by Bazin's younger *Cahiers* colleagues. Welles, on the other hand, perfected deep-focus photography, which presented the spectator with a vast depth of field and preserved the continuities destroyed by Eisensteinian cutting. For Bazin, Welles rescued sound movies from the standard continuity editing techniques of the thirties that had hardened into a visual formula. In addition, thematically Bazin saw Welles's work as "[taking] its place beside the great spiritual landscapes created by Stroheim, Chaplin, Eisenstein, Renoir, Flaherty, Rossellini."[1] But with the exception of this unrestrained enthusiasm for Welles, and to some extent Wyler, Bazin resisted what he considered to be the extremes of his colleagues' claims for cinematic authorship, as he made clear in a 1957 essay ("On the 'Politique des Auteurs' "): in particular, Bazin complained that once a director was hailed as an auteur by a *Cahiers* critic, every film by that director automatically was hailed as a masterpiece, while competent directors such as John Huston could never make a great film according to the same critic because he had not been elevated to auteur status.

Clearly, Chabrol and Rohmer see their text as the definitive establishment of Hitchcock's auteurist credentials. In our references to their "exchange of guilt" theme we tend to forget how much they initiated the discussion of Hitchcock's style. In an important footnote in their Hitchcock book, the authors write that "Hitchcock's style is 'narrative.' His camera chooses, relates, takes sides. Nevertheless, after *Rope*, the arbitrary – for the arbitrary is inevitable – is disguised under the appearance of objectivity."[2] What they prize most in Hitchcock's style is the very "arbitrariness" of the shots: the camera selects what it wants to present and the director makes no pretense of showing an objective reality. Narration – meaning this selectivity of the camera in relation to the development of the movie's content, its story – is thus the source of the director's most impressive effects, and this style is reflected primarily in Hitchcock's use of traveling shots, close-ups, point-of-view shots, and montage. Ultimately this emphasis on the selectivity of the camera brings Chabrol and Rohmer into conflict with the realism of Bazin.

Key to Bazin's theory of realism is the ideal of preserving the unity inherent in the objects or people being photographed. Discontinuity, on the other hand, is the essence of montage. In his seminal essay "The Evolution of the Language of Cinema" Bazin contrasts directors "who put their faith in the image and those who put their faith in reality."[3] By "faith in the image" Bazin means a reliance on montage and/or the effects of lighting, sets, and framing. These directors "impose" their "interpretation of an event on the spectator."[4] By "faith in reality" he means "the image is evaluated not according to what it adds to reality but what it reveals of it."[5] In the silent era Griffith represents the former and von Stroheim the latter. Bazin's essential argument is that sound film would benefit by a re-dedication to faith in reality and an avoidance of the "tricks" of montage.

Welles, of course, is central to Bazin's project. In order for us to fully understand his significance for the critic his style must be contrasted with that of the directors of the thirties. Bazin claims that by 1938 a virtually universal style of editing had been established, one that he calls "analytic" or "dramatic."[6] The montage is not meant to indicate parallel action (Griffith) or poetic metaphor (Eisenstein) but to reflect the dramatic logic of the scene. He even calls such editing "invisible": basically he is designating the continuity editing that clearly delineates the positions of the actors and uses medium shots and close-ups for psychological purposes. *Citizen Kane* ignored this static precedent and substituted what were for Bazin the aesthetically superior techniques of the sequence shot (an entire scene filmed in one take), the wide-angle shot, and, of course, the construction in depth provided by the deep-focus shot – all of which could be and, in *Citizen Kane* (1941) were, combined. Bazin called Welles's style "decoupage in depth," as opposed to fragmented decoupage, and insisted that these long takes provided a "surplus of realism ... a realism that is in a certain sense ontological, restoring to the object and the decor their existential density, the weight of their presence; a dramatic realism which refuses to separate the actor from the decor, the foreground from the background; a psychological realism which brings the spectator back to the real conditions of perception."[7]

Chabrol and Rohmer do not reject Bazin's aesthetics – like him their emphasis is almost always on the content of the shot and the way each shot is photographed, as opposed to the relationship between shots – but they do find it to be incomplete. The two critics also did not underrate Welles – indeed, they were in the forefront of the continued French enthusiasm for him during the fifties, championing *Mr. Arkadin* (1955) and *Touch of Evil* (1958) when these films were ignored by American critics – but they saw a one-sided adherence to his style as leading to a rejection of many cinematic possibilities that, presumably, they intended to explore in their own films.

Robin Wood's discussion of the aesthetic influences on Hitchcock provides a useful perspective on Chabrol and Rohmer's critical project. Wood claims that cinema modifies reality in two ways: through montage and through expressionism, which is a "distortion or deformation of objective reality, 'expression' taking precedence over representation."[8] Obviously Bazin's aesthetic devalues both methods, and Chabrol and Rohmer cannot support their mentor's rejection of two approaches to filmmaking that are so essential to Hitchcock's art. As Wood points out in his 1977 essay on Hitchcock entitled "Retrospective," the director drew consistently upon both traditions – the Russian belief in montage and the German adherence to expressionism – but without the ideological contexts in which these traditions were developed. Wood suggests however that Hitchcock's films can be considered "realistic" if photography is not considered as the historical precedent for cinema but instead the nineteenth-century novel. For the fiction of Dickens and his European contemporaries possesses a realism that is "bound up not so much with literal visual representation as with the audience's involvement in the movement of a narrative, the illusion that we are experiencing 'real life.'"[9] Here Wood redefines realism through its relation to narration, a notion that is at the heart of the Chabrol and Rohmer book on Hitchcock. For the French critics, Hitchcock's films are not repositories of cinematic "tricks" that subvert the audience's relationship to the real world; instead, they are models of how a director creates an alternative reality for the spectator, conditioned not by the location of objects in space and time but by the demands of the story being told.

Yet this "narrative" style, one that is not determined by faithfulness to the real world being photographed but which is "arbitrary" and "descriptive" allows the director to concentrate on images and other visual patterns that serve as symbols for a film's "idea" (p. 146). Thus Hitchcock's style reveals the purity of the continuum between form and theme. In effect Chabrol and Rohmer qualified Bazin's "dramatic" realism with a "narrative" realism; at the same time they continued to respect his "ontological" realism with its emphasis on the physical properties in each shot. (In their discussion of *Rope* they challenge the "psychological realism" Bazin finds in the deep-focus shot.) Chabrol and Rohmer state that

> the current that goes from the symbol to the idea always passes through the condenser of emotion. It is never a theoretic or a conventional connection. The emotion is a means and not an end in itself, as for example it is in the horror plays of the Grand Guignol. This emotion is on the other side of the form, but on this side of the idea.
>
> (p. 112)

Thus Hitchcock's technical finesse is always in service to theme: the camera establishes symbols that, because of the way they are shot, affect the audience emotionally, but the emotions evoked lead ultimately to the idea of the film, its essential meaning. The book's more detailed analyses of form and theme begin with Hitchcock's move to Hollywood, for as the authors point out the director's "system" became more "coherent" as his career developed. They call the elements of this system the "formulas of construction" and assert that we must examine these formulas

> if we want to study Hitchcock's symbolism; it is these formulas that we must keep our eyes on if we venture to use the dangerous word "metaphysics." As we have often pointed out, it is in the form that we must look for the depth of the work and that form is heavy with a latent metaphysic. It is important therefore to consider Hitchcock's work in the same way we would that of an esoteric painter or poet.
>
> (p. 107)

Certainly Chabrol and Rohmer here betray their roots in theology, biblical exegesis, and late nineteenth-century symbolist art and literature, alien sources to today's preoccupation with ideology and intertextuality. Yet their background enables them to concentrate on the formal qualities of Hitchcock's films in ways that are surprisingly relevant to film theory's interest in the language of cinema.

A clear example of their brief but insightful commentary on his British films is their treatment of *Young and Innocent*. Typically, Chabrol and Rohmer concentrate on Hitchcock's use of the camera to create the narrative. As usual, their emphasis is on particular shots as opposed to montage: "The run-of-the-mill plot leaves Hitchcock all the time he needs to linger over the peripheral details of his subject and create an abundance of poetic, funny, or terrifying shots" (p. 51). They are particularly enthusiastic about the tracking shot in the ballroom towards the end of the film:

> [*Young and Innocent*] has the most beautiful forward track to be found in the history of film: the protagonists enter the ballroom of a fancy hotel in which the murderer is probably hiding; though the spectator has previously seen him, all he knows about him is that his eyes twitch. The camera, mounted on a crane, is some forty yards overhead and follows, in a short pan, the entry of the young people into the ballroom, at the far end of which one can see a black orchestra playing a number while couples move about the dance floor. The camera begins a slow, oblique descent, as if searching to frame the orchestra. It does frame it, and it continues to move forward until it takes in only a portion of the orchestra, then only three musicians, and finally only a single musician: the drummer. The camera comes closer still, until only the drummer's face is on the screen. The camera searches for his eyes, finds them, and isolates them. The eyes twitch.
>
> (p. 52)

Chabrol and Rohmer proceed to claim that this shot is even more impressive than the famous track onto the key in Ingrid Bergman's hand in *Notorious*. But they also use *Young and Innocent* to support their other significant strategy: to establish Hitchcock as an innovator of cinematic forms who is independent of and who in many cases antedates Welles. In this instance the technique involved is sound: the film "contains a very successful preliminary sketch of the family scenes in *Shadow of a Doubt*: we hear the same hubbub of conversation, a factor which tends to prove that when it comes to sound, Hitchcock owes less to Orson Welles than is generally believed" (p. 52).

Beginning with their analysis of *Shadow of a Doubt*, they always explore the exchange of guilt motif through its cinematic representation. Crediting Truffaut with having provided the examples, they identify "rhyme" as the formal principle of the film, meaning the same framing shots and camera movements that are used to present Charlie and her uncle, as well as the "doubling" elements in the scenario. In fact, this approach to *Shadow of a Doubt* serves as a paradigm for the remainder of the text's critical formulations as the critics identify the key symbols that Hitchcock's camera selects. For example, in *Spellbound* the authors emphasize parallel lines and the color white. In *Notorious* it is, of course, the key, along with other objects shot in close-up such as alcohol and cups of poison.

Perhaps the section that most clearly delineates the accomplishment of *Hitchcock: The First Forty-Four Films* is the commentary on *Rope*. For here the celebrated long takes would seem to challenge the chief claim of the book that Hitchcock's mise-en-scène is an important alternative to that of Welles. The only expressionistic effect in the film is the changing hues of the sky outside the apartment: there are no point-of-view shots that show the state of mind of a character such as are used at crucial points in *Notorious* from the same period. And of course this is the least fragmented decoupage in Hitchcock's canon. Yet Chabrol and Rohmer seize on this film to make explicit their differences from Bazin. They admit that Bazin's critique of the film is important: Hitchcock's use of a tracking camera in the long takes results in a constant succession of reframings, which therefore does not achieve the effect of Welles's long takes in deep focus that juxtapose at least two images simultaneously. Bazin complained that the reframings merely recreate the classic shot breakdown of the thirties that Welles had rejected. But Chabrol and Rohmer challenge Bazin on just this point: for them Hitchcock is more innovative because his roving camera overcomes an overreliance on the frame itself as the determinant of an image's meaning. Hitchcock's frame is constantly shifting and pliant; Welles's is static and does not really accomplish Bazin's ideal realist objective: "The visual freedom enjoyed by the spectator of a deep-focus shot in *Citizen Kane* is completely theoretical, since only the front or the back of the field will hold our attention, depending on whether the dramatic interest puts the accent on the one or the other" (p. 96). *Rope*, precisely because of its long takes and tracking camera, thus becomes for Chabrol and Rohmer the film that most clearly reveals the differences between the two directors and establishes Hitchcock as a true successor of the first geniuses of cinema: "[*Rope*] contributed in no small way to freeing the film-maker from his obsession with painting and making of him what he had been in the time of Griffith and the pioneers – an architect" (pp. 96–7).

As usual, Chabrol and Rohmer connect the long takes to the film's meaning. The continuity in space and time that they provide allows the director to use lighting, and especially the color of the sky, to delineate the changing emotional atmosphere of the film as the afternoon turns into night. For example, they stress the "anguish" of Farley Granger's character at the piano, an emotional duress emphasized by the twilight outside (p. 94). The two critics are clearly determined to refute the "shallow virtuosity" indictment of Hitchcock's detractors by demonstrating, film by film, this subtle but *continual blending of form and content.*

In their study of *Strangers on a Train, Rear Window*, and the remake of *The Man Who Knew Too Much*, Chabrol and Rohmer determine the "formal postulate," the essential symbolism, that Hitchcock employs to convey his ideas. In the first film they identify the geometric pattern of the circle inscribed over a straight line, the latter indicated by the movement of the train and the amusement park tunnel, the former by balloons, glasses, and the merry-go-round. The "vertigo" induced by these "motifs" in the spectator reflects that of the characters joined irrevocably by "the exchange of guilt" (pp. 107–10). In *Rear Window* the critics earn the distinction of being the first to discuss both the elements of "spectacle" and the theme of alienation in the film by concentrating on Hitchcock's use of confined space as both technical achievement and symbol. (In fact, their entire discussion of this film, while theological rather than psychoanalytic, seems remarkably contemporary in its indictment of voyeurism.) And in *The Man Who Knew Too Much* they demonstrate how the director's mise-en-scène uses time in the same way that *Rear Window* used space: to convey the idea of separation from "the object [the character] desires or fears," an idea exemplified brilliantly by the Albert Hall sequence (p. 140).

In the director's two "Catholic" films, *I Confess* and *The Wrong Man*, the explicitly Christian interpretations are still rooted in the camera's ability to select images and turn them into symbols: the Stations of the Cross in the former (for example, the explicit Calvary references as Father Michael descends the courthouse stairway surrounded by the jeering crowd), the matrix of the "wall" in the latter that assumed importance in the mise-en-scène because of the restricted space of the location-shooting sets and that create the feeling of suffocation experienced by Ballestero. Again, whether Hitchcock uses a discontinuous style (as in *The Wrong Man*) or long takes is not of crucial importance to Chabrol and Rohmer: the selectivity of the camera is the same in either case, choosing what is filmed not to reflect reality but to convey ideas through narrative.

Chabrol and Rohmer's analysis of *To Catch a Thief* demonstrates perfectly that what they value in Hitchcock transcends the montage versus mise-en-scène distinction. Although they claim that the film contains no "well-defined formal challenge," it is characterized by an "abundance of cinematic set pieces" (pp. 130–1). They concentrate on three, and each instance reveals a different aspect of the director's manipulation of reality by the camera. The first is the image of Jesse Royce Landis stubbing her cigarette out in an egg: the camera captures – and emphasizes – an apparently arbitrary gesture that would normally not be noticed, but here it conveys an aspect of Landis's character which could never be described verbally. Chabrol and Rohmer even find a metaphysical significance in the image: "it expresses the idea of the inimicalness, of the fundamental resistance, of things" (p. 132). The second example is the famous cross-cutting between the lovers played by Cary Grant and Grace Kelly and the fireworks, the use of montage to create a metaphor for sexual intercourse, fulfilling Eisenstein's theories with what they call "lightness and humor" (p. 132). Finally, the two critics stress the impact of Hitchcock's use of ellipsis: the fireworks scene is almost immediately followed by the image of Grace Kelly entering Cary Grant's room and demanding the return of her mother's jewels: "It is as if we were emerging from a heavy sleep, which seems to have lasted only a second. Suddenly we are aware of all the time that's gone by. The liaison is extremely simple, but somebody had to have the audacity to think of it" (p. 133). Considering the importance of jump cuts and other elliptical techniques in the films of the *nouvelle vague*, we can understand the enthusiasm of these emerging filmmakers for Hitchcock's manipulation of time in this scene.

Thus a look back at *Hitchcock: The First Forty-Four Films* is a useful practice at this moment in the development of Hitchcock studies, for the first book-length study of the director's work contains far more formal analysis than what is generally supposed. Certainly, it returns again and again to the "exchange of guilt" concept, one deeply rooted in the authors' theological adherence to the notion of original sin. Yet more importantly the text contains an impressive and valuable examination of Hitchcock's creation of an original cinematic language. In their discussion of narration in the director's films and its relation to both decoupage and symbolism, Chabrol and Rohmer established an alternative critical method that supersedes the Eisenstein/Murnau dichotomy and subordinates both montage and mise-en-scène to the selectivity of the director's camera in the process of creating a narrative. It seems to me that both criticism and theory would benefit from considering the implications of this approach, for the relation of narratology to visual style needs to be reviewed and expanded from multiple perspectives. Historically the book is also fascinating in that it defines a moment in film criticism when auteurism was compelled to establish definite critical standards to support the critics' enthusiasm for certain directors, and in particular the enthusiasm among the younger *Cahiers* writers for Hitchcock. Chabrol and Rohmer established standards in their book that supplement Bazin's ideas about realism with a "narratological" realism. It was not a question of supplanting Welles with Hitchcock, but instead a quest to establish Hitchcock as an artist who belongs in the same pantheon of cinematic authorship.

Notes

1   André Bazin, *Orson Welles*, New York: Harper & Row, 1978, p. 65.
2   Eric Rohmer and Claude Chabrol, *Hitchcock: The First Forty-Four Films*, trans. Stanley Hochman, New York: Ungar Publishing Co., 1979, p. 95; Originally published in

1957. Subsequent citations appear in parentheses in the text.

3   André Bazin, "The Evolution of the Language of Cinema," in *What is Cinema?*, vol. 1, ed. and trans Hugh Gray, Berkeley: University of California Press, 1967.

4   Bazin, "The Evolution of the Language of Cinema,", p. 24.

5   Bazin, "The Evolution of the Language of Cinema," p. 28.

6   Bazin, "The Evolution of the Language of Cinema," p. 31.

7   Bazin, *Orson Welles*, p. 80.

8   Robin Wood, *Hitchcock's Films Revisited*, New York: Columbia, 1989, p. 207.

9   Wood, *Hitchcock's Films Revisited*, p. 209.

Chapter 8

HITCHCOCK WITH DELEUZE

Sam Ishii-Gonzáles

Is there any doubt that Hitchcock's stature (both in academia and without) is largely due to the French? Not only did the critics and future filmmakers at *Cahiers du cinéma* first accord him the status of "auteur" – culminating in the first book-length study of the director: Rohmer and Chabrol's 1957 monograph *Hitchcock* (wittily referred to, fifteen years later, as the "original sin" of Hitchcock criticism)[1] – but Raymond Bellour's textual analysis of *North by Northwest*, *Psycho*, and *The Birds* in the late sixties and early seventies helped introduce a cluster of themes and methodological issues that inspired and perplexed cinema scholars for years to follow. This essay will consider another French reading of Hitchcock, one that has not yet received much attention in the Anglo-American world, although this appears about to change. I refer here to the commentary on Hitchcock found in the French philosopher Gilles Deleuze's two-volume study, *Cinema 1:The Movement-Image* and *Cinema 2:The Time-Image* (translated into English in 1986 and 1989, respectively). With interest in Deleuze's writings on the rise this seems a particularly opportune moment to review his philosophy of film and the privileged place he accords Hitchcock's work in this system.[2] The first half of the chapter will elaborate upon the general parameters of Deleuze's semiotics. The second will illustrate his claims through a consideration of several Hitchcock films, including *Rear Window*, *The Wrong Man*, and *Vertigo*. It is this trio of works, I will suggest, which most clearly exemplify the arguments set forth in Deleuze.

"Hitchcock is at the juncture of the two cinemas, the classical that he perfects and the modern that he prepares."[3] Which is to say that Hitchcock, for Deleuze, is at the juncture, or *is* the juncture, between the two representational systems that characterize the ninety-year history of cinema and which he calls the movement-image and the time-image.

To understand what Deleuze means by these terms we need first to consider his engagement with the philosophy of Henri Bergson, especially *Matter and Memory* (1896) and *Creative Evolution* (1907). Deleuze, in fact, begins *Cinema 1* with one of four chapter-length exegeses of Bergson (two chapters in each volume). He does so because he sees an important affinity between the cinema and Bergson's philosophical project: both are concerned with the nature of time and movement.[4] As Deleuze says in response to a question regarding the link for him between philosophy and film: "I liked those authors who demanded that we introduce movement to thought, 'real' movement (they denounced the Hegelian dialectic as abstract movement). How could I not discover the cinema, which introduces 'real' movement into the image?"[5] Of the authors who "introduce movement to thought," for Deleuze it is Bergson who most directly addresses the issue as a philosophical problem.

For Bergson, movement is an expression of change or becoming. It is continuous, qualitative variation and is experienced as such in time or duration (*durée*). Movement and time affirm the impermanence of being, the heterogeneity and mobility of life. This conception is radically dissimilar to the one that typifies much of Western thought (from ancient philosophy to modern physics).[6] This dominant model treats movement and time as analogues to space – i.e., as calculable, quantitative sets. Reality is reduced, is believed reducible, to a series of mathematical points, standardized units of measure to be applied mechanically, a priori.[7] What is presumed, Bergson argues, is that movement can be reconstituted through an analysis of instants (of time) or positions (in space). Think here, for instance, of the paradoxes of motion proposed by Zeno (fifth century BC). Zeno's paradoxes exemplify the tendency of the intellect to abstract reality, to impose a "mental diagram of infinite divisibility" on the flux of reality, to render static or immobile that which is in constant movement or motion.[8] It is this proclivity that leads Bergson to describe consciousness as *subtractive*. We retain only those aspects of the material world that serve our practical needs. At the same time, we mistake this subtracted portion as the whole of reality. This is perhaps the most pernicious effect of our inclination to spatialize time: abstract movement and time are considered real, while concrete movement and time are construed as illusory (e.g., the Platonic distinction between Intelligible and Sensible realms).

But movement and time, Bergson contends, is neither homogenous nor divisible. It is a process whose outcome is neither predetermined nor absolute. As he says of Achilles' arrow, "although we can divide at will the trajectory once created, we cannot divide its creation, which is an act in progress and not a thing."[9] While the arrow is in movement, while it completes its course and its duration unfolds, the event is *virtual* – open to change, alteration, becoming. Let's consider a second example (one even more relevant to our purposes). Bergson contrasts the task of reconstructing a picture puzzle with the act of painting. In the first, the picture is *assembled* rather than *created*. The act of constructing the puzzle has become habituated and no longer entails a specific duration: "theoretically, [it] does not require any time. That is because the result is given. It is because the picture is already created, and because to obtain it requires only a work of recomposing or rearranging." What of the second? Here we cannot say that time (time of the event) is superfluous: "to the artist who creates a picture ... time is no longer an accessory; it is not an interval that may be lengthened or shortened without the content being altered. The duration of his work is part and parcel of his work. To contract or dilate it would be to modify both the psychical evolution that fills it and the invention which is its goal."[10] Furthermore, no one – not even the artist himself – can calculate in advance the result of his endeavors, for the painter is not removed from the act of painting but is intimately bound up with its creation. It is this form of time that interests Bergson (time as transformation or becoming) and it is this form of time that cannot be thought in abstract mechanics.[11]

Now, Bergson does not dispute the practical efficacy of scientific rationality or its axioms. What he does question is their *philosophical* value. There is a necessary distinction, for Bergson, between useful (effective) action and knowledge. Hence, his definition of metaphysics as "mind striving to transcend the conditions of useful action."[12] So how then can we move beyond the reified views that characterize our normal perception?[13] How can we be made to "see" movement and time? Bergson argues that this experience of duration is only grasped intuitively through acts of philosophical or artistic creation – acts that allow us to experience other durations than the ones which suffuse our daily acts and perceptions (circumscribed by what he evocatively calls "the rhythm of necessity"). While we are reading a philosophical text, for instance, it is the process of thought – the emergence of a thesis, its subsequent development and transformation – to which we become attuned. And just as the painter (in our example above) is not detached from the act of painting, neither is the reader simply external to the philosopher's thoughts during the act of reading. Indeed, to the extent that the writer's ideas generate a movement or counter-rhythm, it would be more accurate to say that these ideas inhabit the reader than the reverse. In a Bergsonian intuition of time we experience – as Deleuze writes – a movement that is not our own: "Intuition is ... the movement by which we emerge from our own duration ... to recognize the existence of other durations, above or below us."[14]

With this discussion in mind, it shouldn't be difficult for us to understand how Deleuze's philosophical interest in "real movement" might lead him to a consideration of the cinema. As he points out at the beginning of his study, film is "an ensemble of time relations"[15] and this ensemble generates a movement-image: movement as mobile section of duration. Deleuze, ironically, has to develop this thesis contra Bergson since the latter viewed motion pictures as merely the latest attempt to quantify movement and abstract time (see section four of *Creative Evolution* titled "The Cinematographical Mechanism of Thought and the Mechanistic Illusion"). Bergson's objection, however, is rather easily overcome. As Deleuze points out, Bergson's comments on the cinema are made in 1907 and thus need to be understood as a reference to early cinema with its fixed camera, single-take aesthetic, and its audience engrossed in the simulation of movement. It is in this nascent period that a convincing link can still be made between the motion picture and the motion studies of Marey and Muybridge.[16] Deleuze is more than willing to concede that early ("primitive") cinema has not yet discovered a movement-image. As he puts it, "the image is in movement rather than being movement-image" (*C1*, p. 24). However, this is no longer the case as soon as filmmakers begin to discover more complex forms of movement: the movement generated by the moving camera, by multiple points of view and montage (movement generated through the assemblage of shots). Deleuze writes, "because Bergson only considered what happened in the apparatus (the homogeneous abstract movement of the procession of images) he believed the cinema to be incapable of that which the apparatus is in fact most capable, eminently capable of: the movement-image – that is, pure movement extracted from bodies or moving things" (*C1*, p. 23). At this point the comparison between cinema and, say, photography (or motion studies) becomes untenable, for the latter drains movement from the event – presenting objects and events as immobile sections – while cinema shows us "the thing itself caught in movement."[17] Hence, while a photograph or a series of photographs might serve to illustrate Zeno's paradoxes, film would instantly falsify them by showing how they are impossible to prove as soon as duration is added to the event. Once the cinema learns how to extract and execute movement, it no longer consists of "immobile sections of movement" but, rather, "movement as mobile section." The cinema shows us how the objects and events it depicts are transformed, put into variation or translation, by a series of movement-images.

Deleuze gives as an example the scene in *Frenzy* of Babs and Bob Rusk walking to his apartment. The rhythm created by the montage of shots, by the interplay of sound and silence (the irony of Rusk's line, "a girl like you should travel … see the world"), by the movements of the actors and the camera – the zoom-in on Babs as she momentarily hesitates outside the bar, the tracking shot as Babs and Bob walk through the fruit and vegetable warehouse, the climb up a flight of stairs, the silent retreat of the camera after they enter the apartment – combine to give the sequence its specific power. These series of movements, as Deleuze writes, "[express] something in the course of happening" and that something is the extinguishing of life (*C1*, p. 19). An even better example it seems to me can be found in *Rope,* with its elaborate camera movements conjoined to extreme long takes (the film consists of eleven shots with an average shot length of seven-and-a-half minutes). As V.F. Perkins writes, the suspense of the film, its almost unbearable sense of claustrophobia, is a function both of its extended takes and its increasing restriction of the camera's movement – from a free movement between sitting room, hallway and dining room, to a restricted movement within the confines of the sitting room, and then the cessation of movement in the final minutes of the film.[18] The winding path of the camera makes manifest as well the way in which the transfer of guilt comes to bind one conscience to another (Rupert's "guilt" is nowhere more evident than at the moment when the camera, replicating the trajectory of Rupert's thoughts, "re-enacts" Brandon's and Philip's murder). André Bazin is correct when he says that Hitchcock's use of long takes and staging in depth is qualitatively different from that found in Welles or in the films of the neorealists; however, he is in error when he claims that Hitchcock could have used conventional continuity editing techniques to produce the same film. As Perkins demonstrates, the rhythm of the work (and the meaning this rhythm generates) would be completely altered by substituting analytic break-down for mobile frame. He reminds us as well of the link that Hitchcock forges between character and camera movement so that the latter comes to mimic the psychology of the central characters: Brandon's "arrogant exhibitionism," Philip's "submissiveness" and Rupert's "tentative and fearful probings."[19]

Hitchcock's experimentation with long takes and intricate camera movements gains even more poignancy in his next film, *Under Capricorn,* because of the way these movements are imbricated in the work's central theme: a married couple, Henrietta and Sam Flusky, whose love has become petrified, frozen in the past. When Henrietta, dead to the present, is confronted by a figure from her youth, "a very old friend," she hesitates, uncertain whether he is a subjective vision or an actual dinner guest at her table. Here the windings of the camera conjoined to extended takes underline the distance that separates the couple from one another – they were lost to each other somewhere in the past – but also from the "old friend" Adair and the other characters. These movements indicate a series of obstacles or distances – horizontal movements which convey the debilitating effects of time and memory, vertical movements which remind us (or remind them) of the social gap that "properly" links Henrietta to Adair, and Sam, a former stable boy, to the maid who secretly loves him – which the couple must traverse or overcome to find one another.

Although Deleuze begins *Cinema 1* by disputing the link between film and "the immobile sections + abstract movement" which characterize scientific rationality, this does not necessarily mean that the mobile sections of duration found in the classical cinema immediately allow for an intuition of time in the Bergsonian sense. This is why Deleuze proposes two regimes of cinematographic signs: movement-images and time-images. These two regimes are distinguished by different qualities of duration. Consider Keith Ansell Pearson's description of *durée*: "Duration is experience (it is something lived if not adequately intuited), but equally it is experience enlarged and gone beyond, that is, beyond our dominant habits of representation."[20] The movement-image of classical cinema, we could say, fulfills only the first part of the definition. Here the experience of duration is inadequately intuited: it remains circumscribed by habit or convention. The first volume is thus primarily concerned with demonstrating how the cinema's potential for evoking time and change is circumscribed by a series of rules or procedures that stabilize the flux of movement-images. Think here for instance of the rules of continuity editing and how they establish a "logical" procedure for the linkage of shots. The movement and time generated by this arrangement of shots is predictable, "normal." (We could say that the rules of continuity editing allowed not only film production to become routinized but film viewing as well.) As Rodowick notes, the main types of images derived from the movement-image – what Deleuze calls perception-, affection-, and action-images – function to "direct movement to a discernible cause, trajectory, or point of view."[21] Nowhere is this more evident than in the "action-image" that, as Rodowick suggests, completes the set of movement-images. For while all films combine perceptive, affective, and active movements, the dominant form in classical cinema is the action-image. "The cinema of action depicts sensory-motor situations: there are characters, in a certain situation, who act, perhaps even violently, according to how they perceive the situation. Actions are linked to perceptions and perceptions develop into actions."[22] The focus here is on modes of behavior, and the passage from situations to actions (the bodily response to external stimuli); the conversion of percepts and affects into the embodied perceptions (viewpoints) and affections (emotions) of individuated characters.

The classical cinema thus comes in its own way to duplicate the subtractive tendencies of a situated intentional consciousness. A center of reference develops to constrain the flux of movement-images. This argument returns us to Bergson's critique of the motion picture but with a subtle, and important, difference. While Bergson would argue that film by its very nature is able only to produce the reified perceptions of normal consciousness, Deleuze argues that it does so with great effort – through the implementation of a series of rules for how to compose and arrange the flow of shots. It is only in the modern cinema, however that we find filmmakers willing to experiment with aberrant (unconstrained) movement and new modes of duration. (Here time will be treated as an unknown quality – to be invented or released – rather than the conventional image of time generated in classical cinema.) This modern cinema is the focus of volume two of Deleuze's study. Nevertheless, there are traces throughout *Cinema 1* of an alternate movement and time that is only partly suppressed by the formal strategies of classical cinema. It is here in fact that we find Deleuze's Hitchcock, not quite classical and not quite modern.

So what does Deleuze mean when he says that Hitchcock is at the juncture of the two regimes? According to Deleuze, Hitchcock perfects and moves beyond the classical through the invention of a new type of image, alternately called mental-image and relation-image. "Inventing the mental image or the relation-image, Hitchcock makes use of it in order to close the set of action-images, and also of perception and affection images. Hence his conception of the frame. And the mental image not only frames the others, but transforms them by penetrating them. For this reason, one might say that Hitchcock accomplishes and brings to completion the whole of the [classical] cinema by pushing the movement-image to its limit" (*C1*, p. 204). In Hitchcock we still find perceptions and affections actualized in the embodied perceptions and affections of characters but rather than elide the process of actualization, or naturalize it, he makes this process – the becoming-actual of percepts and affects – the object of an image. (According to Bergson there is a "point of indetermination" which results from our contact with material reality and which occasions an interval, a temporal gap, between a received action and an executed response. Hitchcock, we could say, dwells on this indeterminate point whereas the action-image elides it or masks it by natu-ralizing both the action and the response.) There is thus a shift from physical acts to mental ones. More and more emphasis is placed on the functions of thought. "In Hitchcock, actions, affections, perceptions, all is interpretation, from begin-ning to end" (*C1*, p. 200).

It is in this context that Deleuze suggests an inspired link between Hitchcock's cinema and the concept of signs proposed by the American philosopher-logician Charles Sanders Peirce. (It is from the latter that Deleuze derives the alternate name "relation-image.") Peirce claims that meaningful signs contain a relation between three parts: sign, signified, and interpretant. If we say for instance that the sound of a bell is a sign that the ice-cream vendor is on the street selling his wares, it is because the relation of sign to object (bell = ice-cream vendor) has been established by or for a third (e.g., a small child). Similarly, if stripped bark is a sign that the woods are inhabited by deer (stripped bark = deer) it is because this relation has meaning for a third, in this case a hunter. Thought, in each case, is the result of an interpretative relation drawn between object and sign.[23] "Peirce's theory, based on an analysis of thought rather than language (in the narrow, verbal sense), posits within the signifying process not only an object and its sign but also a third element, the interpretant, or thought, to which the sign gives rise."[24] This is what Deleuze means when he emphasizes the importance of relations (or thirdness) in Hitchcock's cinema: Hitchcock doesn't merely give us objects and their signs but the interpretant or thought, the mental-image, which they generate.[25]

Let's consider an example. *Rear Window* is a film about how a man, L.B. Jeffries, comes to interpret a series of signs – three late night trips in the rain with a suitcase; a knife and saw wrapped in newspaper; an alligator purse and three rings – as an indication that a crime has been committed: Lars Thorwald has murdered his wife. If Hitchcock leaves us uncertain for two-thirds of the film whether a real crime has occurred it is exactly because his focus is on the mental process whereby Jeff comes to believe that a crime has taken place. (As Lisa says to Jeff, "Tell me everything you saw *and what you think it means*.") What Hitchcock wishes us to understand is that Jeff's interpretation is driven by his own desire to demonstrate that marriage can lead one to commit desperate, even criminal, acts. In other words, if Thorwald is proven a wife-murderer, then Jeffries is justi-fied in remaining unattached, a permanent bachelor. That Hitchcock wishes to make perceptible the functions of thought is evident from the filmmaker's own comments on *Rear Window* in an article that he wrote in 1968 when he explains, "it's composed largely of Mr. Stewart as a character in one position in one room looking onto his courtyard. So what he sees is a mental process blown up in his mind from the purely visual."[26] As Bill Krohn points out, it was the director himself who came up with the idea of having the neighbors serve as mirror reflections of Jeffries's own fears and desires. (In the Cornell Woolrich short story upon which the film is based, the protagonist has no profession, no girl-friend, and there is no emphasis, dramatic or psychological, placed on his neighbors.)[27] Not only does Hitchcock show us how Jeffries comes to attribute meaning to what he sees, but also how he erroneously interprets other signs and objects. For example, he misinterprets Miss Lonelyhearts sitting to write a letter as a sign that she is *not* planning to commit suicide, even though such an act is typically taken to have the exact opposite meaning. Jeffries's error serves as a sign of his indifference to events that have no immediate bearing on his own interests. The latter becomes a sign for the viewer, now actively involved in the process of semiosis, the production of meaning.[28] (For Hitchcock, the spectator must also be inscribed within the fabric of relations. Hence, the director's version of suspense which is based on the co-efficient to involve, to implicate.)

If the mental-image is the culmination of the classical cinema, bringing it to a limit point, as Deleuze suggests, I would argue that it functions in this way for Hitchcock as well. In other words, the mental-image does not emerge *ex nihilo* but is developed and perfected by Hitchcock over a course of several decades. (*Rear Window* was Hitchcock's fortieth feature film.) This is not to say, of course, that we don't find traces of the mental-image in his early work. When Hitchcock says that it's the task of the filmmaker – not the actor or the screenwriter – to show us what a character truly thinks or feels, he is already pointing us toward a cinema of thought. Discussing the scene in *Sabotage* (1936) when Mr. Verloc is killed in a confrontation with his wife, Hitchcock tells Truffaut, "The wrong way to go about this scene would have been to have the heroine convey her inner feelings to the audience by her facial expression. I'm against that. In real life, people's faces don't reveal what they think or feel. As a film director I must try to convey this woman's frame of mind to the audience by purely cinematic means."[29] (In this sequence we come to understand the process whereby the knife becomes a sign of retribution first for the wife and then for the husband.) For Hitchcock, "pure cinema" can convey not only acts or emotions but also the mechanisms of thought. Deleuze reiterates this point when he suggests that it is Hitchcock's camera that establishes the mental-image. Describing the opening crane shots in *Rear Window* – which pan around the courtyard and search Jeffries's apartment as he sleeps – Deleuze writes, "It is the camera, and not the dialogue, which *explains* why" (*C1*, p. 201).

That Hitchcock achieves his goal of pure cinema (and the realization of a mental-image) in the late forties and fifties does not require a mystificatory explanation. Hitchcock's long-term contract with producer David O. Selznick ends at a time (1947) when a major upheaval has already begun to undermine some of the core assumptions of classical cinema (e.g., the Italian neorealist use of locations, non-professionals, and elliptical narrative; Welles's re-discovery of the long take and depth of field). Not only does Hitchcock gain his artistic independence but is allowed to keep it because of dramatic shifts in the production and distribution policies of the classical studio system. Hitchcock also establishes a working crew in this period, including the cinematographer Robert Burks, the editor George Tomasini, and the composer Bernard Herrmann. All of these factors encouraged the filmmaker to continue with and extend his own experiments in pure cinema. *Rear Window* (1954), *The Wrong Man* (1957), and *Vertigo* (1958) each display this increased refinement of Hitchcock's aesthetic, and it is these works which most clearly reside in the juncture or gap between the movement-image and the time-image.[30]

Of the three, *The Wrong Man* has received the *least* amount of attention by a considerable margin. The lack of critical attention is quite remarkable considering the voluminous literature on Hitchcock in general and the quality of the film in particular. Students often find the film's somber tone and slow pacing baffling. To many it seems atypical or even non-Hitchcockian. Yet *The Wrong Man* is very much in keeping with Hitchcock's aesthetic preoccupations of this period. Like *Rear Window* (which precedes it by three years) and *Vertigo* (immediately to follow), *The Wrong Man* continues Hitchcock's experiments with a cinema of thought. Indeed, one could claim that these films function as a trilogy of sorts, each focused to a remarkable degree on the perceptual experiences of a character that happens to be, in each case, a (passive) male figure. By "remarkable" I refer to the extraordinary reliance on point-of-view cutting. The percentage of shots that replicate the perceptual subjectivity of the protagonist is extreme, even for Hitchcock. As the filmmaker says to Truffaut, "The whole approach is subjective."[31] (I will qualify this notion of the purely subjective below. Suffice to say for now that this general description of *The Wrong Man* applies just as well to *Rear Window* and *Vertigo*.)

The passivity that characterizes each of the protagonists – Jeffries in *Rear Window*, Manny Balestrero in *The Wrong Man*, and Scottie in *Vertigo* – allows us to draw a distinction between them as well. For the passivity of Manny Balestrero (Henry Fonda) in *The Wrong Man* is less grounded in the diegesis than the characters played by James Stewart in *Rear Window* (bound to a wheelchair, his right leg in a cast) or *Vertigo* (suffering from acrophobia, wearing a corset) and thus brings us even closer to one of the key traits for Deleuze of the modern cinema: "This is a cinema of the seer and no longer of the agent" (*C2*, p. 2). The generic movement that extends perceptions and affections into actions is blocked or delayed. The dispersive or fragmentary is no longer suppressed or sublimated. A new emphasis is placed on seeing and hearing, on pure optical and aural signs (*opsigns* and *sonsigns*). Perception is severed "from its motor extension," affection "from adherence or belonging to characters," and action "from the thread which joined it to situation" (*C1*, p. 215). The characters hesitate, uncertain of how to act or even if they can act. The situation "is no longer sensory-motor, as in [classical] realism, but primarily optical and of sound, invested by the senses, before action takes shape in it" (*C2*, p. 4). Think here, for instance, of the protagonists of neorealism (e.g., Ricci in *Bicycle Thieves*, or the women played by Ingrid Bergman in Rossellini's *Europa '51* or *Voyage to Italy*) or the characters found in Antonioni or Bresson. No longer merely "the subject of movement or instrument of action," these characters encounter a world that remains inassimilable to reified modes of seeing or feeling or being (*C2*, p. xi).

Deleuze, in his comments on *Rear Window*, notes a similarity between Hitchcock's immobile protagonist ("he is reduced as it were to a purely optical situation")[32] and the characters who populate the modern cinema, but he also wishes to make clear the difference that keeps Hitchcock from completely crossing over the divide from classical to modern. The difference is this: Hitchcock provides a narrative rationale for the passivity of his photographer protagonist, whereas the modern cinema removes this diegetic support. (Indeed what happens in Rossellini is that the reality which immobilizes the characters often threatens to erode the distinction between the diegetic and non-diegetic itself – what is a part of the fictional universe and what is not. For example, the tuna fishing sequence in *Stromboli*.) However, it is exactly this kind of narrative explanation that is missing in *The Wrong Man*. Through the course of the film,

Manny remains a passive witness to the nightmarish events in which his life becomes ensnared: his (false) arrest for a series of petty robberies; the subsequent mental breakdown of his wife Rose, reduced by story's end to a state of catatonia. Deleuze's description of the protagonist of modern cinema – "He shifts, runs and becomes animated in vain, the situation he is in outstrips his motor capacities on all sides, and makes him see and hear what is no longer subject to the rules of a response or an action. He records rather than reacts. He is prey to vision, pursued by it or pursuing it, rather than engaged in an action" (*C2*, p. 3) – perfectly describes Manny Balestrero: *he records rather than reacts*.[33] His passivity brings a new dimension to Hitchcock's use of the optical point of view, for while *The Wrong Man* uses the same subjective techniques that we find in his other works of the period, it is neither employed to generate suspense nor to lure the spectator into an identification with the protagonist.[34] Tom Gunning, in comparing the style of Hitchcock to Fritz Lang, has argued that while Lang insists on the primacy of space (prior to its habitation by a character), Hitchcock builds his scenes "out of a character's (or sometimes characters') point of view, sculpting the space with the viewpoint of the character." He suggests that this formal trait "reflects a stronger belief in the centrality of subjectivity."[35] *The Wrong Man* certainly exemplifies this claim on a technical level, but here the "centrality of subjectivity" produces an unexpected result: a disparity between the point of view and the subjectivity to whom they are meant to "belong."

This gap has been interpreted in several ways. Jean-Luc Godard in his 1957 review of the film for *Cahiers du cinéma* suggests that what Hitchcock wishes to convey by these point-of-view shots is the mind's inability to come to terms with what it sees – for example, when Manny is led into a prison cell and locked up for the first time, Godard argues that the series of point-of-view shots of what he perceives conveys that Manny has "strength enough only to see, to register." Manny is, in other words, "seeing without looking." His eyes objectively register the objects that surround him but he does not really see them. His mind is elsewhere, clouded with other thoughts – just as later, during the trial, "*he hears without looking*."[36] More recently, Renata Salecl has argued that the discord between the character and what he perceives is a sign of Manny's psychosis. This explains, according to Salecl, why Hitchcock's usual techniques of cinematic identification fail to create any suspense or involvement: the gap between Manny's perceptions and his subjectivity indicates that Manny himself is split; there is no genuine relation between what he sees and who he is.[37] An ingenious solution, no doubt, but is a solution what's required? (Moreover, one that assimilates everything that is strange, unresolved, and new in this work to recognizable Hitchcockian – or Lacanian – patterns?)

Geoffrey Nowell-Smith, writing about the character played by Monica Vitti in

Antonioni's *L'Avventura*, notes, "The audience is invited to share her point of view, but this point of view is not fully inhabited."[38] Manny Balestrero functions in a very similar way. One never has a sense that Manny fully inhabits (fully owns) the point of view from which he views the world. It is along these lines that one might wish to qualify Godard's reading of the prison cell and trial sequences – for while they seem perfectly plausible (even, inspired) descriptions of these individual scenes, they overlook the similarity between Manny's behavior at these moments and throughout the rest of the film. This is what Rohmer and Chabrol allude to when they suggest that the point-of-view shot in *The Wrong Man* is "only seemingly subjective": "Though we see things with Balestrero's own eyes … the protagonist remains outside us, just as he is outside himself."[39]

What is important about the passive characters that populate the modern cinema for Deleuze is that they allow the filmmaker to explore (or to open up) different connections between character and world. It seems to me that it is exactly this process of discovery that Hitchcock is invested in here. Hence, for example, the remarkable sequence detailing the process whereby Manny is detained, identified, charged, and locked-up for a series of neighborhood robberies. For nearly forty minutes plot gives way to something else: an emphasis on the minutiae of existence and the time between events. Rather than eliminate "insignificant" details they are given their own expressive value, such as the emptying of Manny's pockets (the contents placed, one by one, on the counter: change, pocketknife, rosary beads, plastic comb, six one-dollar bills, Rose's insurance policy), or the camera's focus (simulating Manny's point of view) on his fellow inmates' feet as they are handcuffed and driven to Long Island Jail.[40] That Godard, Truffaut, Chabrol and Rohmer each evoke Bresson (but also Dreyer and Rossellini) in their separate reviews of the film is neither surprising nor gratuitous. More importantly, none of them (in 1957) view this development in Hitchcock as an aberration but, rather, as the logical continuation of his interests. Truffaut: "it is probably his best film, the one that goes furthest in the direction he chose so long ago."[41]

Vertigo, unlike *The Wrong Man*, has achieved the status of a "classic." Yet we should not forget that, at the time of its release, Anglo-American critics and audiences were just as bewildered by *Vertigo* as they were by *The Wrong Man*. If the stronger generic conventions of *Vertigo* make the protagonist's passivity and opacity less difficult for the modern viewer, this should not lead one to overlook the fundamental strangeness of the film (viz., classical cinema): the "contemplative rhythm;"[42] the subordination of plot to situation; the long musical passages without dialogue (nearly thirty minutes consists simply of Scottie pursing Madeleine; the longest stretch without speech of any kind lasts ten-and-a-half minutes); the emphasis on pure opsigns and sonsigns (who watching the film ever forgets the green light that bathes Judy in a shimmering silhouette?).

Vertigo also extends Hitchcock's mental-image in a new direction by showing us how memory intervenes in the mechanism of thought. Here we witness the workings of a subconscious or unconscious memory on the male protagonist, this memory being not only Scottie's of Madeleine – which results in Judy's makeover during the last third of the film – but his memory of the policeman's death that draws him toward Madeleine in the first place. Does he believe that by saving Madeleine he can rewrite the past? Or is he drawn to her *because* she herself is drawn (or so he believes) to a death-by-falling? In fact, there is a radical ambiguity at the center of the text. Increasingly we realize that Scottie himself does not know exactly why he acts in the way that he does. (Until it is too late and we find ourselves at the same point of disequilibrium, as though we too are caught up in something that we cannot control.) Rather than master time and memory, Scottie finds himself ensnared in their vertiginous effects. The circuits that Scottie charts as he follows Madeleine in his car, the 360-degree turn that encircles Scottie and Judy-as-Madeleine: these are spatial *and* temporal signs of the delirium experienced by the protagonist.

> "We travel in space in the same way we travel in time, as our thoughts and the characters' thoughts also travel. They are only probing, or more exactly, spiraling into the past. Everything forms a circle, but the loop never closes, the revolution carries us ever deeper into reminiscence. Shadows follow shadows, illusions follow illusions, not like the walls that slide away or mirrors that reflect to infinity, but by a kind of movement more worrisome still because it is without a gap or break and possesses both the softness of a circle and the knife edge of a straight line."[43]

For Bergson, the process of memory affirms the complex temporal nature of human subjectivity. We are never simply "present" in the "here and now." Our reaction to external stimuli is mediated by different forms of memory (conscious and unconscious, *volontaire* and *involontaire*): the past is reactivated in a present that conditions the future. This complex layering of time illustrates how we are inhabited by time (rather than the other way round).[44] As Deleuze writes, "Time is not the interior in us, but just the opposite, the interiority in which we are, in which we move, live and change." He adds, "In the cinema, there are perhaps three films which show how we inhabit time, how we move in it, in this form which carries us away, picks us up and enlarges us": Dozvhenko's *Zvenigora*, Resnais's *Je t'aime je t'aime*, and Hitchcock's *Vertigo* (*C2*, p. 82). Although he declines to elaborate this claim (in fact, this is the sole reference to *Vertigo* found in *Cinema 2*), we might ask – based on it – why Deleuze maintains that Hitchcock is *beyond* the movement-image but *before* the time-image. If Hitchcock does not quite belong to the modern cinema it is, according to Deleuze, because he still conceives the cinema as an organic totality, a closed system. For Hitchcock, the mental-image is not a break from the perception–action–affection system but its complement and natural extension. It is a demonstration of the cinema's (and the filmmaker's) infinite reach and control, whereas the mental-image found in the modern cinema is "less a bringing to completion of the action-image, and of the other images, than a re-examination of their nature and status" (*C1*, p. 205). Here the mental-image is no longer contained in a closed textual system and the film-maker no longer claims to account for all the affects set in motion by the work. "It was necessary," Deleuze states, "to want what Hitchcock had constantly refused" (*C1*, p. 215).

Deleuze is correct, I think, to suggest that Hitchcock himself would resist the notion that every affect was not determined in advance. But the question is whether he is led to an unforeseen result regardless of intention. Does not the final shot of *Vertigo* – Scottie on the precipice, staring into the abyss – suggest a radical opening rather than closure?[45] Certainly the enormous amount of litera-ture that Hitchcock's films have generated (*Vertigo*, most of all) also suggests this: not a closed text or system but one whose ramifications continue to proliferate and expand with each passing decade.

Obviously, a great deal more can be said about these (and other) Hitchcock films in relation to the concepts of movement and time. That I have only skimmed the surface indicates the complexity and value of these concepts as they apply to Hitchcock and to cinema in general. One of the great strengths of Deleuze's cinema books is that the reader never has the sense that he is proposing an explanation that can be applied indiscriminately from one film to the next. (It is in this context that John Rajchman correctly suggests that Deleuze is "against theory.")[46] Rather, like the thinkers and artists whom he admires, Deleuze wishes to introduce movement to thought, to keep thought in movement. And, it seems to me, this is exactly what he achieves in his *Cinema* books (and exactly what cinema requires). Implicit in Deleuze's cinema books is not the claim that "the power of film is now explained" but the opposite: the power of cinema remains to be thought. Is this not why we return to a filmmaker like Hitchcock over and over again? Not to delineate (or contain) the power of cinema but to discover it?[47]

Notes

I would like to thank Richard Allen, Pavle Levi, and David Owens for their sound editorial advice.

1 Albert J. LaValley, "Introduction," in LaValley (ed.) *Focus on Hitchcock*, Englewood Cliffs, NJ: Prentice-Hall, 1972, p. 2. Pascal Bonitzer playfully argues, twelve years later, that the concept of the auteur itself had been "invented expressly by *Cahiers du cinéma* to honor Hitchcock." "The Skin and the Straw," reprinted in Slavoj i ek [ed.] *Everything You Always Wanted to Know About Lacan (But Were Afraid to Ask Hitchcock)*, trans. Martin Thom, London and New York: Verso, 1992, p. 179.

2 As Jon Beasley-Murray notes, Deleuze's cinema books were met with "incomprehension or mistrust" when first translated in the late eighties. This had to do with paradigm

the concept of the auteur itself had been "invented expressly by *Cahiers du cinéma* to honor Hitchcock." "The Skin and the Straw," reprinted in Slavoj Žižek [ed.] *Everything You Always Wanted to Know About Lacan (But Were Afraid to Ask Hitchcock)*, trans. Martin Thom, London and New York: Verso, 1992, p. 179.

2 As Jon Beasley-Murray notes, Deleuze's cinema books were met with "incomprehension or mistrust" when first translated in the late eighties. This had to do with paradigm shifts within Anglophone film studies (e.g. the shift towards historical research models; the shift from "difficult" modernist texts to works of popular culture) as well as Deleuze's dense or abstruse writing style. The past six years, in comparison, have shown a groundswell of interest in these works. Recent publications including the first book-length study of the *Cinema* books and the first collection of essays have focused exclusively on Deleuze and film. See D.N. Rodowick, *Gilles Deleuze's Time Machine,* Durham, NC and London: Duke University Press, 1997, and Gregory Flaxman (ed.) *The Brain is the Screen: Deleuze and the Philosophy of Cinema*, Minneapolis and London: University of Minnesota Press, 2000, respectively. The Beasley-Murray reference is found in "Whatever Happened to Neorealism? – Bazin, Deleuze, and Tarkovsky's Long Take," *Iris* 23, spring 1997, p. 39. This issue of *Iris* is focused exclusively on Deleuze's film theory.

3 Gilles Deleuze, *Cinema 1: The Movement-Image*, trans. Hugh Tomlinson and Barbara Habberjam, Minneapolis: University of Minnesota Press, 1986, p. x. Originally published in 1983. Hereafter cited as *C1* in the text.

4 For Deleuze, there can be no genuine understanding of the powers of cinema without a consideration of its status as a moving image, an image with a specific duration in time. (This may seem commonsensical but, in fact, there are remarkably few theories of film that actually consider these qualities of the cinematic sign.) It is in this context that Deleuze rejects the attempts by Christian Metz and others to establish a linguistically-based film semiology whereby the shot becomes equivalent to an utterance, etc.

5 Gilles Deleuze, "The Brain is the Screen: An Interview with Gilles Deleuze," in Flaxman, *The Brain Is the Screen*, p. 366.

6 While the seventeenth-century physics of Descartes, Kepler, Newton is a paradigm for Bergson of this type of abstract reasoning he also recognized and was responsive to the innovations in mathematics and science that emerged in his own time. Bergson, let us not forget, is writing in a period in which many of the axioms of scientific theory are being questioned or undermined, e.g., Riemann's challenge to Euclidean geometry, and Einstein's revision of Newton's laws of gravitational motion. Bergson himself was originally trained in mathematics (his first publication appeared in *Nouvelles Annales de Mathématiques* in 1878).

7 "The universe became a system of points, the position of which was rigorously determined at each instant by relation to the preceding instant and theoretically calculable for any moment whatever." Henri Bergson, *Creative Evolution*, trans. Arthur Mitchell, Mineola, New York: Dover, 1998, p. 348.

8 Keith Ansell Pearson, *Philosophy and the Adventure of the Virtual: Bergson and the Time of Life*, London and New York: Routledge, 2002, p. 24.

9 Bergson, *Creative Evolution*, p. 309.

10 Bergson, *Creative Evolution*, p. 340.

11 By placing emphasis on difference or becoming, Bergson wishes to problematize the notion that consciousness is extrinsic to the force of change or that subjectivity somehow precedes or exceeds its existence in time. As Pearson writes, "it is not simply that time is *in us* but rather that we are, and we become, *in it*" (*Philosophy and the Adventure of the Virtual*, p. 168).

12 Henri Bergson, *Matter and Memory*, trans. Nancy Margaret Paul and W. Scott Palmer, New York: Zone Books, 1991, p. 15.

15 Deleuze, "The Brain is the Screen," p. 371.

16 For more on this relation see Rodowick, *Gilles Deleuze's Time Machine*, pp. 9–11.

17 Gilles Deleuze, *Cinema 2: The Time-Image*, trans. Hugh Tomlinson and Robert Galeta, Minneapolis: University of Minnesota Press, 1989, p. 27; originally published in 1985. Hereafter cited as *C2* in the text.

18 V.F. Perkins, "*Rope*," *Movie* 7, February–March 1963, p. 12.

19 Perkins, "*Rope*," p. 12. The rhythmic quality of the film is also discussed in Peter Wollen, "Three Hypotheses," in Richard Allen and S. Ishii-Gonzáles (eds.) *Hitchcock Centenary Essays*, London: BFI, 1999, pp. 75–85.

20 Pearson, *Philosophy and the Adventure of the Virtual*, p. 9.

21 Rodowick, *Gilles Deleuze's Time Machine*, p. 36.

22 Gilles Deleuze, "On the Movement-Image," in *Negotiations 1972–1990*, trans. Martin Joughin, New York: Columbia University Press, 1995, p. 51. This interview (with Pascal Bonitzer and Jean Narboni) was originally published in *Cahiers du cinéma* in 1983. It provides an excellent introduction to Deleuze's project.

23 These examples are drawn, respectively, from Cornelis de Waal, *On Peirce*, Belmont, CA: Wadsworth/Thompson, 2001, p. 70, and Christopher Hookway, *Peirce*, London: Routledge & Kegan Paul, 1985, pp. 122–4. Admittedly, Deleuze's discussion of Peirce is threaded through the latter's complex notions of first, secondness, and thirdness but this should not obscure the essential point which is that, for Peirce, "the sign relation is triadic: signs exemplify thirdness" (Hookway, *Peirce*, p. 121). In other words, Peirce himself was mainly (if not exclusively) concerned with thirdness – which, according to Deleuze, can also be said of Hitchcock.

24 James Hoppes, Introduction to *Peirce on Signs: Writings on Semiotics by Charles Sanders Peirce*, ed. Hoppes, Chapel Hill and London: University of North Carolina Press, 1991, pp. 11–12.

25 Deleuze suggests that Rohmer and Chabrol's concept of "transfer of guilt" can be understood in terms of the relation-image: in Hitchcock, there is never simply an act and its perpetrator (a crime and a criminal) but a third for whom it is staged or who gives it its proper meaning (*C1*, p. 201).

26 Alfred Hitchcock, "*Rear Window*," in LaValley, *Focus on Hitchcock*, p. 40.

27 Bill Krohn, "The Uncertainty Principle," in *Hitchcock at Work*, London: Phaidon, 2000, pp. 132–47.

28 The difference between Hitchcock and Peirce, we might say, is that while the latter assumes that the interpretant sign is produced by or for a rational, reasonable being, Hitchcock does not. For Hitchcock, desire always intervenes in these relations. Our apprehension of the world, the meaning that we extract from (or impart to) the world, is mediated by desire. As Jean Douchet notes in his discussion of *Rear Window*, the logical process of induction and deduction gives way finally to something else, "to feelings of desire and fear" ("Hitch and His Audience," in Jim Hillier [ed.] *Cahiers du cinéma, 1960–1968: New Wave, New Cinema, Reevaluating Hollywood*, trans. David Wilson, Cambridge, MA: Harvard University Press, 1992, p. 151; originally published in *Cahiers du cinéma* in 1960).

29 François Truffaut, *Hitchcock*, revised edition, New York: Touchstone, 1985, p. 111.

30 For myself, Deleuze's statement that Hitchcock prepares for modern cinema makes most sense if by "modern cinema" we mean the sixties modernist cinema of Antonioni, Godard, Resnais, et al. Hitchcock's mental-image does not precede the innovations of Renoir or the neorealists or Welles but is contemporaneous with them.

31 Truffaut, *Hitchcock*, p. 239.

32 Deleuze, "On the Movement-Image," p. 51.

33 Eric Rohmer, in his 1959 review of *Vertigo*, suggests that this film forms a trilogy with *Rear Window* and *Man Who Knew Too Much*, each linked by the passivity of the James Stewart character: "the heroes are victims of a *paralysis* relative to movement in a

30 For myself, Deleuze's statement that Hitchcock prepares for modern cinema makes most sense if by "modern cinema" we mean the sixties modernist cinema of Antonioni, Godard, Resnais, et al. Hitchcock's mental-image does not precede the innovations of Renoir or the neorealists or Welles but is contemporaneous with them.

31 Truffaut, *Hitchcock*, p. 239.

32 Deleuze, "On the Movement-Image," p. 51.

33 Eric Rohmer, in his 1959 review of *Vertigo*, suggests that this film forms a trilogy with *Rear Window* and *Man Who Knew Too Much*, each linked by the passivity of the James Stewart character: "the heroes are victims of a *paralysis* relative to movement in a certain milieu" ("Alfred Hitchcock's *Vertigo*," in *The Taste for Beauty*, trans. Carol Volk, New York and Cambridge, UK: Cambridge University Press, 1989, p. 169). The Fonda character though seems far more intriguing to think about in relation to the Stewart characters in *Rear Window* and *Vertigo* – and in terms of "paralysis" – than the Stewart character in *The Man Who Knew Too Much*. In his review of *The Wrong Man*, Jean-Luc Godard links Manny Balestrero to L.B. Jeffries in their "semi-inertia" and Truffaut in his compares Manny to the protagonist of Bresson's *A Man Escaped*: "Henry Fonda is impassive, expressionless, almost immobile. Fonda is only a look." See Godard, review of *The Wrong Man*, in *Godard on Godard*, ed. and trans. Tom Milne, New York: Da Capo Press, 1972, p. 48, and Truffaut, "The Wrong Man," in *The Films of My Life*, trans. Leonard Maychew, New York: Touchstone, 1978, p. 85.

34 The strangeness of the point-of-view shot in *The Wrong Man* actually led Truffaut to mistakenly claim that the film was a move away from Hitchcock's usual technique of subjective narration: "We are at Fonda's side throughout, in his cell, in his home, in the car, on the street, but we are never in his place" ("The Wrong Man," p. 85).

35 Tom Gunning, *The Films of Fritz Lang: Allegories of Vision and Modernity*, London: BFI, 2000, p. 347.

36 Jean-Luc Godard, review of *The Wrong Man*, p. 50.

37 Renata Salecl, "The Right Man and the Wrong Woman," in Žižek, *Everything You Always Wanted to Know about Lacan*, pp. 185–94.

38 Geoffrey Nowell-Smith, *L'Avventura*, London: BFI, 1997, pp. 41–2.

39 Eric Rohmer and Claude Chabrol, "*The Wrong Man*," *Hitchcock: The First Forty-Four Films*, trans. Stanley Hochman, New York: Frederick Ungar, 1979, p. 151. Originally published in 1957.

40 Hitchcock, at one point during his interviews with Truffaut, asks, "why has it become old-fashioned to tell a story, to use a plot?" Rather than express disdain, however, he expresses allegiance: "nowadays, I'd prefer to build a film around a situation rather than a plot" (Truffaut, *Hitchcock*, p. 203).

41 Truffaut, "The Wrong Man," p. 86.

42 "*Vertigo* unfolds at a deliberate pace, with a contemplative rhythm that contrasts sharply with [his] other pictures, which are mostly based on swift motion and sudden transitions" (Truffaut, *Hitchcock*, p. 246).

43 Rohmer, "Alfred Hitchcock's *Vertigo*," p. 171.

44 Rodowick argues that the "memory-image" found in classical cinema is built on "contrast and opposition" – the present is affirmed by way of the past, memory is the result of a subjective recollection. The memory-image in modern cinema however expresses something quite different: "chiasmus and reversibility" – here temporal distinctions between past and present become difficult to discern and impossible to stabilize by way of an intentional consciousness. (See Rodowick, *Gilles Deleuze's Time Machine*, p. 91). Rodowick develops this argument in relation to the films of Resnais but I would suggest that "chiasmus and reversibility" is also what occurs in *Vertigo*. For a reading of the film developed along these lines, see Chris Marker, "A Free Replay (Notes on *Vertigo*)," in John Boorman and Walter Donahue (eds.), *Projections 4 1/2*, London and Boston: Faber & Faber, 1995, pp. 123–30. In this essay Marker – who made

La Jeteé in homage to *Vertigo* – even compares Hitchcock's film to Resnais's *Hiroshima, mon amour*.

45 We should not forget that the original denouement of *The Wrong Man* was meant to be just as uncertain. When Hitchcock first became attracted to the material Rose Balestrero was still confined in a mental hospital. Therefore, the original ending would have been the shot of Manny exiting her room and walking down a hospital corridor (a shot repeated half-way through *Vertigo* when Midge leaves Scottie in his hospital room) and not the tacked-on final shot of the reunited family now living in Miami, Florida. (This last image was shot by a second-unit crew and features stand-ins for Fonda, Miles and the two child actors.) Six years after the release of the film Hitchcock seems to have completely forgotten this denouement. He says to Truffaut, "as a result of all the trouble, [Rose] lost her mind and was put in an insane asylum. She's probably still there" (Truffaut, *Hitchcock*, p. 235).

46 John Rajchman, *The Deleuze Connection*, Cambridge, MA and London: MIT Press, 2000, p. 115.

47 For other essays which explore the Hitchcock–Deleuze connection see Joe McElhaney, "Touching the Surface: *Marnie*, Melodrama, Modernism' in Allen and Ishii-Gonzáles (eds.) *Hitchcock Centenary Essays*, pp. 87–105; Stojan Pelko, "*Punctum Caecum*, or, Of Insight and Blindness," in Žižek, *Everything You Always Wanted to Know about Lacan*, pp. 106–21; and Angelo Restivo, "Into the Breach: Between *The Movement-Image* and *The Time-Image*,' in Flaxman, *The Brain is the Screen*, pp. 171–92.

Part III

POETICS AND POLITICS OF IDENTITY

Chapter 9

MUSIC AND IDENTITY
The struggle for harmony in *Vertigo*

Daniel Antonio Srebnick

The word *harmony* is usually defined as, one, an agreeable sound, and, two, the adaptation of parts in any system or combination of things intended to form a connected, unified, and aesthetically pleasing whole. We refer to the harmony of a piece of music to indicate the aural integration and unification of its components, or to the harmony of a person to define how functional they are, or how well they fit in with their surroundings. Film with musical accompaniment is perhaps the most appropriate artistic medium in which to discuss both types of harmony because both film and music are temporal, and contain rhythm, tempo, tone, volume, balance, and melody;[1] and linked with film, music can enrich the psychological landscape of a visual narrative.[2] Because of the immediacy with which the viewer experiences these nonverbal aspects of cinematic narrative, film with musical accompaniment can ideally achieve a profound exploration of the specific problem of harmony in personal identity. In many of Alfred Hitchcock's films, music confirms such identity. In *The Thirty-Nine Steps*, the protagonist Hannay realizes that the melody he cannot stop whistling is the entrance theme for Mr. Memory, who knows the secret identity of a spy organization and who will thereby validate the protagonist's own identity and make possible his potential coupling with Pamela. In *The Lady Vanishes*, the protagonist Gilbert, a professional clarinetist and musicologist, must communicate a melody to the British Intelligence agency to uncover the identity of an even more ruthless spy operation; in the process, his own identity, and the greater harmony of his life, are enriched when, like Hannay, he too couples with a woman who is his emotional counterpoint, and who, herself, needs him to bring out her authentic identity.[3] An even more significant and integrated instance of music used in this way in Hitchcock occurs in the 1956 *The Man Who Knew Too Much* (Hitchcock's second version of this film and his second collaboration with composer Bernard Herrmann). The protagonist Jo MacKenna, played by the professional singer Doris Day, saves her son's life by singing the Jay Livingston song *Che Sera, Sera*. Interestingly, she must use the defining element of the old identity as a singer that she has shed – that is, her voice – to re-establish and exercise the defining characteristic of her new identity, that of the protective mother within her family. However, it is in *Vertigo*, with its Herrmann score, that the relationship between music and identity on every level reaches its greatest convergence, and artistically, its greatest success.

The collaboration between Hitchcock and Bernard Herrmann has been analyzed at some length, most notably by Royal S. Brown in his essay "Herrmann, Hitchcock, and the Music of the Irrational."[4] Beginning with *The Trouble with Harry* (1955) and ending with their acrimonious split over the score for *Torn Curtain*, Hitchcock and Herrmann collaborated on nine films[5] and created a body of work in which music and film formed an interdependent relationship that helped define Hitchcock's later œuvre. Brown astutely draws a parallel between the "irrational" world of Alfred Hitchcock's later films and their Herrmann scores. What Hitchcock does for narrative technique in the filmic medium, Herrmann does for film music by introducing many of the chromatic elements that had been explored by the twentieth-century musical avant-garde. As Brown suggests, Hitchcock's films use everyday reality as their point of departure in the same way that Herrmann's music departs from the Western musical principles upon which it is based. Herrmann, following upon the innovations of the musical avant-garde, challenges the sense of harmonious form that such Western musical standards attempt to establish. In *Vertigo*, Herrmann's exploration of complex harmonies, asymmetrical phrase structures, and unique orchestration (the process of arranging a piece of music for the orchestra by assigning notes to different instruments according to range, tone, dynamic, color, and balance) challenges the ear of listeners, thereby further enveloping them in the film's "irrational" world where everything, including identity, is removed from the domain of reason, understanding, and order.

In *Vertigo*, Hitchcock explores the identity conflicts of the film's two central characters: Scottie and Madeleine/Judy. As a result of Gavin Elster's plot to kill his wife, each of these figures is fractured into two separate identities: a "self" and an "alter ego," each struggling for ownership of their respective characters. There is Scottie, the retired detective as well as the obsessed lover; there is the fabricated Madeline, the "wife," as well as the possessed reincarnation of Carlotta Valdes; and there is Judy, the simple salesgirl from Kansas as well as the impostor Madeleine. As a result of these dual identities, the characters are unable to exist as individuals in harmony with themselves or with the social world in which they live. In the film's soundtrack, Herrmann sonically represents their psychological turmoil by introducing contrasting music that has stable tonal centers, such as the "love themes" and the source music that accompanies Midge's scenes, with dense chromatic music that has, or that resolves to, ambiguous tonal centers. Herrmann's prowess lies in his ability to musically underscore the narrative by harmonically, rhythmically, and orchestrationally (his unique combinations often feature two bass clarinets, two vibraphones with rapid tremolo, a Hammond organ with rapid tremolo, and three English horns) instilling a feeling of aural vertigo, literally the unbalance created by a disturbance his score produces in the equilibrium inside the ear of the listener. In so doing, he expands the viewer's role as a visual witness to the narrative to that of an involved and unsettled listener.

Each music composition has its identity confirmed by a theme, rhythm, and/or harmonic structure that is unconsciously felt as a harmonic center: the key or beat in which the composition is based. Every subsequent musical change (a new phrase, chord, beat, meter, or key) can be heard as a shift in sonic identity, an excursion or moment of development away from the harmonic center of the composition. No matter how long or unrelated the excursion may be, the natural tendency of the ear is to wait patiently for the music to resolve back to the harmonic center that it has grown accustomed to and with which it feels comfortable. We also obviously make some associations with what is heard. If a composition is based in a major key with abundant consonant harmonies and/or rhythms, we associate an emotionally affirming identity with the music. Conversely, if the piece is based in a minor key with dark harmonies and/or rhythms, we associate a somber identity with the music. In atonal music, music that uses all twelve pitches of the chromatic scale, the ear is actually situated by the lack of a tonal system. In other words, the atonality ironically becomes the stabilizing tonal system within the ear of the listener. In *Vertigo*, however, the harmonic identity of Herrmann's score is often so ambiguous that the music, like the characters in the film, struggles to find a stable tonal identity upon which it and the listener can comfortably rest. As a result, we feel that the film's chaotic world, the characters that it explores, are on the brink of disorder and, perhaps, destruction.

In an early scene, Gavin Elster describes his wife to Scottie in a way that parallels Herrmann's score. Elster states:

> She'll be talking to me about something, suddenly the words fade into silence. A cloud comes into her eyes and they go blank. She's somewhere else, away from me, someone I don't know. [I] call to her, she doesn't even hear me. Then with a long sigh, she's back. Looks at me, brightly, doesn't

even know she's been away. Can't tell me where or when ... And she wanders ... [She's] someone I [don't] know. She even walk[s] a different way ... [Sits] there a long time without moving.

Like Elster's troubled wife Madeleine, Herrmann's score seems to follow its own arbitrary and inscrutable path. It often builds into dramatic passages that seem to head towards large resolutions but wind up instead languishing in passages featuring ostinatos, clearly defined phrases that are repeated persistently (usually in immediate succession) while various harmonies and melodies are explored by the rest of the orchestra. There is also little order to the sequence of melodies, as tonal and orderly passages quickly become atonal and, at times, approach the chaotic. Yet melody does not seem to be Herrmann's main concern as he rarely establishes melodic phrases that last more than a measure or two in length. They are either repeated so extensively, or modulated in such rapid succession, that they fail to establish definitive or stable tonal centers. Rather, he focuses on the complex harmonies and textures of dense chords with numerous chromatic extensions (e.g., a raised ninth or eleventh), often voicing them ominously in the lower range of the orchestra, and stacking such chords and short motifs on top of one another to create unresolved harmonic tension.

The score of *Vertigo* can thus be divided into four separate areas: (1) dense chromatic music filled with frenetic motifs, arpeggios, and lush chords that rapidly modulate and often fail to resolve; (2) the passages featuring ostinatos that accompany many of the scenes in which Scottie follows Madeleine and Judy; (3) the lush romantic music of the love themes; and (4) the source music that Midge' plays on her stereo. The score alternates among these four musical directions, switching from one to another, often simultaneously exploring more than one, in an effort to establish a chromatic harmonic identity that will restore an order that is escaping the film's narrative.

The first of these categories, chromatic harmony, refers to the harmonic system that uses notes not present in the diatonic scale but which result from the subdivision of a diatonic whole tone into two semitonal intervals, e.g., of G-A into G-G# (the application of this principle to all five whole tones of the diatonic scale produces the chromatic scale, with twelve tones to the octave).[6] It was first extensively explored to great effect by modernist composers such as Wagner and Richard Strauss and, interestingly, coincided in its later incarnations with Sigmund Freud's early work on the unconscious. Like the psychological notion of the unconscious, chromatic harmony seems to delve into a subterranean harmonic world to express the sounds behind, between, and beneath the notes. Chromatic music can sound dreamlike, impressionistic, and/or romantic because melodies and harmonies fluidly develop by half steps (the shortest distance between two notes in the Western diatonic system) in unexpected directions.

Conversely, chromatic harmony can sound disconcerting and unstable because, like the difficulty in exploring one's own unconscious thoughts, the ear struggles with the tension created by the pitches of the chromatic scale. Furthermore, in chromatic music, the lack of harmonic restrictions allows melodies, harmonies, and rhythms to develop in a way that suggests an absence of the order and restrictions that in psychology are associated with the id.[7] Herrmann uses both the dreamlike and abrasive effects of chromatic harmony throughout *Vertigo*. These allow him to explore the psychological implications and effects of harmonic textures and ambiguous tonal centers and, by extension, to underscore the problem of identity found in the narrative. Influenced by the twentieth-century musical avant-garde, Herrmann's music breaks away from traditional tonal systems and seems to follow its own instinctual desires. The score is filled with sinewy motifs, dissonant clusters of two or more adjacent chromatic pitches, chromatically constructed chords, and rapid chromatic modulations that allow him to express something otherwise inexpressible: the notes behind the notes, the aural underworld of the disturbed psychological realm of Hitchcock's characters. The ear of the viewer/listener instinctively waits, hoping that the tension created from these harmonies will resolve or that some other force, perhaps a harmonious musical superego, will emerge to restore the order that has left the score.

The film's striking opening theme – the haunting G augmented arpeggio over E-flat\6 to an E-flat minor/major seventh arpeggio – illustrates Herrmann's most prominent display of the psychological implications of ambiguous chromatic harmony (Figure 9.1). Like the characters in the film, this phrase is harmonically independent and dissonant, simultaneously abrasive and seductive. Although extensively repeated and developed, it is an ambiguous phrase that does not reach or resolve to a stable tonal center.[8] It is, however, a defining musical motif in the film, even though it is heard only in the opening credits, where it achieves full orchestral development, and later during the scene where Judy allows her hair to be dyed blonde as she acquiesces to Scottie's attempt to transform her identity.

The phrase sounds disconcerting for several technical reasons, including:

1   the dissonance of the compound major seventh interval between the E-flat and the D;

2   the dissonance of the diminished sixth interval between the B-flat and the G-flat;

3   the dissonance of the major second interval between the C and the D;

4   the dissonance of the minor second interval between the D and the E-flat;

5   the ambiguity between the major and minor harmonies embedded within the motif (a minor third interval between the E-flat and the G-flat, and the

major third interval between both the G-flat and the B-flat, and the B-flat and the D as well); and

6 the G-flat augmented triad.

The ear is drawn to the dissonance created among these notes, although it struggles with adapting to and ordering these pitches, as well as with adapting to and ordering the ambiguity of the conflicting major, minor, and augmented harmonies. The natural expectation is that one of these pitches will resolve. In fact, the ear's struggle to maintain a harmonic equilibrium with these pitches is what instills something like an aural feeling of vertigo within the listener.

The opening theme is actually two motifs played simultaneously – one that begins ascending and another that begins descending – one arpeggio on top of the other, pulling the phrase and the listener in opposite directions. Like the strained relationship between the self and the alter ego that Hitchcock explores within the narrative, the arpeggios reflect images of each other while struggling for harmonic resolution and dominance in the ear of the listener. However, although the arpeggios pull the listener in opposing directions, we actually hear them as one motif. They seem to coexist as a positive and as a negative, canceling each other out in an attempt to become one unified and stable melody. But they are not unified and stable, and the dissonance and unstable equilibrium of the two arpeggios moves them further apart. No matter how often the arpeggios ascend, descend, or modulate, or seem to approach a stability that is implied by the supporting harmony played by the rest of the orchestra, the phrase is pulled back or pushed to a position outside of any stable harmonic center. As such, the up and down movement of the arpeggio actually resemble Scottie's struggle with his acrophobia. It reflects his fear of and difficulty with ascending, and by extension progress towards the resolution of the narrative whereby Judy and Madeleine's identity, and for that matter his own identity, will be ultimately realized and resolved.

Herrmann frequently explores chromatic harmony in long, drawn-out passages that feature ostinatos, often in the rhythm of the Cuban dance music of the *habanera* (see Figure 9.2).[9] Some of these pieces accompany scenes in which Scottie is following first Madeleine, then Judy. While they are interesting for their harmonic motion, these passages lack significant development to a secure center. Time seems to stand still during these passages, or rather, not to exist at all. Although seeming to be firmly rooted in the tonal centers implied by the ostinato, these passages seem incapable of settling into a definitive and comfortable harmonic identity. Rather, they "try on" various identities by exploring the harmonic tensions and harmonies that are created by modulating the upper notes of the chord, often chromatically, while keeping the bass (or inverted bass)[10] fixed.

Figure 9.1: Vertigo Prelude (orchestral reduction)

Figure 9.2: The Gallery (orchestral reduction)

It is interesting to note the numerous passages throughout the film where Herrmann accomplishes a parallel effect with music that consists of chords modulating to equivalent chords in different keys (major to major, minor to minor, augmented to augmented, diminished to diminished, etc.) without the ostinato. We hear this in the modulating minor chords in the hallway scene at the McKittrick hotel, in the modulating augmented chords when Scottie rescues Madeleine from the bay, in the modulating major seventh chords when Scottie reads Madeleine's letter, and the modulating major chords when Scottie and Madeleine walk along the beach. Like the ostinatos, these passages enable Herrmann to decenter the score from any stable center, allowing it instead to "try on" various identities in the pursuit of stability, moving the score through the same process of transformation as Hitchcock and Samuel Taylor's narrative.

The modulating chords and ostinato passages, like the short chromatic motifs that Herrmann stacks on top of one another, mirror Hitchcock's exploration of his characters' struggles to resolve unstable identities as both music and narrative explore identity and resolution along similar vertical and horizontal lines. For once Hitchcock fractures the identities of the central characters in the last third of the film – the identities of Scottie and the Madeleine/Carlotta/Judy amalgam – placing one (the alter ego) on top of the other (the self), he has in effect imposed a vertical narrative, a layering of superimposed identities, on top of the traditional horizontal narrative progression of the film.[11] As the narrative follows a linear path to its conclusion, the viewer witnesses the two halves of the fractured identities battling for supremacy over their respective characters. This exploration of identity along vertical and horizontal lines in the narrative and musical score engages the viewer/listener both visually and aurally, and we eagerly wait for the instability of both the narrative and the score to resolve. Consciously or not, we become transfixed by the symmetry Herrmann has created between his score and Hitchcock's narrative, as chromatic motifs, modulating chords, and ostinatos languish in arrested states of development where they too remain incomplete and anything seems possible. Further, as the various identities of the characters are stacked like conflicting harmonies on top of one another, it becomes all too apparent that something dangerous is building, both narratively and musically. At any moment, the dissonance that accompanies the vertical and horizontal exploration of identity may become destructive both in the action and the score.

Herrmann suggests this destructive force through the many dissonant polychords (chords that are created by stacking two different chords on top of one another to create a harmony that is made up of more than one complete tonal system) that highlight many of the dramatic moments when Scottie experiences his vertigo: the D major over E-flat minor polychord in the opening scene when Scottie, hanging from the building, looks down; the D major over E-flat minor and D major over B-flat polychords that we hear during Scottie's nightmare when he falls from the tower; and finally the D major over A-flat major polychord when Scottie looks down while climbing the bell tower with Judy in the film's finale. The harmonic chaos created by these polychords fulfills what Hitchcock and Herrmann have been alluding to and potentially building towards: the breakdown of harmonic stability into permanent harmonic chaos.

Musically, the one place that Herrmann's chromatic music cannot go to is the very place that the narrative's love themes (see Figure 9.3) explore: connection, or in musical terms, harmony. This problem in the music is suggested in the dialogue, as Madeleine tells Scottie, "only one is a wanderer, two together are always going somewhere." And she is correct, for the individual with a fractured identity is left to wander apart from others, while a stable person can connect with another, and to the world around them, thereby more fully realizing themselves. The music that accompanies these love scenes appears to be remarkably different to the chromatically infused music that we encounter in the rest of the film. Here, rather than exploring dense harmony through short motifs and harmonic profile, Herrmann seems to develop the "love melodies" – simple, longing, legato themes – along a linear course where the music resolves to lush chords with clear harmonic identities.

This horizontal progression of the music follows the narrative forward to an

Figure 9.3: Madeline's Theme (orchestral reduction)

apparent, albeit temporary, harmonic resolution of both soundtrack and story. Interestingly, the most prominent harmonic resolutions occur during the narrative's most optimistic moments: the first time that Scottie sees Madeleine, when Scottie and Madeleine first kiss, and when Judy emerges from the bathroom after her Madeleine makeover. Yet oddly enough, such harmonic resolution also occurs in somewhat different fashion at the very end of the film after Judy has fallen from the bell tower.[12] All of these scenes offer a brief respite from the chaos of the film, moments when the suspense of the narrative and the tension from the conflicting identities are temporarily reconciled or resolved.

Despite the harmonic reconciliation during love scenes, there is something surprisingly tentative and unfulfilling about these lush, romantic, musical passages.[13] Rather than resolving the tension created by the instability of the rest of the score, the love theme seems to add to it as each new note feels like a slow step around a dangerous and unsupported hidden precipice. Herrmann accomplishes this in large part through his extensive use of a musical technique known as *appogiatura,* a practice whereby a composer places a rhythmically strong dissonant note in place of a harmonic tone. The *appogiatura* enables Herrmann to momentarily delay the resolution of the melody to the appropriate harmony, thereby challenging our expectations and creating an awkward sensation as the melody sounds somewhat separated from its harmonic support. Although melodies develop and resolve, they do so chromatically, so that each new phrase and chord, although lush and lyrical, feels new, unexpected, tenuous, and mysterious. Interestingly, the melodies do not for the most part develop beyond their original four-note length, creating a rigidity that seems to confine and restrict their full harmonic and melodic development. Furthermore, the harmonic resolutions of these melodies and harmonies are so short that the ear does not have time to rest comfortably within the confines of the tonal center and to achieve an aural position that is both comforting and stable.

As the love theme develops, Herrmann introduces new disjointed elements such as the modulating thirds played by the second violins when Madeleine sits by Scottie's fireplace, and the violin and viola ostinato heard when Scottie and Madeleine are at the beach. Although subtle, these new components further disrupt the stability of the love theme by bringing in musical elements that the listener has previously associated with instability. In addition, Herrmann often ends the passages in which he explores the love theme with unstable chords: the G-sharp half-diminished seventh chord when Scottie and Madeleine sit by the fire in his apartment; the A augmented when Madeleine subsequently leaves Scottie's apartment; and the C major seventh that ends Scottie and Madeleine's first outing. As a result, the ear remains suspicious of the validity of the love theme just as the credibility of Madeleine and the love she inspires becomes less certain as the narrative develops. Thus, Scottie's love for the duplicitous, fabricated Madeline has already been challenged in the score before it is challenged in the narrative itself.

The music that has a definitive harmonic identity, and therefore the potential for stabilizing the identity conflict in the film's narrative and score, is actually outside of Herrmann's score in the source music that accompanies Midge's scenes. It is as if Hitchcock and screenwriter Samuel Taylor stretched the landscape of the film to find a musical ground to restore the harmony and stability that has clearly escaped the world and characters that are being explored.[14] Midge, the only grounded character in *Vertigo*, has a firmly established identity that makes her Hitchcock's agent both of psychological stability and of stabilizing music within the narrative. When she is introduced to us in her apartment after the traumatizing and vertiginous opening scene (with its similarly chaotic and unsettling musical motifs and polychords), she is playing a recording of a bright, serene baroque C.P.E. Bach piece (the second movement of a Sinfonia in E-flat, Op.9, no. 2, *c.* 1775) on her portable phonograph. Later, after Scottie has suffered his psychological breakdown, she tries to help him in the sanitarium by playing a record of Mozart's tranquil Andante from the 34th Symphony (*c.* 1780), with its soothing stable tonal centers. Apart from Scottie dismissing the Baroque piece in the film's second scene, Midge is the only character to play or discuss music or the psychological role that it serves. Even the psychiatrist plays no role in this aspect of Scottie's "treatment." As she says to Scottie,

> I had a long talk with the lady in musical therapy and she says that Mozart's the boy for you. The broom that sweeps the cobwebs away. Well, that's what the lady said. You know, it's wonderful how they have it all taped now, John. They have music for dipsomaniacs, and music for melancholiacs, and music

for hypochondriacs. I wonder what would happen if somebody got their files mixed up.

As composers whose lives were contemporaneous with the Enlightenment values of reason and rationality, C.P.E. Bach and Mozart created music that is orderly and consonant and progresses towards stable harmonic centers that reassure and ground the listener. As the above quote illustrates, Hitchcock/Taylor introduce an idea into the narrative that Herrmann musically explores in his score: namely, the psychological impact of tonality. In the earlier British films and pre-Herrmann American films music confirmed identity. It is now apparent however that in late Hitchcock (in particular *Vertigo* and *Psycho*), music not only confirms identity but mirrors the psychological conflict of the self – and what's more, it reaches into the unconscious to influence the struggle as well. In Midge's discussion of the psychological influence of music, Hitchcock confirms what the listener has felt all along: that the disturbing psychological landscape of the film is mirrored by the ambiguous harmony of Herrmann's music, and that Herrmann's exploration of ambiguous harmony parallels Hitchcock's exploration of the psychological struggle of the individual whose identity is in conflict – an individual whose personal and musical files are now, to use Midge's term, "mixed up."[15]

Despite her efforts to stabilize Scottie's harmonic "composition," Scottie and his world remain beyond reach. Just as Herrmann does not allow his music to reach a secure harmonic center, Midge ends up turning off the music in every scene in which she plays it. In her first scene, Midge turns off C.P.E. Bach after Scottie admonishes her not to "be so motherly. I'm not going to crack up," and then adds, "ah, don't you think the music is sort of…"[16] Later, when visiting the unresponsive Scottie in the sanitarium, she turns the music off herself even though she has just remarked that her record player turns off automatically. As she confesses with resignation to Scottie's psychologist, and to the viewer/listener, "I don't think Mozart will help at all."

The only way that Scottie can recuperate is through ascension, by moving onward and upward, as if literally to reverse the psychological "falling" brought on by the fatal falls of both Madeleine and his colleague. Time and again we see him try to overcome what ails him by working from the bottom up. In the film's second scene he tries to overcome his own acrophobia by learning to climb gradually, starting pathetically with the stepladder in Midge's apartment. In a similar way, he believes that the only way he can save Madeleine is to help her piece together and put in order her troubled past. Or, as he states, "If I could just find the key, the beginning, and put it together." (Herrmann, meanwhile, seems engaged in a parallel search for the musical key that will stabilize both the narrative and the score.) Later, in a desperate attempt to recuperate from Madeleine's death and restore his earlier identity, he also physically rebuilds Madeleine from the bottom up in Judy: first the suit, then the shoes, and finally, the makeup and hair, hoping that the psychic and emotional Madeleine will also somehow magically return. However, it is not until the film's conclusion, when Scottie climbs the stairs of the bell tower while attempting to revisit Madeleine's death and verify who she truly was, that we witness his most significant attempt to ascend. Combined, each of these attempts at ascension can be seen as an attempt to progress, to actually reach a higher understanding, or what in Greek tragedy is called *anagnorisis*: a state of mind in which the protagonist will be able to recognize the truth, to resolve all uncertainty, to determine all responsibility, and to firmly establish all identities, including his own.

Just as Scottie gambles and tries to ascend and to reach a place of recognition and understanding – a place where the conflict in the narrative will be resolved and he will find spiritual and psychological peace – so too, in a way, does Herrmann's score. Like the ascending and descending arpeggio motif in the film's opening, the long searching passages with ostinatos, and numerous sections in which motifs are developed, the entire score tries to transcend its ambiguous harmonic identity, its identity conflict, to reach a stable and harmonious tonal center. The conflict between musical styles culminates in the struggle to find a musical structure that will restore order to the narrative. However, like Scottie, the music cannot do so, and returns at the conclusion to the ambiguous and fractured harmony with which it began. At the end of the film Scottie stands alone and looks down at Judy's fallen body as the music resolves to a climactic grounded C major chord that marks the end of the drama. Although he has ascended physically and reached an understanding of Madeleine/Judy's identity and his own as "the set up," Scottie is no closer to the deeper level of resolution, or the *anagnorisis*, he was seeking. He has again been devastated by a death by falling, and the possibility of his recovering from this second blow seems remote at best. Although the film's final chord suggests harmonic resolution, it has come at the highest cost.

In a 1933 interview, Hitchcock stated that in his films "music had to inspire the action." He then goes on to discuss the psychological role of music to "express the unspoken," using the following example:

> two people may be saying one thing and thinking something different. Their looks match their words, but not their thoughts. They may be talking politely and quietly, but there may be a storm coming. You cannot express the mood of that situation by word and photograph. But I think that you could get at the underlying idea with the right background music.[17]

In *Vertigo*, Bernard Herrmann's score accomplishes precisely this and more.

Although there are numerous action sequences, *Vertigo* is notable for its slow pace and lack of dialogue. In fact, much of what transpires in the film occurs outside of the spoken narrative and in the "thoughts" of the characters. It is Herrmann's score that helps to create much of this aspect of the film and simultaneously to underscore much of its intensity. The greatness of the film lies in the dialectic between image, narrative, and sound. It is Herrmann's music that helps fill the space in the film, tying it all together. Interestingly, in this same interview Hitchcock stated that although music has a significant role in his films, the audience must never be conscious of this role. As he indicated: "I might argue that I do not want the audience to listen consciously to the music at all. It might be achieving its desired effect without the audience being aware of how that effect was achieved."[18]

Ironically, *Vertigo* tests the limits of Hitchcock's idea that the audience must not be consciously aware of the impact of a film's music. Although all listeners may not be aware of how Herrmann's score creates and heightens suspense and drama within the narrative, they are consciously listening – both because Midge has told them to in the crucial sanitarium scene and because Herrmann's score is often all that is heard. In truth, Herrmann's score propels the film while expressing that which the narrative and camera cannot: the inexpressible. For as Hitchcock remarks (echoing George Bernard Shaw), music can express feelings and sensations that no other art can. In film, music can be the glue that holds narrative, performance, camera-work, and editing together. It heightens their successes and suggests a level of psychological and emotional intensity that perhaps can only be heard. *Vertigo* thus explores the possibilities of music in filmic narrative as much as it explores the struggle for a harmonious personal identity within the narrative itself. And to the extent that Herrmann's score does both, the viewer/listener leaves having experienced the rich possibilities of the integration of music into narrative cinema.

Notes

I would like to thank the following readers for their editorial comments: Sarah Bernbach; Dr. Judy Lochhead, Stony Brook University; and my deep personal gratitude to my father, Dr. Walter Srebnick of Pace University, who first took me to see *Vertigo* when I was nine and who, twenty years later, read countless drafts of this paper.

1 Sergei Eisenstein, for example, wrote that film achieved these traits through the use of montage. Hitchcock has also used musical metaphors to describe the filmmaking process.
2 I do not use the term "psychological" to differentiate between different types of film, but, rather, to describe film's ability to explore the processes of sense, perception, cognition, emotion, and behavior.

3 Iris's identity as a woman who acts against her true nature and is preparing to marry a man she does not love is one of the film's central themes.

4 Royal S. Brown, "Herrmann, Hitchcock, and the Music of the Irrational," in *Overtones and Undertones: Reading Film Music*, Berkeley: University of California Press, 1994, pp. 148–74.

5 Herrmann wrote a score for *Torn Curtain* but Universal Studios "encouraged" Hitchcock to use a more commercial soundtrack. Herrmann was replaced by John Addison.

6 *Chromaticism* is a broad term that applies to a wide range of harmonic structures. At its simplest, the use of chromatic pitches acts as a "color modifier" of diatonic harmony. After 1900, chromaticism expanded to a harmonic structure in its own right and was brought to its extreme in Schoenberg's atonality and twelve-tone technique, in which the twelve chromatic notes are treated equally as sources of harmony in their own right without any pre-established relationship between them.

7 Just as Freud argued that the mind was made up of a system responsible for our actions (id, superego, ego), so too is music. Music is governed by natural harmonic and rhythmic rules that govern melodic, harmonic, and rhythmic development. We hear the tension created by notes within a chord, a melody, or by an asymmetrical phrase or rhythm and expect them to develop and resolve in a way to which our ear is accustomed.

8 One could interpret the E-flat minor/major 7th chord as a polytonal harmony existing unto itself. However, the way in which Herrmann explores it, highlighting its separateness to illustrate the ambiguity of identity in the narrative, makes a characterization of the minor/major 7th chord as ambiguous and unstable more accurate and functional.

9 The *habanera* is a Cuban dance of Spanish origin whose rhythm is usually 2/4 meter in moderate tempo. It uses a variety of rhythmic patterns (the two most common being ♪♪ ♪ and ♪♪♪ ♪) which inspired many European composers including Debussy, Chabrier, Auber, Albeniz, De Falla, and Ravel.

10 A musical technique where the bass part, traditionally performed by an instrument in a low register, is moved to higher register.

11 Brown traces a similar idea through portions of the score's where there is no harmonic resolution. However, he does not recognize the vertical complexities in Hitchcock's narrative and thus views Herrmann's "vertical synchronicity" as oppositional to Hitchcock's "horizontally created synchronicity" ("Overtones and Undertones," p. 630). As I have argued, both Hitchcock and Herrmann explore identity along vertical and horizontal planes, as it allows them to get at, the source of their irrational subject matter, namely, ambiguous identity.

12 In the Harris/Katz restored version of the film, the opening arpeggio theme is heard at the end of the film. The original version of the film ends with Herrmann's climactic chord.

13 Romantic music is generally characterized by an emphasis on subjective, emotional qualities and by a greater freedom of form and harmony.

14 Elizabeth Weis associates Hitchcock's use of classical source music with social refinement, and by extension, a staple of civilization. See *The Silent Scream*, Rutherford, NJ: Fairleigh Dickinson University Press, 1982, p. 91.

15 Brown astutely writes that "the whole way in which 'present' source music is contrasted in *Vertigo* seems almost to be a comment on the function of film music in general: this invisible music that film audiences have always accepted as an integral part of the movies is almost always associated with the invisible, the bigger-than-life side of what transpires within the filmic narrative." Brown, "*Overtones and Undertones*," p. 643.

16 Brown correctly sees Scottie's rejection of the Bach piece as "symptomatic of Scottie's refusal to accept the normal world" ("*Overtones and Undertones*," p. 642). Even at this

early, pre-Madeline/Judy stage in the film, Scottie is already struggling with an identity in conflict brought about by the traumatic experience of witnessing his colleague's fatal fall.

17 Steven Watts, "Alfred Hitchcock on Music in Films," in Sidney Gottlieb (ed.) *Hitchcock on Hitchcock: Selected Writings and Interviews*, Berkeley and Los Angeles: University of California Press, 1995, p. 244; originally published in *Cinema Quarterly* 2, Winter 1933–4, 80–3.

18 Watts, "Alfred Hitchcock on Music in Films," in Gottlieb (ed.) *Hitchocock on Hitichcock* p. 243.

Chapter 10

THE SILENCE OF *THE BIRDS*
Sound aesthetics and public space in later Hitchcock

Angelo Restivo

Hitchcock, between history and theory

It is a truism by now, of course,: but one could easily imagine writing the history of the discipline of film studies from the sixties onward solely through the critical discourse surrounding the work of Hitchcock. The critical literature would become a kind of barometer measuring the colliding "fronts" and shifting winds of academic discourse from auteurism and formalism, through semiotics and ideological analysis, to the psychoanalytic move and then its appropriation for feminist film theory, and so on. If we continued this "barometric" analogy into the nineties, we would, I think, discern two broad trends in Hitchcock studies. One: the historical turn, in which Hitchcock's films, and particularly those of the American period, are studied in relation to the specific, concrete historical events in which they – like any other work of art, it is presumed – are embedded. As representative of this camp, we can cite the collection *Hitchcock's America*[1] (as well as Robert Corber's important book, *In the Name of National Security*, to which we will return shortly). Two: a thoroughgoing revision of the earlier psychoanalytic models in film studies – which by the late 1980s had become problematic for a number of reasons – in light of the not-widely known later work of Lacan, centering on the difficult concepts of the Real, the *sinthome*, and the drives. Slavoj Žižek has been at the center of this second camp, and the films of Hitchcock – partly, no doubt, because they played such a large role in the formulation of the earlier psychoanalytic models of the filmic textual economy – were his privileged sites of analysis. Briefly, Žižek argues that, while the earlier work of Hitchcock can be seen to successfully regulate desire and integrate it into the social network, by the 1950s we begin to see more and more blockages to this symbolic integration: we move, that is, "beyond the pleasure principle" and toward some more fundamental obstacle to intersubjective meaning, which we can provisionally call "the drives." [2] To understand what is at stake in this move *historically* is one of the aims of this essay; but at this point, suffice to say that Žižek's analyses have the effect of *periodizing* Hitchcock's work, and thus of making – potentially, at least – some sort of historical claim.

In order to see both the strengths and the limitations of these two strands of scholarship, I would propose comparing briefly the work of Robert Corber and Lee Edelman, both of whom deal with the question of homosexuality in Hitchcock's postwar work. Corber presents us with a wealth of historical information on the political uses of homosexuality in constructing the Cold War consensus. [3] In the fifties, "the love that dare not speak its name" was, it turns out, spoken *about* obsessively, from the State Department as a haven for homosexuals easily blackmailed into treason, down to suburbia's "overprotective" mothers who, along with their "cold, distant" spouses, were presumed to be churning out so many potential "recruits" for the mysterious brotherhood. Like "the Communists," homosexuals were both omnipresent and invisible; though it was presumed that – like vampires – they could always spot one of their ilk. Now, given the ideological work that the discourses on homosexuality were charged with in this period, it would make sense to think that they would emerge – in one way or another – in the popular culture of the period. But when Corber gets to reading the Hitchcock films of the period, we often get the sense that the constellation of social discourses is being reproduced in the film *tout court*, with both the narrative and its actants existing in a kind of one-to-one correspondence with history. The problem is then that there is no tenable model that would explain how such a direct reproduction of history in the text could come about. After all, there are a number of forces that are more directly shaping the structure of the film during its production: aesthetic, narrative, and genre conventions, the competences and collaboration of the creative personnel, the problem-solving nature of film production. These, I would argue, form a kind of screen through which historically specific material must pass; they comprise a kind of dream-work, so that the "daily residue" – history itself – will appear only in forms that are disguised or worked-over.

Lee Edelman's work on Hitchcock takes us to the other, more theoretical strand of recent Hitchcock scholarship. In a number of essays ranging in subject from *Notorious* to *The Birds*, Edelman identifies within the textual economies of these postwar films points at which meaning is occluded in the face of some "senseless," and perverse, *jouissance*.[4] In other words, he identifies points where the destructive economy of the drives erupts to disturb the smooth functioning of symbolic, intersubjective exchange, against which eruptions Hitchcock's Oedipal narratives are seen to be the ideological defense mechanism that they (always already) are. What Edelman is interested in, then, is uncovering the ways in which "queerness" is always the trace or the supplement that inhabits any construction of "normality," and history enters the picture insofar as we can then look at manifestations of this process in determinate events, times, and places. But while I find quite compelling overall the power of Edelman's deconstructive move, what remains unexplained is what might be "driving" that change in Hitchcock's work that pushes it in the direction of the drives.

In sum, then, I would position this essay somewhere in between these two positions, and in a sense as trying to mediate them. The questions to be asked are these: Is there any way that these two strands of scholarship can meet in some productive way? Can, for example, the concrete historical developments of postwar America be connected in some specific way to the formal shifts in the work of a Hollywood director? And what kind of model – of textual economy, of history, and of the relation between the two – would enable such a connection to be made?

The sound of Fordism

To begin to answer these questions, I propose that an analysis of the sound aesthetics of Hitchcock's postwar work, culminating in the highly original sound-track of *The Birds*, will be the most productive avenue to take. For in the first place, in Hitchcock's work of the 1950s and up to *Psycho*, we can discern an increasing destabilization of sound–image (and especially voice–body) relations, and thus our periodization of Hitchcock's work, can rest initially on something much more concrete than an already-conceptualized "eruption of the drives." The change in Hitchcock's use of sound – at least in the period from *Vertigo* to *The Birds* – has indeed been noted by Elisabeth Weis, who characterizes the effects of Hitchcock's sound aesthetic in this period as an attempt to move "beyond the subjectivity" of the earlier films, using the soundtrack to break apart the system of spectatorial positioning constructed through point-of-view shots, which then allows the sound to seize the spectator more viscerally.[5] This impulse in the sound aesthetic has, I would argue, a correlative in the structure of the images, a kind of de-realization that occurs as figure and ground, or surface and depth, begin to become difficult to distinguish – as in, for example, the Mount Rushmore sequence of *North by Northwest*, where the "ground" has become liter-ally a "figure," or in the suffusions of red on the surface of the screen in *Marnie*.

There is a second reason for focusing initially on sound aesthetics in this period of Hitchcock's work: sound is centrally involved in the ways that the cinema constructs space, the ways in which the spatial dimensions of the image are conveyed to the spectator. And if we look at the larger historical forces at work during the postwar period, we see that the reconstruction of space – both physical space (suburbia, controlled environments, etc.) and virtual space (television, advertising images, etc.) – is a central national project. Clearly, the scope of this chapter allows only for the presentation of a necessarily condensed view of a complex set of historical developments, and such a broad overview, to be sure, is likely to be politically contentious to some. However, I think we can safely say that after the Great Depression the problem that capitalism faced was the management of consumption, or the coordination of production with consumption. Achieving this involved several things at the level of political economy, including increasing wages and long-term job security, decreasing work hours, and expansion of credit. But it also entailed the construction of the "consumer." Thus, for example, the postwar period saw the emergence of an entirely new conception of marketing – one of whose pioneers was Social Research Inc., which developed out of the University of Chicago's sociology department – which focused not on measuring demand but on stimulating it.[6] Historians such as George Lipsitz have argued that the postwar transformations of urban/suburban geography were deliberate strategies of social atomization; he suggests, for example, that the focus during the postwar boom on highways and the suburban single-family house (rather than, say, on railroads, public transportation, or multi-family inner-city housing) was a strategy to deliberately defuse any lingering social-democratic ideology from the days of the Depression and Popular Front.[7] Finally, this postwar reconstruction of space was thoroughly imbricated in the emergence and widespread dissemination of television in this historical period. For one thing, television provided the ideal means for disseminating not only advertising, but also images of domestic space, expert discourses on diet and hygiene, and so on. Lynn Spigel, in her pioneering work on early television and domestic space, has shown how the postwar economic boom expressed itself in highly spatial terms, in which the television set was seen as a key link to the "outside" within the increasingly controlled spaces of suburbia.[8]

I propose to argue, then, that the connection of a film text to its historical moment is best seen not by casting its characters and narrative as stand-ins for social actants or events, but through an analysis of the specificities and peculiarities of its formal system – in the case of the later Hitchcock, of the sonic dislocations and manipulations that function to problematize the spatial orientations of inside and outside. Michel Chion has conceptualized the destabilization of sound and image in Hitchcock through his concept of the "acousmatic voice" (*la voix acousmatique*), focusing mainly on *Rear Window* and *Psycho*.[9] *Acousmatique*,

Chion explains in his book *The Voice in Cinema*, is an old French word for a sound whose cause is invisible; Chion claims that it has an ancient reference, going back to the Pythagoreans, to the practice of veiling the Master so as not to allow his/her appearance to distract from the spoken word. He then connects this practice to that of the psychoanalytic cure, where of course the analyst is hidden from the analysand. And finally, Chion argues, it is one of the central possibilities of the sound cinema. Why, we should ask, is the idea of the acousmatic voice so conceptually important to Chion that he makes it the inaugural observation in *The Voice in Cinema*? I think that it's because this voice pushes to the limit the cinema's constitutive separation of sound and image. The acousmatic voice results in a blurring of the distinction between what lies within the diegetic space of the film and what lies outside it. For Chion, the acousmatic voice occupies a kind of indefinable, liminal space that has the continual potential to render unreal the comfortable world of the diegesis. Part of this blurring of boundaries comes from the historically specific modes of sound reproduction in the classical cinema: for in monaurally equipped theaters (which accounted for three-quarters of the world's theaters in the late 1950s),[10] the speaker was positioned behind the movie screen; that is, from the center of the space in which the character – speaking or emitting other vocal cues – was absent. As Chion puts it, "it's as if the voice were wandering along the surface, *at once inside and outside*."[11] Finally, Chion uses the concept of the acousmatic to apply to voices and sounds that "seize" the spectator at a primal level. Such a use of sound has the effect of "incorporating" the images; it is, as Chion puts it, "a voice to which the image is interior."[12]

Hitchcock's *Psycho* provides us with an excellent illustration of these concepts, in a scene whose unorthodox sound design is subtle enough to have been generally overlooked (until Chion). I'm referring to the scene when Marion, driving on the highway the day after her theft of the money, "hears" the voices at the office as her theft is discovered. As Marion drives from daylight to dusk to rainstorm to night, we hear the voices in the office she has fled, as her co-worker, her sister, her boss, and her victim gradually realize what she has done. Here we can see precisely how the acousmatic voices incorporate the image of Marion into a sonic envelope. The film here folds in on itself, insofar as the voices have the specificity we would associate with the "real" situation at the office, which diegetically Marion has no access to. Or, to put it another way, the film asks itself to be read as Marion's fantasy, which the soundscape gives the uncanny specificity of reality. At this point, it is important to note that when Michel Chion discusses this sequence, he argues that in fact the sounds *do not* incorporate the image of Marion. Chion argues that the post-production processing of these voices – the filtering and addition of reverb – clearly locates them inside Marion's head. Technically, this is true: but I am arguing that not only the "grains of the voices" but also the specificity of the "dialogue" introduces an uncanny proximity to reality that works to disrupt our sense that it is fantasy.[13] As I will show later, this blurring of inside and outside, this intrusion of fantasy into the diegetic world, is central to understanding the historical dimensions of Hitchcock's work from the fifties onward.

The acousmatic voice in Hitchcock's work occurs as early as 1948, in the opening shot of the film *Rope*. We can recall that the camera initially looks down from a balcony onto a public street, then slowly turns round toward the curtained windows of an apartment, from which we hear a scream. Here the disembodied voice of the murdered boy floats out, unnoticed, into the one view of public space that *Rope* provides us, though the camera has already turned its back on that space. We then cut to the domestic space – Phillip, Brandon, and the limp body of the strangled boy – which the camera will now never leave, and which it will relentlessly survey under a directorial prohibition of editing. While it might be objected here that the acousmatic quality of the scream is quickly taken away by the cut to the limp body that we infer emitted it a moment earlier, two things nevertheless make the notion of the acousmatic here quite useful. First is the "spectral" quality of the murdered David Kentley: he has not, indeed, received a proper burial, and his initial acousmatic scream haunts the film just as his improperly placed corpse sets off a metonymic chain of associations regarding things not in their proper places – the cassone substituting for the dinner table, the dinner table turned into a book display, and so on. Second, and more important, Hitchcock resorts here to one of the very few edits he uses in this film whose express intention was to present the action in a simulation of "real time." From the very beginning, then, the edit forces us to make an inference; or, as Christopher Morris puts it in his recent book, the sign is "cut" from the referent.[14]

Thus, at precisely the moment when Hitchcock makes visible the arbitrary connection between sound and image in the cinema, he also sets up a binary opposition, between cutting (and by extension, the cinema's mandate to *re-present* what it has filmed) and the brute registration of the profilmic reality. Now, *Rope* was made in 1948, at a moment when a new technology of sound and image – television – was emerging as viable; a technology, in fact, which privileged real-time transmission over cinematic representation. And even if few people in 1948 might have envisioned the extent of television's coming impact, not only on the film industry but on culture and society more generally, nevertheless there was already in place a widely held social fantasy surrounding television and its regimes of visuality. As Richard Dienst points out, the problematic underlying television revolved precisely around these social fantasies: of "liveness," of a total "enframing" of the world. Early television, we should remember, had no intrinsic technology for recording the images that it produced as it scanned the world in "real time"; it was, rather, suited to the continual and instantaneous transmissions of "any-spaces-whatevers" for as long as one might be interested in surveying such spaces. As Dienst puts it, television "is not built to produce images (like cinema), but to open and frame fields of visuality;" such a technology requires "a textual protocol that emphasizes reproducible verisimilitude over representational veracity."[15]

This, I would argue, is precisely what Hitchcock intuited about television in the problematic set forth by the very first cut in the film *Rope*. In a sense, *Rope* can be said to allegorize the tension between the cinema and its new competitor. On the one hand, it presents us with a simulation of the "real time" of live transmission. But what that first, symptomatic edit announces are the very limitations of television's regimes of visibility: its inability – within a system in which there is no conceptual "outside" – to register the public dimension of what it surveys.[16] In *Rope*, we leave the world of the cinematic and enter the world of the televisual precisely at the moment when a cry goes unheard in the public space where, just seconds before, a policeman was seen walking across the street. Thus, it is not surprising that the film's resolution, the bringing to justice of Philip and Brandon, occurs by way of another sound event, one that echoes and corrects the film's initial unmooring of sound and image. This is the gunshot that the professor fires out the opened window, followed by the voices of acknowledgment from the unseen crowd in the public space below. With this "shot," the analytical power of the cinema is vindicated: for the shot reveals the way in which the cinema can always get in synch not only with itself – insofar as such a decisive sound/image connection can be used as a clapboard to put picture and sound in synchronization – but with the larger public sphere.

By the mid-fifties, Hitchcock had embraced television. On the large screen, nevertheless, he enthusiastically experimented with the many innovations Hollywood was developing to make the movie-going experience more differentiated from television viewing. Given this fact, one might suppose that these media crossings at least in part turned Hitchcock's aesthetic experimentation in the 1950s into a – conscious or unconscious – exploration of a social system in transformation. *The Birds*, in fact, falls at the end of over a decade of experimentation with image and sound. But the synergy that came from Hitchcock's familiarity with both media is evidenced, for example, in the bold use of the combined track-and-zoom shots in *Vertigo*. For while a technically sophisticated zoom lens was developed by Frank Back in 1946, this lens was used, as John Belton reports, mostly for television work (where the ability to quickly reframe a visual field was invaluable in a "live" medium).[17]

Of course, by now it is well documented that as television extended its reach in the early 1950s, it precipitated a crisis in Hollywood; the declining box-office receipts pushed Hollywood toward the development of a number of wide-screen formats (including such "immersive" systems as Cinerama, Todd-AO, and 3-D), the development of multi-track magnetic stereo sound, and even the rise of new venues for watching movies (the drive-in, for example). In terms of technologies of the image, some of the wide-screen formats "took hold" and became industry standards, so that by the mid-fifties, most theatrical features were exhibited on either a wide -screen achieved by masking the standard 35mm film, or – to achieve an even greater aspect ratio – by using an anamorphic process for shooting and projecting the film.[18] Magnetic stereophonic sound, however, was another story. Since as much as 75 percent of movie theaters refused to invest in stereophonic playback systems, filmmakers were forced to release all films with mixed-down, monaural optical tracks; and, again according to Belton, the inno-vative "fourth track" which was designed to carry surround-sound to envelop the spectators from speakers at the rear, was seldom used because of the difficulties involved in getting its sound information onto the monaural mix.[19] This is why the move toward stereo sound has been called the "frozen revolution." But ulti-mately, from the point of view of the aesthetic development of motion pictures through the 1950s, all of these innovations – in both picture and sound – had important ramifications. In the first place, wide -screen allowed for new systems of editing to emerge: for theoretically, if not in actual practice, the wide screen mitigates the need for cutting to the point-of-view shot. This, as we have seen, was the visual correlative to the "extrasubjective" soundscape that Weis noted as a characteristic of *Vertigo, Psycho,* and *The Birds*. A second and related point to be made is that taken together, all these technological innovations were designed specifically to have the effect of engulfing the moviegoer in spectacle. Technically speaking, innovations in sound were most congenial to this project, insofar as stereophonic sound has the capacity to break down the barrier between the clearly contained diegetic world of the screen, and the space of the auditorium.[20] It is this that Hitchcock achieved in the soundtrack of *The Birds*, through the aesthetics of electronic music and not through the technologies of magnetic surround (now in disuse).

In order, finally, to link an analysis of *The Birds* to larger historical shifts in spatial and social organization in the postwar period, it would be productive to look, however briefly, at Hitchcock's television work, specifically with an eye toward understanding the different (that is, non-cinematic) regime of spatiality that was enacted by television. I propose thus to focus not so much on the actual narrative content of the episodes, but rather on the various framing mechanisms that the television format set forth, and the relationship of those framings to the new forms of commodity presentation that we see in television and its commer-cials.

In his television series, Hitchcock consistently adopted an acerbic tone in rela-tion to the sponsors whose advertising he was introducing in those framing monologues which were a trademark of the series. Thomas Leitch has noted two things about these monologues of particular interest to the argument presented here: one, that these bits were staged in a flat studio space which contrasted sharply with the three-dimensional space of both the presented story and the domestic site of reception; and two, that often in these bits Hitchcock employed "a single stylized (often oversized) prop."[21] Leitch argues that the spatial discontinuity introduced by the frame-monologue works to carve out an ironic space of superiority to the episode's diegesis; but I would argue that these spaces are, in fact, more related to the advertising spaces that generally followed them – which would be in perfect keeping with the idea, alluded to by Leitch, that Hitchcock's presence in these bits is not so much a guarantee of authorship as it is a brand-name logo.

The case of the props is even more interesting: recently, a considerable amount of discussion in psychoanalytic analyses of Hitchcock's films has dealt with what is called "the Hitchcockian object." The discussion about objects had as its impetus the attempt to theorize the famous "MacGuffin," that object or idea, so famous to both scholars and aficionados of Hitchcock, which has no relation to the drama Hitchcock wants the audience to become involved with, but instead is just something to set the plot in motion. While the MacGuffin is an imaginary object – that is, with no real "content" – it requires another type of object, technically a "drive-object," to set in motion the symbolic relations through exchange. An example here might help clarify: in *Notorious*, the wine bottles containing the uranium ore – even beyond their absurdity from the point of view of physics – have nothing to do with the "real story" Hitchcock wants us to be involved in; they are simply a stand-in (imaginary) for any number of other things that could equally have set the story in motion. The key with the *Unica* inscription, however, is – as its inscription suggests – quite singular, and as it changes hands and winds it way through several scenes, it serves to create around it an entire set of social relations and obligations.

The discussion that emerged in the nineties regarding these objects – put forward by Žižek, Dolar, and others – is this: that the numerous charged objects one sees in films made prior to the fifties functioned like the (Lacanian) object *a*. They were exchanged, and so mediated between, private desire and the public space, so as to guarantee the smooth functioning of the symbolic system. (In *Notorious*, whatever violence the characters are perpetrating on one another, the social system continues to hum along, with public civility remaining intact.) But as we move into Hitchcock's "great period," these objects can no longer hold together a system that is now under assault from the formless waves of enjoyment that engulf the films' diegeses, whether via the red suffusions of *Marnie*, the birds in *The Birds*, or the bog of quicksand in *Psycho*.[22] If we add to this observation the fact that in these films we also see a highly schematized, and even "de-realized," mise-en-scène (often achieved through blatant back projection), we end up finding ourselves in a space very much akin to that limbo in which Hitchcock hosted his television series. The Hitchcockian object has now become the oversized prop, as fetishized and disproportionate as the close-ups of toothpaste tubes and mouthwash bottles that would populate the commercials of 1950s television. It would seem, then, that the failure of the object to guarantee coherence of the social field finds as its correlative the newly packaged form of the commodity.

The silence of *The Birds*

This failure of the object to produce a social coherence – and by extension, a public sphere – is in fact something that is explicitly presented in *The Birds*, notably around the many rituals of coffee that recur throughout the film. The taking of coffee (or occasionally tea or brandy) is presented as central to the forging of social links; and coffee cups are one of the things that the birds most consistently zero in on in their various attacks. However, the more one watches this film, the more one is struck by the forced, disconnected dialogue that is exchanged in these rituals. Schoolteacher Annie Hayworth gives "all due respect to Oedipus," but her explanation of Mrs. Brenner's problems seems even more pat than use of the Oedipal complex would be. And when it comes to the conditions of her own life, could it be possible that she doesn't see how pathetically "Oedipalized" it is, with her playing surrogate mother to the sister of a man she can never have? (And all the while, she makes sneering asides about Bodega Bay to Melanie.) Neither does Melanie seem to have any clear sense of her own lack of coherence: she manages to convince herself that the only reason for her going to Bodega Bay is to play an elaborate practical joke (which by any definition of "joke" would not have been funny anyway). But that's really the whole point: an act of aggression and an act of generosity have become indistinguishable. And so the strangeness of these coffee rituals is the way in which they don't quite cover up the hostilities and self-delusions that continually surface. "We're waging a war," the boatsman says in the coffee shop; but what becomes striking the more one attends to the dialogue of the film is the way in which everyday social exchange has turned into a kind of warfare; recall that twice conversations between Mitch and Melanie turn into badgering interrogations.

But it is, as I've indicated earlier, the soundtrack to *The Birds* that offers the most promising avenue in which to pursue the film's position historically, and so we must turn to an examination of it. The sound design of *The Birds* is celebrated for its innovation. In the first place, we have an early case of the extensive post-production processing of sound effects. Second, these sound effects are elaborately orchestrated into a soundscape in which the processed sounds of the birds take the place of an absent musical score. Indeed, the electronic sounds are used musically: in the final assault on the Brenner house, for example, the flapping of wings is orchestrated in waves of crescendo and decrescendo, as the traumatized characters flail at empty space and the sound itself seems to back them into corners. In this way, *The Birds* takes up in the *soundtrack* the problem of diegesis articulated in the *image* at the end of *Psycho*, when the skull of Mother is superimposed over the face of Norman. Namely, how are we to know the point when the soundtrack moves from diegetic (sounds the birds are actually making) to non-diegetic (sound that exists in some space other than the world of the film)? This blurring of the boundary between the film's inside and outside is further evident in the film's strategic use of silence. Of course, I am not talking here about "real" silence; I am referring to those points in the film – especially near the end – when the mix of bird sounds gives way to an eerie electronic hum. This occurs most notably when Mitch opens the door of the house and ventures out to get to Melanie's car. Of the sound in this sequence, Hitchcock said in his interview with Truffaut that he and sound engineers Gassman and Sala were trying to produce "a sound so low that you can't be sure whether you're actually hearing it or only imagining it."[23] We thus come upon the problem of fantasy (imagined sound) derailing the sense, of certainty upon which an older conception of the public sphere rests. And in a way, this blurred boundary is the formal equivalent of the way in which the conversations, described above, have become derailed from the communicative "ideal" by the insistence of the characters' fantasies.

This move in the sound aesthetic, we can say from our vantage point today, was decades ahead of its time. In its subversion of the distinction between inside and outside, it is anticipating a sound aesthetic that would only come to fruition decades later, in the wake of the technology of the Dolby sound mix. As we have already indicated, however, Hitchcock was well aware of the developments in sound technology during the period of the "frozen revolution." It could thus very well be that the intended effect of the 1950s "fourth track" was what Hitchcock was trying to achieve here, but within the constraints of monaural sites of reception. (It would not be until 1975 that Dolby laboratories would introduce a system of four-track motion picture stereo optical instead of magnetic, which, would be affordable to most movie theaters.) Chion argues that Dolby ultimately allowed for a sound mix that so orchestrated its hyper-real sound effects, its electronically processed ambient tracks, and its music in such a way as to relocate the "scene" of the film into the spectators' minds (as if, he argued, each spectator were equipped with a pair of headphones).[24] In a sense then, Dolby allows for the full realization of the potential of the acousmatic voice to unmoor the connections between images. For this "other scene" of the soundscape now allows the images to achieve a degree of independence in their traditional function of establishing the space of the narrative. We can thus argue that with *The Birds*, Hitchcock is finally able to spread the acousmatic voice, so prevalent in his postwar films, out across the soundscape, by displacing the acousmatic onto the birds. In fact, the opening scene of the film announces this displacement: Melanie hears (what to her is) a disembodied whistle while walking in Union Square, turns to see that a young boy is teasing her, but is quickly directed by the soundtrack to attend not to him, but to the cloud of birds in the distance.

Of course, there is a much more famous displacement of sound in this film: it occurs when Lydia runs out of the farmhouse after seeing the dead body and pecked-out eyes of Dan Fawcett. Here, the expected scream cannot emerge from her body, and, as Hitchcock himself said, the squealing of the car on the road stands in place of that scream. There is something more going on here than simple technical bravura; for ultimately this is a film in which all the characters are driven to silence. This is especially evident in the scene in which, after Mitch has elaborately boarded up the house, Lydia, Mitch, Melanie, and Cathy sit in the parlor waiting for the next attack. The scene unfolds in complete silence, broken at first only by – what else? – the quiet clinking of coffee cups as Lydia removes them to the kitchen. We could argue, then, that the pulsating, organic soundscape of bird sounds, the soundscape that lies somewhere beyond the boundaries of the diegesis, has as its prerequisite the fact that something remains unutterable, stuck in the throat, of the humans in the film. (Significantly, in the scene just described, the wordlessness is broken when Cathy announces she is "sick," and Melanie escorts her off-screen to vomit.) Clearly, then, the film is predicated upon the presence of trauma, of that which is unutterable because unsymbolized; but it would be too easy to say that the birds have caused the trauma, rather than that they are its avatars or textual representatives.

To begin to pull some of the strands of the argument together, we can say that the film's soundtrack systematically undermines the distinction between psychic and social space, and that this soundtrack exists against the background of a traumatic silence. The systems of symbolic exchange that were so central to the early work of Hitchcock have collapsed. But to move to the central question with which we began – namely, the connection between the aesthetics of later Hitchcock and its historical moment – we can see that it is precisely the oversaturation of the spaces of everyday life, with the phantasmatic images of the commodity, that provokes this aesthetic reaction. With the shift toward a consumption-driven economic system, a new form of subjectivity is produced, one in which experience has become so privatized that public life is continually haunted by that "silent hum" of private enjoyment. Or, to rephrase the conclusion in terms of the drives, we can say that the refashioning of the commodity in the postwar period – both through an essentially new conception of marketing and a new medium, television, through which to put it in practice – creates an object that is no longer "autonomous" enough to be the object of desire; it is, rather, an object of appetite against which the sphere of intersubjectivity can only be a barrier.

Now, if television is the principal technology and cultural form underlying the emergence of consumer capitalism, we could argue that television's reconfiguration of the space of public discourse would become visible in films of the 1950s and early 1960s. Returning to *Psycho* once again, this is seen in the speech of the psychiatrist: for while his explanation is ineffectual, at the same time it invokes the emergence of the "expert," so vital to the 1950s media's normalization of the practices of everyday life (Is your kitchen modern? Are your pancakes good? Is your son a homosexual? etc, etc.) as to allow the commodity to seamlessly insinuate itself into all aspects of life. We could even argue that the very ineffectiveness of the psychiatric explanation of Norman Bates is what gives it its allegorical power, insofar as the media parade of experts is designed not to move us toward some sort of consensus or provisional truth, but rather to proliferate a bewildering array of options. Along these same lines, in *The Birds*, the textual equivalent to this scene is surely the coffee shop scene: for if the coffee house tradition is now seen by some cultural historians as an essential institution in the emergence of the modern democratic state, in *The Birds* it is simply the site where no explanation is sufficient, where no workable consensus can be achieved. Perhaps the most telling symptom in this scene is the way that the hysterical mother can cut short the speculative discourse about the bird attacks by an appeal to "protect the children." By the 1990s, this had become the principal ideological move in hystericizing public discourse in the interest of social control: here we need only look at the way in which "family values" has become an idiotic quilting point for all political discourse, or at the Communications Decency Act, passed by a Republican Congress, defended in the courts by a Democratic White House, and (for the time being at least) struck down as unconstitutional by the federal courts.

Finally, the soundscape of *The Birds* can be seen to announce, symptomatically, the emergence of a new form of subjectivity (and its concomitant mode of spectatorship), one in which access to the public sphere, so vital to Hitchcock's pre-fifties films, is blocked by the silent hum that might very well be hallucinatory. *The Birds* leaves us in a space where the world has become unthinkable. Significantly, there are only two scenes in the film where we connect to the outside world: the first when we hear an inconclusive and casual soundbite on the radio, and the second in the film's penultimate scene, when Mitch tunes the car radio to a news broadcast. Did audiences in 1963 wonder at all why the characters in the film fail to connect to the broadcast network? In the 1950s, there had appeared an entire cycle of films dealing with mutant species run amuck –

usually ants or grasshoppers, and always because of nuclear radiation – in which the news media, and particularly television, played a critical role in driving home the films' "liberal" moral of the necessity for global cooperation, even if it was always good old American know-how that actually managed to rid us of the pests. But as Hitchcock seems to suggest, the media is radically incommensurate to the task that *The Birds* has set out for us. For that task is nothing less than the imperative to re-think the human, once we have moved "beyond subjectivity.'

Notes

I would like to thank Sam Ishii-Gonzàles and Richard Allen for their invaluable editorial comments on an earlier draft of this essay.

1 Jonathan Freedman and Richard Millington (eds.) *Hitchcock's America*, New York: Oxford University Press, 1999.
2 See, for example, the important second part of Slavoj Žižek's *Looking Awry: An Introduction to Jacques Lacan through Popular Culture*, Cambridge, MA: MIT Press, 1992, pp. 69–122; and his introduction to Žižek (ed.) *Everything You Always Wanted to Know About Lacan (But Were Afraid to Ask Hitchcock)*, trans. Martin Thom, London and New York: Verso, 1992, pp. 1–12.
3 Robert Corber, *In the Name of National Security: Hitchcock, Homophobia, and the Political Construction of Gender in Postwar America*, Durham, NC: Duke University Press, 1993.
4 See, for example, Lee Edelman, "Hitchcock's Future," in Richard Allen and S. Ishii-Gonzàles (eds.) *Hitchcock: Centenary Essays*, London: BFI, 1999, pp. 239–58.
5 Elisabeth Weis, *The Silent Scream: Alfred Hitchcock's Sound Track*, Rutherford, NJ: Fairleigh Dickinson University Press, 1982, chap. 8.
6 For a brief but highly readable account of Social Research Incorporated (SRI), see John Easton, "Consuming Interests," *The University of Chicago Magazine*, August 2001, 16–22.
7 George Lipsitz, "Consumer Spending as State Project," in Susan Strasser, Charles McGovern, and Matthias Judt (eds.) *Getting and Spending: European and American Consumer Societies in the Twentieth Century*, New York: Cambridge University Press, 1998, esp. pp. 132–5.
8 Lynn Spigel, *Make Room for TV: Television and the Family Ideal in Postwar America*, Chicago: University of Chicago Press, 1992.
9 My summary of Chion in this paragraph comes from Michel Chion, *The Voice in Cinema*, trans. Claudia Gorbman, New York: Columbia University Press, 1999, pp. 17–29, 50–2. For Chion on *Rear Window*, see "The Fourth Side" in Žižek, *Everything You Always Wanted to Know About Lacan*, pp. 155–60.
10 See John Belton, "1950s Magnetic Sound: The Frozen Revolution," in Rick Altman (ed.) *Sound Theory, Sound Practice*, New York: Routledge, 1992, p. 156.
11 Chion, *The Voice in Cinema*, pp. 22–3.
12 Chion, *The Voice in Cinema*, pp. 50–2.
13 See Chion, *The Voice in Cinema*, p. 52, for the discussion of the voices during the drive in *Psycho*. To my mind one of the things that makes Chion's concept of the *acousmêtre* so useful is its potentially desconstructive force; and in my reading of Chion, as well as in my readings of filmic sound, I tend to push the concept in such a deconstructive direction.
14 Christopher D. Morris, *The Hanging Figure: On Suspense and the Films of Alfred Hitchcock*, Westport, CT: Praeger, 2002. Morris will go on to argue that the arbitrary nature of

the sign is the principal theme of the film. Morris's book, which draws on the work of Paul deMan and Jacques Derrida, is in many ways provocatively original. But by and large, it leaves "hanging" the question of history that is animating this essay.

15 Richard Dienst, *Still Life in Real Time: Theory After Television*, Durham, NC: Duke University Press, 1994. My summary of Dienst ranges through Chapter 1 of the book; the quotes are on, respectively, pp. 20 and 6.

16 This of course emphatically does *not* mean that television has no political dimension: rather, it suggests that televisual space operates synergistically with the public event, so that the event and the transmission become coextensive. Today, the media event and reality TV both exemplify this fact.

17 John Belton, "Technology and Innovation," in Geoffrey Nowell-Smith (ed.) *The Oxford History of World Cinema*, New York: Oxford University Press, 1996, p. 263.

18 See Belton, "Technology and Innovation," p. 266.

19 Belton, "1950s Magnetic Sound," in Altman (ed.), pp. 157–8.

20 Belton, "1950s Magnetic Sound," *Sound Theory, Sound Practice* p. 154.

21 Thomas Leitch, "The Outer Circle: Hitchcock on Television," in Allen and Ishii-Gonzàles, *Hitchcock Centenary Essays*, pp. 59–71.

22 See, for example, Mladen Dolar, "Hitchcock's Objects," in Žižek, *Everything You Always Wanted to Know About Lacan*, pp. 31–46; and Zizek's introduction to the same volume.

23 François Truffaut, *Hitchcock*, New York: Simon & Schuster, 1984, p. 297.

24 Michel Chion, "Quiet Revolution … or Rigid Stagnation," trans. Ben Brewster, *October*, vol. 58, 1990, 69–80.

Chapter 11

THE MASTER, THE MANIAC, AND *FRENZY*
Hitchcock's legacy of horror

Adam Lowenstein

At one point during *The American Nightmare* (Adam Simon, 2000), a recent documentary that examines the horror film's relation to U.S. social crises of the 1960s and 1970s, director John Landis invokes Alfred Hitchcock as a means of distinguishing horror from suspense:

> When you're watching a Hitchcock movie and you are in suspense, you are in suspense as the direct result of being in the hands of a master – a master craftsman who is manipulating the image in a way to lead you where he wants you to go. And I think that's a kind of comfortable scary feeling, whereas in some of the films we're talking about … when you look at a *Texas Chainsaw Massacre* (Tobe Hooper, 1974) or a *Last House on the Left* (Wes Craven, 1972) … the people making the movie are *untrustworthy*. You're watching it, and you're not in the hands of a master, you're in the hands of a maniac!

Landis voices a long-standing, familiar sentiment which this essay seeks to interrogate: Hitchcock, the reliable master of suspenseful audience manipulation, must not be confused with the untrustworthy "maniacs" responsible for the modern horror film's visceral assault on audiences. This insistence on demarcating Hitchcock's distance from the horror films that are so obviously indebted to him surfaces often in film criticism and trade press discourse, where distinctions between "just a horror film" and "more of a psychological thriller" are remarkably common.[1] So common, in fact, that one of Hitchcock's most enduring legacies could be defined as the line dividing suggestive, tasteful suspense from graphic, tasteless horror in the popular imagination. But what, then, do we make of *Frenzy* (1972), the Hitchcock film that most directly challenges "Hitchcockian" discretion?[2]

Responding to this question entails rethinking not only Hitchcock's contribution to cinema as an affective medium, but also the stakes of film spectatorship as audience confrontation and authorship's role in mediating such confrontations. By analyzing *Frenzy* as something closer to the culmination of Hitchcock's project of manipulating the very senses of his spectators, rather than a regrettable aberration from his signature style, I hope to suggest alternative possibilities for imagining cinema's capacity to confront the viewer. Blurring the boundaries between the "master" and the "maniac" allows us to see the cultural and political significance of cinematic spectatorship beyond the confines of tasteful suspense and tasteless horror.

Showing and suggesting

As Robert Kapsis has noted, *Frenzy*'s critical reputation has fallen precipitously since its initially enthusiastic reception in 1972.[3] While Hitchcock's previous ventures into the horror genre, *Psycho* (1960) and *The Birds* (1963), have amassed sequels, remakes, and cottage industries of criticism, *Frenzy*, by comparison, has remained relatively forgotten or maligned. Kapsis attributes the film's critical downgrading to "the power of both feminist thought and critical attitudes concerning cinematic stylization and restraint in shaping recent assessments of Hitchcock's work."[4] Tania Modleski has already written an eloquent response to those who dismiss the film as nothing more than crude misogyny,[5] so I will focus here on the issue of stylization and restraint. Perhaps no one has stated this case against *Frenzy* as baldly as Donald Spoto:

> The act of murder in Alfred Hitchcock's films had always been stylized by the devices of editing and the photographic wizardry that conveyed a sense of awfulness and of shock without languid attention to detail. But *Frenzy* was designed differently, for *Frenzy* was at once a concession to modern audiences' expectations and a more personal self-disclosure of the director's angriest and most violent desires ... Hitchcock insisted on all the ugly explicitness of this picture, and for all its cinematic inventiveness, it retains one of the most repellent examples of a detailed murder in the history of film ... what finally appeared onscreen was unworthy of the ordinary Hitchcock

restraint and indirectness. The scene gives the impression of a filmmaker eager to push to the limits his own fantasy and to join the ranks of the more daring (but in fact less imaginative) directors, whose excesses were just beginning to fill movie screens in 1971.[6]

Spoto's characterization of *Frenzy* as a disappointing departure from Hitchcock's trademark approach and a shameful surrender to perversities both personal and collective rests on the sharp distinction between showing and suggesting. For Spoto, Hitchcock's genius stems from his "restraint and indirectness," his ability to suggest without showing. *Frenzy* commits the sin of shocking its audience by showing horror in all its "ugly explicitness."

Yet a closer look at *Frenzy* reveals a complex performance of "showing" and "suggesting" without mutual exclusivity, where neither category emerges as the definitive answer to questions of how or why to shock an audience. Contrary to Spoto's account, Hitchcock very deliberately alternates between showing and suggesting in order to highlight their interpenetration. For example, the notoriously graphic rape and murder of Brenda Blaney (Barbara Leigh-Hunt) is followed by a scene where we only *hear* her secretary (Jean Marsh) scream as she discovers the corpse. The spectator's vision in this scene is limited to the nondescript exterior of Brenda's office building, held stubbornly in a static shot. Similarly, the demise of Babs Milligan (Anna Massey) begins as a reproduction of Brenda's murder, with the camera eagerly following along as Babs accompanies the killer Bob Rusk (Barry Foster) to his apartment. But just as Rusk confesses to Babs that she is his "type of woman," the same line he spoke to Brenda earlier, the camera retreats from the scene, descending the stairs and exiting the building in a fluid tracking movement that again flamboyantly denies horrific visual spectacle. Only this time, as we wait for the expected scream as confirmation of what we cannot see, we are thrown instead into the clangorous bustle of the street outside. Amidst the din of the crowded city street we cannot see *or* hear. But this scene, too, has its graphic complement. Babs's body returns later in all of its materiality when Rusk must search her corpse for his lost signature tiepin. Rusk's struggle with the resolutely uncooperative cadaver is both hilarious and harrowing in its insistently vivid display of the material fact of death, where stiff limbs must be manipulated painstakingly and frozen fingers must be pried open arduously, one cracking joint at a time.

These scenes demonstrate the sophisticated intertwining of showing and suggesting in *Frenzy*, but they also intimate how the film refuses to define the sensorium solely at the level of sight. I have already pointed to the crucial role of sound in these scenes, but even sound interacts with senses other than the visual during the course of the film. The noise of Babs's crunching fingers returns later, as Mrs. Oxford (Vivien Merchant) snaps breadsticks in front of her husband,

Inspector Oxford (Alec McCowen), while they discuss Rusk's murders. This pairing of body and food through sound ties the film's audio and visual economies to one of taste, a trajectory developed throughout the film with stark consistency.[7] As if that were not enough, there are also scenes where smell is added to the inventory of prominently displayed senses, as the wrong man protagonist Richard Blaney (Jon Finch) must deal with a jacket that has become rank after an overnight stay in a Salvation Army shelter. And of course, the sense of touch haunts the entire film through the extremely tactile murder method of strangulation. In this manner, *Frenzy* emerges as a remarkably self-conscious meditation on the possibilities of sensory perception. The result of this theme's systematic, almost didactic implementation is a film that underlines the inadequacy of the showing/suggesting binary that continues to organize Hitchcock's critical reputation. *Frenzy* does not simply ask us to open our eyes; it asks us to reshape our idea of what "opening our eyes" could mean.

Dan Auiler's recently published *Hitchcock's Notebooks* supports just such a re-reading of *Frenzy* as an ambitious, major work, rather than Spoto's depiction of the film as the misstep of a senile director at the mercy of private perversions and public hunger for more explicit cinematic spectacle. Auiler reveals details concerning *Frenzy*'s genesis in an aborted 1967 project alternatively titled either *Frenzy* or *Kaleidoscope*, a gruesome serial killer horror film that Hitchcock felt an extraordinary personal commitment towards – a project that moved the director, for the first time since *The Paradine Case* (1946), to pen his own screenplay. Universal's rejection of *Kaleidoscope* and mishandling of *Topaz* (1969) led Hitchcock not to despair, but to assertive action – he bought a controlling share in the company and moved *Frenzy*'s production to London to minimize studio interference.[8] In short, *Frenzy* must be acknowledged as a film Hitchcock very much wanted to make, not a mistake he succumbed to or was bullied into.

Revising authorship

Of course, *Frenzy* cannot be "saved" simply by conflating biography and work – this would merely repeat Spoto's condemnation in reverse. Such a move would also fall perilously close to what is usually recalled as the ideologically naive days of *Cahiers du cinéma* in the 1950s and 1960s – an era when a pantheon of auteurs could be constructed based on the more or less direct expression of their artistic personalities on film.[9] But even as auteurism has been supplanted in film studies in favor of other theoretical methodologies, author-based Hitchcock criticism has persisted and even flourished. Thomas Leitch offers an instructive explanation for this phenomenon by remarking that Hitchcock's multidimensional persona (equal parts auteur, impresario, businessman, and legend) "suggests that revisionist theories of authorship that present the author as nothing more than an effect of the apparatus ... are telling only part of the story."[10] Leitch's comment reflects a new willingness in film studies, explored with increasing frequency during the past ten years or so, to revise the "revisionist theories of authorship" associated with poststructuralist thinkers such as Roland Barthes and Michel Foucault and influentially adapted for cinema studies (via Lacanian psychoanalysis and Althusserian Marxism) by film theory of the 1970s. If the 1970s heralded the "death of the author," then the 1990s and present appear to announce a certain resuscitation of the author. In these new accounts, the author does not die so that the text and/or reader can be born, but lives in the moment the author imagines an audience, and, in turn, as that audience imagines an author. By consulting these new conceptions of authorship alongside *Frenzy*, I will continue questioning the construction of Hitchcock as defender of suspense in the face of horror.

In an important essay tellingly titled "The Revenge of the Author," Colin MacCabe argues for a notion of authorship that reckons with the complexity of filmmaking's production contexts. For MacCabe, the director's significance as an author emerges from his or her ability to organize the film's very first audience – its cast and crew. The director exists "not outside the text but within the process of its production" – a process centrally concerned with the figuring of production personnel *as* an audience.[11] Anthony Shaffer, who wrote the screenplay for *Frenzy* based on Arthur La Bern's novel *Goodbye Piccadilly, Farewell Leicester Square* (1966), has spoken about the illusion that the signature "Hitchcockian" moment belongs solely to Hitchcock himself. Shaffer points out that one of *Frenzy*'s most famously Hitchcockian sequences, the striking tracking shot that leaves Babs's murder scene unseen, was the screenwriter's invention, not Hitchcock's.[12] In addition, Shaffer claims that it was he who reminded Hitchcock of the importance of discretion throughout the film, including winning an argument that the director use a slightly toned-down version of the Brenda Blaney rape/murder. This is not to say that Shaffer (or La Bern, for that matter, whose novel already outlines a number of the film's key sequences) must be acknowledged as *Frenzy*'s "true" author – in fact, Shaffer himself admits that writing *Frenzy* meant writing for Hitchcock expressly, of creating scenes that he imagined would fit the director.[13] I offer these anecdotes to substantiate MacCabe's notion that film authorship depends on the *negotiation* between director and audience, beginning with production personnel. The point is not to itemize Shaffer or Hitchcock's individual contributions to *Frenzy*, but to recognize that "authorship" translates as a network of negotiations, usually organized around the director (but also conceivably aligned with a producer, star, or other personnel), that begins with production, but extends to distribution, exhibition, and reception. In this sense, a crucial component of *Frenzy*'s authorship involves active debate over discretion (and its absence) as a mode of communication between film and audience – a debate begun during *Frenzy*'s production, but continued during its reception.

In "The Unauthorized Auteur Today," Dudley Andrew describes further the author's existence as a relation between audience and director. Andrew (partly paraphrasing Timothy Corrigan) suggests that the author presents a "mode of identification" for the audience, a link to the process of creation. By tying the insights of Gilles Deleuze on temporality to his own suggestions, Andrew concludes, "the word 'auteur,' and the occasional signs left by whatever this word signals, can thicken a text with duration, with the past of its coming into being and with the future of our being with it."[14] The mode of identification offered to audiences by the figure of an author thus includes connections that span time, such as intertextual associations between a number of the director's films. Tom Gunning boldly enacts this type of proposition in his recent book *The Films of Fritz Lang: Allegories of Vision and Modernity*, a massive study composed largely of close readings of Lang's individual films. For Gunning, the author reemerges as a crucial aspect of interpretive practice for the audience, and for the critic. The author exists as "an invitation to reading … precisely poised on the threshold of the work, evident in the film itself, but also standing outside it, absent except in the imprint left behind."[15] What anchors Gunning's study is the firm belief that reading this imprint constitutes a valuable act of scholarship, one that allows audiences and critics to engage authorship by detecting interwoven patterns across a director's œuvre – an encounter not with the biographical author, but with "the language of cinema" as negotiated between viewer and director. In other words, the author's revenge is not reasserting absolute mastery over the meaning of his or her films, but suggesting a set of terms, a number of possible identifications, with which audiences make meaning from those films. To take these identifications seriously as a critic does not automatically denote ideological irresponsibility, where cinema's inscription in larger discourses is simply ignored – instead, it attends to the complexity of acts of reading within such discourses, where cinema's coming-into-being *between* director and viewer is a living negotiation rather than a predetermined certainty.

Revising intertextuality

Frenzy, as a late work from a highly idiosyncratic and well-known director, abounds with complicated intertextual references that invite certain acts of reading from the audience. As always with Hitchcock, these references function partly as a playful game of recognition with viewers, in the manner of his signature cameo appearances. But there is also a more contemplative and confrontational dimension to the intertextual moments of *Frenzy*. They generate the distinct sense that Hitchcock is not just inviting his audience to alter their expectations and responses to his work, but forcing them to.

Like the similarly titled *Psycho*, *Frenzy* features the graphic murder of a woman early on as its shocking centerpiece. But where *Psycho*'s shower scene assaults viewers with sound and speed – a flurry of rapid-fire cuts accompanied by Bernard Herrmann's piercing violins – the demise of Brenda Blaney in *Frenzy* proceeds slowly, repetitively, and almost completely without nondiegetic sound. Marion Crane (Janet Leigh), like *Psycho*'s audience, has only a few seconds to realize what is happening to her. Brenda, along with *Frenzy*'s audience, must contemplate her fate through a long, painful struggle with Rusk. She is given time to rebuff, to plan, to plead, to fight, to surrender, to pray, and finally, to scream, when she realizes that rape will not be the end of her suffering. Even the murder method itself, strangulation, emphasizes slow death in contrast to *Psycho*'s lightning-fast stabbing.

The key to the significance of these differences seems embedded in the conclusions of the two murders. In *Psycho*, Hitchcock dissolves from the bloody water swirling down the shower drain to a graphically matched extreme close-up of Marion's lifeless eye, rotating as if in imitation of the water's movement in the previous shot. Brenda's murder in *Frenzy* also ends with an extreme close-up on her face, but this time we see both of her eyes in the stillness of a freeze frame. This juxtaposition of *Psycho*'s single, moving eye with *Frenzy*'s two motionless eyes highlights how clearly Hitchcock demands that his audience *see* differently during *Frenzy*. We see things explicitly during Brenda's rape and murder that were only suggested during Marion's murder – most notably, the physical mate-riality of both the victim and killer's bodies. Marion's body stays partially obscured behind the literal and cinematic cuts of the shower scene, just as the identity of her killer remains hidden in shadow. *Frenzy*, by contrast, features well-lit close-ups of Brenda's exposed breasts and grotesquely lolling tongue as well as intimate (nearly case history) details relating to Rusk – the streak of hapless dating, the need for love, the sexual psychopathology, the murder method (dispensing quickly with the "mystery" of the necktie murderer's identity), and, perhaps most strikingly, his voice.[16] Where *Psycho* merges Marion's terrified scream and the violence of her killer's stabbing into the high-pitched sound of repetitive violin shrieks, *Frenzy* opts to repeat Rusk's low-pitched growl of "Lovely!" during the rape while Brenda prays softly. In short, Hitchcock presents jarring differences between the two murders in the very places that we brace ourselves for similarities – those places etched in our experience at the level of sensory perception, of sight and sound. The effect is a shocking breach of contract regarding Hitchcock's role as "master of suspense." If *Psycho* represents a watershed in Hitchcock's project of manipulating the sensory responses of his audience,[17] then *Frenzy* represents a stunning reevaluation of that watershed. The line between showing and suggesting has been redrawn, and Hitchcock insures that the audience *feels* the shock of this change. Viewers, who count on Hitchcock for the discreet tingle of suspense, are suddenly betrayed into an encounter with the sensory mortification of horror.

Another major betrayal of audience expectations surrounding suspense and horror occurs much earlier in Hitchcock's career and sheds light on *Frenzy*'s mode of audience address. *Sabotage* (1936) features an (in)famous sequence where the young boy Stevie (Desmond Tester) unwittingly carries a time bomb disguised with film reels across London. The audience is painfully aware of what Stevie cannot know – the ticking minutes before the bomb explodes. Suspense mounts as Stevie encounters numerous obstacles and distractions that prevent the safe completion of his errand. Since Stevie is a sympathetic character developed with affectionate care earlier in the film, the fretting audience still assumes that he will survive – that the contract of suspense will be upheld. Instead, Hitchcock kills Stevie and a busload of innocents when the bomb explodes.

This moment of audience betrayal in *Sabotage* was powerful enough for Hitchcock to reflect upon in writing several years later. In "The Enjoyment of Fear" (1949), Hitchcock invokes the language of the contract (as I have above) to describe the exchange between director and viewer necessary to produce pleasurable fear. The director assures the audience that although they may identify with characters placed in perilous situations in order to feel vicarious fear, they will not "pay the price" for this identification – that once audience sympathy with a character is established, it is not "fair play" to violate it.[18] *Sabotage* violates this agreement not only by killing Stevie, but by combining what Hitchcock refers to as "suspense" and "terror" (p. 121). "Suspense" depends on "forewarning," on audience knowledge of impending threat. "Terror," on the other hand, depends on "surprise," on the abrupt revelation of threat without warning (in this sense, "terror" overlaps the visceral shocks associated with horror). For Hitchcock, terror and suspense "cannot coexist" simultaneously, but must be alternated (p. 119). Yet Stevie's death, he admits, breaks his own rule – it combines forewarning with surprise. The result? "Thoroughly outraged" audiences and critics whose trust had been betrayed, who believed that Hitchcock himself "should have been riding in the seat next to the lad, preferably the seat he set the bomb on" (p. 121).

Frenzy celebrates the breach of contract that stung viewers so painfully in *Sabotage*. Other Hitchcock films ignore the taboo on violating audience sympathies (*Psycho*, of course, most famously), but *Frenzy* lays bare what had been present in Hitchcock's work all along – the interdependence of horror and suspense rather than their mutual exclusivity. For *Frenzy* posits forewarning in terms of audience expectations gleaned from Hitchcock's previous films as well as from his reputation as the master of suspense, and surprise in terms of the staccato rhythm of violation and reinstatement of these expectations. The film revisits *Sabotage* and the lessons learned there, but the goal is to unlearn these same lessons – to foreground outrage in viewer response, rather than evade it through upheld contracts; to blur suspense and horror, rather than alternate them; to fuse the "master" and the "maniac."

Once again, intertextual resonance invites viewers to participate in this project of unlearning. The film Stevie transports in *Sabotage* bears the title *Bartholomew the Strangler*, suggesting that *Frenzy*'s own strangler may be prefigured in this deadly bomb masquerading as a film. The trope of film as bomb, capable of inflicting damage on its audience, provides a striking interface between *Sabotage* and *Frenzy* – the unseen *Bartholomew the Strangler* could be understood as *realized* not only as the shocking explosion but as *Frenzy* itself. When inspector Ted Spenser (John Loder) discovers the *Bartholomew* film tin amidst the wreckage of the bus, a reporter asks him if the charred object is indeed a film tin. "No," Spenser seethes, "sardines." Spenser's equation of film as food along an axis of destructive consumption is fully borne out by *Frenzy*, just as Spenser's undercover identity as a greengrocer is ominously reversed by the greengrocer Rusk's undercover identity as the necktie murderer. Even the unlikely notion of a film entitled *Bartholomew* (!) *the Strangler* has its dark echo in *Frenzy* – our laugh over *Bartholomew*'s absurd title gets caught in our throat as we watch Spenser stare helplessly at the film tin as all that remains of Stevie, just as *Frenzy*'s many laughs maintain an uneasy proximity with real horror. Indeed, if *Frenzy* blurs horror and suspense as tools of audience confrontation, then humor overlays this chaotic cross-pollination as an equally vital mode of viewer self-reckoning.[19] Over and over, *Frenzy* returns to *Sabotage* not to correct what Hitchcock referred to as the "grave error" of Stevie's murder, but to inhabit that error in all its graveness.[20]

Revising the national

The language of the contract is not the only figurative discourse Hitchcock employs in "The Enjoyment of Fear" to discuss the betrayal of *Sabotage*. Another is the language of warfare. Hitchcock posits the difference between terror and suspense as "comparable to the difference between a buzz bomb and a V-2" (p. 118). Suspense, like the noisy buzz bomb, relies on the forewarning provided in the moments between the bomb's release and its impact. Terror, like the silent V-2, generates only surprise when it detonates. "To anyone who has experienced attacks by both bombs," Hitchcock explains, "the distinction will be clear" (p. 118).

Hitchcock draws attention here to apparently personal wartime experience in Britain. The autobiographical reference may seem somewhat odd at first glance, but its presence recalls a significant 1940 incident that helped convince Hitchcock to leave Hollywood temporarily and return to his native soil. One of his former British producers, Michael Balcon, publicly accused Hitchcock of abandoning his country during her most urgent time of national need. Hitchcock felt compelled to reply publicly: "The British government has only to call upon me for my services. The manner in which I am helping my country is not Mr. Balcon's business and has nothing to do with patriotic ideals."[21] In 1943–44, Hitchcock returned to Britain and contributed to three wartime propaganda projects supervised by the British Ministry of Information. He co-wrote and directed two short films about the French Resistance, *Bon Voyage* (1944) and *Aventure Malgache* (1944), and worked briefly as a "treatment advisor" on documentary footage of Nazi concentration camps. The unfinished documentary was known in its time only as "F3080," but in 1985 it was polished and broadcast by PBS as *Memory of the Camps*.[22] Despite these efforts, Hitchcock's references to the war in "The Enjoyment of Fear" suggest that questions of "patriotic ideals" still linger – questions that *Frenzy*, as yet another return to Britain, will recast in terms of demythologized "Britishness" and redefined lines between "Hitchcockian" suspense and "non-Hitchcockian" horror.

Just as *Frenzy* revisits Hitchcock's British film *Sabotage*, it also revisits the subject of Hitchcock's wartime "patriotism." Although claims have been made for Hitchcock's World War II films as unambiguous valorizations of democracy, others have noted the more ambivalent nature of these films' commitment to a democratic cause.[23] *Frenzy*, filmed away from Hitchcock's adopted homeland during the turbulent era of the Vietnam War, performs the kind of savage critique of British national mythology that the independent horror film was simultaneously leveling against American national mythology. World War II may reside in the past, Hitchcock seems to suggest, but the mythology of national consensus that sustains war, just or unjust, thrives in the present.

Not surprisingly, several British critics attacked *Frenzy* for portraying Britain anachronistically, as a function of Hitchcock's outdated state of mind rather than the current state of the nation.[24] What these critics miss is Hitchcock's concern with the national not so much as a matter of contemporary trends, but of deep-seated beliefs and images. This stereotypical archive of "Britishness" was readily available to Hitchcock – indeed, he had performed it for years in the guise of his trademark public persona. But as Thomas Elsaesser has noted, Hitchcock's performance of arch Britishness encompasses the double-edged quality of a British "dandyism of sobriety," where the values of "philistine Victorianism" come under fire precisely because Hitchcock ironically simulates these very mannerisms. Elsaesser argues that Hitchcock's authorial persona as sober dandy represents a "protest against a specifically English concept of maturity" that approaches the "force of a moral stance."[25] In *Frenzy*, the moral implications of this protest extend to the interrogation of proper, "mature" Britishness as the repository of national identity.

The opening of *Frenzy* immediately establishes the terms of national critique the rest of the film will elaborate. A postcard-quality aerial shot of London along the Thames is literally postmarked with an official "City of London" emblem in the upper right of the frame and accompanied by Ron Goodwin's robustly "royal" score. The camera tracks along the Thames as the credits roll, sailing beneath the majestically raised Tower Bridge. The shot is self-consciously picture-perfect, so it is somewhat jarring when it dissolves into the thick black smoke spewing from a passing boat. However, subsequent shots reveal this juxtaposition of ideal Britishness with an iconography of ugliness as the stylistic and thematic fabric of *Frenzy* as a whole. The first lines spoken in the film belong to the aristocratic dignitary Sir George (John Boxer), who addresses a crowd of reporters and onlookers beside the banks of the Thames. Sir George refers to Wordsworth as he promises the return of "ravishing sights" of natural beauty along the river, the restoration of a "clear" habitat that has been polluted by "the waste products of our society." In the very moment that he describes these "waste products" as "foreign," the crowd discovers a strangled female corpse floating in the river. The illusions of purity collapse alongside fantasies of pollution as "foreign" – Sir George worries that the corpse may be wearing his own "club tie."

The crowd of onlookers includes a portly man whose traditional British air mirrors Sir George's. He is dressed in a conspicuously conservative black suit and Victorian-style bowler hat, and although he gives his polite attention to Sir George's speech, he seems much more fascinated by the sight of the corpse and the comments about the grisly doings of Jack the Ripper from fellow observers in the crowd. Could such a man, the very image of upstanding Britishness, prove to harbor unsavory tastes and untrustworthy impulses? He is, of course, Alfred Hitchcock.

Hitchcock's cameo foregrounds *Frenzy*'s challenge to traditional conceptions of British national identity. The film's protagonist, Richard Blaney, is a former Royal Air Force pilot. But instead of the expected noble military hero, Blaney is abrasive, spiteful, and violent. This is a very different "wrong man" than those from Hitchcock's past – when Blaney is placed alongside a character like Roger Thornhill (Cary Grant) from *North by Northwest* (1959), the difference between "wrong man" and simply "wrong" becomes glaring. Similarly, the vibrant English local color associated with Covent Garden does not receive the warmly nostalgic treatment one might expect (especially given the line of greengrocers in Hitchcock's own family background). This is not the Covent Garden celebrated for its working-class rituals, as presented in Lindsay Anderson's documentary *Every Day Except Christmas* (1957) and adapted for other "authentically British" working-class locales in the related films of the British New Wave.[26] Instead,

Hitchcock's Covent Garden mixes the everyday labor of the market with the fantastic labor of murder. This interchange reaches its most literal extremes when Babs's dead body becomes part of a potato truck's cargo. But the green-grocer/killer Rusk embodies Covent Garden's Englishness most thoroughly, and most disturbingly. His rape and murder of Brenda Blaney is bookended by bites he takes from an apple. When he first takes the apple from Brenda he comments, "English, isn't it? Yeah, of course it is." Rusk, like *Frenzy* itself, encourages us to ask, "Is horror understandable as 'English'?" Of course it is.

Conclusion

When we consider Hitchcock's authorship in light of *Frenzy*, rather than divorced from it, the image and legacy of the "master" shifts significantly. A project of suspense becomes imbricated with a project of horror, resulting in a demytholo-gized representation of "Britishness" itself. The very term "Hitchcockian" radiates a different meaning, moving from precisely measured manipulation (with its connotations of "British" restraint) to shocking confrontation. On the eve of *Frenzy*'s screening at Cannes, François Truffaut asked Hitchcock "how a director of suspense and espionage films can compete with everyday life in 1972?"[27] This essay ultimately claims that *Frenzy* answers this question by figuring the relation between film and everyday life not in terms of competition, but of modes of perception. *Frenzy* demands that viewers redefine their ways of seeing Hitchcock, of perceiving his films between showing and suggesting, between suspense and horror. If the "master" *is* the "maniac," then Hitchcock's name can no longer divide the trustworthy "thriller" from the untrustworthy "horror film." "Untrustworthy," in this sense, might finally translate as "alive to the anguish of history."

Notes

Special thanks to Richard Allen, Charles Barr, Sam Ishii-Gonzáles, Tom Gunning, William Paul, Irina Reyn, and David Slocum for their helpful comments and encouragement along the way.

1 Witness, for example, the recent critical scandal surrounding Ridley Scott's *Hannibal* (2000), when expectations for a "thriller" could not be reconciled with unsettling cine-matic elements deemed worthy only of "horror." For a thoughtful examination of the thriller at the crossroads of several genres, see Martin Rubin, *Thrillers*, Cambridge: Cambridge University Press, 1999.
2 Director David Cronenberg responds with a similar question when asked why his visceral horror films refuse to be more discreetly "Hitchcockian" in their presentation of graphic violence: "Have you seen *Frenzy*?" Quoted in Chris Rodley (ed.) *Cronenberg on Cronenberg*, London: Faber & Faber, 1997, p. 41.

3 Robert E. Kapsis, *Hitchcock: The Making of a Reputation*, Chicago: University of Chicago Press, 1992, p. 146.
4 Kapsis, *Hitchcock*, p. 147.
5 See Tania Modleski, *The Women Who Knew Too Much: Hitchcock and Feminist Theory*, New York: Routledge, 1989, pp. 101–14. Modleski offers a valuable corrective to Jeanne Thomas Allen, "The Representation of Violence to Women: Hitchcock's *Frenzy*," *Film Quarterly* 38.3 (Spring 1985), pp. 30–8, who reads the film purely in terms of misogyny. See also Cynthia A. Freeland, *The Naked and the Undead: Evil and the Appeal of Horror*, Boulder, CO: Westview Press, 2000, pp. 168–76, for a reading of the film that ends up strengthening Modleski's overall interpretation, even though Freeland argues against some of her claims.
6 Donald Spoto, *The Dark Side of Genius: The Life of Alfred Hitchcock*, New York: Ballantine Books, 1983, pp. 545–6.
7 For a more detailed examination of the food theme in *Frenzy* and other Hitchcock films, see Dick Stromgren, " 'Now to the Banquet We Press': Hitchcock's Gourmet and Gourmand Offerings," in Paul Loukides and Linda K. Fuller (eds.) *Beyond the Stars III: The Material World in American Popular Film*, Bowling Green, OH: Popular Press, 1993, pp. 38–50.
8 Dan Auiler, *Hitchcock's Notebooks: An Authorized and Illustrated Look Inside the Creative Mind of Alfred Hitchcock*, New York: Avon, 1999, pp. 277–89, 545–50.
9 See John Caughie (ed.) *Theories of Authorship*, London: Routledge, 1993, for a compendium of important writings relevant to film authorship, including those of *Cahiers du cinéma*. For a valuable thinking of the conventional account of authorship associated with *Cahiers*, see James Naremore, "Authorship and the Cultural Politics of Film Criticism," *Film Quarterly* 44.1, Fall 1990, pp. 14–23.
10 Thomas M. Leitch, "The Outer Circle: Hitchcock on Television," in Richard Allen and S. Ishii-Gonzáles (eds.) *Hitchcock Centenary Essays*, London: BFI, 1999, p. 69.
11 Colin MacCabe, "The Revenge of the Author," in *The Eloquence of the Vulgar: Language, Cinema and the Politics of Culture*, London: BFI, 1999, p. 38.
12 Anthony Shaffer, "*The Wicker Man* and Others," *Sight and Sound* (August 1995), p. 28. See Charles Barr, *English Hitchcock*, Moffat, Scotland: Cameron & Hollis, 1999, for an extended discussion of the importance of Hitchcock's screenwriters in relation to his British films.
13 See Shaffer's commentary in *The Story of* Frenzy (Laurent Bouzereau, 2000), a documentary included on the DVD release of *Frenzy* (Universal, 2000).
14 Dudley Andrew, "The Unauthorized Auteur Today," in Jim Collins, Hilary Radner, and Ava Preacher Collins (eds.) *Film Theory Goes to the Movies*, New York: Routledge, 1993, pp. 80, 85.
15 Tom Gunning, *The Films of Fritz Lang: Allegories of Vision and Modernity*, London: BFI, 2000, p. 5.
16 One might include the physical presence of Rusk's smiling mother (Rita Webb) during the film as a knowingly humorous addition to this list – her sweet (and silent) visage seems calculated to be everything Mrs. Bates was not.
17 For an excellent consideration of *Psycho*'s landmark status for "postmodern" viewing practices and new modes of cinematic spectatorship, see Linda Williams, "Discipline and Fun: *Psycho* and Postmodern Cinema," in Christine Gledhill and Linda Williams (eds.) *Reinventing Film Studies*, London: Arnold, 2000, pp. 351–78.
18 Alfred Hitchcock, "The Enjoyment of Fear" (1949), reprinted in Sidney Gottlieb (ed.) *Hitchcock on Hitchcock: Selected Writings and Interviews*, Berkeley and Los Angeles: University of California Press, 1995, p. 120. Subsequent citations appear in parentheses in the text.. For thoughtful close readings of *Sabotage* that are attentive to the issues of audience address I examine later, see Mark Osteen, " 'It Doesn't Pay to Antagonize the Public': *Sabotage* and Hitchcock's Audience," *Literature/Film Quarterly* 28.4, 2000, pp. 259–68; and Susan Smith, "Disruption, Destruction, Denial: Hitchcock as Saboteur," in Allen and Ishii-Gonzáles, *Hitchcock Centenary Essays*, pp. 45–57.

19 The dark encounter between humor and horror in Hitchcock recalls the confrontational tactics of Surrealism. For more on this connection, see Alfred Hitchcock, "Why I Am Afraid of the Dark" (1960), reprinted in Gottlieb (ed.) *Hitchcock on Hitchcock*, pp. 142–5, and James Naremore, "Hitchcock and Humor," chap. 2 in this volume.

20 Quoted in François Truffaut, with the collaboration of Helen G. Scott, *Hitchcock*, revised edition, New York: Simon & Schuster, 1984, p. 109.

21 Quoted in Spoto, *The Dark Side of Genius*, p. 245.

22 See Bret Wood, "Foreign Correspondence: The Rediscovered War Films of Alfred Hitchcock," *Film Comment* 29.4 (July–August 1993), pp. 54–59; and Elizabeth Sussex, "The Fate of F3080," *Sight and Sound* 53.2 (Spring 1984), pp. 92–7.

23 See Ina Rae Hark, "'We Might Even Get in the Newsreels': The Press and Democracy in Hitchcock's World War II Anti-Fascist Films," in Allen and Ishii-Gonzáles, *Hitchcock Centenary Essays*, pp. 333–47.

24 See Peter Hutchings, "*Frenzy*: A Return to Britain," in Charles Barr (ed.) *All Our Yesterdays: 90 Years of British Cinema*, London: BFI, 1986, p. 369. Hutchings reads *Frenzy* as a "compendium of post-war British cinema" (p. 369) – I argue that the film is closer to an interrogation of such national cinema traditions.

25 Thomas Elsaesser, "The Dandy in Hitchcock," in Allen and Ishii-Gonzáles, *Hitchcock: Centenary Essays*, pp. 3–13; quotations from pp. 5 and 11. For a valuable exploration of the figure of the dandy within Hitchcock's films, see Richard Allen, "Hitchcock, or the Pleasures of Metaskepticism," in Allen and Ishii-Gonzáles, *Hitchcock Centenary Essays*, pp. 221–38.

26 In this sense, *Frenzy* mirrors earlier British horror films such as *Peeping Tom* (Michael Powell, 1960), which, as I have argued elsewhere, contest the reassuring assumptions of working-class "authenticity" embraced by the British New Wave. See Adam Lowenstein, "'Under-the-Skin Horrors': Social Realism and Classlessness in *Peeping Tom* and the British New Wave," in Justine Ashby and Andrew Higson (eds.) *British Cinema, Past and Present*, London: Routledge, 2000, pp. 221–32.

27 Truffaut, *Hitchcock*, p. 338.

Chapter 12

HITCHCOCK'S IRELAND
the performance of Irish identity in *Juno and the Paycock* and *Under Capricorn*

James Morrison

Alfred Hitchcock's work, by many accounts, is notoriously apolitical. Especially given Hitchcock's avowals of allegiance to "pure" cinema, it has always been easier for critics to view his work in the context of formalist-aestheticism than to examine the political ramifications his work may substantiate, even despite those avowals. Moreover, when Hitchcock's work has been treated in terms of political or social issues, it has usually been conformed to a traditional modernist template that aligns experimental form with "progressive" ideologies, even in the face of apparently reactionary content. To be sure, if Hitchcock's work has been treated politically at all, it has been seen either as a manifestation of the modernist self-reflexivity that evidently, in these accounts, exceeds politics as such; or else, on the one hand, as a reinforcement of British imperialism or, on the other, as complicit with the institutions of post-World War II America's national security state.[1]

For a filmmaker so apparently committed to shoring up the British or American Empires, however, Hitchcock is notably attentive, in his films, to issues of xenophobia, nationalist insularity, and colonialist domination. Indeed, at times when the prevalent portrayal of Empire in British cinema typically fostered the legitimacy of British domination, Hitchcock's work repeatedly appeared sympathetic to the self-determination of nations under British dominion. The treatment of the Canadian Hannay in *The Thirty-Nine Steps* is a striking example, but the only two of Hitchcock's films to treat Irish themes in a sustained way challenge most suggestively the accepted paradigms for understanding socio-political representation in his movies. One of these films is the 1930 adaptation of Sean O'Casey's play *Juno and the Paycock*; the other is the 1949 film version of Helen Simpson's novel *Under Capricorn*. Both films reflect interestingly on Hitchcock's relation to British Empire, revealing an unusually complex response to national and colonial discourses.

More specifically, both films present nationality as a form of identity linked to performance. The trope of performance is associated in both films with other facets of identity as well, such as race or gender, but it takes on particular resonance in relation to concepts of national identity. Though my use of the idea of the "performative" is intended to be evocative rather than definitive, I do mean to employ the concept with a full range of its theoretical implications. Indeed, the relation here between performance, theatricality, and figuration may seem to require a certain slippage. The notion of the "performative" has, after all, followed a highly adaptable intellectual trajectory in its movement from speech-act theory (in the work of J.L. Austin) to deconstruction (in the work of De Man and Derrida) to feminist theory (in the work of Judith Butler). In its initial formulations, the relation of language and matter – the speech that was also an act – found its fullest shape in figuration, because the symbolic referents named in a trope, Austin thought, inevitably implied an act: the comparison of tenor and vehicle.[2] At the same time, the speech-act itself necessitated a more literal kind of performance, to the extent that the legitimation of speech-acts often depended on forms of authority certified in or conferred by ritual and artifice: those of the state (as in a christening, "I name thee …") or, which may come to much the same thing, those of the law ("I condemn you …").[3]

As Eve Sedgwick and Andrew Parker point out, "the stretch between theatrical and deconstructive meanings of 'performative' seems to span the polarities of, at either extreme, the *extroversion* of the actor, the *introversion* of the signifier."[4] By the time feminism adopted the term "performative," it had subsumed these multiple senses. It names "the ways identities are constructed iteratively through complex citational processes," and it posits an alienated subjectivity to be remade as provisionally whole through the performance of given texts and conventions, or the figural subversion of received discourses.[5] My understanding of the specifically nationalist valences of the performative, relying on each of the senses outlined here, may analogize self and country: the split-self performed as coherent, the splintered nation reconstituted as "whole." However, it is because I do not want to insist on an insuperable correlation between performative *subject* and performative *nation* that I prefer, on the whole, to allow the implications of the concept, with all of its apparent slip-knots, to emerge inductively during the course of the analysis.

The metaphor of theatricality looms large in Hitchcock's work as a whole, as has frequently been noted in the scholarship, but the connection of theatricality to issues of national identity is especially significant in the two films under consideration here that reflect on Irish national identity. *Juno and the Paycock* and *Under Capricorn* are distinctive among Hitchcock's films in elaborating the theme of theatricality at the level of form, *through* the process of adaptation of the theatrical or literary works that are the films' sources. In both cases, instead of transposing the material into traditionally "cinematic" terms, Hitchcock draws attention to the theatrical or artificial nature of the source material itself. Indeed, both films employ stylized settings, mannered performances, exaggerated visual styles that emphasize their theatrical origins, or narrative structures that self-consciously foreground the explicitly *dramatic* heritage of the narratives. Their emotional registers distinguish them from nearly all of Hitchcock's other films, and their generic lineage – the naturalist drama of O'Casey or the historical-romance of Simpson's novel – place them apart from the "suspense-thriller" genre with which Hitchcock is so closely identified. The genre differences of these two films may itself account for their special place in Hitchcock's work. If the "suspense-thriller" allows Hitchcock to employ a high degree of artifice in a manner congruent with the "willing suspension of disbelief" that genre typically enables or demands, these films may testify to the result when Hitchcock brings such characteristic artifice to genres that do not so readily assimilate it. Certainly the most striking feature of these films is their definitive anti-illusionism; incorporating elements of the modernist/expressionist artifice Hitchcock has traditionally been noted for, these films also use such techniques to reflect on national identity as a form of performance that undermines essentialist notions of nationality and thereby implicitly, I argue, subjects the colonial discourses of British imperialism to critique.

Nation and performance in *Juno and the Paycock*

Juno and the Paycock ends with the most direct expression of grief in Hitchcock's work. Having just learned that her daughter is pregnant out of wedlock, Juno (Sara Allgood) has returned to her home in working-class Dublin to find that her family's creditors have taken their furniture. Fast upon these set-backs, she discovers the crowning horror: her son has been murdered as an informant by the Irish Republican Army. Alone in the empty room, beseeching the statue of the Virgin Mary that is all that is left her, she wails in purest grief. The moment is unmatched in Hitchcock's work, at least until the scene in *The Man Who Knew Too Much* (1956) when Jo McKenna (Doris Day) learns of her son's abduction and breaks down in an agony of distress. Both these scenes of maternal grief at the loss of a son are granted an emotional weight through what can only be seen, especially in the context of Hitchcock's work as a whole, as the nearly unique recourse of the relaxation of performative inhibition. So forthrightly do the actors express this grief in both scenes, so boldly do they lay bare the characters' suffering, that the scenes achieve an emotional rawness that presses the bounds of performance. By contrast to Hitchcock's usual demand for underplaying among his actors, the scenes are especially striking instances of an excess of emotional expression, an abdication of performative self-control.

An important difference separates the two scenes, however. Juno's expression of grief repeats line for line the grief-stricken litany, earlier in the film, of the mother of the murdered boy Juno's son has informed on: "O Sacred Heart of Jesus, take away these hearts of stone and give us hearts of flesh. ... Take away this murdering hate and give us thine own eternal love!" The pseudo-Shakespearean oratory of the lines contributes to the sense that this final speech is, precisely, a soliloquy, a repeated performance of a prior, given text, rather than the natural, spontaneous outpouring of feeling the scene's emotional register would seem to imply. Juno herself comments on the fact that the words are not her own; it is, as she puts it, merely her "turn" to recite them. Even at this most desolate moment of the drama, and despite a soaring emotion that appears to break out of the simulation of performance into a transcendent realm of true, pure feeling, the text continues to insist on the performative dimension of the drama.

An important theme in Sean O'Casey's play is that of national identity as a species of performance. In its Synge-like exhibition of an array of Irish types, the play parades a variety of brogues and slangs, and in its election of apolitical but nominally "patriotic" characters, it points up an imaginary basis of national affiliation. Both these points place the play in a lineage of Irish drama running from Yeats and Synge to O'Casey and Denis Johnston, and on to such contemporary Irish playwrights as Brian Friel or Martin McDonagh. In O'Casey, despite the characters' pledged indifference to the national "troubles" that surround them, they perform their own Irishness exuberantly; but because of their removal from political strife, this allegiance defines itself not around political action, but around slogans and sayings, popular mythologies, folk tales, songs, and other types of shared national discourse that may be viewed as ideologically "neutral" by those who recite them. O'Casey's work shows the process by which the characters seek refuge in such mythologies of nation, only to find that, however remote they think the tumultuous politics of nation are from their own lives, they cannot escape their own implication in them. (History is a nightmare, in other words, from which one cannot wake.) Indeed, it is *because* O'Casey seems inclined to locate an essential "Irishness" in his characters that the theme of performance emerges so prominently in his work, or in that of the tradition he joins. The point is not that the complex, irresolvable stratifications of Irish iden-

tity – Catholic and Protestant, Nationalist and Unionist, to cite only the dominant matrices – refute the possibility of a common essence around which Irish
nationality might cohere; rather, it seems to be that because of the prevalence of
a common folk culture, the strife between Nationalists and Britons (to name only
one obstacle to Irish "unity") must ultimately be seen as local squabbling or
regional bloodbaths, without answerability to the "real" identities of the people
or the real needs of the working class.

Each of O'Casey's earliest plays takes shape around one of the major crises of
Irish nationalism of the early twentieth century: The Easter Uprising in *The
Shadow and the Gunman*, the Civil War in *The Plough and the Stars*, and the war for
independence in *Juno and the Paycock*. In each case, O'Casey laments the deferral
of class politics to nationalist politics. In *Juno and the Paycock*, O'Casey portrays an
Irish-Catholic family unjoined by Irish nationalism. This disalliance functions not
only to refute the notion that all Catholics are or were Irish nationalists – the
feature that may well have attracted Hitchcock to this material – but to illustrate
the competing affiliations that complicate the politics of self-interest. In treating
the theme of evasion in O'Casey's work, Raymond Williams connects the
problem of self-interest to performance: "Through all the early plays, it is the
fact of evasion, and the verbal inflation that covers it, that O'Casey at once
creates and criticizes."[6] The "true nature of the endless fantasy of Irish talk" in
O'Casey's plays, according to Williams, inheres in a "formally rhetorical
Communism" that vilifies nationalist political identity as a betrayal of the self-
interests of the working-class.[7] Yet the plays can hardly be said to celebrate
apolitical dispositions, since the effort to escape politics fails as tragically as does
the impulse to engage with politics. For Williams, it appears that there may well
be some "true nature" of national identity that O'Casey's characters miss. The
types of performance Williams finds in the characters' endless bombast, puffery,
and showing off – stereotypical attributes of Irish national identity, of course –
enable them only to "evade" the real circumstances of their material histories. In
Hitchcock's film, these circumstances are conceived in far less stable or unitary
terms.[8]

The metaphor of O'Casey's title laminates performance on identity, but
Hitchcock literalizes the metaphor rather emphatically. In O'Casey, the image of
the peacock evokes a prideful exhibitionism linked to Irish identity by the collo-
quial transcription of the title, which also condenses the metaphor's equilibration
of money with nation. An insistent visual metaphor in the film presents as
peacock-like the baroque megaphone of the phonograph the family acquires
when Captain Boyle wrongly believes they have inherited a bequest, and the
metaphor is played out in a crisp, mercurial dissolve that graphically matches the
image with the terrified face of the son. The shell-shaped megaphone with its
crescent of sinuous grooves suggests the erect feathers of the peacock's tail, and

the gramophone's function in the plot bears out some of the image's association with vanity or aggression to the extent that it represents Captain Boyle's new-found sense of power. The delusory aspect of that power is manifested in the image as well, as it is in the directness of the dissolve that graphically matches the megaphone with Johnny's face. In this superimposition, Hitchcock visually underlines an irony already apparent in the play's text, that of the family's obliviousness to Johnny's impending fate, but in presenting it with such overdetermined force, Hitchcock juxtaposes two distinct national attitudes. Johnny's nationalism is rooted in traditional notions of patriotism, of a valued tradition to be preserved: "Haven't I done enough for Ireland?" he wails, and the plaint brings with it a set of assumptions about Ireland-as-motherland, about the myths of the Gaelic pastoral to be defended against the onslaught of British imperialism.

In the superficially good-natured whimsy of its folk attitudes, on the other hand, the family's nationalism bears no traces of any such reactionism. The performative community they achieve as they sing along with the record on the gramophone is explicitly nationalist and exclusionary – "If you're Irish, come into the parlor. … So long as you're from Ireland there's a welcome on the mat" – but if O'Casey's point is the incommensurability of folk nationalism and political nationalism, Hitchcock's seems to be the *inextricability* of the two attitudes. Assuming that Irish resistance to British rule sought, among other things, to protect a rural, traditional heritage (Gaelic myth) from an encroaching modernity (British imperialism), the most striking function of the gramophone is to wed the metaphorics of rural poesy (the image of the "paycock") to the rise of industrial commerce. Despite the military past signified in his title, Captain Boyle eagerly accepts the imperatives of an ascendant consumer culture that allies power with purchase, and with it, accepts the commodification of folk traditions through mechanical reproduction. The play's setting in an industrial slum has already revealed the anachronism of the pastoral in the wake of the modern, an effect Hitchcock emphasizes in "opening up" the play, through shots of the desolate city. Considering the inevitability of severe regulation of production, import and export levied by the colonizer upon the colonized – and the consequent likelihood that the gramophone would have to have been a product of England – the pleasure the family takes in the commodity is shown as evidence of their own complicity in imperial domination or their failure to recognize their own self-interests.[9]

The insinuating quality of the dissolve suggests the workings, rhetorically speaking, of both the comparison of metaphor and the obliteration of displacement. Figurally, the two images of the dissolve invite comparison through their superimposition; literally, in any dissolve, one image displaces another. The graphic match of the gramophone and Johnny's face emblematizes both the powerful claims of Irishness that hold Johnny in thrall – the father's strutting "paycock"-like posturing before which he is powerless, the folk culture that signifies what is to be preserved – and the imperial authority that swallows him. The boldness of the technique links the scene to the film's other metaphor, also rendered in a severe, extended dissolve that leads into the final scene. This dissolve superimposes the statue of the Virgin Mary over the image of Juno, and combines the apparent didacticism of its rhetoric with an ambiguity of meaning that suggests a strongly parallel example from Hitchcock's later work. In *The Wrong Man* (1957), the unjustly accused Manny heeds his mother's injunction to pray, and a high-lit shot of a crucifix dissolves into a close-up of Manny, which is then painstakingly matched in an elaborate dissolve to the face of the actual robber. The didactic meaning is clear: Manny's prayer is answered, the real criminal is exposed. The figural meaning, however, cannot so readily resolve the doubleness the trope necessitates. The visual trope suggests not a culminating redemption but the image of a split self – two faces interlinked – fulfilling an earlier metaphor in the film, a fractured mirror reflecting Manny's face. In *Juno and the Paycock*, the iconographic figurine is readable, like the gramophone, as an emblem of commodification, but it does not lend itself to the same didactic clarity, since the stark, tragic elevation of the final scene overwhelms what might have appeared as its most immediate available meaning: the admonition that Juno take solace in her faith. Considering the emphatically heightened register of Allgood's performance at this moment in the film, the icon seems to be presented more as a gauge of tragic destiny than as a source of potential redemption.

The final soliloquy is, quite literally, a speech-act. It *performs* an act which it nominates only through imitation, neither fully connotative nor strictly denotative. In her reiteration of another mother's grief, Juno takes on the burden of the troubles that surround her. *She is what she does*, and the final scene is notable for the starkness of its execution. The camera retreats with solemn deliberation, as we watch Juno trudge heavily across an empty room. Despite the pseudo-inspirational image of the figurine, it is the sense of emptiness that this last shot punctuates, both through the distance of scale and the stifling of sound. The recording appears to be direct sound, and Hitchcock achieves an effect worthy of early Renoir by allowing the room's emptiness to swallow the actor's lines. It is not just, then, the quality of performance that makes the moment so decisively *performative*; rather, the scene returns us to the origin of performativity in speech-act theory, where act is seen to be determined not by prior, essential being, but by an identification with an objectified Other, in imitation of external convention rather than obedience to inner edict. Judith Butler's influential adaptation of speech-act to gender theory effectively evokes the tenor of this scene (and reminds us as well of its gender specificity): "an identity tenuously constituted in time, instituted in an exterior space through a *stylized repetition of acts*."[10] On this image, with a desolate flourish, the picture fades.[11]

Metonymy and theatricality in *Under Capricorn*

Like *Juno and the Paycock*, *Under Capricorn* occupies an unusual place in Hitchcock's work. In the recently published *Hitchcock's Notebooks*, the editor reflects tradition by referring to *Under Capricorn* as a "disappointment,"[12] but other critics, Chabrol and Rohmer among them, have found in its highly charged, distinctive atmosphere something like the "key" to Hitchcock's work. Given the film's reputation as a rather static, talky costume-drama, it is surprising that the critics of *Cahiers du cinéma* would have so championed it, considering their surpassing disdain for the genteel tradition-of-quality historical melodrama it at least superficially resembles. However, the film makes sustained use of two crucial means, with an equivocal but entrenched significance in cinematic representation: metonymy and theatricality. Indeed, the film proposes an unusual relation between these modes of operation with important implications for the treatment of theme, particularly, in this case, the representation of ideologies of nation.

The opening shots of the film reveal the most pertinent terms of this relation. Under the credits, we see a map of Australia, and in the first several shots a series of sites representing the space of Australia while an archly authoritative voice narrates significant details in the history of Britain's colonization of New South Wales, from Captain Cook's "discovery" of the country in 1770, to the imposition of a policy of penal importation, to King William's appointment of a new governor in 1831. "And" – intones the orotund voice, invoking the authority of narrative convention to mask the gaps in history – "here our story begins!" The notably broad and somewhat fanciful version of this history provided by the grandiloquently disembodied voice has its analogue in the images that accompany it. The map stands in contrast to other well-known maps in the lore of film nation, such as the one that introduces *Casablanca* (Michael Curtiz, 1942). Similarly accompanied by a god-like voice-over, that map is charted, contextualized, and stratified. It presents a more holistic geographical framework in which to locate the space of "Casablanca," representing it in relation to surrounding spaces, and it is graphically circumscribed by explanatory markings that appear on the screen without visible human intervention.

Given such strategies of representation, it is difficult to avoid the conclusion that a territorial version of nationhood, dependent on given zones that foster and dictate colonial discourses, is being blithely universalized across a site – "Africa" – that need not, of course, have been subject to such conceptions. The map functions, in other words, as an index of spatial stratification whose simultaneous function as a guarantor of colonial dominion is thereby denied. The map in *Under Capricorn* is de-stratified and de-contextualized. It is not shown in relation to other points of geographical reference, and aside from the assignment of random names of coastal cities, no inland settlements or territories on the map are charted. In thus projecting Australia as an unsettled "dark continent," the map exposes a contradiction on which colonial discourse is predicated, which it is typically at pains to conceal. The map erases any signs of aboriginal habitation and signifies "Australia" as an open, unmarked, unoccupied territory, standing in presumed readiness to be colonized, but it also reveals that the boundaries of the colonial enterprise are not timeless frontiers that have always really been there, waiting to be fulfilled by the manifest destinies of dominion and the progressive ideals of history itself. Rather, they are revealed as constructed territories, lines on a map, to be drawn by the violent interventions of colonial power.

Unlike the map of *Casablanca*, the map of *Under Capricorn* foregrounds its status as a "sign." It is quite obviously a page in a book, as evidenced by an unhidden wrinkle running through it and a printed page-border enclosing it. By contrast to the pristine graphic emblem of *Casablanca*, that of *Under Capricorn* presents itself not as an incorporeal symbol, free of material, worldly influences, but as a mundane object, rife with them; and the insistent artifice of the first shots of Australia realizes the anti-illusionist impulse of the presentation of the map. In one of these shots, an obvious miniature with a windmill's mechanical wheel spinning wanly at the left of the frame, the only other motion is that of a British flag waving at the right, and while the monochromatic coloration of the shot – a luminous, irreal blue dominating the composition – emphasizes the flag by its color contrast, it also draws attention to the general artifice of the film's opening. The flag is a sign of colonial presence, to be sure, but its metonymic status is evidenced by its segregation in the shot, and the voice-over immediately articulates a crisis of colonial power: "The colony exported raw materials. It *imported* materials even more raw: Prisoners – many of them not guilty – who were to be shaped into the pioneers of a great dominion." Accompanying this spoken text is the closest shot of the sequence, a canted low-angle of a group of convicts being herded ashore (a shot that will recur significantly in a different context at the end of the film). Here the shot and the narration both archly call into question the agency of the colonizer. Far from the familiar mythic figures of imperialist vigor, glorified explorers forging an uncharted terrain that is theirs by the assumptions of Manifest Destiny, these "pioneers" are themselves figures of abjection, whose conquest of the new world is seen not in light of idealist determination but of anterior servility. The colonists are not *already* "pioneers," any more than the map asserts the idealist priority of imperial territory. Rather, they are to be "shaped" into "pioneers"; that is to say, these colonists are themselves subject to colonial force, their role as colonizer itself an edict decreed, to be performed by sovereign will. Thus, the revealed artifice of the film's opening visuals is fulfilled by this thematic emphasis in the plot.

Without wishing to suggest any essential affinity between the rhetoric of cinematic representation and the ideology of nationhood, I do want to propose that both rely for certain forms of their power on tropes of metonymy or synecdoche.[13] To the extent that these figures underlie any act of representation, and to the extent that the ideology of nation depends on representations to sustain itself, the link may be a purely formal one. Given the importance of cinema in establishing and defining many twentieth-century nationalities, however, the connection appears to go beyond the strictly formal. In the development of cinema, the discovery of synecdoche in the variability of shot scales displaced a prior holism: the nearly exclusive reliance on the long shot in the first decade of film. Even that holism was figurative, of course, requiring that the large-scale, unedited image stand in for an absent whole, the "world" looming beyond it, rhetorically implied by the image's very existence, only the acceptance of which could make the image compelling to a viewer. The invention of editing and variation of shot scale presaged the *loss* of a "whole," then, but in acknowledging the synecdochic or metonymic basis of cinematic representation, it promised a new, virtual, imaginary one. Fragmenting the primitive "whole" into a complex order of parts – the hand or the face that was to be taken for the real presence of a whole body, for instance – the cinema gradually developed a language that compelled the accumulation of fragments into an embracing plenitude, whether it be the unities of classical editing, the syntheses of Eisensteinian montage, or some other theoretical alternative.

Discourses of nationalism also work to generalize part to whole, and whether this process is violently upheld or only zealously pledged, it typically requires that the whole, to achieve or to usurp its imaginary unity, be thought apprehensible through its parts: the individual citizens collocated into group identities, the "states" (or other local district) subsumed into the "union" (or other metonymic totality), or the national symbol – the map, the flag, the armband – that seizes its narrative authority or its auratic sanctity through its supernal reference to the teeming yet still unreduced "whole." A doctrine of imperialism, such as that of Britain, will often have to address its own implicit challenges to national holism. Does the need for expansion imply prior incompletion? Of course not: it *fulfills* an ideal unity always already in place. And the violence of colonialism is, among other things, the violence of rampant metonymy, its formal trajectory reversed so that the part no longer appears to gesture toward an absent or conceptually inconceivable whole, but the whole swallows the constituent parts that will serve to shore it up, and have been abiding through primitive epochs of regression and benightedness in anticipation of their culmination within the empire as it always was and ever shall be.

Three images in *Under Capricorn* take on a particularly bristling significance in this context: a shrunken head, a wooden placard, and an unseen horse. The shrunken head, presented in strikingly emphatic close-up at three points in the film, carries associations of ritual, monstrousness, aboriginal violence, a *blackness* practically equivalent (if the theoretical excess of the sign did not refute the easy correspondence) to the "primitive." "There is a traffic in such things here," mutters Sam Flusky, an Irish convict deported to Australia, accosted in the street by a seller of heads. Flusky's crime is at issue in the plot: he is said to be a murderer, and lives with mysteriously acquired wealth on a remote estate, with a withdrawn, alcoholic wife, Hattie. The plot twins Hattie's rehabilitation with the rejuvenation of their marriage through the equivocal agency of Charles Adair, a visiting Irish "gentleman," nephew to the governor. The shrunken head conjures a "black market" and thus signifies the legislation of a primordial nativism by the allegedly civilizing encroachments of the colonizers. But the transaction is complex. The seller approaches Flusky with an air of furtive conspiracy, stealthily revealing the swaddled head as if he were exposing or offering a sexual opportunity, and when Flusky rebuffs him violently, the seller shouts recrimination, accusing Flusky of being a murderer.

As evocations of the primitive often will, the encounter carries strong suggestions of the unspeakable and the illicit, and these are given reign by the curious refusal to specify – as if the colonizer could readily comprehend the primitive instinct – why the head might be a desired commodity (talismanic power? aphrodisiac potency?). Thus, its real function is to serve as a gauge between colonizer and colonized, even as the whole plot resists the schematism of the binary opposition. The seller deems Flusky a suitable customer because of his troubled relation to the Empire – he has been "a guest of Her Majesty" in prison, he is known to have been a criminal, and he is affiliated with the colonial dominion of Ireland – but Flusky lashes out because of his identification with the colonizer, an instinctive disgust at the primitive ritual of the colonized, which is called upon to justify their subordination.

On his first visit to the Flusky mansion, Adair notes a signboard with the name of the house: "Minyago Yugilla." Not recognizing the language, he asks the driver what it means. The driver curtly translates: "Why weepest thou?" The words, not surprisingly in the Hitchcock movie perhaps most deeply invested in the thematics of rebirth and renewal, connote the Christian contexts of resurrection. They refer to the New Testament story of Christ's resurrection, wherein an angel appears at Christ's tomb and asks Mary Magdalene, "Woman, why weepest thou?" (John 20:12–13).[14] The thematic resonance of these words in the film, with their associations of insufficient but ultimately restored faith, is less important here than the generalized signifier of Christianity that couches the allusion in an unknown language. The signboard functions, in part, as a generic marker, evocative of the Romanticist Gothic convention of the named house (as in *Rebecca* – "Last night I dreamt I went to Manderlay again" – but with closer associations to *Wuthering Heights*). But its perhaps less insinuating function is also its more suggestive. If the shrunken head, a grotesquely literalized synecdoche, figures the demonic primitivism that vindicates the rationalizing forces of colonialism, the sign disables a clear distinction between "primitive" and "civilized," pagan and Christian, pre-colonized and colonized Australia. David Cairns and Shaun Richards examine the construction of linguistic difference in English imperial ideology, concluding as follows:

> The Welsh, Scots and Irish must ... be seen to speak English as evidence of their incorporation within the greater might of England, but they must speak it with enough deviations from the standard form to make their subordinate status in the union manifestly obvious. What cannot be acknowledged is their possession of an alternative language and culture.[15]

Hitchcock's film distinguishes not at all (except in the stylized accents of Joseph Cotten and Ingrid Bergman) between British "English" and Irish "English," but this reference to aboriginal language even further undermines any sense of polarization by alluding to the *triadic* structure of the relation between British, Irish, and aboriginal people. Named by the colonized, the house is inhabited by the colonizers, but they have been colonized too. Shown in effulgent close-up, the placard may merely suggest the missionary intervention that so often strove to bring enlightenment to "backward" peoples so that they could learn to welcome their enslavement as another phase in their "advancement," but it also implies a certain theoretical compatibility – or at least refuses to assert incommensurability – between the "native" languages of the land, the habitation of the colonists, and the overarching spiritual codes of the colonizers.

The final image in this triad, the horse, is all the more suggestive for remaining unseen. To this extent, it is a clear marker of the film's highly "theatrical" climate. The action involving the horse could easily have been exploited to introduce decisively cinematic momentum, but by consigning the action with a great show of deliberation to the space off-screen, Hitchcock courts a willed "staginess" in the treatment of the material. Films, after all, typically work to deflect the viewer's attention from the fact that there *is* any space, theoretically speaking, that may remain beyond the camera's purview. If the previous two images operate as synecdochic or metonymic emblems of the colonized territory's aboriginal people – themselves all but invisible in the film – the horse signifies the lost past of a bucolic Ireland. Flusky was the stable-boy in Ireland with whom the formerly aristocratic Hattie fell in love (another variation on *Wuthering Heights*), and the first flush of their love is imbricated with the argued, demands simultaneous polarization and identification of colonizer and colonized.[16]In *Under Capricorn*, the polarization dissolves into shared political power while the identification disappears into just such poetic nostalgia, and both are subsumed under the rubrics of fabrication and averment. If the Irish are themselves colonized people, they share political power with the colonizer (the governor is Irish); the aboriginal people are colonized people, but they are identified with the Irish as sharing a position of subordination. As the "pioneers" of this "great dominion," then, the Irish identify across colonial lines, refuting both the polarization and the stable identity imperial ideology requires, and emerging as the very term, in the relation between British Empire and Australian colony, that disrupts the magisterial certainty of the colonial imaginary.

The dominant formal maneuver in the of *Under Capricorn* is the long take, and the domination of this technique by contrast makes the few close-ups in which the first two of these metonymic/synecdochic images are presented, and the off-screen space occupied by the third, all the more weighted with significance. The development of the mobile long-take in the work of directors such as Murnau, Renoir, Ophüls, Dreyer, Wyler and Welles typically precluded the preponderance of the close-up – though in most cases, the preclusion was called upon, as in *Under Capricorn*, to cast a nimbus of significance upon the rare close-ups (think, for instance, of the ending of Dreyer's *Ordet* [1955]). For André Bazin, of course, this development toward the long take culminated the evolution of the language of cinema in a triumphant comprehension of real time, apprehension of real space, and mobilization of long-shot scales in the name of the spectator's greater freedom of observation. What Bazin celebrated in the long take, clearly, was a *new* rhetoric of holism, especially in contrast to the very literal fragmentations of time and space of classical decoupage. In this light, the long take should certainly emerge as the favored prosthetic of the colonial gaze, just as the grandiosity of CinemaScope might well be seen to realize the noumenal idealism of its vast embrace.[17]

Yet Hitchcock's highly specialized uses of the long take in *Under Capricorn* paradoxically work against the holistic rhetoric the technique might be supposed to promote. At times, some of the long takes provide a sense of the unobstructed, unfettered access to space that could support such a supposition. In the shot of Adair's first visit to the house, a shot that lasts nearly ten minutes and ends with the emphatic cut that announces Hattie's first entrance, the camera tracks, pans, and pirouettes with effortless agility from room to room, suggesting its successful conquest of intricate interior space, from the infernal kitchen where the domineering maid cracks a whip to keep her underlings in line, to the cavernous foyer where more genteel social manners obtain. Distinctions of color and visual texture in the mise-en-scène give such contrasts dominating force within the shot, undermining any rhetorical unity that the refusal of editing might be supposed to introduce, and the long range of the camera's dizzying movement, far from guaranteeing optimum access in the penetration of the house's space, introduces spatial disorientation by exceeding the standard reference points typical of shots more restricted in their temporal range and motion. The unconcealed theatricality of the set design, the emphatic artificiality of the house front, is worth noting here as well, since the penetrating gaze of the camera draws attention, by contrast, to its seeming flatness.

Another telling example occurs in a long take after the dinner scene where the camera follows Sam and Adair as they talk about Hattie, but then breaks away from them suddenly and scales to a second-floor balcony, where Hattie languishes. Once again the agility and the breathless virtuosity of the shot assert the camera's mastery, but once again its outcome is ambiguous. Sound cues, for instance, do not let us know whether Hattie hears what the men are saying, and her separateness and solitude are heightened by the fact that she is shown in the same shot as, and in such apparent proximity to, their conversation. If an ordinary function of the long take is to show characters in relation to one another, associated by social context within integrated space (as in Renoir *pace* Bazin), Hitchcock uses it here, on the contrary, to suggest disconnection and disorientation, to emphasize a character's isolation.

For Bazin, the absence of editing in the long take gave it a theoretically holistic character that produced "an image of the world on its own terms." Hitchcock's reliance on the extremes of the close-up and the long take, however, results in a certain rift in representation, an incommensurability, precisely, between the isolated object of the close-up and the integrated field of its self-presence – or, to put it in the terms most significant to the argument here, between figure and meaning. If the close-up works to delimit objects in a metonymic relation to an imagined or projected whole – one that might only, theoretically, be fulfilled in the ascendancy of the long take – the point in *Under Capricorn* would seem to be how *little* integrated these close-ups are into the dominant formal framework of the film. The first close-up of the head is especially striking in this regard, because it breaks the narrative illusion so decisively: the camera glides in for the close-up, and the actor holding the head folds back its covering in a very deliberate, theatrical gesture, clearly intended to assist the camera's gaze.

The use of the long take in the film, far from appearing to fulfill an imaginary unity in its rejection of editing, makes the viewer constantly aware of *absence*, especially through the repression of the reverse-field editing so necessary to achieving classical continuity. In the scene after Sam's arrest where Hattie resolves to go to town to intervene on his behalf, a reverse-shot, looking away from the house front, shows a dense wood. The effect is strikingly dissociative, because not only does the wood look substantially more "real" than any other location in the film, but the shot is one of the few reverse-shots in the film. Like the use of the long take, the practice of reverse-field editing is typically understood as working to construct a virtual, holistic reality through the integrated relation of shots. Here, however, Hitchcock "lays bare the device" by juxtaposing a clearly artificial set, the house, against a putatively "real" space, the wood, and in the collision of shots, remarking the rhetorical incommensurability of artifice and reality.

Under Capricorn has been widely charged with a quality of oppressive "staginess," characterized as a talky, static melodrama. Hitchcock's previous experiment with the long take, *Rope,* typically escapes this charge, despite its one-room setting and actual theatrical source, perhaps because of its more sustained use of the "cinematic" long take, while *Under Capricorn* suffers by comparison because of entrenched assumptions about the imperative realism of the historical costume-drama. But that is exactly the point: *Under Capricorn* joins a small group of Hollywood movies (including Max Ophüls's *The Exile* [1947] and Fritz Lang's *Moonfleet* [1955]) in challenging these assumptions, replacing the sweep and spectacle of the genre with emotional stasis and self-conscious theatricality. By manipulating the evidently holistic long take into a figure of ellipsis, placing important action such as the horse's fall off-screen, and otherwise emphasizing off-screen space as a structuring-absence, Hitchcock severs the assurance of connection between part and whole, sign and signifier. Metonymy still dominates, but the *failure* of part to stand in for whole exposes as false the systems – of representation, of political ideology – that would have it do so. In its prevalence of defamiliarized artifice, *Under Capricorn* raises a pressing question: if history itself is a construct, what can the colonizer's idealism be but delusion?

Conclusion

Hitchcock's spy thrillers figure nation-as-MacGuffin: they bid for a certain apolitical status through a universalizing appeal to the needs of narrative pleasure. The spectator agrees, ostensibly, to accept national identities as given, archetypal, universal, rather than as local, distinctive, ideological, and agrees to enter the illusionist atmosphere of a popular, crowd-pleasing genre. However, it is this very attitude, routinely promoted by Hitchcock himself, that enabled his films to comment quite specifically, and at least covertly politically (over and over again in the course of his career), on historical crises of nationality: the international anxieties of pre-World War II Europe (in the 1934 version of *The Man Who Knew Too Much, The Thirty-Nine Steps, Sabotage, The Lady Vanishes*), the insular landscapes of Cold War America (in *Strangers on a Train* or *North by Northwest*), or the yet-again international context of late Cold War, neocolonial intrigues (in the 1956 version of *The Man Who Knew Too Much* or *Topaz*). The treatment of the IRA in *Juno and the Paycock,* significantly, is the closest Hitchcock comes to the spy thriller template in either of the films treated here; it seems, strikingly, almost like a dry run for the scene of the stalking of Annabella Smith in *The Thirty-Nine Steps*. In many of these cases, it is hard to say whether the conception of nationality as a formalist, generic convenience or as an ideological, political construct is the determining factor or the final dominant effect, but the illusionist basis of the spy thriller, welcoming a version of nationality as theatrical conceit, could always be seen, in any case, to render the question moot.

Though the atypical examples of the two films considered here reflect quite directly upon the more typical ones, and thereby call for a rethinking of the political valences of Hitchcock's films more generally, the question must remain bracingly moot in relation to *Juno and the Paycock* and *Under Capricorn* too, at least to the extent that, however important it is to unravel the implications of national and political representation in Hitchcock's films, the complexity of their imbrications is likely to prevent easy final analyses of the political ethics – critical of the evil, or complicit with the good? Of the devil's party, or harbingers of failed or actual virtue? – that these films ultimately express. (The traditional binary division in such ethics, of the type Nietzsche was not alone in hoping to get beyond, itself calls for further thought on the matter.) These two films are distinguished from Hitchcock's more characteristic work not least in their decidedly less punitive atmosphere: neither the IRA nor the unionists are finally called to account in *Juno*, since there is enough suffering to go around, and *Under Capricorn* shares with *Marnie* the lone distinction in Hitchcock's work of achieving closure through such means as acceptance, understanding, and forgiveness. The "transference of guilt" (Hitchcock's time-honored theme) may simply be understood to be so general in colonial conflict that there is little point in assigning individual blame. That idea, to be sure, has surfaced often enough in twentieth-century international culture to exculpate colonial violence, and certainly, in both these films, if "performance" never quite succeeds in conferring liberation, it is also what sometimes enables individual subjects not to comply fully with the entrapment that accompanies the regimes of any politics these films are able to project.

In point of fact, that haunting image of Juno crossing the empty room, for all its rhetorical power, is not the final image the viewer of *Juno and the Paycock* sees on screen. That honor goes to a picture of a cartoon planet with a cartoon goddess-figure astride it, the logo of "British International Pictures." An image accompanied by a standardized jingle, especially after the tragic heights achieved at the end of the film – an *Irish* narrative, after all, about terrible injustices attendant upon nationalist conflicts, with the question of *British* internationalism a very pertinent one given the context – this image registers as notably discordant. British International was one of several companies that appeared in the late 1920s following a parliamentary decree of minimal quotas upon British film production, to prevent the British cinema from becoming merely an arm of the Hollywood film industry. Thus, despite the pledge of "international" interest in the company's name, and despite Scottish collaboration in its formation, it took shape around a somewhat panic-stricken anxiety about national integrity. The production through this outfit of films such as Hitchcock's about Irish experience may have fulfilled (or even defined) the company's stated "international" aspirations, but it also reflected (and, possibly, enforced) the lack of a "native" cinematic tradition in Ireland itself.[18] It would be heartening indeed to believe that the crushing insensitivity of this last fade – a very direct transport from the sublime to the ridiculous – and of this final symbolic assertion of proprietary rights, enacted a speech-act parallel to Juno's in the film proper: to nominate, to expose, the murderous frivolity, in the face of Juno's tragedy, of such puerile gestures of ownership; to *speak from* the position of colonial power of both the brute oppression and the overwhelming sterility of that power, in the hope of hurrying its decay.

Notes

Thanks to Maria Pramaggiore and Deborah Wyrick for comments on earlier drafts.

1   These two tendencies are exemplified in William Rothman's *Hitchcock, The Murderous Gaze*, Cambridge, MA and London: Harvard University Press, 1982, and Robert J. Corber's *In the Name of National Security: Hitchcock, Homophobia, and the Political Construction of Gender in Postwar America*, Durham, NC: Duke University Press, 1993. Toby Miller attempts to counteract such approaches by arguing that Hitchcock's *The Thirty-Nine Steps* "had homologous relations to the social world," "39 Steps to 'The Borders of the Possible': Alfred Hitchcock, Amateur Observer and the New Cultural History," in Richard Allen and Sam Ishii-Gonzàles (eds.), *Alfred Hitchcock, Centenary Essays*, London: BFI, 1999, p. 319. That Miller finds it necessary to make this claim at all indicates the strong anti-political bias in much of the work on Hitchcock's films.

2   J.L. Austin, *How to Do Things with Words*, London: Oxford University Press, 1962, pp. 103, 120–1.

3   Erving Goffman, *Forms of Talk*, Philadelphia: University of Pennsylvania Press, 1981, p. 145.

4   Andrew Parker and Eve Kosofsky Sedgwick (eds.), *Performativity and Performance*, New York: Routledge, 1995, p. 2.

5   Parker and Sedgwick (eds.), *Performativity and Performance*, p. 2.

6   Raymond Williams, *Drama from Ibsen to Brecht*, New York: Oxford University Press, 1969, p. 150.

7   Williams, *Drama from Ibsen to Brecht*, p. 153.

8   It is significant that Hitchcock found himself drawn to this work by a playwright with so ambivalent a response to Irish nationality, but it is equally striking that, despite O'Casey's move to England shortly before the film's production, O'Casey can hardly be called, in any simple way, a "Briton." Many Irish playwrights wrote far more critically of Irish nationalism, and O'Casey is equally critical of Irish unionism. (The opening speech of *Juno* contains the play's most clearly endorsed political sentiment, a call for Irish identity that circumvents the nationalist/unionist binarism.) It is worth noting, all the same, that despite the complexity of its treatment of these issues, Irish nationalists burned the film in protest on the streets of Limerick shortly after its release. Cf. Harold Bloom (ed.) *Modern Critical Views: Sean O'Casey*, New York: Chelsea, 1987, p. 177.

9 It is worth remembering here that the politics of importing and exporting goods was crucial in the relation of Ireland to the United Kingdom. The two famines of the 1800s took place in large part because of the export by non-residential landowners of quantities of food that would have been more than sufficient, if retained, to end starvation, a fact that would surely have been known to both O'Casey and Hitchcock.

10 Judith Butler, *Gender Trouble: Feminism and the Subversion of Identity*, New York: Routledge, 1990, p. 140.

11 This ending departs from the play, where Joxer and Boyle return after Juno's last soliloquy for one last round of expansively Irish colloquy. The departure from O'Casey's text further punctuates the performative aspect of Juno's own last words in Hitchcock's film.

12 Dan Auiler, *Hitchcock's Notebooks: An Authorized and Illustrated Look Inside the Creative Mind of Alfred Hitchcock*, New York: Avon, 1999, p. 154.

13 In the ensuing discussion, the reader may find the terms "metonymy" and "synecdoche" conflated. Even in classical rhetoric, the tropes have often been treated as very closely congruent, and in discussion of cinematic figuration, they have both been linked routinely with the same formal procedures, such as the close-up, the dissolve, superimposition, editing in general, and so on. In what remains the most systematic treatment of cinematic figuration, discussing the interrelations of metaphor, metonymy, and synecdoche, Christian Metz remarks as follows: "The important thing is not to wish [types of cinematic figuration] would coincide, but to work on the ways in which they intersect" (*The Imaginary Signifier: Psychoanalysis and the Cinema*, trans. Celia Britton, Annwyl Williams, Ben Brewster, and Alfred Guzzetti, Bloomington: Indiana University Press, 1982, p. 194).

14 This signifier may also be read as specifically Catholic, since the Protestant Bible usually translates the phrase in question less grandiloquently, as "Woman, why are you weeping?"

15 David Cairns and Shaun Richards, *Writing Ireland: Colonialism, Nationalism and Culture*, Manchester: Manchester University Press, 1988, p. 11.

16 Peter Childs and R.J. Patrick Williams, *An Introduction to Post-Colonial Theory*, New York: Prentice-Hall, 1997, p. 70.

17 See Roland Barthes, "On CinemaScope," trans. Jonathan Rosenbaum; and my own commentary, "On Barthes On CinemaScope," both in *Jouvert* 3.3 (Spring) 1999, http://social.class.ncsu.edu/jouvert/u3:3/bath.htm.

18 For a discussion of Hitchcock and British International, see Tom Ryall, *Alfred Hitchcock and the British Cinema*, Urbana: University of Illinois Press, 1986, pp. 45–51. For a discussion of the development of Irish cinema, especially in a colonial or post-colonial context, see John Hill, Martin McLoone, and Paul Hainsworth (eds.), *Border Crossing: Film in Ireland, Britain and Europe*, Ulster and Belfast: BFI, 1994, pp. 112–73.

Chapter 13

HITCHCOCK AND HOM(M)OSEXUALITY

Patricia White

The emergence of Hitchcock's work as a test object for queer writing on film, recalling its centrality to psychoanalytic feminist criticism in the 1970s and 1980s, raises important questions about authorship and discursive authority in queer studies, as well as the relationship between feminist and queer critical projects. What "authorizes" our work. Which proper names determine what is proper to it? Is it symptomatic that one of the first topics on the agenda of gay and lesbian film scholarship would be – the father? Or, to borrow his post-struc-turalist nickname, courtesy Raymond Bellour, "Hitchcock the Enunciator."[1] Alfred Hitchcock presents: lesbian and gay film theory.

Two anthologies, *Inside/Out* and *Outtakes*, feature major essays on Hitchcock's films, and a third, *Out in Culture*, devotes a dossier to "Hitchcock and Homosexuality." At least three books that explore the topic in depth have been published to date.[2] Laura Mulvey's incisive and widely applicable analysis of visual pleasure and the female image in narrative cinema, an analysis developed in part from a closer look at Hitchcock's films, has exerted enormous influence in film and feminist studies since the mid-1970s.[3] Does recent scholarly publishing indicate that an epistemological claim of equivalent force can be made about Hitchcock and homosexuality? A number of fruitful directions have been pursued. Queer theory pre-empts what might crudely be understood as the "misogyny" question in Hitchcock to take on homophobia – as well as to elabo-rate the nuances of connotation, the discourse of aestheticism, the byways of perversion, and the displacement of politics. Addressing all of these important topics under the rubric of authorship, queer methodology parallels that of feminism, turning canonical works and exemplary geniuses inside out.

Yet in pursuing this parallel, it is important to point out that "Hitchcock and homosexuality" might appear gender-inclusive while effectively marginalizing women, much as does the generic term "man," or indeed that enemy of the generic, "queer." The tendency of the master's films to trace scenarios of male subjective crisis and integration has been well documented, not least by Bellour and his feminist commentators, and in numerous of these dramas critics have detected a tantalizing touch of queerness, if also of pathology.[4] Hitchcock murderers who have been implicated as crypto-homos – besides the thrill killers in *Rope* (1948) and the eponymous *Strangers on a Train* (1951), Uncle Charlie in *Shadow of a Doubt* (1943), Norman Bates in *Psycho* (1960), and Bob Rusk in *Frenzy* (1972) – can be seen as achieving the extra-legal and transgressive power the author usually reserves for himself. If I will have occasion below to dispute the claim made by Robin Wood, arguably Hitchcock's most prominent gay critic, that Mrs. Danvers, the impressive housekeeper of *Rebecca* (1940), "appears to be the only lesbian in the Hitchcock canon," certainly her loneliness is indisputable. Moreover, her power and authority are notably circumscribed by her narrative function and her gender.[5]

Luce Irigaray used the neologism hom(m)osexuality, its spelling punning on *homme*, "man," and *homo*, "same," to designate "a single practice and representation of the sexual" pervading Western discourse, marking with the term the invisible standard of male subjectivity and interrogating the function of woman as signifier of sexual *difference*.[6] As Teresa de Lauretis elaborates, hom(m)osexuality is "the term of sexual *in*difference, the term (in fact) of heterosexuality."[7] In retaining the word homosexuality, understood as lesbian or gay sexuality, and adopting Irigaray's neologism, de Lauretis intends "to re-mark both the incommensurable distance between them and the conceptual ambiguity that is conveyed by the two almost identical acoustic images." [8] That the two terms tend to dissolve into the same, the *homo*geneous, problematizes the very representability of lesbianism. In this chapter I want to explore this "conceptual ambiguity" in recent Hitchcock criticism and, through a brief reading of Hitchcock's *Stage Fright*, to suggest a different approach to lesbian representability and authorship.

Irigaray writes, "Hom(m)o-sexuality is played out through the bodies of women, matter, or sign, and heterosexuality has been up to now just an alibi for the smooth workings of man's relations with himself."[9] Her definition might be a provocative summary of how femininity relays male concerns in the Hitchcock text. Mulvey describes an alignment among spectator, male character, and the look of the camera played out through the body/sign "woman" in *Rear Window* (1954), *Vertigo* (1958), and *Marnie* (1964). This erotics of self-referentiality is further embedded in the discourse of authorship. Kaja Silverman detects what she in fact names as "a radically dispersed and decentered 'hom(m)osexual' economy" in the critical writings of Raymond Bellour, "one that installs "Hitchcock-as-director ... as the point of apparent textual origin."[10] Bellour's reading of the chain of male authorial stand-ins in the opening of *Marnie* genders the critic's position as well as the author's, inscribing a circuit of male author-ity. In *The Women Who Knew Too Much: Hitchcock and Feminist Theory*, Tania Modleski provides as astute a critique of Hitchcock's male commentators as she does of the gender politics of his films. Citing William Rothman's claim that the director "compels the blindest viewer to bow before the terrifying power his camera commands," Modleski comments on the posture of "male masochism" the assertion calls to mind, even as she reminds us of "Eve Sedgwick's remarks about the 'masculinizing potential' of submission to another man [through which] it becomes possible for the male viewer to achieve a rough equality with the director."[11] Excluded from such power games, she suggests, Hitchcock's female viewers and critics can disrupt the "smooth workings of man's relation with himself."

If hom(m)osexuality can designate the collaboration between Hitchcock and his male exegetes and acolytes, enough hints of homo*sexuality* exist in the œuvre to claim the attentions of avowedly gay (male) critics. In *Rope* and *Strangers on a Train*, the œuvre's most "overt" representations of homosexuality, the viewer's alignment with the author extends to his evident identification with gay-coded characters, albeit ones who are implicated with murder, fascism, and the phallic order. Indeed, homosexuality and homophobia are intertwined in a manner characteristic of the economy of hom(m)osexuality. Even the films' crimes uphold a regime of male power and exchange. In *Strangers on a Train* Bruno and Guy barter the symbolic murder of the father, the idealized Oedipal crime, for the murder of the woman, the everyday Oedipal crime.[12] In *Rope*, Brandon and Philip attempt to consolidate their symbolic power by committing a murder that is at once a sexualized act between them, an affirmation of the father/teacher and his doctrine, and the narrative move that binds them in a thread of identifications running from virtuoso auteur to viewer-voyeur.

In what follows I shall look closely at the rhetorical strategies of two of the most fascinating readings of Hitchcock's queer texts to suggest how gay male critics may be implicated in this display of male authority. In his breathtaking close reading "Anal *Rope*," D.A. Miller both reveals and re-inscribes the terms of the technical operation of hom(m)osexuality in the Hitchcock text. While I cannot do justice to his rhetorical brilliance here, in essence, Miller argues that there is an overdetermined relation between the much-discussed technical experiment of *Rope* – the long takes, the cuts often not-quite-hidden on a man's backside – and the tacit homosexuality of Philip (Farley Granger) and Brandon

(John Dahl), the elegant young men who kill and hide the body of their friend David before their other dinner guests arrive. The fact that homosexuality cannot be denoted under the appropriately named Code results in what Miller diagnoses as a "pandemic of homosexual signification": anything might be recruited to connote (male) homosexuality in this text.[13] The camera's unblinking eye represents the desire of the homophobic male viewer addressed by the film for denotative proof – in short, for "the spectacle of 'gay sex'" (p. 130). But of course such surveillance also prevents the act from ever taking place (p. 133). The anxious male viewer both wants to see and wants to avoid seeing – what? In Miller's reading, the cut itself, a figure for the anus. Although the essay does not refer to Mulvey's account of castration and the politics of vision, it ultimately comes to turn on the "facts" of male anatomy. Miller asserts that the castration anxiety of the heterosexual male is what sustains his identity as such – only by fearing loss is self-possession assured (p. 135). If female difference reassures by the absence of the penis, then male homosexuality renews anxiety through the *indifference* represented by the anus. The threatening signifying surplus the gay male enjoys is ambiguously figured by the chest or cassone where the victim's body has been stashed (p. 138). What is hidden in the piece of furniture upon which Brandon and Philip serve their dinner guests, Miller asks? Bluntly put, a sexually penetrated male body with an erect penis (he has been strangled, from behind) – a sight that is withheld just as Hitchcock hides one of the film's few cuts, this time seamlessly, on the action of opening the chest. These bodily signs, taken together, would denote "the negation of castration" that the heterosexual male both fears in his homosexual other and desires for himself. For Miller this explains why, "with little in the ostensible narrative or generic conventions to forbid displaying the corpse," the contents of the chest are never revealed, are rendered precisely ob-scene, the spectator permitted to keep his eyes wide shut (p. 137).

Stowing the resplendently imagined, albeit dead, gay male body in the space of exchange between heterosexual author and spectator on opposite ends of the narrative address, Miller re-inscribes a singular male standard of signification even while displacing its signifier of singularity, the phallus, by doubling the anatomical supports of (gay) masculinity in the possession and use for pleasure of both penis and anus. Displacing the phallus, he also displaces women, who are defined in relation to it.

Miller persuasively claims that the film erects a signified "heterosexuality," in the character of the boys' teacher Rupert (Jimmy Stewart), "whose only necessary content is not a desire for women, but the negation of the desire for men" (p. 128). This heterosexuality without women follows to the letter the logic of hom(m)osexuality. Women cannot receive what Miller calls male homosexuality's "exemption" from "the problematics of castration" (p. 137), and the spectacle of dead female bodies remains a generic and narrative convention displayed elsewhere in Hitchcock's films, reassuring to the male spectator if outside the scope of the critic.

But to each his own. Miller is not obliged to offer a feminist analysis of Hitchcock's film; his interests lie elsewhere. And femininity is at best marginal to *Rope*. Of the victim's fiancée Janet, Miller comments, "Arthur Laurents's script focuses as little and with as little interest on the character as Hitchcock's camera does on the body" (p. 126). Yet Miller's metaphor of (male) anus as cut cuts feminist film theory and its considerable insights out of the picture as well. *Homo*sexuality is reserved for the *same* sex, the male. Implicitly the woman can represent only difference, that is, heterosexuality. The anus deconstructs sexual difference (the opposition phallus/lack), but access to this supplement is reserved for male members. The male anus is a sign of *différance*, Derrida's term for the deferring power of difference. Femininity is definitively different from the phallic, the female anus at best redundant.

Evidence that an explicit analysis of gender difference *is* compatible with "anal" readings of Hitchcock's films can be found in Lee Edelman's "*Rear Window*'s Glasshole."[14] A rhetorical tour de force like "Anal *Rope*," a debt which it acknowledges, Edelman's essay appears in Ellis Hanson's collection *Outtakes* next to a new essay by Miller on *Suddenly, Last Summer* that acknowledges Edelman's piece in turn.[15] Within the context of such male specularity, femininity, and indeed feminist film theory, actually figure quite spectacularly. Unlike *Rope*'s Janet, *Rear Window*'s heroine in haute couture Lisa Fremont (Grace Kelly) is highly visible (even if the hero would rather look elsewhere), and she is clearly not "frigid," an adjective that Miller applied to Janet. Invoked in the first line of Edelman's essay, feminist theory provides its point of departure. Yet the return is too much delayed. For Edelman, getting to the bottom of Mulvey's claims means interrogating what is left out of her reading of classical cinema. For him this is not female spectatorial pleasure, as it is for Modleski and other 1980s feminist critics of Mulvey, but, again, anality. In performing this reading of what is hidden, femininity remains consigned to the world of appearances, emblem of the visible, of difference: masculinity.

Rear Window, Hitchcock's story of a photojournalist recovering from a broken leg who avidly follows the goings-on across his Greenwich Village courtyard, already gives, in its title, something on which Edelman can rest his case. Going against an extensive body of criticism of the film that anatomizes its reflexivity about vision, Edelman privileges darkness. The fades to black that structure the film's editing and the blinding red flashes from Jeffries's camera when he tries to defend himself from the intruding wife-murderer Thorwald (Raymond Burr), are read as figures for the anus, which when cut from the picture excludes all that dis-orders and de-means.

How does the woman become tied to this operation? Her body, perpetually on display, not only bears the mark of castration, but also displays the occlusion of the alternative anal libidinal economy structuring the film, and, the reading implies, insofar as *Rear Window* is a meta-movie, structuring the cinema itself. Edelman uses the term Freud's Wolf Man coined for female genitalia, the "front bottom," to pinpoint the function that Lisa's display of castration (in her superbly cut dresses) has for Jeff. Her difference connotes heterosexual genitality, a reassuring distinction ensured by the Symbolic, barring off the primary reversibility and indistinction of anality, whose figures are the hole, the zero. Here the woman's looks refer man to himself in a double move: she reassures him of his intactness by lacking the phallus, which lack also covers over the metonymic displacement of his anus by hers. Yet the anal realm, although situated before/beyond sexual difference, is distinctively masculinized. A relay of looks that Edelman uses to illustrate his argument shows Lisa gesturing behind her back to indicate to Jeffries Mrs. Thorwald's wedding ring in her hand. Thorwald finally returns the voyeur's gaze when he looks out to see whose attention Lisa's gestures are trying to attract. The seemingly triangulated logic of hom(m)osexuality (which requires female participation) returns to a version of phallic singularity: female difference signifies sameness – male specularity. Here, anality, ostensibly something else, not one but zero, "an otherness that, once made visible, threatens to make us thereafter see double ... disturbing the either/or logic of a castratory clarity" ultimately does the same (p. 86). Femininity is either/or; masculinity both/and.

The clarity of the movies' "window on the world" entails keeping the rear view in darkness. In this reading, the foundational gesture of the filmic apparatus is covering its "behind," the behind of vision, a gesture masculinized by its attachment to Hitchcock's authorship and to the precarious position of his surrogate Jeffries in *Rear Window*, who covers his ass as he remains wedded to his chair, staring vigilantly out of the rear window.

The deconstructive trope of turning around on oneself that Edelman's reading of anality and vision performs is aptly figured in the threatened reversibility of *Rear Window*'s gaze. Turning around on oneself is also characteristic of narcissism, and the self-referentiality of deconstructionist readings such as Miller's and Edelman's, miming as it does Hitchcock's own reflexivity, nevertheless places the female reader in an awkward position. For the film is about more than Symbolic violence – it is not a matter of indifference that it is a woman's body, that of Thorwald's wife, which is cut to bits, reduced to a formless mess, in the apartment across the way. If Hitchcock's woman is a signifier of genitality and reproduction, the woman who is "cut" as castrated covers for the woman who is dismembered, equated with waste. Edelman argues that the clean-up of the cut-up woman is staged to cover the "clean-up" that Hitchcock's technique –

montage as "pure cinema" – performs upon the waste or darkness figured by anality (p. 78). Not only is the gruesome fate of the woman merely an alibi for a male-coded operation in this reading, but the considerable agency that Modleski argues the film's heroine wields is also bracketed.[16]

Femininity is pressed into symbolic service in Edelman's essay, yet despite this attentiveness the woman still signifies difference, as bearer of the bleeding wound that is now *comforting* rather than threatening.[17] In short, she stands in for castration, not only in the Freudian but also in the Mulveyan context: castration as feminist film theory's blinding (and implicitly heterosexist) conceptual insight. Edelman is then in a position to deconstruct the anal cut from which castration has hitherto been cut off. Does feminist theory, which Edelman positions in some sense analogously to the female body in its cut-and-dried literalism, also fall prey to critical indifference? Let us return to the first sentence of his essay.

> We have learned, and learned perhaps all too well, as a result of the feminist, psychoanalytically oriented theorization of narrative cinema, to observe the dynamics of power that inflect the masculinist desire to see … This lesson can work … complicitously with the seductions of dominant cinema to keep us from seeing a no less significant – and no less significantly male-associated – desire to *escape* the phallic regime … in which presence and absence define male and female antithetically.
>
> (p. 72)

Complicit with the dominant cinema it critiques, feminist film theory's didacticism requires supplementation. On the next page Edelman invokes "the anus as site of a cut, as D.A. Miller has taught us to see it" (p. 73). The two theorists have found the ultimate master of "anality" in Hitchcock himself.

Acknowledging that the desire for a beyond – or a behind – is "no less significantly male-associated," Edelman does not elaborate on the significance of this acknowledgment. The male-associated desire (to see) that is illuminated by feminist theory is a phallogocentric one. The male-associated desire to escape the phallic regime, associated with anality, is a potentially radical one. But it gains significance precisely through a specific kind of "male association." Gay male Hitchcock criticism makes a bid, that is, for prestige, for authority, most directly through the author himself. Getting behind Hitchcock to deconstruct but also to display authority is an hom(m)osexual act.

There is much more to learn than the lesson of castratory vision from feminist film theory, a discourse that has for many years extended its reach beyond the "cut" of sexual difference to questions of narrative, fantasy, history, genres, audiences, and, yes, authors. These inquiries have in common the shift from "woman" in the singular to *women*, in the plural, as social subjects of cinema. This epistemological distinction, as elaborated by Teresa de Lauretis in *Alice Doesn't*, is also the condition of lesbian theorizing, for, as de Lauretis writes elsewhere, "it takes two women, not one, to make a lesbian."[18] Ultimately feminist film theory proffers concepts with which to differentiate lesbian readings of classical cinema from hom(m)osexual ones.

Within feminist Hitchcock criticism, Modleski's *The Women Who Knew Too Much* explores the tension between the often-disturbing representation of woman and of the violence done to women on-screen and the complex pleasures of women in the audience. Her book's afterword, "Hitchcock's Daughters," relates scenarios of female complicity and resistance in Hitchcock's *Stage Fright* (1950) to the ambivalent position of female viewers. *Stage Fright*, which features two top-billed female stars, one of whom investigates the other's secrets, can also be read outside Modleski's familial frame. I argue that the film stages lesbian desire in a manner resonant with Hitchcock's (and possibly Code-era Hollywood's) most important lesbian film, *Rebecca*,[19] and that it engages in an authorial contest that also characterizes that earlier film.

Let me make clear that I am not interested here in "saving" Hitchcock for lesbian studies. By this formulation I am alluding to Modleski's critique of Robin Wood's avowed motives in revisiting his seminal work on Hitchcock. Wood asks: "Can Hitchcock be saved for feminism?" and Modleski writes, "His very language, implying the necessity of rescuing a favorite auteur ... suggests that the question is fundamentally a rhetorical one."[20] She argues that "the strong fascination and identification with femininity revealed in the movies subverts the claims to mastery and authority not only of the male characters but of the director himself."[21] Her prose demonstrates that the male critic's claims – his rescue missions – are also vulnerable to a feminist reading. Similarly, I want to suggest that claims for mastery – including gestures that appear to relinquish it – in "anal" criticism of Hitchcock are disrupted by the differences women make. Leaving questions of rescue, if not of rhetoric, aside, I might describe the operation of lesbian representability in the Hitchcock text as a kind of ghost authorship. In other words, lesbian readings remain unauthorized, yet those that are compelling respond to definite presences, to echoes of an alternative voice, in the films.

If Hitchcock's homos are the flip side of his hetero heroes, taking the perverse inflections he gives to Jimmy Stewart or exploits in Cary Grant to the longed-for limit – murder – Hitchcock's lesbians, if they can be claimed by the author at all, are more covert, more marginal, less easily assimilated to dramas of transgression and restoration of order. Suzanne Pleshette barely manages to light Tippi Hedren's cigarette before meeting a violent death in *The Birds*, and Marnie simply will not be pinned down.[22] In *Rebecca*, as I've argued above, Danvers is not granted a place in the circuit of meaning, exchange, and identification that binds author to spectator/critic. In "Hitchcock's Homophobia," for instance, John Hepworth does what he accuses *Rebecca* of doing, dismissing Danvers as a "creepy," "crazy" dyke. Rebecca herself is not even represented in the film that bears her name, and the film's heroine bears no name of her own.

There is an irony in the fact that the lesbian Hitchcock narrative returns again and again to *Rebecca* – Oscar winner in 1940 but, by the director's own admission, "not a Hitchcock picture." Modleski demonstrates that the dismissal of *Rebecca* by Hitchcock and certain of his admirers has to do with its "novelettish" quality, its feminine aspect.[23] *Rebecca* is not a Hitchcock picture because it owes too much of its style and preoccupations to other authors: Daphne du Maurier, the writer of the best-selling gothic novel upon which it was based; David O. Selznick, the producer who brought Hitchcock to Hollywood and assigned him to direct this follow-up to his great woman's picture *Gone with the Wind* (1939); and even the female readers and potential viewers who would only "authorize" a faithful version of a book that was perceived to be faithful to their own experience. Finally, as Modleski's influential reading of the film suggests, there is a signature on the film that rivals Hitchcock's; that of "Rebecca," an uncast – uncastable – figure, signifier at once of the hero's misery and the heroine's – not to mention Danvers's – obsession. That Rebecca is a lesbian, or that she represents one of classical Hollywood cinema's most powerful inscriptions of the lure and the threat of lesbianism, has been persuasively argued by Rhona Berenstein and other critics.[24] The paradox of *Rebecca* – the Hitchcock picture that lends itself most readily to lesbian interpretation is "not a Hitchcock picture" – illustrates the challenge of positing a relationship of lesbians to classical cinema under the rubric of authorship.[25]

Stage Fright is not a Hitchcock picture – not one that gets talked about much.[26] The film is most likely to be remembered as a Marlene Dietrich vehicle, though *Stage Fright* is not a Dietrich picture either – or not one of the first rank. This curious sense of a film at cross-purposes is, to me, what makes it interesting. In *Stage Fright*, I argue, lesbianism is staged through a shift in narrative and visual conventions usually reserved for male/female relationships, a shift made possible by the film's generic relation to the women's picture, its status as one of *Rebecca*'s successors. The film undermines Hitchcock's customary authority by jamming the machinery of male narration. It lends itself to an un-authorized lesbian reading by failing to contain Dietrich's star image, which also makes a diegetic appeal to the female spectator through the character of the film's protagonist Eve, who watches her every move.

Stage Fright was made for Warner Bros. right after *Rope* and *Under Capricorn*, Hitchcock's first independent ventures, and just before *Strangers on a Train*. But rather than being discussed as part of a "queer period," it is considered something of a misfire, a "minor" Hitchcock: a black-and-white murder mystery, filled with eccentrics, filmed in England and set in the world of the theater. Truffaut put his finger on the problem when he remarked to the director: "*Stage Fright* ... added little or nothing to your prestige."[27] Hitchcock was attracted to the project because of the theatrical setting, but, in a letter to Jack Warner, the director complains of the technical limitations of the London sound stage, contrasting the experience with his experimental freedom with color and long takes in the films he had just finished. "The nature of the subject forces me to cut it up much more than I would have liked."[28] The cutting back on authorial technique might be extended to *Stage Fright*'s casting

The film features an unlikely leading couple: Jane Wyman and Marlene Dietrich receive top billing, and their male co-stars follow on the same title card. Wyman had won the 1948 Oscar for *Johnny Belinda* and Dietrich was shaping her postwar cabaret star persona. *Stage Fright* follows the efforts of ingenue drama student Eve Gill (Wyman) to secure evidence that musical theater star Charlotte Inwood (Marlene Dietrich) has murdered her husband and framed Eve's would-be boyfriend Jonathan (Richard Todd) – who is actually in love with Charlotte – for the crime. The audience's belief in Charlotte's guilt is overdetermined from the outset. Not only do we hear the accused man's version of the story, as he persuades Eve to protect him from the police, we see it – in a lying flashback that is never replaced by a "correct" one that would restore narrative order. In setting up as an enunciator an unreliable character – not only a psychotic villain, but a villain who, in Hitchcock's words, is a flop[29] – the director cashes in on male narrational authority, throwing the weight of the cinematic apparatus behind it by visualizing the story. Critics felt utterly betrayed by the lying flashback, as it breaks the cinema's implicit pact between male author, character, and spectator. Modelski notes that Jonathan's version is credible because it embodies "the lie about women's guilt that fuels patriarchal cinema." Eve's enunciative and investigatory role is much more prominent in the film (Jonathan goes into hiding). While striving to uphold the lie, she precisely reverses the process of transferring guilt to the woman and facilitates punishment of the man, the false authority who becomes a rather spectacular victim of the apparatus. Jonathan is trapped on the stage and we again share his point of view – just as the theater's safety curtain is about to crash down upon him, presumably to cut him in two.

Despite the revelation of Johnny's guilt, Charlotte is never entirely vindicated, at least on the level of plot. But *Stage Fright* manages to expose the very question of the woman's guilt as little more than a plot hook. Given the overwhelming presence Dietrich brings to the role, whether Charlotte is guilty or innocent of any mortal crime is almost a moot point. I would argue that the film's real interest resides elsewhere, in her performance and its reception, most notably by Eve – in the relation between women.

While Modleski delights in Charlotte's treachery as a female strategy of resist-ance, she dismisses Eve as a good girl, a dutiful daughter. A feminist reading that sees pairs of women as opposites will miss Eve's function as figure for female spectatorial fascination, for interpretation and desire. For the film's ostensible narrative of one woman's conspiring to prove the guilt of another quickly becomes, as does *Rebecca*, the history of an obsession. Eve goes to great lengths to get near Charlotte, bribing her lady's maid and dresser to allow her to take her place. The position authorizes Eve's constant eavesdropping upon and uninter-rupted gazing at Marlene Dietrich in various stages of undress. *Stage Fright* has more in common with *All About Eve* than its heroine's name and its 1950 release date. Both are stage-door melodramas about a woman who makes up a story in order to gain access to an admired star. Unlike *All About Eve*, in which the estab-lished and the ambitious actress are presented as equally talented and it is the investigating woman who has her secrets, in *Stage Fright* we seem to know all about Eve, and Dietrich's superiority is awesome. Eve's interest in Charlotte cannot be explained as mere identification, as the ambition plot might favor. Simply by being in the same film with Dietrich, Wyman's character is rendered nearly as bumbling and incompetent a figure as Joan Fontaine's in *Rebecca*. Indeed Hitchcock reports that Wyman burst into tears upon viewing Dietrich's glam-orous appearance in the rushes. She greatly annoyed him by gradually improving her own appearance, by refusing to stay in character as a Cockney maid.[30] But since her character Eve is, after all, merely impersonating the maid, Wyman's dropping the disguise allows her to stay in character as the fascinated actress. She is the woman's picture heroine transfixed by an image of woman, and Charlotte in turn eventually recognizes her companion's uncommon qualities. The film presents us with a woman engaged in an investigation of the other woman with a persistence that, like that of Jimmy Stewart in *Vertigo*, to take an extreme example, appears excessive to its narrative objective and can only be explained as the playing out of desire.

Yet the heroine cannot simply accede to the role of hero; it is as a lady's maid that Eve gains access to Charlotte. De Lauretis has argued that classical narrative grants to man the function of narrative actor and consigns woman to the zone of narrative space, acted upon.[31] In both *Rebecca* and *Stage Fright* the narrative func-tion "Woman" – object of desire and fascination – is occupied by an intangible figure who cannot quite be contained within it. Rebecca is absent and seemingly all-powerful, and Dietrich's star-image exceeds her appearance in any single role. Both films include a second heroine who takes up the narrative position usually occupied by the hero, the figure of spectatorial identification who drives the story forward. Her access to this role in both films depends upon a third, supporting female character, whose class difference throws lesbian difference into relief. Joan Fontaine starts out as a lady's companion; she tries to establish herself as leading lady in response to Mrs. Danvers's dismissal of her. Nellie, Charlotte's maid, contemptuously asks Eve if she has ever done any character acting. Classical cinema cannot sustain two heroines in the mold of "Woman" because that would deny her uniqueness, her fetish status. The investigatory woman, like the lesbian critic, is charged with figuring out the meaning, allure, and mystery of Woman. Although this quest can never be resolved on the level of a narrative driven by the motor of sexual difference, it is nevertheless powerfully figured in the text's incoherencies. The mysterious Rebecca, or Dietrich-as-Charlotte, becomes excessive to heterosexualized narrative when the position from which she is viewed shifts to that of the other woman. Her story no longer makes sense as the complement of male desire, the position in which films such as *Marnie* or *Vertigo* attempt to place her.

The doubling of the heroine function and the alternative story of desire inscribed within *Stage Fright* open up a space in the presumed hetero-normativity of classical cinema. In a film about performance in which everyone plays a role, heterosexual relations are consistently mocked by everything from Eve's parents' oddball marriage to Charlotte's show-stopping production number of Cole Porter's "The Laziest Girl in Town," in which she sings of her lack of interest in men. The film's running joke is at the expense of the man Eve is eventually paired with instead of Jonathan, the detective investigating the case (Michael Wilding), whose last name, Smith, and middle initial, O., earn him the nickname Ordinary. As in *All About Eve*, it is through the trope of female spectatorship that desire is attached to narrativity.

The representation of Eve's spectatorship is the film's primary visual support for this lesbian reading, emphasizing female difference not as an expression of sexist duality, as Modleski's slotting of the two female characters might suggest, but as the condition of desire. In contrast to his dissatisfaction with Wyman's efforts to make herself over to be attractive next to, or perhaps to, Dietrich, Hitchcock had no problem tolerating Dietrich's authoring of her own image in the film. He quipped: "Marlene was a professional star—she was also a professional cameraman, art director, editor, costume designer, hairdresser, makeup woman, composer, producer, and director."[32] If Hitchcock first grants Dietrich authority, and then mocks it as feminine excess, Donald Spoto adds, "She was ... the only actress ever allowed substantial creative freedom on [Hitchcock's] set. She would appear early each morning and ... instruct the cinematographer on the proper lighting for herself."[33]

Indeed Charlotte is shot in classic frontal Dietrich style, perpetually gazing towards an unseen mirror and thus towards, but never directly at, the spectator. She does not return the looks of the other characters. Eve stands at her side, attention riveted, in the traditional admiring male position. This configuration within the frame, along with the repeated scenes of her eavesdropping just outside Charlotte's door, mirror the position Eve takes up as dresser, standing in the wings at the theater, repeatedly positioning Eve as the privileged spectator whose female gaze is directed at the female movie star. Witty two-shots of Dietrich and Wyman pair seemingly incompatible female types and capture the relay of the look between them (Figure 13.1). When Charlotte does turn away from the mirror to give Eve an appreciative once-over, it is when Eve appears not in her maid's costume but in a dress and hat that mimic Charlotte's own.

Figure 13.1: Jane Wyman and Marlene Dietrich in *Stage Fright* (1950)

Dietrich, who is depicted as capricious, narcissistic, and cavalier, hits a very touching note in her final scene alone with Eve in her dressing room, a scene that starts out like a pick-up and finishes a frame-up. "We shall probably never see each other again, ships that pass in the something or other … I like you, you're so sweet and patient," says Charlotte, offering Eve money and a lift. The sincerity of this private moment is credited by Eve's subsequent betrayal. She leads Charlotte into a room where a microphone has been concealed and gets her to reveal an incriminating knowledge of the murder. This conversation is heard over the theater's sound system – the betrayal enabled, even called forth, by the appa-ratus of public performance. But the scene brings tears to Eve's eyes as she emerges, stricken, onto the stage, only to shrug off Ordinary's comforting pat and to collapse sobbing when her father applauds her performance. Charlotte dismisses this "terrible scene with a lunatic girl" with the poise of a woman who has discarded a too-demonstrative lover.

Dietrich is one of the most iconic figures in the history of cinema: a much-analyzed symbol of sexual allure and inscrutability, an icon of performance, famous for mannish clothes and many lovers of both sexes. Dietrich's later films, including *Stage Fright*, deploy a self-consciousness and even humor about her image. For these and other, obvious, reasons she is also a lesbian icon of the first magnitude. The Dietrich star-image in this film provides an authorial signature to rival that of the director: *Stage Fright* is not *only* a Hitchcock picture. As her co-star Richard Todd remarked, "If you asked me who directed *Stage Fright*, I'd have to answer Dietrich, the performances at least. She was the one with the theatricality and know-how and experience and generosity."[34]

Rather than pointing to a unitary, authorial source of meaning – indeed the lying flashback undermines the male character's function as authorial double, *Stage Fright* valorizes the multiplicity of readings, the respect for innuendo, theatricality as know how, the self-authorization of the fan. As in *All About Eve*, the story of Eve is here retold as that of a stage-struck girl. She takes her place among the curious crowds outside Charlotte's house, fascinated by the figure of a scandalous woman. The film's emphasis on role-playing inscribes the female spectator in a fantasy of investigating, rescuing, comprehending Woman. *Stage Fright* cites, and performs, the Marlene Dietrich mystique in a manner offered specifically to her female fans. Repeated scenes in her dressing room offer a parade of Marlene props – feather, furs, fashions, veils, and cigarettes, without the fetishistic build-up that Mulvey argued male spectatorial investment required. Eve is the star's dresser; she gets to have a nominal role herself in the creation of the image. Finally, the ultimate meaning of the scandal of Charlotte Inwood is revealed in the hordes of presumably women fans – this is, after all, London, where the intensity of female fanaticism is notorious – who flock to the theater in ever-greater numbers to behold her. Charlotte's own desire finds its most unambiguous expression in her hasty return to the stage after the murder in order to give her public what it wants.

If a lying flashback dupes the spectator, the characters are duped by a blood-stained dress that appears to corroborate Johnny's story of Charlotte's guilt. Eve's father fixes on the absurd idea of getting Charlotte to betray herself by having displayed before her, as she performs onstage, a doll wearing a dress stained with blood, an image, Modleski notes, of her own castration. Does Charlotte's horror stem from recognition of femininity as bleeding wound, or from the damage done to her Christian Dior gown? Reception accounts of the film mention Dior nearly as often as Hitchcock. To comment on the clothes is of course to interpret the film according to the criteria of a woman's picture, and

Dietrich herself leads us in this direction. According to her daughter Maria Riva, Dietrich's verdict on the film was the following: "The hair is very bad – the whole picture – too 'old lady little curls.' I always have said that the British can't make women's films." Dietrich thus archly sidesteps the Hitchcock myth and concludes: "I should have listened to myself."[35] My aim is not to authorize a female narcissistic discourse in place of a male one, of course, but to emphasize that a reading of *Stage Fright* in terms of Hitchcock's authorship would miss at least half the fun.

In concluding her book with a discussion of *Stage Fright*, Modelski challenges the attitude of authorial acknowledgment that Rothman assumes in *Hitchcock: the Murderous Gaze*. She writes:

> If ... we would seek to prevent being absorbed by male authority and male texts, we must risk punishment and withhold the authorial acknowledgment the texts exact. Feminist critics must refuse to bow before the camera's "terrifying power" and, instead, *affirm* the theatrical, "treacherous" aspects of these "seductive" texts – those parts which "know" more than their author, those moments ... when woman resists capitulation to male power and male designs.
>
> It all comes down to a question of interpretation, which ... involves a struggle for survival.[36]

In this chapter I have suggested that the interpretive strategies we bring to critical explorations of Hitchcock and homosexuality have similarly high stakes. While Robin Wood, who puns on Rothman's title in his essay "Hitchcock's Murderous Gays," may remain invested in authorial acknowledgment, Edelman and Miller's queer deconstructive method might well be defined as "the affirmation of aspects of texts that know more than their author." But "knowing more than the author" can itself be seductive, and in their essays woman is still cast as a clear-cut signifier of sexual difference. In fashioning a lesbian and gay film studies that goes beyond hom(m)osexual studies, we must be attentive to formations of spectatorship, stardom, genre, and agency that challenge more purely textual authorities, formations in which women have clout. In *Stage Fright*, Charlotte Inwood is never ultimately pinned down. "I'm what you'd call an accessory, I suppose," she sighs. Who better than Dietrich to remind us of the power of accessories? While inciting my lesbian reading of *Stage Fright*, she reminds me: Hitchcock was not acting alone.

Notes

1 Raymond Bellour, "Hitchcock, the Enunciator," trans. Bertrand Augst and Hilary Radner, *Camera Obscura* 2, pp. 66–92.

2 Robert Corber, *In the Name of National Security: Hitchcock, Homophobia, and the Political Construction of Gender in Postwar America*, Durham, NC: Duke University Press, 1993; Theodore Price, *Hitchcock and Homosexuality*, Metuchen, NJ and London: The Scarecrow Press, 1992; Robert Samuels, *Hitchcock's Bi-textuality: Lacan, Feminism, and Queer Theory*, Albany: SUNY Press, 1998

3 Laura Mulvey, "Visual Pleasure and Narrative Cinema," *Screen*, 16.3, 1975, pp. 8–11.

4 Raymond Bellour and Janet Bergstrom, "Alternation, Segmentation, Hypnosis: Interview with Raymond Bellour," *Camera Obscura* 3 and 4, pp. 71–103. On male homosexuality and pathology in Hitchcock, see John Hepworth, "Hitchcock's Homophobia," and Robin Wood, "The Murderous Gays: Hitchcock's Homophobia," in Alexander Doty and Corey K Creekmur (eds.) *Out in Culture: Gay, Lesbian, and Queer Essays on Popular Culture*, Durham, NC: Duke University Press, 1995, pp. 186–96, 197–215.

5 Wood, "The Murderous Gays," p. 206.

6 Luce Irigaray, *This Sex Which Is Not One*, trans. Catherine Porter, Ithaca, NY: Cornell University Press, 1985, p. 172.

7 Teresa de Lauretis, "Sexual Indifference and Lesbian Representability," *Theatre Journal* 40.2, May 1988, p. 156.

8 De Lauretis, "Sexual Indifference and Lesbian Representability, p. 156.

9 Irigaray, *This Sex Which Is Not One*, p. 172.

10 Kaja Silverman, *The Acoustic Mirror*, Bloomington: Indiana University Press, 1988, p. 204.

11 Tania Modleski, *The Women Who Knew Too Much: Hitchcock and Feminist Theory*, New York: Methuen, 1988, pp. 118–19. Rothman responds, "I knew I was ... taking the risk of appearing too self-effacing," but objects strenuously to Modleski's having "dismissed me .. as the ultimate male masochist for bowing so obsequiously to Hitchcock-the-master." He appears to have missed Modleski's point about the potentially self-aggrandizing nature of male critical claims on the auteur, while her "obtuseness" and "mean spiritedness" presumably caused her "to altogether miss the thrust," namely, " that a life-and-death struggle for authorship is waged, symbolically, in the readings that comprise [*Hitchcock: The Murderous Gaze*]." William Rothman, "Some Thoughts on Hitchcock's Authorship," in Richard Allen and Sam Ishii-Gonzáles (eds.) *Hitchcock Centenary Essays*, London: BFI, 1999, p. 37.

12 For astute feminist and queer readings of this film, see Sabrina Barton, " 'Crisscross': Paranoia and Projection in *Strangers on a Train*," in Doly and Creekmur, *Out in Culture*, pp. 216–38, and Robert Corber, *In the Name of National Security*, pp. 62–82.

13 D.A Miller, "*Anal* Rope," in Diana Fuss (ed.) *Inside/Out: Lesbian and Gay Theory*, New York: Routledge, 1991, p. 124. Subsequent citations appear in parentheses in the text.

14 Lee Edelman, "*Rear Window*'s Glasshole," in Ellis Hanson (ed.) *Outtakes: Essays on Queer Theory and Film*, Durham, NC: Duke University Press, 1999, pp. 72–96. Subsequent citations appear in parentheses in the text. See also Edelman, "Piss Elegant: Freud, Hitchcock, and the Micturating Penis," *GLQ*, 1995, vol. 2, pp. 149–77.

15 D.A Miller, "Visual Pleasure in 1959," in Hanson (ed.) *Outtakes*, pp. 97–125.

16 Modleski concludes, "Lisa Fremont is anything but helpless and incapable," noting the film's "emphasis on the woman's mobility, freedom, and power" (*The Women Who Knew Too Much*, pp. 76–7).

17 It is difficult, without adducing extensive passages, to convey Edelman's argument adequately. He refers to "the order of visual productivity in the form of continuity editing and the hetero-genetic castration fetish: that is to say, in the form of what I call Lisa Fre/montage," a formulation that condenses a number of key elements ("*Rear Window*'s Glasshole," p. 83).

18 Teresa de Lauretis, *The Practice of Love*, Bloomington: Indiana University Press, 1994, p. 92. On the distinction between woman and women, see de Lauretis, *Alice Doesn't: Feminism, Semiotics, Cinema*, Bloomington: Indiana University Press, 1984.

19 Patricia White, *Uninvited: Classical Hollywood Cinema and Lesbian Representability*, Bloomington: Indiana University Press, 1999.

20 Modleski, *The Women Who Knew Too Much*, p. 3.

21 Modleski, *The Women Who Knew Too Much*, p. 3.

22 See Lucretia Knapp, "The Queer Voice in *Marnie*," in Doly and Creekmur, *Out in Culture*, pp. 266–81. Supporting characters whose dress and demeanor overlaps with lesbian coding (tweeds, for example, and an air of brisk competence) appear elsewhere in Hitchcock's films: *Suspicion* (1941) even includes a couple. See Rick Worland, "Before and After the Fact: Reading and Writing Hitchcock's *Suspicion*," *Cinema Journal* 41.4, 2002, and my discussion of lesbian coding and supporting characters in chapter five of *Uninvited: Classical Hollywood Cinema and Lesbian Representability*.

23 Modleski, *The Women Who Knew Too Much*, p. 43.

24 Rhonda Berenstein, "'I'm Not the Sort of Person Men Marry': Monsters, Queers, and Hitchcock's *Rebecca*," in *Out in Culture*, pp. 239–61, and "Adaptation, Censorship, and Audiences of Questionable Type: Lesbian Sightings in *Rebecca* (1940) and *The Uninvited* (1944)," *Cinema Journal* 37.3, spring 1998, pp. 6–37. See also White, *Uninvited*, pp. 64–72.

25 The only generally acknowledged lesbian "author" in classical Hollywood history is director Dorothy Arzner, and even in her case the auteurist argument is contested. See Judith Mayne's fascinating rethinking of authorship, lesbianism, and Arzner's career, *Directed by Dorothy Arzner* (Bloomington: Indiana University Press, 1994). Of course, the argument for broadening the concept of authorship beyond directors is compelling, especially if we wish to consider not only lesbians but any women at all, as well as many categories of men, who were and continue to be all but excluded from that profession.

Of course, *Rebecca* is very much a Hitchcock picture, one of his best. Discussing the film's authorship, Richard Allen reminds us that du Maurier's lesbianism is one of the authorial ghosts we are glimpsing in this powerful text. See Richard Allen, "Daphne du Maurier and Alfred Hitchcock," in Robert Stam and Alessandra Raengo (eds.) *A Companion to Film and Literature*, New York: Blackwell, forthcoming 2003.

26 For an informative account, see Michael Walker, "The Stolen Raincoat and the Bloodstained Dress: *Young and Innocent* and *Stage Fright*," in *Hitchcock Centenary Essays*, pp. 187–204.

27 François Truffaut, with the collaboration of Helen G. Scott, *Hitchcock*, revised edition, New York: Simon & Schuster, 1984, p. 189.

28 Correspondence included in exhibition at the Museum of Modern Art.

29 Truffaut, *Hitchcock*, p. 191.

30 Truffaut, *Hitchcock*, p. 191.

31 De Lauretis, *Alice Doesn't*, chapter 4.

32 Donald Spoto, *The Dark Side of Genius: The Life of Alfred Hitchcock*, New York: Ballantine Books, 1983, p. 334.

33 Spoto, *The Dark Side of Genius*, pp. 334–5.

34 Richard Todd quoted in Steven Bach, *Marlene Dietrich: Life and Legend*, New York: William Morrow, 1992, p. 340.

35 Maria Riva, *Marlene Dietrich*, New York: Ballantine Books, 1992, p. 607.

36 Modleski, *The Women Who Knew Too Much*, p. 199.

Part IV

DEATH AND TRANSFIGURATION

Chapter 14

DEATH DRIVES

Laura Mulvey

The cinema is death 24 times a second.

Jean-Luc Godard

When I first watched Douglas Gordon's *24-Hour Psycho* at the Hayward exhibition *Spellbound* in 1996, I realized gradually that its use of slow motion had implications beyond the mesmeric images, which seemed to hover somewhere between the stillness of the photograph and the movement of the cinema. I found myself caught in a reverie that wove its way in and out of the events on the large, suspended, screen: *Psycho* itself, Hitchcock's own film history, the history of cinema in general. As Amy Taubin's illuminating catalogue essay pointed out, *24-Hour Psycho* opened up a Hollywood genre movie to the aesthetics of slow motion and thus to the traditions of the avant-garde film.[1] To put *Psycho* so firmly within the fold of art is also to celebrate the most successful of the films in which, across the whole of his career, Hitchcock tried to combine industry and experiment. But, inexorably, a reverie triggered by *24-Hour Psycho* must be affected by the presence of death that pervades it. In Douglas Gordon's reworking, in *Psycho* itself, in Hitchcock's films more generally, stories, images, and themes of death accumulate on different levels, leading like threads back to the cinema, to reflect on its deathly connotations as a medium and ultimately on its own mortality. Just as *Psycho*, in 1960, marked a final staging post in the history of the vintage Hollywood film industry, *24-Hour Psycho*, like an elegy, marks a point of no return for the cinema itself.

In 1960 films were still viewed primarily in cinemas, although television screening had gradually crept in as a new mode of exhibition and consumption. During the twenty years leading up to the cinema's centenary in 1995–96, video had transformed the ways in which film could be watched, introducing the spectator to a new kind of control over the image and its flow. *24-Hour Psycho* is, as much as anything, a celebration of the radical new possibilities offered by video viewing. At the same time, around 1996, new digitally based technologies were clearly about to give a new twist to the viewing patterns initiated by video. *24-Hour Psycho*, as Amy Taubin noted, was a product of the new video-based viewing patterns. Douglas Gordon had happened to reverse his *Psycho* tape to freeze-frame the scene in which Norman watches Marion through the peephole, and then had discovered the beauty of the film when run at two frames per second. In an art gallery, the spectator watches Gordon's reflection on the slow motion effect, unable (as in the cinema) to intervene in the projection flow. But *24-Hour Psycho* is also a significant, and *public*, meditation on new forms of *private* spectatorship. Anyone who wants is now able to play with the film image and, perhaps, in the process, evolve voyeurism and investment in spectacle into something closer to fetishism and investment in repetition, detail and personal obsession. Gordon's own discovery of another dimension to the film image, as he slowed his machine to examine a highly self-reflexive moment of voyeurism, can stand symbolically for this shift in spectatorship. *24-Hour Psycho* may represent an elegiac moment for the cinema, but it also marks a new dawn, the beginning of an "expanded cinema," which will grow in possibility as electronic technologies are overtaken by digital ones.

Amy Taubin noticed the way that the work, beyond its slow motion, seems to take the cinema, paradoxically refracted through an electronic medium, back to its own materiality and yield up the stillness of the photogram itself:

> By slowing the film down to a 13th of its normal speed, Gordon shows us not a "motion picture" but a succession of stills, each projected for about half a second. We become aware of the intermittency of the film image and the fragility of the illusion of real time in motion pictures.[2]

Here the cinema can find a way back to its essential stillness and the double temporality to which Taubin refers. While the flow of the image at 24 frames a second tends to assert a 'now-ness' to the picture, stillness allows access to the time of the film's registration, to its "then-ness." This is the point, essentially the single frame or photogram, where the cinema meets the still photograph, both registering a moment of time frozen and thus fossilized. André Bazin expands the idea of the photograph's frozen moment of time to the cinema's extended time:

> The film is no longer content to preserve the object, enshrouded as it were in the instant, as the bodies of insects are preserved intact, out of the distant past, in amber ... Now, for the first time the image of things is also the image of their duration, change mummified as it were.[3]

Watching *Psycho* at the beginning of a new century adds to this sense of mummification, partly because of artificially heightened temporal consciousness, but also because a decisive gap now stretches out, relegating the great days of the Hollywood studio system, not to the recent past, but to history. *Psycho* stands on the nearest edge of that divide. Metonymically it reaches back to the chronicle of cinema with which Hitchcock himself is so inextricably imbricated.

Hitchcock's *Psycho* was already a "minimalist" film. In *24-Hour Psycho*, the elongation of the film's running time inevitably obscures its startling, graphic, use of plot and narrative structure. Structure merges with form and form with thematic content in a way that was perhaps only possible for a film made outside the constraints of the studio system in unprecedented production conditions. Pared down to the limit, the story structure draws attention to itself as though revealing the skeletal shape of narrative usually concealed by surrounding clutter. There is nothing new in the generic plots Hitchcock draws on in *Psycho*. In their reworking, however, he found the bold patterns that relate stories to the spaces in which they take place – their links to traditional forms of story telling – and touched that narrow border where collective "pools" of cultural reference overlap with more sophisticated psychoanalytic material discussed by Freud. In all these different but interconnected spheres, the rendering of ideas into visual form is of the essence. Plot finds realization in topography; psychoanalysis draws liberally on spatial metaphor. *Psycho* reflects on plot structures in their own right and on the translation of these non-cinematic forms onto the cinema screen.

Psycho takes the plots that characterized Hitchcock's English thriller series, which he continued to recycle in Hollywood, and uses them in a way that is shocking both in its novelty and in its strange familiarity.[4] Peter Wollen argued, in a short but suggestive article in 1981, that *Psycho* combines two plot types - the fairy-tale and the detective story - and the two types differ in their relation to time. The fairy-tale is linear and horizontal. A journey into no-man's land that should lead, through adventure, to marriage, the sense that "civilization anywhere is a thin crust." Closing with the villain's defeat and the hero and heroine "to be married," this plot characteristically takes the hero away from home, to found a new home at the end. The process is progressed by movement forward through space and time. In the detective story, as Wollen observes, citing Michel Butor, " there is always a double story, the story of an investigation ends with the telling of another story embedded in it, the story of a crime. The narrative of one story concludes with the narration of another."[5]

In *Psycho*, Marion's journey takes her, not to marriage as she intended, but to death. The investigation into her death leads back in time to the discovery of an "Ur-death," a long-guarded secret: the crime of matricide. The two plots, usually superimposed in the Hitchcock thriller, here, in the Hitchcock horror, are run in sequence, separated by Marion's murder.

These two conjoined plots in *Psycho* are the vehicles for moving, frightening stories and moments of pure horror. They also have an affect on the overall aesthetics of the film. The formal patterns built into these plots manage to reach the surface across character and event. It is as though Hitchcock thought in terms of the graphic quality of his stories, as though, in addition to transposing his shots from a graphic, storyboarded form to celluloid, he visualized the patterns of his plots in terms of line and contour. A journey, a protagonist's movement along a road, figures the narrative's linear development, linking form to content. Similarly, the concept of a mystery, the secret to be discovered, may be figured by an enclosed space, for instance, a house. These topographies, of course, are far from specific to cinema or to Hitchcock. But in translating the themes, forms and metaphors of popular storytelling, he rendered them visually and physically into mise-en-scène, for the spectator's eye and then for the mind's eye. *Psycho*'s sparseness and the separation of the two plot patterns enhances their visibility.

Although these two plot patterns divide the larger framework of *Psycho*'s narrative, they are themselves framed by two brief opening and closing moments in which the camera takes over as the film's narrator.[6] *Psycho* opens with a series of camera movements that select an upper window in a Phoenix hotel and move through the window to penetrate the space and privacy of the couple inside. This act of penetration prefigures subsequent violations of space throughout the rest of the movie, of which the violent intrusion into the enclosed space of the shower, combined with the knife's penetration of Marion's body, are only the most remarkable and shocking. But although the camera subsequently latches onto smaller, or minor, movements of story, character or point of view, this opening sequence sets in motion a transcendent drive towards an end that is only realized in the film's closing sequence. With a long, slow tracking movement, the film reaches the image that allows it to come to a halt: the close-up of Norman/Mother looking straight into camera. Just as the audience's look is drawn into that first movement, detached from any diegetic point of view, so it is inscribed into its last. Movement reaches towards stillness and then towards the dead: Mother's skull appears superimposed briefly on Norman's features and they merge.

But the film marks "THE END" with its ultimate shot, which encapsulates movement stilled, the animate transformed into the inanimate, the organic into the inorganic: the last image of Marion's car subject to an abstract pattern of black and white lines, echoing the film's opening and closing credit design. These motifs – movement and stillness, the animate and the inanimate – find fictional equivalence in the two "hybrid" plots of *Psycho*. At the center of the film, another "narrating" shot organizes the transition from one plot segment to the next. In a complicated amalgam of three separate sections of film, the camera moves from Marion's eye, motionless in death, across the motel room, passing over the $40,000, to rest on the Bates house on the hill. As Norman runs out, shouting "Mother, Mother," the transition from a journey stilled by death to the enigma locked away in the house is achieved and figured on the screen. From the journey's horizontal movement, mapped into space by the heroine's desire and abruptly halted by her death, to the mystery which is to be investigated, concealed in the enclosed, vertical space of the house which represents the unspeakable bond between mother and son.

With *Psycho*, Hitchcock brought death to the foreground of the plot and its visualization on screen. Here he was able to strip away the armature of romance with which Hollywood, and popular storytelling in general, sugared the sight and site of violent death. In the fairy-tale, the villain's death was an essential component in narrative closure to be followed by the hero and heroine united and living happily ever after. In most Hitchcock thrillers, the villain's pursuit and death has a similar structural function. But Hitchcock often concentrates such a degree of spectacle, suspense and drama in the death of the villain that it constitutes the visual climax to the film as a whole. Its complex staging often takes place in public so that the spectacle has its own built-in or ready-made audience, for example, the dance-hall in *Young and Innocent*, the fairground in *Strangers on a Train*, the Albert Hall in both versions of *The Man Who Knew Too Much*, the presidents' heads in *North by Northwest*. *Blackmail*, *Murder!*, *Saboteur*, and *To Catch a Thief* all end with, or threaten, death by falling as a public spectacle. As the spectacle of death constitutes the high point of many Hitchcock plots, the end of the villain's life comes to condense with "The End" of the story itself. In a sense, these extraordinary tableaux, animated by suspense and anxiety, overwhelm the actual closing moments of a movie. The ultimate figuration of narrative closure, the "formation of the couple" (or in Vladimir Propp's terms "function Wedding") takes up comparatively little and unspectacular screen time.

In *Psycho*, the spectacle of death is detached from the film's end, its conventional narrative purpose of eliminating a villain. The scene in the shower has a dual function: Marion's death closes the story of her journey; her murder then initiates the enigma, the investigative phase of the plot. Taking place, as it does, in the center of the movie, the double function of Marion's death confirms, from a formal perspective, the "hybridity" of *Psycho*'s plot. But there is a significant stylistic shift in the staging of death in *Psycho*. As a murder, it must, of course, be secret. As the climactic moment of Marion's story, as its "ending," her death is given a spectacular staging but one that is purely cinematic. The complex, almost baroque, surroundings and the theatricality that have contributed to the spectacle of death in so many earlier Hitchcock movies have disappeared, leaving only the formal whiteness of the shower, the woman's naked body, the flow of blood and water, and the screech of the violins. The sense of death as public spectacle has been replaced by a more abstract, cinematic, spectacle. It is the cinema spectator alone who can interpret this complex montage sequence, which renders this spectacle of death as cinematic spectacle. Although the montage sequence had many successors, it is hard to think of precedents in the cinema that followed the conversion to sound. It is tempting to imagine that, when Hitchcock asked Saul Bass to design the sequence, he thought of films he had watched at the London Film Society during the late twenties, and of the way in which Eisenstein translated the eruption of violence into fragments of film and turned shock into the cinema of attractions.

Of course it was natural for Hitchcock to think of death as spectacle: public execution in London had ceased only about fifty years before he was born. Hitchcock always seemed to feel that the audience for the spectacular aspects of his films would be wandering somewhere between peep show, roller coaster and gallows. While the closing death of the villain lies directly in this lineage, the act of murder is more complex and essentially secret. Marion's murder constitutes a formal, cinematic, shocking centerpiece for *Psycho* as a whole; it initiates the second, investigative, section of the film. Marion's death also marks "The End" for the journey that had driven her story so far. As such, it indicates, from a formalist perspective, the interchangability of narrative stasis as death and narrative stasis as marriage. In order to get married Marion steals $40,000, leaves Phoenix and drives to California to join her fiancé. The journey is represented sketchily, mostly filmed in a studio. But the figure of "the road," the graphic element in this segment of the story, marks the movement between the parental home (the static, establishing structural point of Marion's narrative) and the desired new home and marriage (the static, closing, structural point the narrative). However the stasis to which Marion's story returns is that of death, not of marriage.

In his 1920 essay "Beyond the Pleasure Principle," Freud discusses the instinct or drive that overwhelms the pleasure principle, always seeking to find a way back to "an earlier state of things" to the inorganic and ultimately, he argues, to death. Throughout the essay, the stimulation to movement, inherent in the instinct, jostles with its aim to return, to rediscover the stillness from which it originally departed. Reading the essay, especially in the context of its relevance to narrative, the term "drive" takes on an extra resonance. Peter Brooks has described Freud's concept of the death instinct as his "master plot" and has used it to analyze the problem of narrative's own drive to find a return to stillness and the inorganic after its initial animation under the aegis of desire. As these instincts are always striving to return to a previous state and are fundamentally conservative in nature, they assume, as a disguise, the appearance of movement, of progress and change:

Conservative instincts are therefore bound to give a deceptive appearance of being forces towards change and progress, whilst in fact they are merely seeking to reach an ancient goal by paths alike old and new ... it would be a contradiction to the conservative nature of the instincts if the goal of life were a state of things which had never yet been attained. On the contrary, it must be an old state of things, an initial state from which the living entity has at one time or other departed and to which it is striving to return by the circuitous paths along which its development leads.[7]

In this paragraph, Freud's use of metaphor, invoking "paths" and "departure" alongside "return" and "initial state," resonates with the topographies of narrative, suggesting that life itself is subject to similar patterns. These are the elements that allow Peter Brooks to perceive a "master plot" at stake:

We emerge from reading "Beyond the Pleasure Principle" with a dynamic model that structures ends (death, quiescence, non-narratability) against beginnings (Eros, stimulation into tension, the desire of narrative) in a manner that necessitates the middle as a detour, as struggle toward the end under the compulsion of imposed delay, as an arabesque in the dilatory space of the text.[8]

The type of story into which Marion departed from Phoenix should, according to the conventional pattern, end with marriage, with a new home symmetrical to the one left behind. Here the stasis of the story's ending is inscribed into its spaces: the home brings stillness with it as the movement of the journey comes to its end. Form and content reflect each other. But, as Brooks points out, if the end of a story is realized as death, the metonymy of the narrative chain, of its journey through the space of telling, finds a more vivid realization in metaphor. Narrative end and human end literally coalesce; narrative "ending" not only implies the silence and stillness associated with death, but that this death-like property of "the end" may well literally be figured by a final death in the narrative:

The more we inquire into the problem of ends, the more it seems to compel an inquiry into its relation to the human end.[9]

There is a homology that connects the terms "stillness," "death", and "ending," which takes the cinema back to its own secret stillness, the death that lies concealed within it. When the camera plots its "pivot" shot, moving the *Psycho* story into its second phase, it departs from a close-up of Marion's face as she lies on the bathroom floor. The eye, whose involuntary flickering is a guarantee of life itself, is fixed in an inanimate stare. As the camera pulls back, it seems impossible to tell whether or not Janet Leigh is there, acting the stillness of death, or whether, in a trick shot, Hitchcock replaced the actress with a still photograph of her face. Just when the image's stillness seems necessarily to derive from a photograph, a single drop of water falls in front of the camera. Its effect is to re-animate the image, to create a contrast with the inanimate, the inorganic matter, the corpse, which the camera then leaves behind. As the camera moves to the window, it displaces Marion's story and her dead body onto the enigma "Mother" and then, ultimately, onto her dead body. This sequence prefigures *Psycho*'s triple ending: Lila's discovery of Mrs. Bates's corpse, the stillness that envelops Norman/Mother at the very end of the story, and the final shot of Marion's car, reiterating death as the drive of narrative.

Peter Wollen concludes his article on "Hybrid Plots in *Psycho*" as follows:

> *Psycho*, I think, is the most extreme case of a film … in which the fairy-tale is not simply a hybrid with the tale of detection, but is also transformed into a different type of story which, following Freud, we can call a tale of the uncanny.[10]

The uncanny has long made a significant contribution to popular culture and certainly prefigured the genre of "horror" with which Hitchcock was experimenting in *Psycho*. During the "gothic" period, abandoned sites of human habitation provided a style, vocabulary and topography for this sense of nameless dread. During the period when he was developing the *Psycho* project, Hitchcock had been impressed by the success of the French import *Les Diaboliques* (Henri-Georges Clouzot, 1954) and by Roger Corman's adaptation of the stories of Edgar Allan Poe into low-budget movies for American International Pictures. The new horror genre bore witness to continued public interest in the uncanny and its license to explore areas of dread and superstition that had been banished by the rational and the everyday. This is an uncanny that turns towards the archaic and the gothic. Freud's interest in the topic seems to have been triggered by his desire to refute Ernst Jentsch's 1906 article "On the Psychology of the Uncanny,"[11] in which the effect is associated, in the first instance, with "the new and unfamiliar." For Freud, there could be little or no interest for psychoanalysis in the new. Only the return of the repressed, the sense of something ancient, that had once been known and reassuring but had become a source of dread, would be located in the unconscious rather than the conscious mind and could be of psychoanalytic interest. In *Psycho*, the aesthetics of the uncanny have their roots in that emblem of the ancient and the repressed: the maternal body and its decay.

Freud's interest initially focuses on two meanings of the German word *heim-lich*. The first has various associations with the homely, the familiar; the second with the secret, something that must be concealed and kept out of public sight. The two, while apparently unconnected in meaning, are connected by topography: the home *encloses* and thus gives comfort while the secret is *enclosed* and thus hidden.[12] These two meanings condense together in the last image of *Psycho*'s pivot shot, bringing together in a single figuration the dual significance that the Bates house will have for the rest of the film. It is Norman's home, his Mother's home, yet it is also the place where the story's ultimate enigma lies hidden. But the secret concealed in the Bates house conforms with two further aspect of the uncanny. Initially, Freud argues, the body of the mother is the first "home," and thus familiar, but with the passing of time this *heimlichkeit* has become archaic, *unheimlich*. Second, Freud comments on the uncanniness of the corpse. Mrs. Bates, of course, condenses both, so that the film's imagery is, in the last resort, associated with the maternal uncanny. There seems to be almost a touch of parody in Hitchcock's manipulation of these themes, especially with the Bates house's gothic connotations, evoking the "haunted house" in its *design* and *mise-en-scène*. Even the motel, "left behind" when the highway moved, has this sense of the once familiar that has been extracted, like a ruin, from the flow of life; Norman's everyday performance of his chores seem to take on an aura of repetition compulsion.

While topography connects the space of the home to the space of secrets, the secrets are the product of the home, the domestic, the family. As Norman explains:

> *This place* is my home … *this place* happens to be my only world. I grew up in that house up there. I had a very happy childhood. My mother and I were more than happy.

Behind Norman's words lie the trauma and repression that, in Freud's terms, turn the *heimlich* space (homely/concealed) into the *unheimlich* space of the uncanny. The bond between mother and son, on the one hand, the most normal of relations, is, on the other, easily distorted into the perverse, so that the home conceals deviance and then the enigma: the crime of matricide. Lila's investigation of the Bates house, the enclosed space of the uncanny, is also an incursion into the privacy of Norman's world. The point-of-view tracking shot with which Hitchcock stages Lila's journey up the hill cuts between her look and the house itself, which seems to draw her, just as her curiosity drives her, towards its secret. When Lila enters Mrs. Bates's bedroom, her pressing concern for her sister is temporarily suspended. At the same time, the inexorable movement of the plot, carrying her towards and into direct, face to face, encounter with Mrs. Bates, also falters. Lila's curiosity roams freely around the house. On a literal level, these scenes build suspense through delay, but they also elongate her journey through the uncanny. Although her point of view organizes the sequence, it is no longer attached to the tracking shot that has taken her to the door. Her look becomes a surrogate for the spectator's desire to see inside this forbidden and frightening space. Mrs. Bates's bedroom is, of course, maintained as if she were alive: washbasin, fireplace, and her clothes all ready for use. But the only sign of human presence is the strange fossil-like trace of a body left on the bed. Hitchcock isolates two details: first a tracking shot moves into a close-up of a perfectly lifelike china reproduction of hands folded on a cushion; second, Lila is suddenly startled by her reflection in a mirror. Freud mentions both, the lifelike reproduction of limbs and the sudden sight of one's own reflection, in his consideration of various uncanny phenomena. Norman's bedroom, with its objects suspended somewhere between childhood and adolescence, is subjected to Lila's curiosity, recalling Freud's phrase:

> From the idea of "homelike" and "belonging to the home," the further idea is developed of something withdrawn from the eyes of strangers, something concealed, secret. [...] According to [Schelling], everything is *unheimlich* that ought to have remained concealed but has come to light.[13]

Inexorably, Lila's detour comes to an end, and the movement of this segment of the film returns to its ultimate uncanny: Mother's preserved corpse in the cellar.

Until the very last moment, the film preserves an element of doubt that prepares the way for the film's actual secret: that Mrs. Bates is both alive and dead. When Lila finds Mrs. Bates in the cellar, the old woman seems to move, to respond to her voice and her touch. Then, as the corpse turns and the skull looks directly into the camera, the swinging light bulb continues to act out the illusion in which the inanimate body is fleetingly animated. This fleeting moment is, in a certain sense, a gesture of horror in which the blurred boundary between the stillness of the corpse and its fake movement is enacted with truly gothic effect. But the theme of stillness, and now stillness condensing with the stasis of narrative closure, is finally enacted in Norman's mind through his own, internal, blurring of the inanimate with the animate. This final drama is introduced by the psychiatrist's summing up ("Norman had to keep alive the illusion of his mother being alive"). His speech leads to the image of Norman in his cell, and "Mother's" decision to remain completely still. ("I'll just sit and stare like one of his stuffed birds.") In the last resort, the second segment of *Psycho* condenses the conventional death drive ending, the image of the mortal body, which returns in the film's last image of Marion's car emerging from the swamp, with a more disturbing blurring of the boundary between the animate and the inanimate, the living and the dead. And this, after all, is the boundary that the cinema itself blurs.

During the fifties, Hitchcock's big budget pictures had expanded, along with other A movies of the time, into increasingly elaborate spectacle. These high production values, with top stars, color, wide-screen and location shooting, are exemplified in *To Catch a Thief* with its Technicolor and VistaVision, its sweeping helicopter shots of the Riviera, costumes by Edith Head and investment in stars that Hitchcock later either wouldn't ("I don't want to give Cary Grant 50% of the picture") or couldn't ("We can't get Grace because she's off in Monaco being a Princess, isn't she?") equal. In these fifties films, and with Grace Kelly in particular, Hitchcock streamlined the star iconography of the "cool blonde." Production values went hand in hand with the highly censored eroticism that was symptomatic of America at the time as it celebrated its status as "democracy of glamour" in its cold war with Communism. This is the cinema, with its witty, self-conscious voyeurism, that fell away with *Psycho*. The crisis in the Hollywood film industry, caught at a crossroads, faced with its own mortality, offered Hitchcock the opportunity to write its epitaph, but also to transcend its conventions and create something startling and new.

Like its plot structure, *Psycho* was a hybrid, the joint product of Hitchcock's film and television enterprises. Like its central shot, *Psycho* is a pivot, a package deal put together by MCA that prefigured the industry's imminent shift away from studio-based production. With *Psycho*, the scale of the production shrinks to a short rehearsal period, a tight schedule and budget ($800,000), with certain shots or scenes privileged for more complex staging, effectively a return to the studio and to black and white film stock. Hitchcock could then put on the screen ideas that his big Hollywood movies had only hinted at. The glamorous beauty of his blonde stars had, perhaps, veiled the other, repressed, side of the female body, the mother. In *Psycho*, "mother" as site of horror and madness brings back memories of Uncle Charlie's phobia in *Shadow of a Doubt,* made at the height of American anxiety about "Momism." In *Notorious*, Mrs. Sebastian, who prefigures the psychic structures of *Psycho*, adds foreign-ness to the material uncanny. If the star as spectacle had neutralized these anxieties, she had not kept them completely at bay. But if there is an element of social comment hidden in *Psycho*, its aesthetic comment is, in the last resort, more significant. Able to exploit to the full a purist desire to strip away the fiction film's unnecessary ornament, Hitchcock could reveal the presence of death in narrative, as spectacle and in the cinema's own illusion of movement. As he had said at the start of his thriller cycle in the thirties:

I aim to provide the public with beneficial shocks. Civilization has become so protective that we are no longer able to get our goose bumps instinctively. The only way to the remove the numbness and revive our moral equilibrium is to use artificial means to bring about the shock. The best way to do this, it seems to me, is through a movie.[14]

Notes

1 Amy Taubin, "Douglas Gordon," in Philip Dodd (ed.) *Spellbound. Art and Film*, London: South Bank Centre, 1996.

2 Taubin, "Douglas Gordon," p. 72.

3 André Bazin, "The Ontology of the Photographic Image," in *What Is Cinema?*, ed. and trans. Hugh Gray, Berkeley: University of California Press, 1967, p. 15.

4 See Charles Barr, *English Hitchcock*, Moffat, Scotland: Cameron & Hollis, 1999, pp. 148, 185.

5 Peter Wollen, "Hybrid Plots in *Psycho*," in *Readings and Writings. Semiotic Counter Strategies*, London: Verso, 1982, p. 35.

6 See Raymond Bellour, "Neurosis, Psychosis, Perversion," *Camera Obscura* nos. 3–4, summer 1979, pp. 105–29, for an alternative segmentation of *Psycho* which gives due importance to the opening and closing camera movements.

7 Sigmund Freud, "Beyond the Pleasure Principle," in *Standard Edition of the Complete Psychological Works of Sigmund Freud*, vol. XVIII, London: The Hogarth Press, 1954–74, p. 38.

8 Peter Brooks, *Reading for the Plot. Design and Intention in Narrative,* New York: Vintage, 1985, p. 105.

9 Brooks, *Reading for the Plot*, p. 105.

10 Wollen, "Hybrid Plots in *Psycho*," pp. 38–9.

11 Ernst Jentsch, "On the Psychology of the Uncanny," *Angelaki* 2: 1, 1995.

12 See Anthony Vidler, *The Architectural Uncanny: Essays in the Modern Unhomely*, Cambridge, MA: MIT Press, 1992.

13 Sigmund Freud, "The Uncanny," in *Standard Edition*, vol. XVII, p. 225.

14 Charles Barr, *English Hitchcock*, p. 147.

Chapter 15

OF "FARTHER USES OF THE DEAD TO THE LIVING"
Hitchcock and Bentham

Miran Bozovic

In this chapter I will discuss the "farther use of the dead to the living" in Hitchcock's *Psycho*, in particular, the dead body of Mrs. Bates and its "farther use."

The stuffing of dead human bodies and their subsequent animation is not something that originates with Norman Bates. There is in fact a quite respectable philosophical background to human taxidermy and bringing stuffed bodies back to life that reaches back to the beginning of the nineteenth century. Thus, in her post-mortem fate, in her "after-life," Mrs. Bates is not alone; her resurrected body has at least one distinguished historical predecessor, namely the stuffed body of the British utilitarian philosopher, Jeremy Bentham.

Auto-thanatography

It was Bentham's last wish that, after his death, his body be publicly dissected, and then preserved and exhibited. The ideas behind this somewhat extraordinary wish were elaborated in his work entitled *Auto-Icon; or, Farther Uses of the Dead to the Living*.[1]

While other philosophers who reflect on death are mostly concerned with the destiny of the soul after the death of the body, Bentham, in *Auto-Icon*, is concerned exclusively with the destiny of the dead body, that is, the body from which the soul has left. Accordingly, whereas other philosophers' reflections on death most often take the form of meditations on the immortality of the soul and completely disregard the post-mortem fate of the body, Bentham's reflections on death take the form of meditations on the body – first and foremost on his own dead body – and disregard the destiny of the soul.

As a treatise on the author's own dead body, Bentham's *Auto-Icon* is perhaps the only work of its kind; it thus constitutes its own genre, for which Bentham coined a new term. For the description of one's own death and the subsequent fate of the body he proposed the term "auto-thanatography" (p. 2) as a natural sequel to one's autobiography.

While people generally find the very thought of death and the dead body revolting, by contrast, in Bentham's eyes, it is the dead bodies – bodies of animals and humans, preserved after death "in the torrid regions of Africa," "in the ice of the poles," "in the ruins of Herculaneum and Pompeii," "in rocks," and in "bogs, impregnated with tannine matter" – that provide "valuable materials for thought" (p. 1). While others, as a rule, rarely talk about death, particularly not their own, Bentham says of his own death, and of the fate of his body after death, that "for many a year the subject has been a favourite one at my table" (p. 2).

Although Bentham wrote *Auto-Icon* shortly before his death and referred to it as his "last work" (p. 1; note by the editor), he betrays in the treatise no fear of death: instead, he reflects on his own death just as objectively as he reflects upon everything else, that is, from the point of view of its possible utility. Although he usually writes in a cold and dull manner, this utilitarian sage, when writing his auto-thanatography, becomes lively for the first time and does not even try to hide his enthusiasm in contemplating the post-mortem fate of his body. As a utilitarian, he was exclusively interested in how he could be of use to his fellow humans even after death, that is, in what way even his dead body could contribute to the happiness of the living. As he wrote already in 1769, he wished "that mankind may reap some small benefit in and by my decease, having hitherto had small opportunities to contribute thereto while living."[2]

Other philosophers, such as Nicolas Malebranche or George Berkeley, similarly display no fear of death, but Bentham's lack of fear stems from different causes. It is, perhaps, not hard to face death if we share Berkeley's belief that the soul is "naturally immortal"[3] and that "the Resurrection follows the next moment to death."[4] The latter idea constitutes one of the "several paradoxes" that follow from Berkeley's radical theory of time. If, as a mind, I only exist as long as I perceive, then, of course, the moment I cease to perceive – that is, the moment I fall into a totally dreamless sleep or lose consciousness – I should cease to exist. Subsequently, in order to avoid this conclusion, Berkeley introduces his theory of time. According to Berkeley, what constitutes the time of each individual mind – and each individual mind has its own wholly subjective time, that is, there is no absolute time – is "the succession of ideas" in the mind.[5] It follows that the moment there is no succession of ideas, there is no time either. But if, when there is no longer any succession of ideas, there is also no time, then between death (the moment when I lose consciousness) and the resurrection (the moment when I regain consciousness) there is no time for me not to exist.[6] Thus, what Berkeley is claiming is not that *I* myself do not exist in the interval separating my death from the resurrection, but rather that the *interval* itself does not exist. Since he believed that the "intervals of Death or Annihilation" were "nothing," is it any wonder that he got a friend to assist him in hanging himself because he was curious to know "what were the pains and symptoms ... felt upon such an occasion"?[7]

It might be even less difficult to face death if we were to share Malebranche's belief that "at death we do not lose anything."[8] According to Malebranche, in addition to the material body, which is inaccessible and inefficacious, we possess yet another "ideal" or "intelligible body"; and it is only the latter body that is capable of acting on us. It is not simply that the ideal body begins acting on us after death, when we have lost the material body; rather, the ideal body acts on us all along. Thus, although we believe that it is our material body that causes pain in us when we are injured, for example, it is in fact the ideal body that is causing the pain. Since, according to Malebranche, the soul can be united only to that which can act upon it, it follows that the soul is not, and cannot be, united to the material, but only to the ideal body. The ideal body is "more real" than the material body; moreover, unlike the material body, which no longer exists after death, our ideal body is "incorruptible,"[9] and we therefore possess it even after we have lost the material one. Since death cannot separate us from the ideal body, to which we are really united, but only from the material body, which even while still alive was incapable of acting on us and was thus actually dead even before death, it is clear that "at death we do not lose anything": "therefore death which separates the soul ... from this insensible body ... is not to be feared at all."[10] Furthermore, since the body that acts upon us even while the material body is still alive is precisely the body that also acts upon us after the material body's death, it follows that, in Malebranche, the resurrection *precedes* death itself.

Incidentally, there is an apocryphal story – quoted by Thomas De Quincy in his brilliant essay (*On Murder Considered as One of the Fine Arts*) (1839) – according to which Berkeley is supposed to have caused Malebranche's death. When Berkeley called on the famous philosopher in Paris he found him in his cell cooking. A dispute arose about the latter's system. Berkeley urged Malebranche to retract his doctrine of occasional causes, while the latter stubbornly stood his ground – "culinary and metaphysical irritations united to derange his liver: he took to his bed, and died."[11] Berkeley thus came to be considered as "the occasional cause of Malebranche's death."[12]

If, on the other hand, we share Bentham's uncertainty about the ontological status of the soul after the death of the body, that is, if the "soul, existing in a state of separation from the body" cannot even be said to be a "real entity," it may well turn out to be only a "fictitious entity."[13] And if our entire post-mortem fate is that of "a senseless carcass,"[14] then there clearly is not much we can hope for in the afterlife. While Malebranche's post-mortem fate is not dependent upon the fate of the dead material body, Bentham's post-mortem fate is not dependent upon the fate of the soul; while Malebranche, in *Entretiens sur la mort*, views his own post-mortem fate as one of the immortal soul, which, even after the death of the material body, remains united to the ideal body, Bentham, by contrast, in *Auto-Icon*, sees his post-mortem fate solely in terms of his dead body. Although this body will remain soulless even after the resurrection, it will nevertheless be precisely this body that Bentham will claim as "his own self."

The auto-icon art

According to Bentham, the conventional disposal of the body after death goes not only against utilitarian wisdom but also against common sense: not only is it a "source of evil" for the living – "undertaker, lawyer, priest – all join in the depredation" (p. 1) – it also deprives them of the good they might otherwise have obtained from the dead.

Where, according to Bentham, can a "farther use of the dead to the living" be found? What is the good that can be extracted from the dead? In what way can the dead, through their bodies, contribute "to the common stock of human happiness" (p. 2)?

After death, human bodies can serve two purposes: one "transitory" and the other "permanent." The transitory purpose is "anatomical, or dissectional," and the permanent one is "conservative, or statuary" (p. 2). "The mass of matter which death has created" should not simply be disposed of, but should be used "with a view to the felicity of mankind." Bearing in mind his "greatest-happiness principle," Bentham argues that the dead body can be put to the best use if "the soft and corruptible parts" are employed "for the purpose of anatomical instructions," and "the comparatively incorruptible part" converted into "an Auto-Icon" (p. 2).

Let us first look at the "transitory," that is, "anatomical, or dissectional" purpose of dead human bodies. It might seem unnecessary for the utilitarians to have to persuade anyone about the utility of the dead in teaching anatomy – by now most of us will admit that by dissecting and studying the bodies of "the insensible dead" "the susceptible living" may be spared numerous severe pains. Yet, in Bentham's time, this position was not widely shared. As Ruth Richardson observes, in Great Britain during this period, the only legal source of bodies for medical dissection were the bodies of hanged murderers. The dissection, performed by a surgeon-anatomist, was considered part of the punishment, an extension of the hangman's task.[15] Consequently, anatomists acquired a particularly low reputation in public opinion and the act of dissection itself was viewed with suspicion. The dissection of murderers was made compulsory by the 1752 Murder Act, in which dissection is described as a "further Terror and peculiar Mark of Infamy."[16] But since the bodies from this source clearly were in scarce supply, to satisfy the ever-increasing demand of the anatomy schools, the so-called "bodysnatchers" (or "the resurrectionists," as they were also known) emerged and began digging corpses up from their graves and selling them to anatomy schools. Bodysnatching was not technically a crime of theft – dead bodies were not thought to belong to anyone by law, and consequently "could neither be owned or stolen" – but was considered merely as an offense against public morality.[17] However, the most notorious of the bodysnatchers, Burke and Hare from Edinburgh, mentioned also by Bentham in his *Auto-Icon*, did not simply dig up dead bodies, but actually murdered their subjects with the intention of selling their bodies to anatomists.

It is in this historical context that Bentham's extraordinary last will must be understood. Bentham left his dead body to his friend and disciple, Dr. Thomas Southwood Smith; it thus became his property and could not be stolen from him with impunity. He was to dissect it and use it

> as the means of illustrating a series of lectures to which scientific & literary men are to be invited ... These lectures are to expound the situation structure & functions of the different organs ... The object of these lectures being two fold first to communicate curious interesting & highly important knowledge & secondly to show that the primitive horror at dissection originates in ignorance.[18]

Bentham left his own body to an anatomist for dissection at a time when there was a growing demand for corpses in the medical schools, but only a scant supply, since only convicted criminals could be dissected. Indeed, corpses were so much in demand and so scarce in supply that murder began to pay. According to Bentham, it was "the pecuniary value attached" to the corpses that "created murderers in the shape of Burkes and Hares."[19] Rather than an empty gesture of a capricious philosopher, who had lost his mind in old age, Bentham's donation of his body was an "exemplary bequest," intended to inspire others to bequeath their bodies for dissection after death, and thus ultimately to make murder unprofitable.[20] Southwood Smith executed Bentham's last will faithfully, and dissected his friend's body in front of his disciples and medical students. Before the dissection, he gave a long oration over the corpse entitled *A Lecture delivered over the remains of Jeremy Bentham*.[21]

The idea that dissected human bodies, having once served their "transitory" purpose, should be preserved, that is, put to their "permanent," or "conservative, or statuary" purpose, is urged by Bentham as follows:

> What resemblance, what painting, what statue of a human being can be so like him, as, in the character of an Auto-Icon, he or she will be to himself or herself. Is not identity preferable to similitude?[22]

Since nothing resembles an individual as well as that individual resembles him or herself,[23] the bodies of the dead need to be preserved as their own most adequate representations. While one is usually represented after death by various icons, that is, "resemblances," "paintings," and "statues," preserving the body makes it possible for anyone to become his or her own icon, that is, an "auto-icon." The term "auto-icon," invented by Bentham, is, as he says, "self-explanatory"; it means "a man who is his own image."[24] Thus, Bentham's auto-icon is a paradoxical sign that is identical with its denotatum, a sign that is itself its own denotatum. Let us briefly recall a typical difficulty concerning the dead human body in medieval philosophy. If the rational soul is the only substantial form of the human body, then the dead body, that is, the body that the soul has left, cannot be said to be identical with the living body. If, however, the dead body on the cross cannot be said to be identical with Christ's body, then it cannot be a fit object of worship.[25] For the utilitarian sage, however, this dilemma would present no difficulty; as he tersely puts it: "a man's Auto-Icon is his own self."[26] Converted into an auto-icon, the "comparatively incorruptible part" of the matter created by death is identical with the living body and therefore a fit object of worship (or scorn), to the extent that people, while still alive, will take into account the judgment they will receive after death in the eyes of their fellow men when deciding upon any course of action: "What will be said of my Auto-Icon hereafter?" (p. 7). Converted into an auto-icon, every man could, even after death, continue to represent himself, to be "his own image." Since each man would be "his own statue" (p. 2), auto-iconism would, of course, "supersede the necessity of sculpture" (p. 4); that is, since each man would be "his own monument" (p. 4), "there would no longer be needed monuments of stone or marble" (p. 3).[27] The art of auto-iconism, in short, would provide "likenesses more perfect than painting or sculpture could furnish."[28] Bentham is thus interested in the dead body in the same way that Thomas De Quincy is interested in murder – as the object of "one of the fine arts."

Bentham set a personal example not only for the "transitory," that is the "anatomical" purpose, but also for the "permanent," that is the "statuary" purpose of dead human bodies: in his will, he directed Southwood Smith, after he had performed the dissection and anatomical demonstrations, to reassemble his bones into a skeleton, place on it the head, which was to have been processed separately, and then clothe the skeleton "in one of the suits of black usually worn by me" and sit it "in a Chair usually occupied by me when living." Thus clad, the skeleton was to be equipped with "the staff in my later years borne by me" and put in "an appropriate box or case."[29] As a result, Bentham can still be seen today exemplifying the "permanent" purpose of dead human bodies: he sits as "his own statue" in a glass and mahogany case in a corridor of University College London – and still represents himself more than a century and a half after his death.

While the conservative preparation of the trunk and extremities amounted to no more than ordinary taxidermy – the skeleton is tied together at the joints by copper wires, wrapped in straw, hay, tow, cotton wool, wood wool, with a bunch of lavender and a bag of naphthalene added for good measure[30] – the auto-iconization of the head required a special treatment. That special attention should be paid to the head is clear: "the head of each individual is peculiar to him," says Bentham, "and, when properly preserved, is better than a statue."[31] Accordingly, it was advised that the head be treated like the heads of indigenous New Zealanders, that is, by exsiccation. (A head, processed in this way, can be seen, for example, in Hitchcock's *Under Capricorn*.) In striving to contribute to human happiness, then, a civilized man was not to scorn the "savage ingenuity" of "the barbarous New Zealanders," who have "preceded the most cultivated nations in the Auto-Icon art" (p. 2). The eyes, one of the "soft and corruptible parts" of the body, did not have to present a problem, since artificial eyes would be made out of glass and would not be "distinguishable from those which nature makes" (p. 2).

A curious irony had it that the auto-iconization of Bentham's body failed precisely at the head. Although Southwood Smith faithfully followed Bentham's instructions, the desiccated head was markedly dissimilar to the head of the living Bentham, and the anatomist therefore had a wax replica made to replace it. Although "identical" to the head of the living Bentham, the original head of the auto-icon was no longer "similar" to it, and Bentham, converted into an auto-icon, no longer resembled himself. It was, then, the wax replica that turned out to be more "like" Bentham than Bentham, in the character of an auto-icon, was "like himself." However, as it is the head that, according to Bentham, is what is "peculiar" to each individual, Bentham's auto-icon, with its wax head, turned out to be no "better than a statue." The irony of this lies not only in the fact that it was the example of Bentham himself that proved that an individual is not neces-sarily his or her own most adequate representation after death, but also in the fact that in considering how to preserve his own head after death, Bentham was led to toy with the idea of experimenting in "the Auto-Icon art" of the New Zealanders: he planned to obtain a human head from an anatomist and dry it out in a stove in his house.[32] It is not clear if the experiment was ever actually carried out, although Bentham, in his *Auto-Icon*, does somewhat cryptically refer to experiments in "the slow exhaustion of the moisture from the human head," which have been going on "in this country," and "which promise complete success."[33]

Dialogues of the dead

How exactly were the auto-iconized dead supposed to "contribute to the happiness of the living"? Besides their numerous other uses – moral, political, economical, genealogical, architectural, phrenological (p. 3), and so on – the auto-icons were also supposed to benefit the living through their "theatrical, or dramatic use" (p. 12).

Auto-iconism would make possible an entirely new kind of theater, in which the auto-icons themselves would perform as actors. On the stage, the auto-icons would speak and gesticulate; they would be animated either from within (moved by "a boy stationed within and hidden by the robe") or from without ("by means of strings or wires," operated by "persons under the stage"). By special contrivances, it would seem as if the auto-icons breathed and as if their voices, lent by actors, issued from their own mouths; since the skin on their faces "would be rendered of a more or less brownish hue," as a result of "the process of exsiccation," they would need to wear stage make-up (p. 13). Thus, for the ultimate good to be extracted from them, the dead would have to be, as it were, brought back to life.

The only roles the dead would play would be themselves. Thus, for instance, Shakespeare's *Julius Caesar*, staged according to Bentham's principles of auto-iconism, would feature Julius Caesar himself, that is, his auto-icon, in the title role. "What actor can play Julius Caesar better than Julius Caesar, in the character of an auto-icon, can play himself?" is how the first sentence of Bentham's manifesto of the auto-iconic theater would no doubt read. All the roles in this theater would thus be the posthumous equivalent of Hitchcock's personal appearances in his films (in which the director plays himself). Moreover, the auto-iconic theater would also make it possible for the characters that actually lived centuries and continents apart to meet on stage face to face.

It is in this spirit that Bentham briefly sketches some dialogues that could be staged in the auto-iconic theater. The dialogues are categorized according to different disciplines, such as ethics, mathematics, politics and so on (pp. 14–15). Each of the performers discusses his own work and his achievements. The performers include thinkers as ancient as Confucius, Aristotle and Euclid, and as recent as John Locke, Isaac Newton, and d'Alembert. In all the draft dialogues, there is one name that persistently pops up, that of Bentham himself. Bentham would thus appear in all these dialogues and of course play himself just like Hitchcock appears in each of his films and plays himself. But unlike Hitchcock, who assigned himself brief walk-ons in his films, Bentham reserves for himself absolutely pivotal roles in which he would compare his various achievements to those of leading authorities in each particular field. Bentham also works out the choreography of the corpses on the stage, down to the smallest details: when all the representatives of a particular discipline were gathered on the stage, Bentham would enter and be greeted in the name of all the performers by one of the interlocutors who would then introduce Bentham to each of the others and briefly sketch the principal achievements of each in his respective discipline (p. 13). The following exchange on ethics is a good example of the typical course of these dialogues. "The sage of the 1830th year after the Christian era," that is, Bentham himself, says to "the sage of three centuries and a half before the same," that is, Aristotle:

> In your work on morals, at the very outset of it, you bring forward the observation, that good in some shape or other, is the end in view of all men. Two thousand years have passed, and in all that time, nothing has been done on the subject by anybody else. Nobody has given a precise and clear import to the word corresponding to good, by translating the language of good and evil into the language of pleasure and pain.
>
> (p. 14)

Nobody but Bentham himself, of course, who considered paraphrasis – namely, replacing words referring to abstract and obscure entities, the reality of which is merely "verbal," with words referring to perceptible, really existing entities, such as pleasure and pain – to be one of his most important achievements. More or less the same story is repeated also in Bentham's dialogues on mathematics with Euclid and Newton (p. 15), on politics with John Locke (pp. 14–15), and so forth.

The body and *Psycho*

In Hitchcock's *Psycho*, Norman Bates's attitude to dead bodies is no less utilitarian than Bentham's own, for, like the philosopher, Norman believes, as we read in the novel, "in the preservative powers of taxidermy."[34] He does not leave his mother's dead body to natural decay and corruption, but digs it up from the grave, stuffs it, and preserves it as her own most adequate representation. Like his stuffed birds – ravens and owls – so Norman's mother becomes after her death "her own image" or "her own statue." Admittedly, the auto-icon of Mrs. Bates assembled by Norman looks somewhat less lifelike than the auto-icon of Bentham, but we should bear in mind that the latter owes its lifelike appearance primarily to the fact that Bentham's desiccated head was later replaced by a wax replica, into which glass eyes were inserted. Artificial eyes were the only concession Bentham was prepared to make within his strict principles of auto-iconism: that is to say, the only part of his body that he did not insist on preserving as auto-iconic after death were his eyes. Instead, Bentham had a pair of glass eyes, later to adorn his desiccated head, made in his own color twenty years before his death that he used to carry around in his pockets and show to his friends.[35] In contrast, Norman Bates keeps the dried head on the auto-icon of his mother and leaves its eye sockets empty, rather than betray the principles of auto-iconism. Thus, even though Mrs. Bates, in the character of an auto-icon, no longer resembles herself, nevertheless in Norman's eyes she represents herself more adequately than Bentham does.

Nor does Norman leave the bodies of his other two victims, Marion and detective Arbogast, to natural decay and corruption, but drops them into the swamp, where corpses can remain more or less preserved over long periods of time. (The fact that swamps were places where bodies were known to have been preserved in the past is also mentioned by Bentham.[36]) Thus, even if they had been brought to light many years after their deaths, Marion and Arbogast would still have represented themselves; no less than Mrs. Bates, they would still have been "their own images," "their own statues." Naturally auto-iconized, their bodies would perhaps have looked even more lifelike than the taxidermically treated body of Mrs. Bates. So, Norman is still experimenting in "the Auto-Icon art."

Norman manifests a utilitarian attitude not only toward dead bodies but also toward taxidermy itself, that is, to the very procedure by which the dead are rendered useful to the living. As he observes, "stuffing things" is an inexpensive hobby: "It's not as expensive as you might think," he says. "It's cheap, really. You know, needles, thread, sawdust. The chemicals are the only things that cost anything."[37] Furthermore, while the good is being extracted from the dead by Norman at minimal costs, it is also "more than a hobby": while people normally take up hobbies "to pass the time," Norman Bates goes about stuffing things "to fill it."[38] Thus, even before they can be put to their "farther use," the dead are already of benefit to him: "stuffing things" is what, in itself, gives him a sense of personal fulfillment, satisfies him – stuffing the dead, in short, is what he lives for.

Norman's pragmatic attitude toward dead bodies draws not only on the tradition of utilitarianism, but on its immediate precursors as well. He does not leave the death of bodies, which he will later put to "farther use," to chance: it is the bodies of his victims that he stuffs and auto-iconizes. The stuffed ravens and owls most likely have not died of natural causes, but, like Mrs. Bates, must have been killed. In his utilitarianism run wild, Norman therefore resembles the infamous assassins Burke and Hare, who murdered people so that their bodies could be used for utilitarian purposes, that is, for anatomical instruction. But while the bodies of Burke's and Hare's victims served Bentham's "transitory," that is, "dissectional, or anatomical" purpose, the bodies of Norman's victims – his mother as well as the ravens and owls – serve Bentham's "permanent," that is, "conservative, or statuary" purpose. When Burke was caught, he was sentenced to be hanged and publicly dissected; that is, the one who had engaged in murder to serve utilitarian ends was himself, in his turn, murdered and his own body put to its "farther use to the living." In fact, Burke's body was used not only for "transitory" but also for "permanent" purpose: the presiding judge decreed that after the execution and subsequent dissection of his body, Burke's skeleton should be reassembled and preserved in memory of his atrocious crimes.[39] Thus, Burke can still be seen today. Displayed in the Edinburgh University Museum, even today he continues to represent himself, even today he continues to be "his own image," his own icon. Is not this exemplary punishment also the one to which Hitchcock, in *Psycho*, condemns Norman Bates by showing him in the end just sitting and staring vacantly, uncannily like the stuffed figures of his mother and Bentham? Does it not seem, then, as if Norman has been stuffed while still alive, since all he is capable of doing henceforth is *representing* himself? Ultimately, Norman comes to realize this himself, when, in the novel, he decides, through his mother's voice, that the best thing for him to do is to pretend to be a stuffed figure: "a harmless stuffed figure that couldn't hurt or be hurt but merely exist forever."[40] Isn't Norman, then, condemned to exemplify, with his body, "a farther use of the dead" even before his death?

And finally, Norman also puts the stuffed body of his mother, that is, her auto-icon, to its "theatrical, or dramatic use." As we have seen, Bentham would have wished to have his philosophical monologues staged after his death in the form of dialogues between himself and various illustrious dead thinkers. It was precisely in order for him to be able to play himself in these "dialogues of the dead" that Bentham had his body auto-iconized. These dialogues did not take place, mainly because with the exception of Bentham's own body, the bodies of those with whom he would have wished to converse after death were not preserved. Nowadays, that is, more than a century and a half after Bentham's death, such a performance should, in principle, be possible, although the selection of Bentham's co-actors and interlocutors would be rather limited. Apart from Bentham, the only eminent sages that could play themselves after their death would be, for instance, Lenin (one can easily imagine a dialogue between Bentham and Lenin, let us say, on ontology, in which the two interlocutors would jointly mock Berkeley and his belief in the nonexistence of matter, with Bentham probably quoting from his *Fragment on Ontology*, and Lenin from his *Materialism and Empirio-Criticism*), Ho Chi Minh, Mao Zedong, Kim Il Sung, and a few others.[41] In contrast, Norman Bates puts Bentham's fantasy of the auto-iconic theater into practice: his fantasy scripts are not taking place merely in his head, that is, in the form of imaginary conversations or interior monologues. Rather, they are *acted out* in the form of dialogues between himself and his dead mother, who in his little theater plays herself, while Norman animates her body (or her auto-icon) and lends it his voice. "What actor can play my mother better than my mother, in the character of an auto-icon, can play herself?" is how, no doubt, the first sentence of Norman's own version of the Benthamite manifesto of the auto-iconic theater would read.

Notes

1 Jeremy Bentham, *Auto-Icon; or, Farther Uses of the Dead to the Living. A Fragment. From the unpublished MSS. of Jeremy Bentham*. Subsequent citations appear in parentheses in the text.

2 Quoted in Thomas Southwood Smith, *A Lecture delivered over the remains of Jeremy Bentham*, London: Effingham Wilson, 1832, p. 4.

3 George Berkeley, *A Treatise Concerning the Principles of Human Knowledge*, ed. Jonathan Dancy, Oxford: Oxford University Press, 1998, p. 156.

4 George Berkeley, "Letter to Samuel Johnson," March 24, 1730, in M.R. Ayers (ed.) *Philosophical Works*, London: Dent, 1992, p. 354.

5 Berkeley, "Letter to Samuel Johnson," p. 354. See also Berkeley, *A Treatise Concerning the Principles of Human Knowledge*, p. 138.

6 For a fuller account of Berkeley's theory of time, see Ian C. Tipton, *Berkeley: The Philosophy of Immaterialism*, London: Methuen, 1974, pp. 271–96; George Pitcher, *Berkeley*, London: Routledge & Kegan Paul, 1977, pp. 206–11; A.C. Grayling, *Berkeley: The Central Arguments*, London: Duckworth, 1986, pp. 174–83; David Berman, *George Berkeley: Idealism and the Man*, Oxford: Clarendon Press, 1994, pp. 61–70; and E.J. Furlong, "On Being 'Embrangled' by Time," in Colin M. Turbayne (ed.) *Berkeley: Critical and Interpretative Essays*, Minneapolis: University of Minnesota Press, 1982, pp. 148–55.

7 Berkeley, *Philosophical Commentaries*, in Ayers (ed.) *Philosophical Works*, p. 308; "Some Original Memoirs of the late famous Bishop of Cloyne," in A. Friedman (ed.) *Works of Oliver Goldsmith*, 5 vols., Oxford: Oxford University Press, 1966, vol. 3, p. 35; quoted in David Berman, *Berkeley: Experimental Philosophy*, London: Phoenix, 1997, p. 38.

8 Nicolas Malebranche, *Entretiens sur la mort*, in *Oeuvres complètes de Malebranche*, 20 vols., ed. André Robinet, Paris: J. Vrin, 1972–84, vols. 12–13, p. 410.

9 Malebranche, *Entretiens sur la mort*, p. 405.

10 Malebranche, *Entretiens sur la mort*, pp. 409–10.

11 Thomas De Quincy, *On Murder Considered as One of the Fine Arts & On War*, London: The Doppler Press, 1980, p. 19.

12 For more on this point, see A.A. Luce, *Berkeley and Malebranche: A Study in the Origins of Berkeley's Thought*, Oxford: Oxford University Press, 1967, pp. 208–10.

13 See Bentham, *A Fragment on Ontology*, in *The Panopticon Writings by Jeremy Bentham*, ed. Miran Bozovic, London: Verso, 1995, p. 120n.

14 Bentham, *Auto-Icon*, p. 7. Subsequent citations appear in parentheses in the text.

15 Ruth Richardson, *Death, Dissection and the Destitute*, London: Routledge & Kegan Paul, 1987, p. 34.
16 Quoted in Richardson, *Death, Dissection and the Destitute*, p. 37.
17 Richardson, *Death, Dissection and the Destitute*, pp. 58–9.
18 Bentham MSS. Box 155, University College Library; quoted in C.F.A. Marmoy, "The 'Auto-Icon' of Jeremy Bentham at University College, London," *Medical History* 2, 1958, p. 80.
19 Bentham, *Auto-Icon*, p. 7.
20 Ruth Richardson and Brian Hurwitz, "Jeremy Bentham's Self Image: An Exemplary Bequest For Dissection," *British Medical Journal* 295, July 1987, p. 195.
21 See note 2 above.
22 Bentham, *Auto-Icon*, p. 3.
23 For Diderot and Rousseau, for example, it is exactly the opposite that holds true: nothing resembles an individual *less* than that individual resembles him or herself. See Diderot's description of Rameau's nephew: "Rien ne dissemble plus de lui que lui-même" ("Nothing is less like him than himself"). Denis Diderot, *Rameau's Nephew*, trans. Leonard Tancock, Harmondsworth: Penguin, 1966, p. 34. Also, Rousseau's description of himself: "Rien n'est si dissemblable à moi que moi-même." Jean-Jacques Rousseau, *Le Persiffleur*, in *Oeuvres complètes*, ed. Bernard Gagnebin and Marcel Raymond, Paris: Gallimard, 1959, vol.1, p. 1108.
24 Bentham, *Auto-Icon*, p. 2.
25 For an account of the controversy, see Anthony Kenny, *Aquinas*, Oxford: Oxford University Press, 1980, p. 47. For an ingenious solution, see Master Eckhart, *Did the Forms of the Elements Remain in the Body of Christ while Dying on the Cross?*, in *Parisian Questions and Prologues*, trans. Armand A. Maurer, Toronto: Pontifical Institute of Mediaeval Studies, 1974, pp. 71–5.
26 Bentham, *Auto-Icon*, p. 10. Subsequent citations appear in parentheses in the text.
27 Literary examples of "auto-iconization," or, of one's turning into one's own statue or one's own monument at the moment of death, of course, abound. See, for example, Malcolm Bradbury's description of Voltaire immediately before his death: "He's become his own statue, transfigured himself into his own waxwork, grown into his own bust." Bradbury, *To the Hermitage*, London: Macmillan, 2000, p. 478. See also Ernest Hemingway's description of the seemingly dying F. Scott Fitzgerald: "Back in the room Scott was still lying as though on his tomb, sculpted as a monument to himself." Ernest Hemingway, *A Moveable Feast*, New York: Simon & Schuster, 1996, p. 166.
28 Bentham, *Auto-Icon*, p. 5.
29 Bentham MSS. Box 155, University College Library; quoted in Marmoy, "The 'Auto-Icon' of Jeremy Bentham at University College, London," p. 80.
30 See Marmoy, "The 'Auto-Icon' of Jeremy Bentham at University College, London," p. 85.
31 Bentham, *Auto-Icon*, p. 2. Subsequent citations appear in parentheses in the text.
32 See John Bowring, *Autobiographical Recollections*, London: H.S. King, 1877, p. 343; quoted in Marmoy, "The 'Auto-Icon' of Jeremy Bentham at University College, London," p. 78.
33 Bentham, *Auto-Icon*, p. 2. Subsequent citations appear in parentheses in the text.
34 Robert Bloch, *Psycho*, London: Bloomsbury, 1997, p. 149.
35 See Marmoy, "The 'Auto-Icon' of Jeremy Bentham at University College, London," p. 84n.
36 See Bentham, *Auto-Icon*, p. 1.
37 Richard J. Anobile (ed.) *Alfred Hitchcock's Psycho*, London: Pan Books, 1974, p. 78.
38 Anobile (ed.) *Alfred Hitchcock's Psycho*, p. 78.
39 See Richardson, *Death, Dissection and the Destitute*, p. 143; see also p. 340, n. 52.
40 Bloch, *Psycho*, p. 152.

41 Like Bentham, these men were all "auto-iconized"; even after death, they all continue to represent themselves. In one significant respect, they can even be said to represent themselves more adequately than Bentham does: unlike Bentham's auto-icon, their embalmed bodies are indubitably "better than a statue." Yet, even though they are all unquestionably "their own statues" or "their own monuments," they are nevertheless nothing more than just that, that is, *monuments* to themselves. What Bentham — and Norman Bates — would probably have found objectionable about all these auto-iconized thinkers is that they all, as a rule, represent themselves as *dead*, that is, as corpses: even though they look exactly the same as they did when they were still alive, they nevertheless lie like dead people with their eyes closed, whereas Bentham himself is sitting upright in a chair, his (glass) eyes opened, his hat on his head and his walking stick in his hands, as if he had just sat down, or as if he were just about to rise from his chair and leave for his daily walk before breakfast — in a word, as if he were *alive*. While Bentham's auto-icon is flexible at the joints (if necessary, it can even be dismantled), the rigid, embalmed corpses would be impossible to animate or to bring back to life even on the stage. So in the auto-iconic theater, in which the dead are brought back to life by the staging of dialogues between them, Lenin, Ho Chi Minh, Mao Zedong, and Kim Il Sung could only play themselves at the moment of their deaths. It is perhaps because they only represent themselves as dead that their embalmed bodies have not superseded "the necessity of sculpture," but on the contrary, have inspired innumerable likenesses that represent them as living, even though, according to Bentham, their bodies are without question "better than a statue." Although these others may "contribute to the happiness of the living," not *all* the good has been "extracted" from them. They offer "anatomico-moral instruction" (Bentham, *Auto-Icon*, p. 7), but do not serve any "theatrical, or dramatic" purpose. It is therefore questionable whether the "extracted" good in fact outweighs "the evil done" (Bentham, *Auto-Icon,* p. 1), that is, the expenses. For example, until a short time ago, Lenin's mausoleum laboratory in Moscow employed a staff of almost one hundred scientists — histologists, anatomists, biochemists, physical chemists, and opticians — who maintained the embalmed corpse around the clock, treating it with special chemicals and by means of equipment worth several million dollars (see Ilya Zbarsky and Samuel Hutchinson, *Lenin's Embalmers*, trans. Barbara Bray, London: The Harvill Press, 1998, p. 181). In contrast, Bentham's auto-icon has been restored only twice since 1832: on both occasions, the moth-eaten clothes were simply cleaned and patched up, and the stuffing replaced (see Richardson and Hurwitz, "Jeremy Bentham's Self Image: An Exemplary Bequest For Dissection," p. 196).

Chapter 16

IS THERE A PROPER WAY TO REMAKE A HITCHCOCK FILM?

Slavoj Žižek

In any large American bookstore it is possible to purchase a volume of the unique series *Shakespeare Made Easy* edited by John Durband and published by Barron's: a "bilingual" edition of Shakespeare's plays, with the original archaic English on the left-hand page and the translation into common contemporary English on the right. The obscene satisfaction provided by reading these volumes resides in how what purports to be a mere translation into contemporary English turns out to be much more. As a rule, Durband tries to formulate directly, in everyday locution, (what he considers to be) the thought expressed in Shakespeare's metaphoric idiom. Thus "To be or not to be, that is the question" becomes something like: "What's bothering me now is: Shall I kill myself or not?" And my idea is, of course, that the standard remakes of Hitchcock's films are precisely something like *Hitchcock Made Easy*: although the narrative is the same, the "substance," the flair that accounts for Hitchcock's uniqueness, evaporates. Here, however, one should avoid the jargon-laden talk on Hitchcock's unique touch, etc., and approach the difficult task of specifying what gives Hitchcock's films their unique flair.

Or – what if this uniqueness is a myth, the result of our spectator's transference that elevates Hitchcock into the Subject Supposed to Know? What I have in mind is the attitude of over-interpretation: everything in a Hitchcock film has to have a meaning, there are no contingencies, so that when something doesn't fit, it's not his fault, but ours – we didn't really get it. While watching *Psycho* for the twentieth time, I noticed a strange detail during the final psychiatrist's explanation: Lila listens to him enraptured and nods two times with a deep satisfaction, instead of being shaken by the final confirmation of her sister's meaningless death. Was this a pure contingency, or did Hitchcock want to suggest a strange libidinal ambiguity and rivalry between the two sisters? Or consider the scene of Marion driving in the night on her escape from Phoenix just before reaching the Bates motel, when she listens to the imagined voices of her boss and the millionaire who bought the house furious at her deception. Marion's expression is no longer anguished, rather, what we perceive is a strange manic smile of a deeply perverse satisfaction, an expression that uncannily resembles the very last shot of Norman-mother, just before it dissolves into the skull and then the car appears out of the swamp. So, in a way, even before actually meeting him, Marion already becomes Norman. A further feature that confirms this point is that her expression emerges when she is listening to the voices in her head, exactly like Norman in his last shot. But the supreme example is the scene when Marion checks in at the Bates motel: while Norman has his back turned against her, inspecting the row of keys to the rooms, she furtively looks around to get an idea which city to put down as her residence, sees the words "Los Angeles" as part of a newspaper headline and writes them down. We have here two hesitations coinciding: while Marion hesitates as to which town to write (which lie to tell), Norman hesitates as to which unit to put her in (if it's number one, this means that he will be able to observe her secretly through the peephole). When, after some hesitation, she tells him "Los Angeles," Norman picks up and gives her the key of unit number one. Is his hesitation a simple sign that he was considering her sexual attraction and then finally opted to pursue her, or is it that, at a more refined level, he detected in her hesitation that she is about to tell him a lie, and then countered her lie with an illegal act of his own, finding in her small crime the justification for his own? (Or is it rather that, upon hearing that she is from LA, he thinks that the girl from such a decadent town can be an easy pick?) Although Joseph Stefano, who wrote the scenario, claims the creators had in mind only the growing sexual attraction that Norman felt for Marion, there remains the shadow of a doubt that the coincidence of two hesitations cannot be purely contingent.[1] This is called true love in theory. So, out of this true love, I claim that there *is* a unique Hitchcockian dimension.

The Hitchcockian sinthom

My first thesis is that this unique dimension is not to be sought primarily at the level of the narrative content. Its original locus is elsewhere. Where? Let me begin by contrasting two scenes from two non-Hitchcockian films. There is one memorable scene in the otherwise dull and pretentious film directed by Robert Redford, *A River Runs Through It* (1992). Of the two preacher's sons, we are all the time aware that the younger one (Brad Pitt) is on a path to self-destruction, approaching catastrophe because of his compulsive gambling, drinking and womanizing. The thing that keeps the two sons together with their father is fly-fishing in the wild Montana rivers. These Sunday fishing expeditions are a kind of sacred family ritual, a time when the outside threats to family life are temporarily suspended. So when they go fishing for the last time, Pitt achieves perfection: he adroitly catches the biggest fish ever. However, the way he proceeds is presented with a shadow of constant threat: Will the dark river bend where he spots the great trout swallow him? Will he reappear after he slips into the fast water? Again, it is as if this potential threat announces the final tragedy that occurs shortly afterwards (Pitt is found dead, with his fingers broken, on account of his gambling debts).

What renders this scene from *A River Runs Through It* rather ordinary is that the underlying threatening dimension is directly reinscribed into the main narrative line, as an index pointing towards the final catastrophe. In contrast, Peter Yates's outstanding *Breaking Away* (1979), a gentle comedy-drama about the coming of age of four high-school kids in Bloomington, Indiana, in the final summer before they face the inexorable choices of jobs or college or the army, resists this temptation. In one of the memorable small sequences, Dave, one of the kids, on a racing bicycle engages in a high-speed highway duel with a semi-trailer truck. The uneasy effect is here the same as in a couple of scenes involving swimming in an abandoned quarry, in which kids jump into deep dark water with bits of sharp stones hidden beneath the surface: Yates suggests the constant possibility of sudden catastrophe. We wait for the terrible accident to happen – for Dave to be hit and crushed by the truck or for one of the kids to drown in the dark water or to hit some sharp stone when jumping into it. No catastrophe in fact occurs, but the hints of one – its threatening shadow evoked just by the general atmosphere of the way the scene is shot, not by any direct psychological references, like the uneasiness felt by kids – make the characters seem strangely vulnerable. It is as if these hints lay the ground for the very end of the film, when we learn, from the legend on the screen, that, afterwards, one of them died in Vietnam, and another had a different accident. This tension between the two levels is what I want to focus on: the gap that separates the explicit narrative line from the diffused threatening message delivered between the lines of the narrative.

Let me introduce here a parallel with Richard Wagner. (Is not the ring from Wagner's *Nibelungen* the greatest MacGuffin of all times?). In his last two operas, the same gesture is performed: towards the end of *Göetterdäemmerung*, the dead Siegfried, when Hagen approaches him in order to snatch the ring from his hand, threateningly rises his hand; towards the end of *Parsifal*, in the midst of Amfortas's lament and refusal to perform the ritualistic unveiling of the Grail, his dead father Titurel also miraculously lifts his hand. Features such as this attest to the fact that Wagner was a Hitchcockian *avant la lettre*. In Hitchcock's films, we also find the same visual or thematic motifs imposing themselves through an uncanny compulsion and repeating from one film to another, in totally different narrative contexts. Best known is the motif of what Freud called *Niederkommenlassen*, "letting [oneself] fall down," with all the undertones of melancholic suicidal fall – a person desperately clinging by his hand onto another person's hand:[2] the Nazi saboteur clinging to the good American hero's hand from the torch of the Statue of Liberty in *Saboteur*; in the final confrontation of *RearWindow*, the crippled James Stewart hanging from the window, trying to grab the hand of his pursuer who, instead of helping him, tries to make him fall; in *The Man Who Knew Too Much* (remake), in the sunny Casablanca market, the dying Western agent, dressed as an Arab, stretching his hand towards the innocent American tourist (James Stewart) and pulling him down towards himself; the finally unmasked thief clinging to Cary Grant's hand in *To Catch a Thief*; James Stewart clinging to the roof funnel and desperately trying to grasp the policeman's hand stretching towards him at the very beginning of *Vertigo*; Eva Marie Saint clinging to Cary Grant's hand at the edge of the precipice (with the immediate cut to her clinging to his hand in the sleeping car's berth at the end of *North by Northwest*).

Upon a closer look, we become aware that Hitchcock's films are full of such motifs. There is the motif of a car on the border of a precipice in *Suspicion* and in *North by Northwest*. In each of the two films, there is a scene with the same actor (Cary Grant) driving a car and dangerously approaching a precipice; although the films are separated by almost twenty years, the scene is shot in the same way, including a subjective shot of the actor casting a glance into the precipice. (In Hitchcock's last film, *Family Plot*, this motif explodes in a long sequence of the car that rushes down the hill, its brakes tampered with by the villains.) There is the motif of the "woman who knows too much," intelligent and perceptive, but sexually unattractive, with spectacles, and – significantly – resembling or even directly played by Hitchcock's own daughter Patricia: Ruth Roman's sister in *Strangers On a Train*, Barbara Bel Geddes in *Vertigo*, Patricia Hitchcock in *Psycho*, and even Ingrid Bergman herself prior to her sexual awakening in *Spellbound*. There is the motif of the mummified skull which first appears in *Under Capricorn* and finally in *Psycho* – both times, it terrifies the young woman (Ingrid Bergman, Vera Miles) in the final confrontation. There is the motif of a gothic house with big stairs, with the hero walking up the stairs where, in the room, there is nothing, although he previously saw a feminine silhouette in the first-floor window. In *Vertigo*, it is the enigmatic episode of Madeleine seen by Scottie as a shade in the window and then inexplicably disappearing from the house. In *Psycho*, it is the appearance of the mother's shadow in the window – again, bodies which appear out of nowhere and disappear back into the void. Furthermore, the fact that in *Vertigo* this episode remains unexplained opens up the temptation to read it as a kind of *futur antérieur*, as already pointing towards *Psycho*: is the old lady who is the hotel-clerk of the house not a kind of strange condensation of Norman Bates and his mother, i.e, the clerk (Norman) who is at the same time the old lady (mother), thus giving in advance the clue to their identity, which is the big mystery of *Psycho*?

Vertigo is of a special interest, insofar as, in it, the same sinthom of the spiral that draws us into its abyssal depth repeats itself and resonates at a multitude of levels: first as a purely formal motif of the abstract form emerging out of the close-up of the eye in the credits sequence; then as the curl of Carlotta Valdes's hair in her portrait, repeated in Madeleine's haircut; then as the abyssal circle of the staircase of the church tower; and, finally, in the famous 360-degree shot around Scottie and Judy/Madeleine who are passionately embracing in the decrepit hotel room, and during which the background changes to the stable of the Juan Batista Mission and then back to the hotel room. Perhaps this last shot offers the key to the temporal dimension of "vertigo": the self-enclosed temporal loop in which past and present are condensed into the two aspects of the same endlessly repeated circular movement. It is this multiple resonance of surfaces that generates the specific density, the "depth," of the film's texture.

Here we have a set of (visual, formal, material) motives which "remain the same" across different contexts of meaning. How are we to read such persisting gestures or motifs? One should resist the temptation to treat them as Jungian archetypes with a deep meaning – the raising hand in Wagner expressing the threat of the dead person to the living; or the person clinging by another's hand expressing the tension between spiritual fall and salvation. We are dealing here with the level of material signs which resist meaning and establish connections which are not grounded in narrative symbolic structures: they just relate in a kind of pre-symbolic cross-resonance. They are not signifiers, nor the famous Hitchcockian stains, but elements of what, a decade or two ago, one would have called cinematic writing, *écriture*. In the last years of his teaching, Jacques Lacan established the difference between symptom and sinthom: in contrast to symptom a cipher of some repressed meaning, sinthom has no determinate meaning. Sinthoms give body, in their repetitive pattern, to some elementary matrix of jouissance, of excessive enjoyment – although they do not have sense, they do radiate jouis-sense/enjoy-meant.[3] According to Stalin's daughter, Svetlana Alliluyeva, the last gesture of the dying Stalin, significantly preceded by the cast of the evil gaze, was the same gesture as in Wagner's last operas, the gesture of threateningly raising the left hand:

At what seemed like the very last moment Stalin suddenly opened his eyes and cast a glance over everyone in the room. It was a terrible glance, insane or perhaps angry and full of fear of death and the unfamiliar faces of the doctors bent over him. The glance swept over everyone in a second. Then something incomprehensible and terrible happened that to this day I can't forget and don't understand. He suddenly lifted his left hand as though he were pointing to something up above and bringing down a curse on us all. The gesture was incomprehensible and full of menace, and no one could say to whom or what it might be directed. The next moment, after a final effort, the spirit wrenched itself free of the flesh.[4]

What, then, did this gesture mean? The Hitchcockian answer is: *nothing*. Yet this nothing was not an empty nothing, but the fullness of libidinal investment, a tick that gave body to a cipher of enjoyment. Perhaps the closest equivalent in painting is the protracted stains which *are* the yellow sky in the late van Gogh or the water or grass in Munch: this uncanny massiveness pertains neither to the direct materiality of the color stains nor to the materiality of the depicted objects – it dwells in a kind of intermediate spectral domain of what Schelling called *geistige Koerperlichkeit*, the spiritual corporeality. From the Lacanian perspective, it is easy to identify this "spiritual corporeality" as materialized jouissance, "jouissance which turned into flesh." Hitchcock's sinthoms are thus not mere formal patterns: they already condense a certain libidinal investment. As such, they determined his creative process. Hitchcock did not proceed from the plot to its translation in cinematic audio-visual-terms. He rather started with a set of (usually visual) motifs that haunted his imagination, which imposed themselves as his sinthoms; then, he constructed a narrative that served as the pretext for their use. These sinthoms provide the specific flair, the substantial density of the cinematic texture of Hitchcock's films: without them, we would have a lifeless formal narrative. So all the talk about Hitchcock as the "master of suspense," about his unique twisted plots, etc., misses the key dimension. Fredric Jameson said of Hemingway that he selected his narratives in order to be able to write a certain kind of (tense, masculine) phrase. The same goes for Hitchcock: he invented stories in order to be able to shoot a certain kind of scene. And, while the narratives of his films provide a funny and often perceptive comment of our times, it is in his sinthoms that Hitchcock lives forever. They are the true cause of why his films continue to function as objects of our desire.

The Case of the Missing Gaze

The next section concerns the status of the gaze. The so-called post-theorists (cognitivist critics of psychoanalytic cinema theory) like to vary the motif of how writers of "theory" refer to mythical entities like the (capitalized) Gaze, entities to which no empirical, observable facts (like the actual cinema viewers and their behavior) correspond – the title of one of the essays in the *Post-Theory* volume is "The Case of the Missing Spectator."[5] *Post-Theory* relies here on the commonsense notion of the spectator (the subject who perceives cinematic reality on the screen, equipped with his or her emotional and cognitive predispositions, etc). Within this simple opposition between subject and object of cinematic percep-tion, there is, of course, no place for the gaze as the point from which the viewed object itself "returns the gaze" and regards us, the spectators. Whereas what is crucial for the Lacanian notion of gaze is that it involve the reversal of the rela-tionship between subject and object. As Lacan puts it in his *Seminar XI*, there is an antinomy between the eye and the gaze, i.e, the gaze is on the side of the object, it stands for the blind spot in the field of the visible from which the picture itself photo-graphs the spectator; or, as he puts it in *Seminar I*, whose uncanny evoca-tion of the central scene of *Rear Window* is sustained by the fact that it was held in the same year that Hitchcock's film was shot (1954):

> I can feel myself under the gaze of someone whose eyes I do not see, not even discern. All that is necessary is for something to signify to me that there may be others there. This window, if it gets a bit dark, and if I have reasons for thinking that there is someone behind it, is straight-away a gaze.[6]

Is this notion of the gaze not perfectly rendered by the exemplary Hitchcockian scene in which the subject is approaching some uncanny threat-ening object, usually a house? There we encounter the antinomy between the eye and the gaze at its purest: the subject's eye sees the house, but the house – the object – seems somehow to return the gaze. No wonder, then, that the post-theorists speak of the "missing gaze," complaining that the Freudo-Lacanian Gaze is a mythical entity nowhere found in the actuality of the spectator's experience: this gaze effectively is missing, its status is purely fantasmatic. At a more funda-mental level, what we are dealing with here is the positivization of an impossibility which gives rise to the fetish-object. For example, how does the object-gaze become a fetish? Through the Hegelian reversal from the impossi-bility of seeing the object, into an object which gives body to this very impossibility: since the subject cannot directly see the true object of fascination he accomplishes a kind of reflection-into-self by means of which the object that fascinates him becomes the gaze itself. In this sense (although not in an entirely symmetrical way), gaze and voice are "reflective" objects, i.e., objects that give body to an impossibility (in Lacanian "mathemes": an under-minus small phi).

In this precise sense, fantasy proper is not the scene itself that attracts our fascination, but the imagined/inexistent gaze observing it, like the impossible gaze from above for which old Aztecs drew gigantic figures of birds and animals onto the ground, or the impossible gaze for which details of the sculptures on the old aqueducts of Rome were formed, although they were unobservable from the ground. In short, the most elementary fantasmatic scene is not that of a fascinating scene to be looked at, but the notion that "there is someone out there looking at us"; it is not a dream but the notion that "we are the objects in someone else's dream." Milan Kundera, in *La lenteur*, presents as the ultimate sign of today's false aseptic pseudo-voluptuous sex, the couple feigning to make love anally close to a hotel pool, in view of the guests in the rooms above, faking pleasurable cries but effectively not even accomplishing the penetration – to this he opposes the slow gallant intimate erotic games of eighteenth-century France. Did not something similar to the scene from *La lenteur* effectively take place in Khmer Rouge, Cambodia when, after too many people died from purges and starvation, the regime, eager to multiply the population, ordered each first, tenth, and twentieth day in the month a day for copulation: in the evening, married couples (who otherwise had to sleep in separate barracks) were allowed to sleep together and compelled to make love. Their private space was a small cubicle isolated by a half-transparent bamboo curtain; in front of the row of such cubicles, Khmer Rouge guards were walking, verifying that couples were effectively copulating. Since the couples knew that not making love was considered an act of sabotage to be severely punished, and since, on the other hand, after a fourteen-hour workday, they were as a rule too tired effectively to have sex, they pretended to make love in order to dupe the guards' attention: they made false movements and faked sounds. Is this not the exact inverse of the experience from the pre-permissive youth of some of us, when one had to sneak into the bedroom with the partner and do it as silently as possible, so that parents, if they were still awake, would not suspect that sex was taking place? What if, then, such a spectacle for the Other's gaze is part of the sexual act – what if, since there is no sexual relationship, it can only be staged for the Other's gaze?

Does not the recent trend of "-cam" web-sites which realize the logic of *The Truman Show* (in these sites, we are able to follow continuously some event or place: the life of a person in his/her apartment, the view on a street, etc.) display this same urgent need for the fantasmatic Other's gaze serving as the guarantee of the subject's being? "I exist only insofar as I am looked at all the time." Similar to this is the phenomenon, noted by Claude Lefort, of the television set which is always turned on, even when no one effectively watches it – it serves as the minimum guarantee of the existence of a social link. The situation is here thus the tragi-comic reversal of the Bentham - Orwellian notion of a panopticon society in which we are (potentially) "observed all the time" and have no place to hide from the omnipresent gaze of the Power. Here, anxiety arises from the prospect of not being exposed to the Other's gaze all the time, so that the subject needs the camera's gaze as a kind of ontological guarantee of his being.

Hitchcock is at its most uncanny and disturbing when he engages us directly with the point of view of this external fantasmatic gaze. One of the standard horror movie procedures is the "resignification" of an objective shot into a subjective one. What the spectator first perceives as an objective shot — say, of a house with a family at dinner — is all of a sudden, by means of codified markers like the slight trembling of the camera, the "subjectivized" soundtrack, etc., revealed as the subjective shot of a murderer stalking his potential victims. However, this procedure is to be supplemented with its opposite, that of the unexpected reversal of subjective into objective shot: in the midst of a long shot unambiguously marked as subjective, the spectator is all of a sudden compelled to acknowledge that there is no possible subject within the space of diegetic reality who can occupy the point of view of this shot. So we are not dealing here with the simple reversal of objective into subjective shot, but in constructing a place of impossible subjectivity, a subjectivity which taints the very objectivity with a flavor of unspeakable, monstrous evil. An entire heretic theology is discernible here, secretly identifying the Creator Himself as the Devil (which was already the thesis of the Cathar heresy in twelfth-century France). The exemplary case of this impossible subjectivity is the "subjective" shot from the standpoint of the murderous Thing itself upon the transfixed face of the dying detective Arbogast in *Psycho*, or, in *The Birds*, the famous God's eye view of the burning Bodega Bay, which is then, with the entry into the frame of the birds, resignified, subjectivized, into the point of view of the evil aggressors themselves.

Multiple endings

There is yet another, third, aspect that adds a specific density to Hitchcock's films: the implicit resonance of multiple endings. The most obvious and well-documented case is, of course, that of *Topaz*: before deciding on the ending that we all know, Hitchcock shot two alternative endings, and my point is that it is not sufficient to say that he simply chose the most appropriate ending. The ending we have now rather in a way presupposes two others, with the three endings forming a kind of syllogism, i.e, Granville (Michel Piccoli), the Russian spy, telling himself, "They cannot prove anything about me, I can simply leave for Russia;" "But the Russians themselves now do not want me, I am now even dangerous to them, so they will probably kill me;" "What can I do then if in France I am outcast as a Russian spy and Russia itself no longer wants me? I can only kill myself." There are, however, much more refined versions of this implicit presence of alternative endings. Already the denouement of Hitchcock's early melodrama *The Manxman* (1929) is preceded by two scenes which could be read as possible alternative endings (the woman kills herself; the lover never returns). Hitchcock's masterpiece *Notorious* owes at least a part of its powerful impact to the fact that its denouement should be perceived against the background of at least two other possible outcomes that resonate in it as a kind of alternative history.[7] In the first outline of the story, Alicia wins redemption by the film's end, but loses Devlin, who is killed rescuing her from the Nazis. The idea was that this sacrificial act would solve the tension between Devlin, who is unable to admit to Alicia his love for her, and Alicia, who is unable to perceive herself as worthy of love. Devlin admits his love for her without words, by dying in order to save her life. In the final scene, we find Alicia back in Miami with her group of drinking friends: although she is more "notorious" than ever, she has in her heart the memory of a man who loved her and died for her, and, as Hitchcock put it in a memo to Selznick, "to her this is the same as if she had achieved a life of marriage and happiness." In the second version, the outcome is the opposite; here, we already have the idea of a slow poisoning of Alicia by Sebastian and his mother. Devlin confronts the Nazis and flees with Alicia, but Alicia dies in the process. In the epilogue, Devlin sits alone in a Rio cafe, where he used to meet Alicia, and overhears people discussing the death of Sebastian's wanton and treacherous wife. However, the letter in his hands is a commendation from President Truman citing Alicia's bravery. Devlin pockets the letter and finishes his drink. Finally, the version we know was arrived at together with a finale that implies Devlin and Alicia are now married. Hitchcock then left this finale out, to end on a more tragic note, with Sebastian, who truly loved Alicia, left to face the Nazis' deadly wrath. The point is that both alternative endings (Devlin's and Alicia's death) are incorporated into the film, as a kind of fantasmatic background of the action we see on the screen: if they are to constitute a couple, both Devlin and Alicia have to undergo the "symbolic death," so that the happy ending emerges from the combination of two unhappy endings, i.e, these two alternative fantasmatic scenarios sustain the denouement we actually see.

This feature allows us to insert Hitchcock in the series of artists whose work forecast today's digital universe. Art historians have often noted the phenomenon of old artistic forms pushing against their own boundaries and using procedures which, at least from our retroactive view, seem to point towards a new technology that will be able to serve as a more "natural" and appropriate "objective correlative" to the life-experience the old forms endeavored to render by means of their "excessive" experimentation. A whole series of narrative procedures in the nineteenth-century novel announce not only the standard narrative cinema (the intricate use of "flashback" in Emily Brontë or of "cross-cutting" and "close-ups" in Dickens), but sometimes even the modernist cinema (the use of "off-space" in *Madame Bovary*), as if a new perception of life was already here, but was still struggling to find its proper means of articulation, until it finally found it in cinema. What we have here is thus the historicity of a kind of *futur antérieur*: it is only when cinema was here and developed its standard procedures that we could really grasp the narrative logic of Dickens's great novels or Flaubert's *Madame Bovary*.

And is it not the case that today we are approaching a homologous threshold: a new "life experience" is in the air, a perception of life that explodes the form of the linear-centered narrative and renders life as a multiform flow even in the domain of the "hard" sciences (quantum physics and its multiple reality interpretation, or the utter contingency that provides the spin to the actual evolution of life on Earth – as Stephen Jay Gould demonstrates in his *Wonderful Life*, the fossils of Burgess Shale bear witness to how evolution may have taken a wholly different turn).[8] We seem to be haunted by the chanciness of life and alternate versions of reality. Either life is experienced as a series of multiple parallel destinies that interact and are crucially affected by meaningless contingent encounters, the point at which one series intersects with and intervenes into another (see Altman's *ShortCuts*), or different versions/outcomes of the same plot are repeatedly enacted (the "parallel universes" or "alternative possible worlds" scenarios – see Kieslowski's *Blind Chance*, *The Double Life of Veronique*, and *Red*. Even "serious" historians recently produced a volume, *Virtual History*, that reads the major events of the Modern Age, from Cromwell's victory over the Stuarts and the American War of Independence to the disintegration of Communism, as hinging on unpredictable and sometimes even improbable chances.[9] This perception of our reality as one of the possible – often even not the most probable – outcomes of an "open" situation, this notion that other possible outcomes are not simply canceled out but continue to haunt our "true" reality as a specter of what might have happened, conferring on our reality the status of extreme fragility and contingency, implicitly clashes with the predominant "linear" narrative forms of our literature and cinema. They seem to call for a new artistic medium in which they would not be eccentric excess, but its "proper" mode of functioning. The notion of creation also changes with this new experience of the world: it no longer designates the positive act of imposing a new order, but rather the negative gesture of choice, of limiting the possibilities, of privileging one option at the expense of all the others. One can argue that the cyberspace hypertext is this new medium in which this life experience will find its "natural," more appropriate, objective correlative, so that, again, it is only with the advent of cyberspace hypertext that we can effectively grasp what Altman and Kieslowski – and, implicitly, also Hitchcock – were effectively aiming at.

The ideal remake

These reflections, perhaps, also suggest what a proper remake of a Hitchcock film would be. To try and imitate Hitchcockian sinthoms is an exercise in advance condemned to failure; it is to remake the same narrative results in a *Shakespeare Made Easy* output. So there are only two ways left. One is indicated by Gus van Sant's *Psycho* which, paradoxically, I am inclined to consider a failed masterpiece, rather than a simple failure. The idea of an exact frame-by-frame remake is an ingenious one, and, in my view, the problem is that the film does not go far enough in this direction. Ideally, what the film should strive for is to achieve the uncanny effect of the double: in shooting formally the same film, the difference would have become all the more palpable: everything would have been the same – shots, angles, dialogue – and, nonetheless, on account of this very sameness, we would all the more powerfully experience the fact that we are dealing with a totally different film. This gap would have been signaled by barely perceptible nuances in the style of acting, in the choice of actors, in the use of color, etc. Some elements in van Sant's film already point in this direction: the roles of Norman, Lila (portrayed as a lesbian), and Marion (a non-maternal, withdrawn, cold bitch in contrast to the big-breasted maternal Janet Leigh), even Arbogast and Sam, nicely indicate the shift from late fifties to today's universe. While some added shots (such as the enigmatic subjective shots of a cloudy sky during the two murders) are also acceptable, problems resurface with the more brutal changes (like Norman's masturbation while he peeps on Marion before slaughtering her – one is tempted to make the rather obvious point that if he were able to arrive at this kind of sexual satisfaction, there would have been no need for him to accomplish the violent *passage à l'acte* and slaughter Marion!); to top it all, some scenes are completely ruined, their impact completely lost, by a change to Hitchcock's precise framing (for example, the key scene in which, after leaving her office with the money, Marion at home prepares to escape). Hitchcock's own remakes (the two versions of *The Man Who Knew Too Much*, as well as *Saboteur* and *North by Northwest*) point in this direction: although the narrative is very similar, the underlying libidinal economy is wholly different in each of the subsequent remakes, as if the sameness serves the purpose of marking the Difference.[10]

The second way would be to stage, in a well-calculated strategic move, one of the alternative scenarios that underlie the actualized Hitchcock, such as a remake of *Notorious* with Ingrid Bergman surviving alone. This would be a proper way to honor Hitchcock as an artist belonging to our era. Perhaps, more than the direct "homages" to Hitchcock of De Palma and others, the scenes that announce such a proper remake are to be found in unexpected places, like the one in the hotel room, the place of crime, in Francis Ford Coppola's *The Conversation*: Coppola is certainly not a Hitchcockian, yet the investigator inspects the room with a Hitchcockian gaze, like Lila and Sam do with Marion's motel room, moving from the main bedroom to the bathroom and focusing there on the toilet and the shower. This shift from the shower (where there are no traces of the crime, where everything is clean) to the toilet sink, elevating it to the Hitchcockian object that attracts our gaze, fascinating us with its premonition of some unspeakable horror, is crucial here (recall Hitchcock's battle with censorship to allow the inside view of the toilet, from where Lila picks up a torn piece of paper with Marion's writing on it, the proof that she was there). After a series of obvious references to *Psycho* apropos the shower (quickly pulling open the curtain, inspecting the hole in the sink), the investigator focuses on the (allegedly cleansed) toilet seat, flushes it, and then the stain appears as if out of nowhere, blood and other traces of the crime overflowing the edge of the sink.

This scene, a kind of *Psycho* reread through *Marnie* (with its red stain blurring the screen), contains the main elements of the Hitchcockian universe: it has the Hitchcockian object, which materializes some unspecified threat, functioning as the hole into another abyssal dimension (is flushing the toilet in this scene not like pushing the wrong button that dissolves the entire universe in science-fiction novels?). This object that simultaneously attracts and repels the subject can be said to be the point from which the inspected setting returns the gaze (is it not that the hero is somehow regarded by the toilet sink?). Coppola realizes the alternative scenario of the toilet itself as the ultimate locus of mystery. What makes this mini-remake of a scene so effective is that Coppola suspends the prohibition operative in *Psycho*: the threat *does* explode; the camera *does* show the danger hanging in the air in *Psycho*, the chaotic bloody mess erupting from the toilet. Furthermore, is not the swamp behind the house in which Norman drowns the cars containing the bodies of his victims a kind of gigantic pool of excremental mud, so that one can say that he in a way flushes the cars down the toilet – the famous moment of the worried expression on his face when Marion's car stops its immersion in the swamp for a couple of seconds effectively signals the worry that the toilet did not swallow the traces of our "crime"? The very last shot of *Psycho*, in which we see Marion's car being pulled out of the swamp, is thus a kind of Hitchcockian equivalent to the blood re-emerging from the toilet sink – in short, this swamp is another in the series of entrance-points to the pre-ontological Netherworld.

And is not the same reference to the pre-ontological Underworld operative also in the final scene of *Vertigo*? In pre-digital times, when I was in my teens, I remember seeing a bad copy of *Vertigo* – its last seconds were missing, so that the movie appeared to have a happy ending: Scottie reconciled with Judy, forgiving her and accepting her as a partner, the two of them passionately embracing. My point is that such an ending is not as artificial as it may seem. It is rather in the actual ending that the sudden appearance of the Mother Superior from the staircase below functions as a kind of negative *deus ex machina*, a sudden intrusion in no way properly grounded in the narrative logic, which prevents the happy ending.[11] Where does the nun come from? From the same pre-ontological realm of shadows from which Scottie himself secretly observes Madeleine in the florist's.[12] It is the reference to this pre-ontological realm that allows us to approach the quintessential Hitchcockian scene which was never shot – precisely because it renders the basic matrix of his work directly, its actual filming undoubtedly would have produced a vulgar, tasteless effect. Here is this scene that Hitchcock wanted to insert in *North by Northwest*, as reported in Truffaut's conversations with the Master:

> I wanted to have a long dialogue between Cary Grant and one of the factory workers [at a Ford automobile plant] as they walk along the assembly line. Behind them a car is being assembled, piece by piece. Finally, the car they've seen being put together from a simple nut and bolt is complete, with gas and oil, and all ready to drive off the line. The two men look at each other and say, "Isn't it wonderful!" Then they open the door of the car and out drops a corpse.[13]

Where does this corpse emerge, or fall, from? Again, from the very void from which Scottie observes Madeleine in the florist's – or, from the void from which blood emerges in *The Conversation*. (One should also bear in mind that what we would have seen in this long take is the elementary unity of the production process – is then the corpse that mysteriously drops out from nowhere not the perfect stand-in for the surplus value that is generated "out of nowhere" through the production process?)

This shocking elevation of the ridiculously lowest (the Beyond where shit disappears) into the metaphysical Sublime is perhaps one of the mysteries of Hitchcock's art. Is not the Sublime sometimes part of our most common everyday experience? When, in the midst of accomplishing a simple task (say, climbing a long line of stairs), we are overwhelmed by an unexpected fatigue, it all of a sudden appears as if the simple goal we want to reach (the top of the stairs) is separated from us by an unfathomable barrier and thus changed into a metaphysical Object forever out of our reach, as if there is something which forever prevents us from accomplishing it. And the domain where excrement vanishes after we flush the toilet is effectively one of the metaphors for the horrifyingly sublime Beyond of the primordial, pre-ontological Chaos into which things disappear. Although rationally we know what happens to our excrement, the imaginary mystery nonetheless persists – shit remains an excess with does not fit our daily reality, and Lacan was right in claiming that we pass from animals to humans the moment an animal has problems with what to do with its excrement, the moment it turns into an excess that annoys us.[14] The Real in the scene from *The Conversation* is thus not primarily the horrifyingly disgusting stuff re-emerging from the toilet sink, but rather the hole itself, the gap which serves as the passage to a different ontological order. The similarity between the empty toilet sink before the remainders of the murder re-emerge from it and Malevitch's *Black Square on White Surface* is significant here: does the look from above into the toilet sink not reproduce almost the same "minimalist" visual scheme, a black (or, at least, darker) square of water enframed by the white surface of the sink itself? Again we, of course, know that the excrement which disappears is somewhere in the sewage network – what is "real" here is the topological hole or torsion which "curves" the space of our reality so that we perceive/imagine excrement as disappearing into an alternative dimension which is not part of our everyday reality.

Hitchcock's obsession with a spotless bathroom is well known, and it is significant that, when, after Marion's murder, he wants to shift our point of identification to Norman, he does this with a long rendering of the careful process of cleansing the bathroom. This is perhaps the key scene of the film, a scene that provides an uncannily profound satisfaction of a job properly done, of things returning back to normal, of a situation again under control, of the traces of the horrifying netherworld being erased.[15] One is tempted to read this scene against the background of the well-known proposition of Saint Thomas Aquinas according to which a virtue (defined as a proper way to accomplish an act) can also serve evil purposes: one can also be a perfect thief, murderer, extortioner, i.e, accomplish an evil act in a "virtuous" way. What this scene of cleansing the bathroom in *Psycho* demonstrates is how the "lower" perfection can imperceptibly affect the "higher" goal. Norman's virtuous perfection in cleansing the bathroom, of course, serves the evil purpose of erasing the traces of the crime; however, this very perfection, the dedication and the thoroughness of his act, seduces us, the spectators, into assuming that, if someone acts in such a "perfect" way, he should be in his entirety a good and sympathetic person. In short, someone who cleanses the bathroom as thoroughly as Norman does cannot be really bad, in spite of his other minor peculiarities. (Or, to put it even more pointedly, in a country governed by Norman, trains would certainly run on time!) While watching this scene recently, I caught myself nervously noticing that the bathroom was not properly cleansed – two small stains on the side of the bathtub remained! I almost wanted to shout: hey, it's not yet over, finish the job properly!

The endings of *Psycho*

I never found convincing the standard explanation of the Leftist theorists who cannot help but to love Hitchcock: yes, his universe is male chauvinist, but at the same time he renders visible its cracks and as it were subverts it from within. I think the social-political dimension of Hitchcock's films is to be sought elsewhere.

Let us take the two closures at the end of *Psycho* – first the psychiatrist wraps up the story, then Norman/Mother delivers the final monologue of "I wouldn't even hurt a fly!" This split between the two closures tells us more about the deadlock of contemporary subjectivity than a dozen essays in cultural criticism. That is to say, it may appear that we are dealing with the well-known split between expert knowledge and our private solipsistic universe, deplored by many social critics today: common sense, a shared set of ethically engaged presuppositions, is slowly disintegrating, and what we get are two points of view. On the one hand, the objectivized language of experts and scientists which can no longer be translated into a common language accessible to everyone, but which is present in it nonetheless in the mode of fetishized formulas that no one really understands yet which shape our artistic and popular imaginary (Black Hole, Big Bang, Superstrings, Quantum Oscillation ...). On the other hand, the multitude of lifestyles that fail to commune with one another so that all we can do is secure the conditions for their tolerant coexistence in a multicultural society. The icon of today's subject is perhaps the proverbial Indian computer programmer who during the day excels in his expertise, while in the evening, upon returning home, lights a candle to the local Hindu divinity and respects the sacredness of the cow.

However, upon closer look, it soon becomes apparent how this opposition is displaced at the end of *Psycho*. It is the psychiatrist, the representative of cold objective knowledge, who speaks in an engaged, almost warmly human way, his explanation full of personal tics and sympathetic gestures. Norman, withdrawn into his private world, is precisely no longer himself, but totally possessed by another psychic entity, the mother's ghost. This final image of Norman reminds me of the way they shoot soap operas in Mexico: because of the extremely tight schedule (the studio has to produce each day a half-hour installment of the series), actors do not have time to learn their lines in advance, so they simply have hidden in their ears a tiny voice receiver, and a man in the cabin behind the set simply reads to them instructions on what they are to do (what words they are to say, what acts they are to accomplish, etc.) – actors are trained to react immediately, with no delay, to these instructions. This is Norman at the end of *Psycho*, and this is also a good lesson to those New Age types who claim that we should drop the social masks and set free our innermost true selves – well, we see the final result in Norman who, at the end of *Psycho*, effectively realizes his true Self and follows the old Rimbaud motto from his letter to Demeny ("Car je est un autre. Si le cuivre s'eveille clairon, il n'y a rien de sa faute"): if Norman starts to talk with the strange voice of his mother, it's none of his guilt. The price I have to pay in order to become "really myself," the undivided subject, is total alienation, becoming an Other with regard to myself: the obstacle to my full self-identity is the very condition of my Selfhood.

Another aspect of this same antagonism concerns architecture: one can also consider Norman as the subject split between the two houses, the modern horizontal motel and the vertical Gothic mother's house, forever running between the two, never finding a proper place of his own. In this sense, the *unheimlich* character of the film's end means that, in his full identification with the mother, he finally found his *heim*, his home. In modernist works such as *Psycho*, this split is still visible, while the main goal of today's postmodern architecture is to obfuscate it. Suffice it to recall the "New Urbanism," with its return to small family houses in small towns, with front porches, re-creating the cozy atmosphere of the local community – clearly, this is the case of architecture as ideology at its purest, providing an imaginary (albeit "real," materialized in the actual disposition of houses) solution to a social deadlock which has nothing to do with architecture and all to do with late capitalist dynamics. A more ambiguous case of the same antagonism is the work of Frank Gehry: why is he so popular, a true cult figure? He takes as the basis one of the two poles of the antagonism, either the old-fashioned family house or a modernist concrete-and-glass building, and then either submits it to a kind of cubist anamorphic distortion (curved angles of walls and windows, etc.) or combines the old family home with a modernist supplement, in which case, as Fredric Jameson pointed out, the focal point is the place (the room) at the intersection of the two spaces. In short, is Gehry not doing in architecture what the Caduveo Indians (in Lévi-Strauss's magnificent description from his *Les Tristes tropiques*) were trying to achieve with their tattooed faces: to resolve through a symbolic act the real of a social antagonism by constructing a utopian solution, a mediation between the opposites? So here is my final thesis: if the Bates Motel were to be built by Gehry, directly combining the old mother's house and the flat modern motel into a new hybrid entity, there would have been no need for Norman to kill his victims, since he would have been relieved of the unbearable tension that compels him to run between the two places – he would have a third place of mediation between the two extremes.

Notes

1 During the public discussion at the Hitchcock Centenary Conference organized by the Department of Cinema Studies, New York University, October 13–17, 1999.

2 See Sigmund Freud, "The Psychogenesis of a Case of Homosexuality In a Woman," *The Pelican Freud Library, Volume 9: Case Histories II*, Harmondsworth: Penguin Books, 1979, p. 389.

3 For a more detailed account of this Hitchcockian sinthom, see Slavoj i ez (ed.) *Everything You Always Wanted to Know About Lacan (But Were Afraid to Ask Hitchcock)*, London: Verso, 1993.

4 Svetlana Alliluyeva, *Twenty Letters To a Friend*, New York: Simon & Schuster, 1967, p. 183.

5 David Bordwell and Noel Carroll (eds.) *Post-Theory*, Madison: University of Wisconsin Press, 1996.

6 Jacques Lacan, *The Seminar, Book I: Freud's Papers on Technique*, New York: Norton, 1988, p. 215. I rely here on Miran Bozovic, "The Man Behind His Own Retina," in i ez (ed.) *Everything You Always Wanted to Know About Lacan*.

7 See the fascinating report in Thomas Schatz, *The Genius of the System*, New York: Hold & Co., 1996, pp. 393–403.

8 See Stephen Jay Gould, *Wonderful Life*, New York: Norton, 1989.

9 See Niall Ferguson (ed.) *Virtual History*, London:macmillan, 1997.

10 Perhaps the greatest achievement of van Sant's remake is the scene of final credits, which follows the shot that ends Hitchcock's film and goes on for several minutes – a continuous crane shot showing what goes on around the car being dragged out of the swamp, the bored policemen around the towing truck, all this accompanied by a soft guitar repeating in an improvised way the main motif of Herrmann's score. This feature supplements the film with the unique touch of the nineties.

11 Is this sudden appearance not similar to Wagner's *Tristan und Isolde*? Towards the very end of the opera, after Tristan's death, Isolde arrives and plunges into a death trance. The break occurs with the arrival of a second ship, when the slow progress all of a sudden accelerates in an almost comic way – in five minutes more events happen than in all the previous opera (a fight, the death of Melot and Kurwenal, etc.) – similar to Verdi's *Il Trovatore*, where in the last two minutes a whole package of things happen. Such unexpected intrusions just before the ending are crucial for the reading of the underlying tensions of a narrative.

12 When Lesley Brill claims that the shrunken head in *Under Capricorn* is a kind of underworld creature trying to drag Ingrid Bergman back into hell, one is tempted to say that the nun which appears at the very end of *Vertigo* belongs to the same evil netherworld – the paradox being, of course, that this is a *nun*, a woman of God, who embodies the force of Evil that drags the subject down and prevents her salvation.

13 François Truffaut, *Hitchcock*, New York: Simon & Schuster, 1984, p. 257.

14 It's similar with saliva: as we all know, although we can without problem swallow our own saliva, we find it extremely repulsive to swallow saliva which was spit out of our body – again, a case of violating the Inside/Outside frontier.

15 Hitchcock's obsession with cleanliness is well-known: in an interview, he boasted that he always leaves the restroom so clean that no one would have guessed, upon inspecting it, that he was there before. This obsession also accounts for the obvious pleasure-in-disgust Hitchcock finds in the small filthy details that characterize the Cuban mission in Harlem in *Topaz*, like the official diplomatic document stained by the grease from a sandwich.

INDEX

275